Wisdom
from
The Greater Community

V O L U M E   I I

Wisdom from *The Greater Community*

VOLUME II

SECOND EDITION

THE GREATER COMMUNITY
BOOK OF TEACHINGS

Marshall Vian Summers

WISDOM FROM THE GREATER COMMUNITY: *Volume II*

Book design by Alan Bernhard
Argent Associates, Boulder, Colorado

Printed on recycled paper

ISBN: 978-1-884238-64-2 *Wisdom from the Greater Community: Volume II*
Library of Congress Catalog Card Number: 90-61254

This is the second edition of *Wisdom from The Greater Community: Volume II*

The books of the New Knowledge Library are published by
The Society for The Greater Community Way of Knowledge.
The Society is a religious non-profit organization dedicated to presenting
and teaching The Greater Community Way of Knowledge.

Wisdom from the Greater Community: Volume II along with its companion texts
Steps to Knowledge and *Wisdom from the Greater Community: Volume I*
comprise the first level of study in The Greater Community Way of Knowledge.

PUBLISHER'S CATALOGING IN PUBLICATION

Summers, Marshall.
   Wisdom from the greater community : spiritual preparation for
humanity's emergence into the greater community / Marshall Vian
Summers. — 2nd ed.
   p. cm.
   ISBN (v. 1) : 978-1-884238-11-6.
   ISBN (v. 2) : 978-1-884238-64-2

   1. Society for The Greater Community Way of Knowledge —
Doctrines. 2. Spiritual life — Society for The Greater Community
Way of Knowledge. I. Society for The Greater Community Way of
Knowledge. II. Title.

BP605.S58S86 1996   299'.93
                                                      QBI96-20379

To order the books of the New Knowledge Library or to receive information about The Society's audio recordings, educational programs and contemplative services please write:

The Society for The Greater Community Way of Knowledge
P.O. Box 1724 • Boulder, CO 80306-1724 • (303) 938-8401

Dedicated to those individuals who recognize

the world's emergence into the Greater Community

and who feel the need to prepare.

Wisdom
from
The Greater Community

*Y*OU ARE SENT TO THE WORLD FOR A PURPOSE, to contribute your gifts which will emanate from your Knowledge. You have come here for a purpose, to remember your True Home while you are in the world. The great purpose that you carry is with you at this moment, and it will arise in stages as you undergo the preparation that we are providing for you.

Contents

INTRODUCTION

*I*N THIS SECOND VOLUME of *Wisdom from the Greater
Community*, you will take another great step towards learning what Knowledge and Wisdom mean in the larger arena
of life that is called the Greater Community. This will bring you to
a new beginning and a new threshold, a beginning and a threshold
that were never available before to humanity. Humanity is now at the
threshold of the Greater Community, of which it has always been
a part. Now humanity has an opportunity to learn its true heritage,
the nature of its evolution and its greater challenge and promise of
life within a larger arena that contains intelligent life in uncountable
forms and expressions.

You are here at this new beginning. This is no accident. You
were sent here for this purpose. This is the meaning of your being
here. The world's emergence into the Greater Community is the
context within which you can fully experience and learn to express
the nature of your greater purpose and your greater identity.

Humanity is emerging into the Greater Community. Greater
Community forces are in the world today. This is the reality in which
you now live, and for this you will need a greater Knowledge and a
greater Wisdom. You already possess this Knowledge within you, for

the Creator has endowed you with the Knowing Mind, which you will need to experience and to call upon increasingly as the revelation of your real purpose and the meaning of your existence here unfold step by step.

In this second volume of *Wisdom from the Greater Community*, we introduce to you new thresholds of learning, new arenas of application and a greater opportunity to experience the reality of Knowledge and the importance of its expression and contribution in the world. Here you will have the opportunity to begin to learn about the Greater Community, about the mental environment, about the meaning of discernment and discretion, and the great application of The Greater Community Way of Knowledge as it pertains to every aspect of your life as you know it today and as you will need to know it in the future.

We bring this great Teaching to you from the Creator, for this Teaching represents a new testament of the Creator's presence and will within the world and a new expression of your Divinity and your intrinsic association and relationship with life around you. We bring with us a promise, a confirmation and a great challenge. The promise is that your purpose and your calling in the world may become fully realized within the context of the world's emergence into the Greater Community. Here you will finally come to understand why you have a unique nature and a unique design. This will enable you to discover who your Designer is. The confirmation is that you will come to realize what you know and what you have always known, and this will restore to you your self-respect, your ability to love and the greater strength that has been given to you. And, yet, we bring you a challenge as well, a challenge to learn what Knowledge and Wisdom mean within the Greater Community and why they are necessary both to heal the great problems that humanity faces within the world and to face the greater challenge of encountering intelligent life from the Greater

Community.

Come with us, then. Come to receive and come to give. Come to learn and come with the willingness to experience and to explore with an open mind. The Greater Community Way of Knowledge is not here to fulfill the past or even to explain the past. It is here to bring you into the present and to prepare you for the future. This is why you have come into the world, and this will give meaning and direction to all that you have done thus far. The Greater Community Way of Knowledge will give you a new foundation to fully realize why you are here and who sent you.

*To move towards
realizing the real
depth and purpose
of your life,
you must move away
from ambition.*

One

AMBITION

T IS WONDERFUL TO ATTAIN PERSONAL GOALS and to acquire things. It is wonderful, but only for a short time. Securing these things carries with it a great price, part of which you pay at the outset and part of which you pay later. The price can be quantified in terms of strain, dishonesty, desire, greed, or other such problems and errors that can accompany the attainment of any goal, even if it is a worthwhile one. But the greatest price of personal goals and acquisitions is that they disengage you from Knowledge within yourself. Here your preoccupations override your true determination, your true inclinations and your inner voice, which is speaking to you throughout the day to help guide and protect you and to counsel you in matters great and small.

It is wonderful to have that moment of accomplishment when you say to yourself, "I set out to do this thing and I did it!" But how long does that moment last? And what does it bring with it? Is it not followed by the anxiety of how that acquisition or accomplishment will be protected or expanded? Does it not bring an emptiness that makes you feel that you must establish a new goal, a new place to reach, something new to strive for? Your success here is very brief and is quickly replaced by new questions and new anxieties.

Yes, you may have great encouragement from the world, and many people may applaud your achievements, but how long does the pleasure of this last? Only a few moments, surely. And is it a pleasure to swell with pride when others are acknowledging you for your great endeavors? Is it a pleasure to receive compliments when your own internal questioning and needs have not yet been fulfilled? So, you set out to strive again, dealing with many adversities, planning, working feverishly to attain another height which will give but only a momentary pleasure and sense of satisfaction. Indeed, consider the costs, both before and after the achievement if it is made, and then weigh this against the pleasure or satisfaction that are yielded as a result.

If you can look at this honestly and clearly, using your own life as a demonstration as well as the demonstration of others, surely you will see what a vain and desperate pursuit this is, how little is accomplished that is lasting and meaningful and how little happiness is generated in the world. Even if you have sought to accomplish something and have done so in as ethical a manner as possible, without incurring injury or harm upon others, what has it cost you? Has not life passed you by—the simple pleasures and wonderment, moment to moment, missed while you were intensely engaged in reaching your goal? And while you are now attempting to reach your next goal, are you not painfully aware that you are missing something? Are you not painfully aware that perhaps this latest pursuit is really not worth it? Perhaps owning or possessing that thing or this new ability is really not such a great accomplishment after all.

You must consider these questions, and consider them you will, especially at times of disappointment and especially when success, if it is achieved, is followed by emptiness and fearful questioning, "What should I do now? What is left for me?" Indeed, if the goal was not achieved, you are left to question yourself. At first, perhaps, you will question your value or the value of others with whom you were involved. But if you are honest, you will come to question your own priorities and your own motivations. What led you to initiate this pursuit? What has kept you going? Is it really valuable? Is it really what you have come here to do? These fundamental questions are answered by an experience—an experience that at the very outset can be quite painful, as it is painful at times to touch upon something that has been waiting for you for oh so long. But the pain of this is quickly replaced by greater insight and a realignment within yourself once you have hit upon an essential truth. These experiences are the result of moments of introspection often begun by grave disappointment and carried out in times of reappraisal.

To move in a new direction, to move towards realizing the real depth and purpose of your life, you must move away from ambition. Here one of the first things that confronts you is the question, "What do I do now?" as if what you do represents who you are. For many people, this great disorientation is fraught with anxiety and the fear that without all their personal goals, nothing will be accomplished, nothing will happen, that there will be no happiness, no achievement, no value and no relationships—just emptiness and despair. This would be the case if Knowledge did not live within you. If Knowledge were not with you, all of your value would be derived by what you do and what you possess. But Knowledge does live within you, a living reality beyond your personal desires and fears, beyond your personal ambition and personal anxiety, beyond even your individuality. It lives within you. It is great. It is still.

Knowledge is living within you, but like your heart that is beating and your organs that are functioning, you are not aware of it. Throughout your whole life, your body works with very little awareness on your part, with very little appreciation and very little understanding. Knowledge is like that. It is working in you every minute, but it goes unnoticed because it is not part of your plans and ambitions. It is not part of your struggle to acquire things, to be someone and to defend yourself against loss. It goes unrecognized. Yet, even in this state it is serving you. Though most of its service goes unheeded, it is still protecting you, and at times it will override even your personal prerogatives in order to save you from a great calamity. Yet, it does not intrude upon your personal life. It simply carries out its function to protect and sustain you and to move you in the direction of self-realization. It is a Greater Mind within you.

So, while you are busy with your plans, goals, fears, anxieties and all of the fantasies and ideas that accompany them, Knowledge lives within you. But you are not with Knowledge. Disappointment brings you to Knowledge because, even if it is only for a brief moment, it illustrates the futility of many of your pursuits. This gives you pause to reconsider your motives and your primary endeavors. This re-evaluation, in turn, can lead you to experience something new that has been within you all along.

This discovery points you in a different direction, a direction that few have traveled. Therefore, it is mysterious. Its pathway is not unknown, however, because there are individuals who have journeyed that way and, though they made many errors in their journey, they paved a way for you. To move in this direction, ambition cannot go with you because at first you will not know where you are going, what you will do or even why you are doing it. Though you may assign personal reasons in order to justify your involvement, your justifications and definitions will sooner or later prove to be inadequate to justify why you are choosing this way.

In choosing The Way of Knowledge you enter into the Mystery. In choosing the way of ambition you follow the ambitions of others. Here you will have a great deal of company. As you follow your own ambitions, you will judge yourself and others very harshly, calling this group winners and that group losers, this group good and that group bad, all the while trying to be in the winning group.

To choose a different way, you must first stop — stop the ceaseless striving to have this, to be that, to attain this and to avoid that. You must stop driving yourself and be still for a time until you can sense that there is a different direction for you to go. This begins a period of critical fusion. For quite a while you will be wandering about in the desert, so to speak, not certain where you are going or what you are doing. Yet, you are actually going somewhere if you do not interfere.

The true way is not the way of personal ambition, so it defies definition. Everyone who has traveled this way has gone through a period of wandering about, bumping into things, uncertain of where they are going and why they are going there. Nobody can map this part of the journey. In light of your former ambitions and all of the standards and values that went with them, you may appear quite foolish — stupid and foolish, like a lost soul. But you are not lost. You are not nearly as lost as you were before, when you were struggling with yourself every day, beating yourself into submission to have and to do and to be all those things that you thought were necessary for your happiness. You were lost then, for you were not available to Knowledge. Even if you valued honesty, you could not be fully honest with yourself before because you could not sense your deeper inclinations. You could only misrepresent yourself to yourself and to others.

Now you feel more honest but less certain. Now perhaps you feel more connected to yourself, but you will have fewer definitions by which to live. This is a time not to make a great many decisions. This is a time to remain open and maintain a simple life — simple employment and simple involvements. This is the time to stay out of a primary relationship if you are single. This is a time to refrain from changing a primary relationship if you are in one. This is a time of internal re-evaluation. But it is not a mental process.

As you wander around, or seemingly so, you will actually find over time that you are following a certain direction and that there are certain clues along the way and little guides and things that are helping you. Though your way is still ill defined and seemingly incomprehensible, you are actually moving in a certain direction.

The mistake that people make here is that they try to bring their ambitions into the situation. Now they think that they are going to achieve spiritual heights. Now they think that they are going to have spiritual relationships. Now they think that they are going to have spiritual wealth, spiritual power and spiritual prestige. When this happens, people redefine themselves all over again and are lost. Now they are doubly lost, for they think they are doing something very genuine when in fact they are just acting out their ambitions once again. It is more difficult now to recognize this because everything can seem very edifying. But it is no different from the person who is out to make a million dollars. It just looks more edifying, and so it is more difficult to realize it is but another form of self-deception.

If you can keep ambition at bay and remain in a state of unknowing and uncertainty, then your way will be revealed, and you will slowly follow it. As you continue, you will recognize that you are following a certain direction and that you are going there for purposes that you can experience even if you cannot yet define them. You will also realize that you are not traveling alone, for companions will come to join you. If you can refrain from ambition and self-definition here, then you will move more powerfully, and Knowledge within you will increasingly become a source of guidance, inspiration and protection that you can experience. Without your attempt to harness and direct your life, Knowledge will emerge. This doesn't mean you are being weak or passive. It simply means that you are attending to something greater. Here you take your former self-determination and apply it to your desire to have Knowledge and to live a life of greater truth. That is the commitment. If this is being followed honestly and sincerely and if you are willing to work for it, then you will be able to generate sufficient energy to move forward on the Path of Knowledge.

During this transitional time, everything becomes redefined. Yet, many things don't become defined for a long time. This is a period when you must find freedom from your own self-definitions, which is a very real kind of freedom. You must become free of all your beliefs and assumptions about the world and about other people and free of all the judgments and grievances that attend them. This is a freedom you can experience. Only here, once you have traveled sufficiently in this direction, can you begin to really see that ambition is a form of personal hell for people. Whether they win or lose in their great pursuits, there is little joy, little empathy with life, little affinity with others and little satisfaction. It all comes to look very tragic.

As you travel in The Greater Community Way of Knowledge, you will see, particularly in the lives of others who inspire you, that great things are achieved when people are allowing a greater Knowledge to emerge within them and are combining that with practical skills in their field of endeavor. This produces something of lasting value. Their activity consumed them, but in a different way. You see that sometimes they achieved some rewards and recognition for their accomplishments, but often they did not. They were following something else. They were participating in a Greater Reality to achieve something. Sometimes they produced things of practical value. Sometimes they produced only Mystery. Their personal goals were not the driving force. Their desire to do something, be something and have something was not where their power came from. That is not why they were engaged. Yes, in most cases some of their own personal ambitions were involved, but they were not predominant. Personal ambition has never created anything of value in the world. Only a greater initiative, born of Knowledge within individuals and combined with the Knowledge of others who are working in concert with them, can produce something of greater value.

For those who have chosen The Way of Knowledge and are in the "wandering in the desert" phase, there is little assurance that they will produce anything of value at any time for anyone. There is no assurance of success. There is no fame, no glory and no wealth. They will not win love or money. They do not know what they will get out of the situation. They are only doing it because they must do it. Either their former life proved to be too painful or they experienced something else calling them — usually a combination of both. What they will produce, they cannot say. Who they will be, they cannot say. What they will have, they cannot say. It is up to the Greater Power now. They are standing by, willing to carry on whatever is necessary. They are truly motivated. Their result is beyond them. They can now be primary participants in achieving a concrete result or a mysterious result, whatever it may be, but they don't know what they are creating. They are only participating in creation now. Now they have greater promise. Yet, there are many pitfalls along the way. They can make many errors, particularly if they try to regain control and determine the nature and the direction of their pursuit. But if they do not do this, they will come to realize the reality of Knowledge, the direction of Knowledge and the expression of Knowledge in their individual lives.

To experience Knowledge, you must follow Knowledge. To value Knowledge, you must follow Knowledge. To comprehend Knowledge, you must follow Knowledge. You cannot stand apart from it and have an understanding of it at all. You cannot accurately say, "Well, I had an experience of intuition and that is all it is." Knowledge is greater, much greater. You must follow it to know it. And to know it, you will have to proceed without ambition.

To begin this journey, you must have your own ambitions fail. Actually, they do not fail. You simply begin to realize what they are and what they produce. This looks like failure because you think that without your ambitions you are nothing and are going nowhere. So, the experience of failure attends this great recasting of your life. As you proceed, a Greater Mind within you will begin to emerge and will be the source of your direction, your accomplishment and your meaning. This you cannot find. You can only participate and learn as you go.

How simple and yet how difficult this is for people who, because they are disassociated from God, are attempting to be God in their own lives. Either they willfully take control of their lives or they give up in submission to an idea of God, a distant God, a God who will not advise them. Either of these extremes, and all of the positions in between them, are governed by ambition. The dominating person is willing to be responsible. The submissive follower is not willing to be responsible. But they are in the same category because of what motivates them.

To know that Knowledge is real, to understand its presence and its expression in your life, you must follow it — not thinking that it will do everything for you, but realizing that it will give you the things that you need to do. It will move you towards certain things and away from others. It will allow an opportunity for new people to join you and for old ones to depart. This happens without ambition.

Think of ambition like this: It is an attempt to make separation work. It is an attempt to make your individual, self-created self satisfactory. This pursuit must fail for you to begin to realize that you have a greater life that exists without your self-definition but that needs your assistance and all of your energy for its expression. This is a new life, a new impulse, a new motivation. It is rare because few have undertaken it. It is great because it extends beyond the boundaries of human ambition. It is mysterious because its source is beyond the world. It is helpful because it yields a greater result and generates satisfaction in people.

The next time you ask yourself, "What do I really want?" ask yourself a different question. Ask yourself, "What would I seek if I did not want anything?" Ask yourself this different question, and new questions will come to mind to ask. This is a different kind of questioning and leads in a different direction. If you believe that your attempts at fulfillment are satisfactory, then go spend time with people who are further along in their pursuit than you are and see what kind of results they are producing. Look at the quality of their lives. Look at the degree of their satisfaction. Look at their ability to be in relationship, to experience affinity and community. Do they inspire you or does what they own inspire you? It will be no different for you. Win or lose, you will miss the essence of life. That is why you must choose again and ask a new kind of question of yourself.

The man and woman of
Knowledge
want economy because
they need time
to focus on Knowledge
and on learning
greater things.

Two

POSSESSIONS

NOW WE SHALL SPEAK ABOUT OWNING THINGS and having things in the world. First of all, let us say that there is nothing you could possibly possess that is nearly as valuable or that in any way can compare with the value of Knowledge and Wisdom. You must develop Wisdom in order to experience Knowledge and carry it with you. When we speak of possessions, do not think we are giving them this value. Do not think that they hold this esteem in our view.

We speak of possessions because owning things is part of being in the world. There are things that are useful and beneficial and provide comfort and joy to a certain degree. And of course there are many things that are quite useless and merely serve as distractions or are damaging in and of themselves. Since you all have to own things, let us talk about ownership and give you the understanding that what is most important is that you set your sights on the reclamation of Knowledge and on developing the relationships that can express Knowledge effectively.

In your world, there seem to be almost unlimited things to own and to do. Certainly, there is enough to fill up your time completely, and this is occurring all around you. People are obsessed with things. They are consumed by things. They purchase things. They own things. They fix things. They trade things. They sell things. They buy more things. Then they buy things to fix the things they already have, and it goes on and on and on. And of course the more you own, the more you must support what you own and, therefore, you must work harder in order to keep what you have and, hopefully, to buy more. So, this buying and owning becomes totally dominating. It overshadows the greater questions of life and seems to ameliorate the suffering individuals feel as a result of living a life that is unknown to them and to others. The abuse of ownership is everywhere. Its manifestations are there for you to see. The ways that people relate to their possessions and how they relinquish themselves to their possessions can be recognized in many, many forms of expression.

Is it bad to have things while so much great abuse is going on? Is it bad? The answer to this requires some explanation. The answer is yes, it can be bad. Having many things is a great disadvantage, not because it is bad in and of itself, but because it takes your mind away from other things which are more important, and it keeps you disassociated from yourself. The world in which you live is devoted to owning and affording things. Indeed, people are esteemed by how much they have, how hard they work for it, how they have accumulated it, and so forth. The accumulation of possessions is an ever-increasing burden and an ever-dominating focus, overshadowing the possibility of living a true life.

Owning things can be bad. However, owning things is a fact of life, and you must own some things in order to function successfully in the world. Here you recognize that you are not an ascetic. You have not chosen an ascetic life, nor do you live in monasteries. You have to own many things in order to function in the world, so where do you draw the line? That is the question. The question is not whether it is good or bad to have things. The question is where to draw the line.

Here we must once again return to Knowledge, for only Knowledge knows what you need and what you don't need. If you can open yourself to Knowledge, wait for Knowledge and abide with Knowledge, then you will have an opportunity to know where to draw the line for yourself. Without this, you will attempt to imitate other people based upon whatever values you hold to be more virtuous. You will try, once again, to live out a set of standards based upon your own value system or based upon the value system of someone else which you think is better than yours. But you cannot draw the line here. Here you are again functioning purely from trial and error. When you are functioning from trial and error, disappointment is with you constantly. It is very hard to sort things out if this is the only means you are choosing.

By ownership, I am not only speaking of physical things. I am also talking about ideas. So, let me speak about this so that we can have a larger view of what ownership really is. Some people collect objects. Others collect ideas. Part of the attraction of collecting ideas is having exciting thoughts and having the thrill of having an insight, which is like the thrill of buying a new thing—perhaps a new garment, which you have the thrill of wearing for a few days, and then it just becomes a garment, one more thing. People often value insights in the same way. They have an insight, and oh, they are excited, and they think it is so meaningful. They walk around proudly with it and share it eagerly with their friends. Then after a few days, well, it's just another thought to add to millions of other thoughts that are already there. So, having insights is like buying a new dress or a new pair of shoes. The thrill is gone quickly and you have one more thing.

Owning things is not merely collecting objects; it is also collecting ideas. Many people collect ideas. They are always searching for new ideas, and when they find new ideas they say, "Oh, this is so interesting! What an interesting idea! Fantastic!" They read a new book and say, "Oh, a great book! Oh, what tremendous insights!" They are excited about this book for a few days, and then they go on to other new, exciting and interesting things. It is like buying bric-a-brac. The only difference is one is physical and the other is mental. But it is all accumulation. People can have a great many ideas they have collected, even an enormous collection of ideas on a particular subject. There are always more to collect, of course, because in the realm of ideas you don't run out. But what you find in the realm of ideas is that after awhile most ideas are like other ideas. The differences between them are not so great. It is the same with objects. After awhile, one is like another — it is all stuff!

Some people think owning things is disdainful, and so they go and collect ideas. Some people collect spiritual practices. Other people collect spiritual artifacts. Collect, collect, collect — whether it is objects or ideas — collect, collect, collect, until you are swollen and glutted with all this, and it all seems to fill up the emptiness within you that is a calling for Knowledge.

When someone comes to study The Greater Community Way of Knowledge, often they are eager for new ideas. "Oh, I want new ideas!" They read *Wisdom from the Greater Community*. "Oh, new insights! New ideas! Fantastic!" Or they say, "Oh, I've heard this before." It is like their other collection of insights. It is all more ideas to them. More ideas, more ideas. Or perhaps it is more insightful experiences. "Oh, I had a great experience!" And then when the experience wears off they say, "There's nothing left here for me. I'll go on to new things."

Many people approach the Teaching in this way, with the idea of collecting more things. Or perhaps their pursuit is more desperate. Perhaps they are looking for an answer. They must have the answer. They are not interested in collecting ideas, but they must have something that will give them relief. So, they read *Wisdom from the Greater Community*, and they find something that gives them relief, but it only gives relief for a few days. Then their pain returns, and they say, "Oh, well. This program is not for me. I have to find something else. It has not taken my pain away. It has not given me relief." So they go on to new things.

Some people approach this Teaching to collect new ideas, new insights, and so forth. Some people even think that if they have these ideas, they will be able to make more money and buy more things. Other people come because they seek relief, an escape from their difficulties, and they are desperately looking. The strange thing is that they will all be disappointed. The Way of Knowledge is not about accumulating things or escaping things, not at all. That is why we make *Steps to Knowledge*, the first level of study, available to people. It contains enough Wisdom to exceed most needs, if it is studied adequately, applied wisely and brought into the realm of relationships.

What it also does, interestingly enough, is expose people's motives for studying it. If you are studying *Steps to Knowledge* in order to have more ideas, new insights or to keep the excitement going and if you continue in the preparation, you will be able to become aware of your motives. At some point, you will come to realize that your motives and the offering of *Steps to Knowledge* are not the same, so either you must abandon the preparation in order to serve your motives or abandon your motives in order to participate in the preparation. At some point, people reach this juncture and their whole motivation for study has to be completely re-evaluated.

The real motivation for studying *Steps to Knowledge* is mysterious. The real reason you do it is that you must do it. That is Knowledge. Only Knowledge can motivate you to find Knowledge. Other interests—accumulation, acquisition, escape, excitement, love—cannot take you to Knowledge. Even love, which in most people's minds is an exciting experience rather than a living Spiritual Presence, will not take you to Knowledge because you find out on the Path of Knowledge that you have some very unloving and difficult experiences. It is not all wonderful, glorious, exciting and spiritual. It is hard. "Oh, my God! What is happening to me? I was a nice person; now I don't know what I am!"

All of these other motivations for studying The Way of Knowledge must be re-evaluated because they do not take you to Knowledge. You go to Knowledge because you must go to Knowledge. It is like a deep, deep instinct beyond your wants, fears and personal preferences. It is like a homecoming. You are drawn in and are willing to make the sacrifices. You are willing to take on the challenges and are willing to make the re-evaluations. Why? Because you *must* do it. The preparation is not promising you a great love life, abundance, a new car or a new personality, where you trade in the old personality for a new personality, one that is more fun. No! That is acquiring possessions.

Acquiring possessions is like eating food: If you eat too much, you'll get stuffed and have stomach problems. If you buy too many things or ideas, you'll get stuffed and you will have health problems and mental problems, and so forth. Whether you are trying to find truth or stimulation, acquiring things begins to make you sick and you must return to simplicity, which is abiding with Knowledge. Abiding with Knowledge is so simple that it utterly confounds people because they are trying to get something, have something, escape something or experience something. Knowledge *is*. It is not a commodity. It is not a set of thrilling ideas. It is not a group of spiritual objects.

At the beginning of *Steps to Knowledge*, it says, "Knowledge is with me. Where am I?" If you could fully understand this lesson, you would learn half of the entire preparation right there. "Where am I? What am I doing?" So, when we speak of possessions, we are talking about everything that everyone is trying to get out of life. As you try to get things out of life, life escapes you. This is frustrating!

Some night when it is clear and the stars are shining brightly, look up at the sky and ask yourself, "What do I want to get out of that?" Speak to the stars and say, "Okay. Give it to me! I want the experience of Universal Wisdom or complete affinity with life. Give it to me!" And the stars are just there. They neither come towards you nor go away from you. They neither yield nor retreat. They are there for you.

People do *Steps to Knowledge* and they say, "Okay! When am I going to get it? Where is the reward? I'm here! I'm practicing, sort of. Where is the reward?" At some point, if they persist in their preparation, they will come to realize that the problem is not with the preparation; the problem is with their motives. You see, without its possessions, your personal mind literally has nothing to hold it together. Its whole sense of identity is based on what it owns, what it thinks, and what it is associated with. Because it is artificial, it must have all these things and keep renewing them or it begins to shrink and fall apart. So, we let it shrink, not drastically but slowly, not to punish it, but simply to redirect the mind to develop a different set of abilities and to gradually gain a different focus and orientation — an orientation away from accumulation towards profound experience, so that one day when you look up at the stars, the stars are there for you and you are there for them.

The possession issue, by the way, accounts for much of the difficulty that people experience in relationships. Here people enter relationships and they have all these expectations about what they are going to get and how they are going to get it and what they deserve, and so forth. So, their ability to actually experience another person and to experience kinship becomes very limited. After all, how can you have the experience of kinship if you have this huge agenda about what you are going to have and who you are going to be and how it is going to work out, and so forth?

Having all of these expectations and this motive for accumulation disables you from being able to experience another. It disables your discernment; it disables your perception; it disables real evaluation based upon compatibility and shared direction. If you enter the relationship without all of these motives for accumulation, things could be clear for you, very clear. But for the person who is governed by these motives, it takes years to come around to the obvious — and then only after many expectations and desires have been disappointed. So, you can see that disappointment is an important part of learning, but it cannot be the only part of learning.

Let us come back now to see where to draw the line in owning things. If you are following me thus far and are thinking about what I am telling you, thinking about it as it relates to you and not to other people, then you can say, "Where do I draw the line? I have to have a certain number of things in order to function well in the world, and I have to have a certain number of ideas, insights and good experiences in order to function in the world. Now, where do I draw the line because I know I can keep buying things and bringing them home until my home is stuffed to the ceiling with things. I can keep accumulating ideas, insights and happy experiences until my mind is filled to the ceiling, stuffed with things. I know I can do that. Where do I draw the line? Where is the balance?"

First of all, find out what you really need and what you really use. What you really use and what you really need are very related. This applies both to the possession of objects as well as to the possession of ideas. What do you really use? What do you really need? People assess their needs for things that give them comfort and often they think some of their possessions will be needed some day, but not today or anytime soon. What do you need now? When you begin to ask this question and seriously consider it, you will see that you don't need a great deal. Yet, the things that you do need should be very good. The objects in your possession should be well made and durable. The ideas with which you associate should be abiding and helpful, so much so that you cannot exhaust them easily. Many of the ideas and insights that people accumulate for their own edification are easily exhausted and have no abiding value; they have no depth and cannot provide meaning. They are either self-gratifying or are only initially stimulating, and beyond that they can offer no more.

What you need is based on what you use. That is the first criterion. If you own thirty garments, and you only use five, then what are the other twenty-five for? And why are they occupying time and energy in your life? This also carries over into relationships because certain people collect relationships the same way that other people collect books, coins, plants, paintings, clothes, or whatever. What relationships are really important to you? This fundamental question requires an honest response.

Next, ask yourself if owning this thought, this object or this insight or being in this relationship feels correct to you? Not "Can I justify it because of its benefits?" but "Does it feel correct?" This is calling upon your experience now, not simply your ideas, because many things can be justified that are not good for you and only prove to be a burden.

The third criterion is to appeal to Knowledge to show you what to do. This is important if the first two do not yield a decisive decision. Here you are asking to be shown. "Show me what I need to do. Show me what is important." Remember, you only need a certain number of objects, ideas and relationships, but they must all be very important and must have great value because they will be sustaining you mentally and physically. So, it is not a question of denying all possessions, all relationships and all ideas or opening yourself to everything that comes your way. Those are two extremes. Neither is a healthy path. Learning discernment and discrimination is a major part of every person's development, if it is based upon true association. I am speaking of *true* association.

What possessions do you really use? Which ones do you really need? Why own anything else? What ideas are really helping you? Which ideas have depth and are important? Why do you need to entertain other ideas? What relationships are really essential for your development and support your spiritual growth? What are you doing in relationships that cannot do this? This sorting out creates real economy. Economy is essential because it gives you enough reserves of vitality — time, energy and motivation — to direct yourself towards greater things.

People who are dominated by too many ideas, too many relationships or too many possessions cannot enter a greater arena of understanding or accomplishment. They are carrying too much baggage. Their lives are full. Their concerns have overtaken them. There is nowhere for them to go. All they can do is service their possessions. They will go no further. They will be identified with their possessions, whether they are objects, ideas or people. They will be filled up 100%. You cannot add anything to them. Nothing new can enter. They are closed to life. They are, in a sense, taking care of the museum of their life. They are museum curators of their own life, keeping track of everything that has been collected so far. What a dusty and dismal existence! They look at the sky and they don't see it. After all, if your life is about preserving your personal museum, why have a universe anyway? It is just scenery. Why ask greater questions? Why feel your pain and your yearning for greater things?

The man and woman of Knowledge want economy because they need time to focus on Knowledge and on learning greater things. They cannot be bogged down with objects, ideas or people that are not part of their greater pursuit. This is economy, and this is important. As you progress and study The Greater Community Way of Knowledge, gradually things fall away, not because they are bad but simply because they are no longer needed. You cannot use them. You don't want to carry a lot of extra baggage. Your life, in a sense, is becoming streamlined. Your burden is getting lighter. Now you can assume greater responsibilities.

As you can see from my presentation, the idea of possessions is much more inclusive than what you may have considered before. This new understanding is very important because The Greater Community Way of Knowledge represents the transformation of relationships and the entrance into a new life and a new kind of experience. You cannot make this journey if you are carrying too much baggage. You can only carry what you really need. Then you can step faster and more lightly and feel less oppressed by what you are leaving behind.

When you are presented with new objects or given opportunities to buy new things, acquire new ideas, meet new people, or participate in new activities, ask yourself, "What do I really need and what do I really use? What is essential?" Part of this you can answer yourself. Sometimes you must appeal to Knowledge, not simply to tell you the answer because Knowledge does not engage in a lot of conversation, but to demonstrate it. Particularly in very important decisions, the way to go must be demonstrated because an idea is not enough. You must see it, know its value and see that it is totally relevant to your life and to your needs. This comes through demonstration.

People pester Knowledge with all kinds of questions. Often they want to accumulate more insight, more ideas, and more people. More, more, more! But Knowledge is silent. What Knowledge will do is set up a learning situation that will help the person come to terms with the real issues at stake. This is because Knowledge is

not like a little errand boy that brings you everything you want—
like room service! Knowledge is the Master. You are the student.
Yet, people often begin their study acting like they are the master
and Knowledge is the student. Somewhere in the process the entire
order of authority becomes reversed—often very gradually and
sometimes with very big steps.

Wisdom from the Greater Community: Volume I states that God's
first purpose is to unburden you. That sounds like a nice idea. But
think about what it really means. What it really means is that the
whole acquisition motive must become reversed. If you are going
somewhere in life, you cannot take everything with you. You can
only take what you need, and this unburdens you. This gives you
time, energy, mental freedom and the ability to establish new ideas
and new alliances. This redefines and redirects your entire relationship with objects in the physical world. This new relationship is not
based on fantasy and past association now. It is based on usefulness
and real value. This creates a healthy relationship with the physical
world, with people and with ideas.

Some people have wondered, "Why would I study The
Greater Community Way of Knowledge? I do not really want to
read books anymore." The reason is that The Way of Knowledge
gives you a few things to deeply consider, rather than simply pump-
ing more ideas into your mind and keeping it stimulated. Consider
the idea, "Knowledge is with me. Where am I?" You could spend
many years on this one idea alone. One idea! You cannot exhaust
that idea. It is revolutionary. "Alone I can accomplish nothing."
This is another revolutionary idea. It could change the world if it
were contemplated and allowed to alter your experience of yourself
and the world. Then you are no longer what you own. You are
aligned with something invisible and mysterious which is the guiding principle of all life.

Our pleasure is great.
Our pains are small.
Your pleasures are small.
Your pains are great.

Three

PLEASURE

PLEASURE IS A FOCAL POINT of most people's minds. It requires attention. Like possessions, pleasure is something that dominates people's awareness, time and energy. Like possessions, pleasure is something that can be bad. Again, you must look at what pleasure is and where you draw the boundaries that determine whether you participate in something that is truly pleasurable or whether you do not.

It is a pleasure for us to speak and to convey to you a greater body of Knowledge as well as a Greater Community perspective, which you and your race will need in order to progress. Our pleasure in this is born of the fact that a gift is being given to you through us. This is the greatest pleasure. This is the pleasure that has no boundaries and does not wear off. It is a pleasure that can be conveyed and resonated through many minds. Therefore, it grows rather than diminishes as it is passed along. It is a pleasure born of Knowledge. It amplifies itself. It is a pleasure unlike any other pleasure that you can find.

All other pleasures weaken once they are broadcast. They diminish. Like a pebble thrown into a pool, the rippling effect becomes weaker and weaker as it spreads out. The pleasure that we speak of, however, has the reverse effect. It is more like planting seeds. As these seeds take hold in minds that are fertile with the desire for Knowledge and the recognition of the need for Knowledge, they grow and flourish there to bear fruit, once again spreading their seeds to new minds that are fertile for Knowledge. They in turn bear fruit, and so on. Therefore, this greater pleasure propagates itself and yields ever greater fruits as it is given and received.

But what about the pleasures of the world and all the myriad pursuits that are undertaken to acquire them, to keep them and to ward off their dissipation? What of these? Clearly, given the excesses that you see about you, the pursuit of pleasure can be seen as utterly destructive and demeaning. Examples of this are so common and take so many forms that you need but look at human life around you to see their many expressions. So, do you say to yourself, "I will eschew pleasure altogether"? The problem with this approach is that you do this for pleasure. Here you are merely changing your avenue or kind of attempt for pleasure. If it is a pleasure to give up pleasure, how do you give up pleasure? Is pleasure only an avoidance of pain? If so, pain will attend you and follow you like a shadow, for pleasure and pain are very associated. Therefore, if you seek pleasure to avoid pain, you produce more pain, which requires more attempts at pleasure, which produces more pain, and so forth. Is pleasure always associated with pain?

These are all very important questions to consider. Your basis for considering them is to take stock of your life and to evaluate your investment in pleasure and what it is costing you. This evaluation can only take place when you can view things and review your own experience objectively. The desires, fantasies and philosophies regarding the acquisition of pleasure are so ever present, so inflated and so subjective that it is very difficult to gain any kind of honest appraisal. However, your experience will not betray you if you are able to interpret it correctly, which you can do if your desire for truth is strong and if you are willing to review or re-evaluate anything that is necessary, even if it is painful to do so. The pain of re-evaluation is not nearly as great as the pain of avoidance. The pain of recognition is minute compared to the pain of seeking substitutes or trying to lose yourself in pursuits that can only mask or conceal your deeper needs and the suffering that is the result of their denial.

So, what are the criteria for determining which pleasures are worthwhile and which are not? Let us give you an idea to consider, for you must consider ideas. Simple answers can never satisfy this inquiry. We give you an invitation for study and contemplation, appraisal and re-evaluation. These are answers that mean something because they take you somewhere. They do not merely pacify you. They actually lead you into a new arena of understanding. Regarding any pleasure that you find attractive and are thinking of pursuing, consider the cost involved. This is particularly important regarding pleasures in the world, which constitute most of the pleasures that you can think of. We shall speak of these and then we shall speak about the pleasure of Knowledge, which is very different from the pleasures of the world.

Like possessions, you need some pleasures in the world. Whether it is possession of things, ideas or relationships, you need some of them. Yet, they need to be important. They need to yield something of real value to you, and the value that they yield must be greater than your investment in them. This holds true for any kind of pleasure that you find attractive or wish to pursue. Given the investment of time and energy — which includes money, of course, for this represents time and energy — how much does that pleasure yield to you? How great are its fruits? Pleasure is an investment. What does it yield? An honest appraisal of your own experience will provide genuine guidelines for this, as will the promptings of Knowledge within you, which will seek to engage you in those activities that are most beneficial, forsaking all others that merely rob you of your time, energy and attention.

Simple pleasures are valuable if the investment in them is not too great and if they yield something of real value. Let us give you an example. It may be a great pleasure to stand by a beautiful river as it passes by. That is a simple pleasure, small in comparison to the pleasure of Knowledge, but genuine nonetheless. However, if you must travel halfway around the world to have this experience, then the investment in this simple, momentary pleasure is clearly inappropriate. Yet, people travel halfway around the world to observe some natural feature or to see some spectacle in order to have a pleasurable moment. Their reward is very small in comparison to their great investment.

Most of the pleasures that are damaging to people are damaging because the investment is great and the reward is very small. In many cases, there is no reward at all. There is only investment and reinvestment. Here we have the contrast between fantasy regarding the pleasure and the real experience. How often have you been disappointed by the real experience of something because the anticipation was so great and so inflated and you had invested so much? Then the real experience came, and it really was not that fine after all. Observe little children around Christmas, how their anticipation and their expectations are so great. The investment of time, energy and attention is so great, but after the gifts are all unwrapped, there is disappointment. The investment is great. The reward is small. Consider how many times you were disappointed by things that you had hoped would be wonderful and magnificent. Why the disappointment? Because the investment was great and the reward was small. Recall experiences where you made an investment of yourself and there was no reward at all.

Often the cost of pursuing a pleasure cannot be accounted for at the outset because when the pursuit robs you of your awareness of yourself, of your interaction with life and of your appreciation of your own existence, such a great price goes unnoticed. Yet, people pay it because they are depressed and angry and lack value and meaning in their lives. They are paying the price all the time. They often associate their suffering with other things, so they seek greater pleasures, which exact great prices, and their dilemma and depression become deeper. In fact, their depression can become so deep that it is like a dark cell with no windows where no light can penetrate.

High expectations and great disappointments can dominate a person's life. The expectation of romance in relationship exacts an exorbitant price, both immediately in terms of time, energy and attention and in a long-range sense. People lose so much over this pursuit and how little is their reward—a few moments of self-inflated pleasure or self-abandonment or a few moments of physical sensation, none of which can be maintained for long. The reality of the relationship can seem very depressing in contrast to the thrill of romance. That is because people invest in the romance and not in the relationship. If you invest a great deal in something that yields very little, you will suffer and your pain will be great. If you invest in something that can yield a great deal, has lasting value and will grow as a result of your participation, then your pains will be small and your investment will be good.

The question then isn't, "What should I do to make myself happy?" The question can be cast in a different way. Consider another question, for example, "Where can I invest myself that will yield the greatest results for myself and others?" This is a much more objective question, for it requires an appraisal based upon your own experience. If the appraisal is based only upon your expectations, you will have no basis for appraisal. Expectations are hope based upon disappointment. How can this be an honest appraisal? But if you ask yourself, "How can I invest myself in such a way that it produces the greatest results or the most value for myself and other people?" it will orient you more towards an objective approach than if you only ask, "How can I make myself happy?" If you don't know how to make yourself happy, your approach will be much more subjective and will be fraught with great expectations. It is more difficult to get an honest appraisal with this approach.

Investment is in terms of time, energy and awareness. You want your reward to give you greater awareness, greater affinity with life and a greater sense of your value and purpose in the world — not the value and purpose that you invent for your own delights, but the value and purpose that are intrinsic to your being here. This value cannot be exhausted. It will not leave you and will only grow as greater attention, time and energy are devoted to its expression and experience. Our pleasure is great. Our pains are small. Your pleasures are small. Your pains are great. It is a matter of investment and appraisal. Preparation in The Greater Community Way of Knowledge reverses this trend. It goes against the ways of the world and sets a new example for human development and achievement.

Now, let me introduce another idea regarding pleasure. This relates to the idea that true value offers a reward that grows and yields benefits for yourself and others. Real pleasure is associated with achievement. You cannot escape this. It is a fact. Things are valued because they are useful according to the purpose that you hold. If something yields value according to your purpose as you understand it, you will value it. Even if your purpose is false and self-deceiving, you will value it nonetheless. Value and pleasure are therefore highly associated. You cannot separate them. If something does not serve a purpose that you value, then it will not yield pleasure for you. Even if it yields happy sensations and a momentary reprieve from the stress of being in the world, it will not be greatly valued. Something that is greatly valued yields a deeper kind of pleasure because it is life affirming. If the value is genuine and if the purpose with which it is associated is genuine, it will yield a greater and more lasting value.

For example, recall in your life those brief moments or interludes where you experienced your own worth, not in a self-congratulatory way but in a genuine way. In spite of your efforts or denials, you experienced your own value—a moment of experiencing affinity with life. The value of these experiences is so great in contrast to all other experiences that they stand out in your memory like sharp points of light against a backdrop of empty space. Like the heavens above you, they are brilliant in contrast to the mundane level of experience. They outshine all of the momentary pleasures that you have accumulated over time. They yield more value in their momentary expression than years and years of attempting to derive value from other things. The investment in them was small. The reward is great and expanding.

Therefore, the path of true fulfillment reinvests you in things that produce great value for you and for others. Here your approach must transcend your own personal wishes and needs because if your pursuit is selfish, it cannot yield greater rewards. It is being identified with little things and little pleasures which exact great prices, both immediately and residually over time. They darken your life, cast clouds over your mind and obstruct the greater possibilities that are waiting for you.

How do you know what a great or small pleasure is? Your experience will tell you if you are able to view it honestly with a willingness to change or readjust things in your life. Knowledge is the barometer here. Even if you are uncertain what Knowledge is, you nonetheless feel drawn towards certain things and resist other things. You can resist Knowledge and be drawn towards things that are of no value, but this happens at the surface of your mind. Your deeper feelings and deeper experiences will always orient you in a true direction. Even if you misinterpret the direction, even if you resist going there, your deeper nature will take you towards that which is most beneficial for you. You will feel greater pleasure as you move in this direction and greater confusion, anger and disappointment as you move away from it.

You see, underneath all of your desires and attempts at self-gratification you have a natural homing device within you that brings you towards those individuals, experiences and involvements that are essential for your development. These things yield greater rewards. Whatever difficulties you may encounter in pursuing them, those difficulties are small in contrast to the rewards which they produce. As you approach these things, you will need to hold this in faith because you have not yet experienced the rewards themselves, and at times the investment can seem too great or too burdensome. In fact, it is very small. You must find this out through experience. This requires time and faith. So, you say to yourself, "Following in this direction is very difficult, but I have a sense that it will yield something of great value. I cannot tell you what that will look like, but I must follow it because I know I must."

Remember, only Knowledge will take you to Knowledge. Other motives will become revealed and must be altered or abandoned. Knowledge will take you to Knowledge. A sense of true value will take you to those things of true value. A sense of greater pleasure will take you to things that produce greater pleasure. They all lead away from the many other things which can only mock the greater meaning that only a greater pleasure and a greater value can yield. Here you step out of the seemingly hopeless predicament in which humanity is mired.

At times the way seems lonely and uncertain, but something in you is guiding you forward. Here you must follow a greater calling, a calling you cannot understand, a calling you have not yet learned to appreciate, a calling whose trials and tribulations, though seemingly large in the moment, are in fact small compared to the greater rewards awaiting you. How can you be certain that you are doing the right thing? How can you be certain? You can only be certain because you know you must proceed. This knowing comes from deep within you. It does not happen in the realm of your personality. It is not a compulsion. It is not a violent or persistent personal need. It is something greater within you.

As small pleasures and things of no pleasure are abandoned, you will find that there will be emptiness in your life. Allow the emptiness to be there. Do not fill it in with new things. Part of your life should always be empty. This creates a vacuum effect, allowing greater experiences to come to you, allowing your boundaries to be expanded, enabling you to progress forward and to develop your true capabilities. Small pleasures fill up the mind entirely so there is no room for anything to enter. Great pleasures always create more space, so there is always room for new experience and a deepening of the understanding of the meaning of your life.

To study The Greater Community Way of Knowledge is to reorient yourself to the true meaning of your life. You will take many small steps along the way as you proceed. Your other motives and your other attachments will become sharply contrasted so that you will be able to perceive them in a more objective manner. This takes faith, for here you are walking away from things that you have believed before to be of great value, and you are moving in a direction that you cannot yet justify. You are going there because something in you is telling you that you must.

You can only find the rewards by achieving them, for rewards are based upon achievement. With momentary pleasure, there is no achievement; there is only a great price for a moment of satisfaction, a moment of self-abandonment or a moment of delight. You only have to look at the human condition around you and in your own life to see the complete demonstration of this.

If you seek great pleasure, then seek great value. Invest yourself in that which yields a greater reward. How do you know what this is? This is demonstrated by the needs of the world and by your own inner need. People stand around saying, "Who am I? What should I do in my life? I don't know what to do." They are looking at themselves personally. If you look at the world, the world needs you. It needs talent, ability and contribution. It needs genuine relationships. It needs investment. The world, if it is attended to, will call this out of you and eventually you will find the avenue of expression and contribution that is yours to claim.

This invests you in that which produces a greater value and a greater pleasure. Here pleasure is a deep satisfaction and confirmation of your life. Yet, it transcends even this definition because it has a resonating effect within you and beyond you as well. So, do not look at yourself personally and say, "Well, what do I want and how will it make me happy?" Look at the world and ask, "What does the world need and what can I give?" Within your personal mind, you will not understand your own meaning and you will not recognize the greater calling for your contributions to be given. But the world demonstrates this. When the outer need and your inner need converge and join, then you will be able to recognize the avenue that you should pursue.

A true life draws 100% of a person's energy, but it does this gradually because people are not capable yet of giving 100%, even if they hold this to be a valuable thing to do. Gradually, your investment will deepen and the rewards will be greater. This will draw you away from other pursuits and interests which yield very little and require a great investment. Only those little pleasures that require a small investment will be able to survive. They can have a valuable role to play. It is still a pleasure to look at the stars or stand by the stream or enjoy your garden or enjoy something that you do that is pleasurable. The reward is small, but it has not taken the place of your greater pursuit in life.

Following The Greater Community Way of Knowledge readjusts all things so that you are able to devote yourself to great values and great rewards and yet have those small pleasures that are necessary for your momentary convenience and personal value. There is no conflict here. However, going from a life of small pleasure and great investment to a life of great pleasure and small investment represents a complete reversal. This reversal must be carried on gradually. Within this is a tremendous period of re-evaluation and rededication that will affect every aspect of your life and everything that you value or hold dear. This is very confusing at times, for you no longer identify with things that were formally pleasurable to you, but you do not know what will take their place. If you are wise, you will not attempt to replace them but will allow the changing focus and direction of your life to illustrate to you the greater value that is awaiting you.

This is going from poverty to wealth, for wealth is investing yourself in that which yields the greatest benefit for yourself and others. Poverty is investing greatly in things that yield little or no pleasure or value. Wealth and poverty are not about how big your house is or what kind of automobile you drive or how much money is in your pocket or what your wardrobe looks like. Wealth and poverty are very different here. In this different light, the wealthy seem poor and often the poor seem wealthy. This, then, gives you a genuine reference point with which to gauge value in the world. Again, your life is part of the demonstration and the demonstration is being carried on all around you. Here you will see such great investment in things that yield little or no value and exact such an enormous price. Look, listen and observe, but do not yet come to conclusions because there is more looking and observing to do.

We wish to share with you the greater pleasure that we experience in keeping Knowledge alive in the world and in reinforcing Knowledge within you. Our presence, then, provides a contrast. This Teaching provides a contrast. Contrast is necessary for you to be able to discern that which is meaningful from that which is not. This discernment is necessary to have in order for you to re-evaluate your life and to set yourself in a new direction born of your true inner need and the needs of the world. This produces a greater pleasure almost immediately because it confirms the meaning of your life. Here you do not need to deceive yourself to have what you want. The relief that this provides is both immediate and long term. It is life affirming. Here the value that you seek is not for you alone, for it transcends your personal needs. Here the emphasis is on giving and not on taking from life, and so the rewards are far greater.

So, review your own investment in pleasure. Itemize the things that you are attempting to acquire or secure for yourself. Look at the investment. Look at the reward. Ask yourself, "Is this reward worthy of the investment?" Do not deceive yourself in thinking that you can circumvent the investment. There is a price for everything. All rewards, all value and all achievements require an investment. Some people are greatly invested in confusion so that they won't have to commit themselves to anything. To them, commitment is pain and confusion is a kind of relief even though it produces no value. Here the emphasis needs to move away form survival to achievement, which is a revolution that takes place within the mind.

As the world teaches you what not to value, your Knowledge and the exemplary life of certain individuals provide a contrast. Studying The Greater Community Way of Knowledge provides a contrast. Once the contrast is recognized, you will have no doubt which way to choose. Once the choices are made plain to you and you can see them as they really are, there is no choice at all. When we say that freedom is no choice, it does not mean that there is no choice. It just means that the choice is so obvious that it is as if there were no choice at all.

When you are attempting to choose between two things that are alluring and you cannot decide, then you have not yet come to recognize the investment and the reward. Often people are bogged down because they are trying to choose between two things, neither of which is the way to go, and so they go back and forth, back and forth, trying to weigh the benefits and the liabilities, and so forth. They cannot proceed by doing this.

If you want to know what real value is and how it can be attained, learn about and associate with individuals who are demonstrating it in the world. You cannot find it on your own. Become a student of Knowledge if you wish to have Knowledge. You cannot get it any other way. You cannot purchase it with money. You cannot learn it through simple ideas. You must develop a capacity for it, a desire for it and learn to receive it and apply it wisely. This is investing yourself in the greatest pleasure, which is the greatest achievement.

*If you are
to serve others,
then you must be served,
and you must learn
what being served*

Four

SERVING OTHERS

*S*ERVING PEOPLE IS AN IDEA THAT IS FAMILIAR TO YOU, but we must give you a larger vision of what it means. We must also caution you about the errors and assumptions that are generally made when people approach this idea and consider it for themselves. Serving people can become a great excuse, or it can become a great opening. It can be used to justify things that cannot be justified, or it can be used to support things that are truly worthy. What is the difference here? The difference here is one of preparation, temperament and motive.

Preparation determines how far you have come in The Way of Knowledge, how honest you are with yourself, how much you are aware of your own tendencies and difficulties and how much you are aware of the environment and its influences, including your primary relationships. Preparation determines how much you know, the degree of clarity that you have established, and so forth.

Next, it is a question of temperament. Temperament will determine what your predisposition is—how you interpret your own behavior and the behavior of others and how you respond to the world according to your nature. If you have discovered your nature, your temperament will determine if and how you can work with it constructively.

Thirdly, it is a question of motive. Why do you seek to contribute to other people? What kind of motives do you have for yourself? What kind of motives have you assumed mindlessly from other people? Motive is always very important in gaining discernment. You will have false motives until your motives become true, and your true motives must be discovered because the false ones will fail. This is where maturity and advancement will play a great part in your success. Anyone can say, for instance, "I am here to serve people. My purpose is to serve people. I know I must serve people." This generally meets with approval because it is a virtuous idea. But your motive determines everything. If you are personally motivated, the result of your actions will carry with it confusion, division of loyalty, fearfulness, anxiety, uncertainty, and so forth.

However, if your motivation is born of a deeper spiritual inclination, which we call Knowledge, then you will have an entirely different approach, and the results and the rewards will reflect this. If Knowledge is not the guiding principle in your motives, then you will not be able to bring about a spiritual transmission—you will not be able to activate Knowledge in another—and you will not be able to produce the beneficial results that will be truly lasting. Even your personal motivation to help others is born of your desire for self-gratification. Even your desire to serve people or to relieve suffering in others may be born of your desire to fulfill an aspect or an idea of yourself. This motivation is fundamentally selfish in nature. These personal motives will override the benefits that you are trying to achieve, and as a result, your giving will be fraught with uncertainty, fearfulness and restraint.

Everyone has personal motives to do good things. This is understandable. We are not saying these motives are evil; we are saying they simply must be set aside for something greater to emerge. The world has many problems, and it calls for selfless action. However, you must prepare for this, and you must grow with it as you proceed. Then something greater can be given to you. Then when you feed the hungry, relieve suffering, attend to the sick or provide valuable resources for other people—whatever the field or avenue of your expression—the Spiritual Presence will be expressed and transmitted. This is the greatest gift. This is mysterious. You cannot learn this in school. You can only prepare for it.

Those who have an association with the Greater Community, who are drawn and called by the Greater Community, and whose nature reflects the Greater Community, must study The Greater Community Way of Knowledge. This Teaching is especially for them. These people will not find their way anywhere else. Perhaps they will want the preparation to be different than it is. This is usually the case. When you find something that is a real answer to your real question, it often does not meet with your expectations. It does not seem to provide the desired things. And it requires things of you that perhaps you are not prepared to give or that you had not thought of giving. That is why understanding your motive and nature are so important here.

You cannot teach The Greater Community Way of Knowledge effectively to individuals who do not have this inner association. They will attempt to use it as a form of therapy for themselves. Or they will use it to gain power, advantage, relationships, wealth, and so forth. It will be lost and wasted on them. They can neither claim it, understand it nor use it. This Teaching offers something far greater than even these things which are so highly valued and which are, in some cases, quite necessary. But you must have this Greater Community orientation inside of you. If not, then you must seek a different teaching and a different way. But if this Teaching is for you, then claim it you must and claim it you should, whether it seems to meet your expectations and preferences or not.

If you are to serve others, then you must be served, and you must learn what being served really means, both in its practical and obvious aspects and in its mysterious aspects as well. You must be served, and you must accept the service that is yours to accept. Then you will learn what service you must give, who it is meant for and how it can be expressed. Then you will be able to understand as well the difficulty that people have in receiving the true answer to their request for help, rejuvenation and fulfillment.

People incessantly ask the same questions: "Who am I? Why am I here? Who is with me? What must be done?" These are the essential questions. These are the questions that underlie all of the "Why this?" and the "Why that?" questioning. People are seeking for their true identity, and they are seeking for their Spiritual Family because true identity cannot be known outside the context of true relationship.

In studying The Greater Community Way of Knowledge, people are seeking for their relationships beyond the boundary of humankind as well as within it. Their requirements are somewhat different from other people's. Their Knowledge accounts for more than humanity alone, regardless of their ideas, fantasies or preferences. Many people are interested in the Greater Community but only as a form of escape from their own practical and emotional dilemmas. Yet those who know that the Greater Community is their life and their destiny must attend to what we are saying very carefully. Perhaps you who are reading this book already know that this applies to you. If so, then open yourself to receive this gift. Learn to be served. Learn to receive. Learn to set aside your preferences and requirements about what service must be for you. Many things that you want for yourself are not necessary while other things must be given and given in a way that you had not expected or that you cannot anticipate.

If you can learn to be served, then you will learn what service is. This will ignite your desire to give, and it will also give you the

Wisdom to learn how to give, to whom you must give and from whom you must withhold your gift. This is Wisdom. This must be learned as well. If you can patiently learn to be served, then your desire to give will grow naturally and the Wisdom that must attend it for it to find its fruitful expression in the world will grow as well.

For this, you will need a community of students of Knowledge. You will need others to demonstrate to you those things that must be cultivated, nourished and developed within yourself and those things that must be restrained or curtailed altogether. Until something is brought into the context of relationship, it is not yet fulfilled. It is only a potential. That is why The Way of Knowledge brings you into relationship.

Perhaps you don't want to come into relationship or the only kind of relationship you think you want is a romantic relationship. This is quite common because people often think that romantic relationship accounts for all of their relationship needs, and as a result they have such great expectations here. But in fact, romantic relationship is a very small part of your relationship needs overall.

This becomes quite evident in The Way of Knowledge, for here you will need individuals to teach you what is true and what is untrue. Here you will need others to help demonstrate to you what you need to see so that you can see objectively, which is easier to do with others than by yourself. They will teach you how to see yourself objectively as you learn to reflect upon your own actions and thoughts and the nature of your interaction with others. This is a very slow learning process. The essential steps must be taken and are often difficult to learn and to decipher.

As we have said many times, The Greater Community Way of Knowledge is not an individual pursuit. It brings you into community, to show you that you are joined with life and that you need to join with specific people in specific ways for a specific purpose. This is where people tend to feel threatened and withdraw because they want to have everything but give very little of themselves. Even their giving is to make themselves richer. It is true that real giving will make you richer, but your real wealth is discovered through the reclamation of Knowledge. It is not counted in how many assets, friends and pleasures you have acquired in life. All of these are constantly threatened and are easily lost. But the reclamation of Knowledge cannot be lost unless it is neglected or denied, and even then it will abide with you and go with you wherever you go.

People say many things that are true, but they do not understand the truth in what they say. They interpret things according to their personal motives, you see. People say, "I must serve others. I must find my spiritual truth. I must develop my intuition." You can say all the right things for all the wrong reasons. It is motive, preparation and temperament that are important.

If you truly want to serve others, and if you recognize that this is needed in order for you to reclaim your value and your gift and to discern your true nature, then you must learn to be served—not according to your dictates but according to what the answer itself calls you to do and to receive. For instance, if The Greater Community Way of Knowledge is the answer, then you must learn to receive it, to practice it and to comprehend it according to its methods. Certainly, how you approach it will be determined by your nature, your motives and your temperament, but nonetheless, you must develop according to its dictates. When people try to learn The Way of Knowledge according to their own personal motives, they will fail, but their failure will elude them until its real costs become known.

That is why we say if you wish to serve others, you must learn to be served. This is learning to receive. This is learning to accept. This is learning to discern. It is not blindly opening yourself to what is offered. It is learning to work with what is offered. If you do this, you will be able to discern your own nature. You will be able to recognize your motives. And you will be able to proceed in your preparation, becoming stronger, wiser and more mature. Maturity here is being able to recognize what is true and what is false and to separate them and choose accordingly. Time, practice and wise decisions bring this about, as well as the great assistance from your essential relationships—your relationships with other people and your relationship with your Spiritual Family, whose help and guidance are unknowingly received and utilized so that their benefits can be known. When you depart this life, you will be able to see more clearly why certain things happened for you and who was behind it after all.

As you learn to be served, you will learn that your gift is meant for certain people and for certain situations to achieve certain kinds of results. Over time, if you have been learning to discern your nature and your motives, you will be able to discern other people's natures, however different from yours, and their motives as well. People's natures vary, but their motives do not. People's motives, no matter how they are individually interpreted and expressed, fall into two categories: There is personal motivation, which is an attempt to make individual identity more secure, more distinct and more autonomous. And then there is the motivation of Knowledge, which will bring about a very different result. The uniqueness that Knowledge will emphasize in you has to do with your gift and your service. It will teach you that you are joined to all life in the world in order to carry out a specific role.

You see, the world is a place of doing. It is not a place of being. Where you have come from before coming to the world is a place of being. So, you "be" there and you "do" here. Who you are here is what you do. Who you are there is who you are. This is a world where things must be done. It is a world of action and movement. That is what makes it temporary. You are here to do things. You are here to achieve certain things, both physically and internally as well. If you are to translate being into doing, then you must learn both how to be and how to do. It is not that you do not focus on being in the world. It is that you translate being into doing so that in whatever you do, you are able to express the essence of your nature and the mysterious force of Knowledge. This is the highest expression of service, whether you heal the sick as a physician or change people's automobile tires, whether you create art to inspire people or work on preserving the environment.

Whatever your form of service, if Knowledge is being communicated, you are giving a tremendous gift, far exceeding your particular activity and whatever you may produce. This is because something is passing through you and being given to others. You are like a conduit of Knowledge here. But you are also a functional person carrying out specific activities.

Therefore, the personal part of you is not sacrificed. It is elevated and given its rightful place within the larger context of your life. Then, as you proceed, you will do extraordinary things for people—sometimes knowingly, sometimes unknowingly. And many of the motives that you had previously—of what you were going to do for people and what it was going to do for you—will have departed or been worn away. As you progress in The Way of Knowledge, your motives will change, and your nature will be enhanced and become known to you. And you will develop the Wisdom to receive your gift effectively and to guide its expressions in the best way possible.

So, hold onto the idea that you are here to serve others. Nurture this idea. But open yourself to learning to be served. You cannot serve others if your development is being neglected, obstructed or denied. How do you learn to be served? By identifying and receiving the answer that is being given to you as the result of your request to know your purpose, your meaning and your direction in life. The answer is always a form of preparation. At a certain stage of your development, there will be a specific training or preparation for advancement. Before this, there is learning lessons, interacting with others and making mistakes in life. But at a certain point, it becomes a formal preparation. This preparation requires practice and dedication; it has structure and form, and so forth. Perhaps you will go through several different preparations of this kind until you find the one which will carry you across the bridge from your personal reality into a Greater Reality which is waiting to be discovered.

Here you must learn a practice, a spiritual practice. Here you must learn discernment. Here everything that you have learned before must come together with greater focus and self-determination. Here you are applying yourself wholeheartedly while you are carrying out a process that transcends your understanding. Here you are developing your abilities in tangible ways, and you are opening yourself to the Mystery, which is beyond your comprehension. If this can be achieved, others will be served because you have been served.

*The
personal mind
serves as a
medium between
physical life
and your
spiritual reality.*

Five

WORKING WITH THE MIND

OCUSING AND WORKING WITH THE MIND is a very important topic for those who are undertaking a spiritual practice and who are seeking to comprehend the nature of the mental environment in which they live. There are many questions regarding how the mind should be approached. Most people follow the mind like resigned servants. Others struggle against the mind as if it were an evil force or a great nuisance that they must contend with. For many people, the mind is either approached as something that is followed unquestioningly or is considered to be an adversary.

When you undertake a spiritual practice, you soon discover how chaotic your mind is and how your thoughts vary from one thing to another without any kind of consistency or purposeful direction. You come to recognize that there are certain patterns of thinking which lead to patterns of behavior and that this is part of your conditioning from being in the world. So, working with the mind is a great challenge. To be able to still the mind, focus the mind and direct the mind's great resources is a tremendous challenge and one that requires preparation, practice and application.

Let me begin now by giving you an idea of what a healthy

relationship with your mind can look like. You have this mind that seems to overtake you, distract you and dominate you. It seems to govern your feelings and direct your actions, almost on its own. You begin to realize this when you begin to recognize that you have a vantage point beyond the mind from which you can observe and direct it. After all, if you can observe the mind and direct the mind, you cannot be in your mind. You are out of your mind, so to speak. This is a very important discovery and will lead you to realize that you have a relationship with your own mind. Up until this time, you were not aware of this relationship. The mind simply told you what to think and what to do and you did that, rarely thinking that perhaps you had a choice in the matter. Your mind was stimulated. It responded, and you did whatever it directed you to do.

However, when you reach the point where you realize that you can stand outside your mind and observe and direct it, then you will realize that you have a relationship with your mind. It is at this point that the mind can seem to be a great adversary and a great nuisance. You wish it weren't there! Or, perhaps you wish it were more compliant to your newfound will and preferences. Some people think of the mind as a great machine which is programmed to do certain things and it does those things repetitively and responds to the environment in predictable ways. Others consider the mind to be something evil that they want to get away from, as if it were the source of all of their suffering and misery. Still others think that the mind is a wonderful thing that they can harness, use and apply—a tremendous energy or resource that they will try to harness and use to produce the things that they want. So, they try to change the mind's thinking and program the mind themselves.

All of these approaches will fail and are doomed with many, many problems. None of them represent a healthy relationship with the mind. They hold that the mind is either a tyrant, a nuisance, or a servant. This does not represent a healthy relationship. Would you want to have such a relationship with another person? Would you want another person to be a dominating influence, a nuisance or a servant? Of course not, if you want a healthy, cooperative relationship. Even though you and your mind are not on equal footing, you have a relationship nonetheless, and your mind can serve a greater purpose if it is trained to do this. The mind has a certain range of responsibility, but beyond that range it cannot function effectively. The mind primarily is here to govern the body and to enable you to interact with the environment. However, for the mind to do this effectively and constructively, you must learn to work with it—not to avoid it, dominate it, conquer it or be subservient to it.

You have a personal side and an Impersonal side. They together have a relationship. This relationship is something that will take a great deal of time to cultivate. As you proceed, you will realize that the personal mind needs some things. It needs certain kinds of comfort and stimulation in order to remain healthy. You realize that the Impersonal side also need certain kinds of comfort and stimulation to remain healthy and functional. Here the mind can serve you, and you can also serve the mind.

If you think of your relationship with your physical body, it is easier to see that it is a wonderful mechanism that is capable of doing marvelous things. It enables you to participate in the world directly. The body has its aches and its pains, and it has its needs and its discomforts. If it is approached in a healthy way, you will see that the body is a tremendous asset which allows you to carry out something of great importance in the world. Of course, most people do not have this approach to the body. It also is seen either as a tyrant, a nuisance or a servant. If the body is a tyrant, then its needs and appetites govern you completely, and you feel miserable and helpless in the face of it all. If it is a nuisance, then you tend to react to the body in a harsh and destructive way, forcing it to do things to try to prove to yourself that you can overcome it. This also happens when you treat the body like a servant.

Your relationship with your body is very much like your relationship with your mind, with some important differences. First,
your mind is more permanent than your body; it will exist beyond
your physical life. Second, the mind is far more complicated and far
more powerful than your body. It interacts in a mental environment
that transcends the physical environment. Therefore, it is impossible
to have the mind be your servant. However, it is possible for the
mind to serve you, but the relationship has to be far more cooperative. Servants are generally treated with a minimal amount of respect
and regard and a great deal is asked of them. This cannot be a healthy
approach to the mind, nor can it be a healthy approach to the body.
Both have their needs and both have their great services. Yet the
mind provides a greater service than the body, for the personal mind
serves as a medium between physical life and your spiritual reality. It
interacts with both of these great domains and serves as a membrane
through which information can pass from your spiritual reality into
physical life.

This can only be realized and experienced if the mind is held
to be a great servant and a great mechanism for service in the world.
It cannot be your personal servant. You cannot use it simply to acquire more money, more love and more advantages. When this is the
case, you do not respect its greater abilities or its greater meaning. To
use the mind for selfish ends such as these will only bring disaster to
you. That is why we point instead to a greater form of development
for the mind. How is this development achieved? Development is
achieved by following a preparation for training and discernment
that you have not created for yourself. This preparation has been provided in many forms. For those who respond to the Greater Community and have a relationship with the Greater Community, The
Greater Community Way of Knowledge has been provided. The Way
of Knowledge is an appropriate means to train the mind and also to

generate a healthy relationship with the mind.

Because the mind is a limited mechanism, though far more expansive than the body, it poses certain problems. First of all, it must be trained properly and wisely. It cannot be trained for purely personal reasons, for it must serve a Greater Reality and a greater need within you. You will need to redirect some of your thoughts, but Knowledge within you must be the source of this instruction. You, personally, cannot do it. Likewise, you personally cannot make the body do things that the body cannot do without creating great harm to yourself physically.

The mind, then, is a great resource, but you need to have a healthy relationship with it. This means that you provide certain things that the mind needs. The mind needs a certain degree of stability. It needs a certain degree of protection from adversity. It needs stimulation. It needs what we call "rethinking." So, let me now talk about rethinking.

Consider your personal mind like a great vat of concrete that is all wet and viscous. If you do not stir it and keep it moving, it hardens into a certain form. Once it hardens, it is very difficult to make it fluid once again. So, it is very important that the mind is stimulated. Its greatest stimulation will come from Knowledge, for as the mind is brought into service to Knowledge, it is continually stimulated with new ideas and new experiences and the requirement that things be re-evaluated according to their relevance to present time. This keeps stirring the mind, so to speak, and keeps it fluid. It keeps it young, fresh and active. If the mind is allowed to harden, its ability to respond to new influences, new information and new relationships becomes severely hampered. Past a certain point, it is not able to respond to new things at all. This is when the mind ceases to be a living organism. This is when having a healthy relationship with the mind becomes very, very difficult.

If the mind is following Knowledge—which means that your

mind is attending to a Greater Power within you, a Greater Power that it can neither design nor harness—it is required to rethink things over and over again. Without service to a Greater Power, people will not rethink their ideas. They will only fortify their position. Rethinking means that you must redefine your position and in some cases abandon it altogether. Rethinking is a necessary part of education. Certainly, when you think of your education, even in a formal sense in your schooling, you will realize that the courses or programs of study that were most stimulating required you to rethink and to entertain different perspectives and points of view, consider new facts and alter your position or take no position at all.

In order for the mind to be able to rethink, it must have something beyond itself to which it is responding and which it is serving. The only thing that this can be is Knowledge within you. Therefore, the mind's healthy relationship is with Knowledge, which is like the "real you" behind you, the real Being behind the temporary person. This sets things in right order. This sets things in the right order with yourself physically as well, for the body is meant to serve the mind, and the mind is meant to serve Knowledge, or Spirit. This is a tremendous change from being in an individual human state of mind, where the mind is made to serve the body and spirituality is thought to serve the mind, if it is thought of at all. Therefore, to develop a healthy relationship with the mind, you must focus on Knowledge and allow the mystery of Knowledge to exist within you.

The mind needs certain things that are concrete in order to establish a foundation or a belief system. Without a belief system, the mind is in a state of chaos and cannot be focused in any direction. This is what insanity is—when the structure of the mind, or the structure of thinking, has broken down to a point where even the will of Spirit cannot work through it. Here the mind has fallen into disarray and dysfunction. Therefore, the mind needs certain assumptions and familiar surroundings, at least to a certain point, in order to function effectively. Just like the body needs food, water, shelter and clothing and a certain amount of soothing, the mind needs reassurance, compatible relationships, a stable environment, at certain points, and new ideas. These are its needs. Neglect these needs, and the mind will fall into disarray, and you will not be able to have a healthy relationship with it.

You can have certain ideas that the mind holds to, and this is fine. You can have certain relationships that stimulate the mind, and this is necessary although few people, indeed, have this as a benefit. But you must have something that the mind can serve, that stimulates it and that exists beyond it. This keeps the mind fluid, which allows rethinking to occur. This allows the mind to be active and alive. This enables you to establish a healthy relationship with the mind. Unless this relationship is being cultivated, you cannot work with the mind. You will either try to take it over or you will be running from it.

Let us bring this into the realm of spiritual practice, for here is where you encounter the mind directly. When you are learning the way of stillness, which produces an environment in which Knowledge can emerge within you, you realize that the mind is constantly thinking, constantly moving, distracting you, taking you away, and so forth. You find here that as it is doing this, you are actually within your mind, for your reference point is still in your mind, and so wherever it goes, you go. In practice, you are trying to bring yourself back to a position of objectivity and observation, but the mind takes off, and it takes you with it. It goes here, there and everywhere. It thinks about things that are grand, and it thinks about things that are ridiculous, and it imagines all kinds of scenarios—little dramas in which you then find yourself. It is like a television that is running all the time.

So, in spiritual practice, how do you deal with the television running all the time? Here you set a certain focal point for yourself.

It is like tuning the television into one kind of frequency or channel. You have to learn to do this, and only practice will enable you to do it. You have to have a focal point, and your mind has to have a focal point as well. In the Steps to Knowledge program, there are many different focal points that are introduced. For instance, you are asked to focus on the word RAHN. The mind continues to go all over the place, but you bring it into focus on this word and this sound. There are other focal points: the Fire of Knowledge within you, a still point within you, your breathing, a part of your body. You can do this with your eyes closed or with your eyes open. This brings the mind into focus, which amplifies its power and establishes for you a position outside the mind. Focusing establishes and enables you to experience this position outside the mind.

Over and over, you practice hundreds and thousands of times, like practicing musicians who must practice scales over and over again. They never give up this practice. You must practice focusing the mind in your spiritual practice. As you do this over time, the mind becomes less chaotic. It becomes more uniform and more compliant to whatever you ask it to do. It also demonstrates its needs to you so that you can recognize what it needs. For example, the mind needs a certain amount of similarity. It can't be dealing with new things all the time. It needs to rest on things that are familiar. At the same time, the mind needs new ideas and new stimulation. The mind needs to fall in line behind Knowledge. These things all have to be balanced together, and this will require skill and Wisdom on your part. If you ask the mind to have new experiences all the time, you will wear it out and it will not be able to function. It cannot integrate new information continuously and will end up going into revolt against you if you are too oppressive with it.

So, there is a question of balance here. Knowledge provides this balance because Knowledge provides new information and stim-ulation and then long periods of stillness. During these periods of stillness, the mind is allowed time to integrate itself. Rethinking is allowed and encouraged. There is stimulation, and there is time for adjustment, rethinking and reassociation. In this way, like taking steps, the mind can grow and progress while maintaining its inner stability. Then, even its most familiar and cherished ideas are able to grow slowly. They are not blown apart. These adjustments are made slowly and carefully, as if you were building something with a very conscientious approach. Then, in time, the mind begins to think *for* you. It has a foundation upon which to exist. Its needs are being honored and served, and it is being kept stimulated and redirected.

Consider another example: Consider that your mind is like a government that is not functioning very well, as most governments in your world are not. If you want to change the government and you want it to be more productive, more kind, more efficient, and more stable, how will you approach this? Will you march in with your armies and conquer it and force every aspect of it into submission? This is how certain people approach their minds when they undertake spiritual practice. Or will you neglect it and say, "Well, it will forever be a great inefficient body and all you can do is try to live with its inefficiencies and do the best you can." You do that and what changes? Nothing.

So, how do you regovern a government? How do you regovern the mind? These questions are similar. The mind has many aspects that interact with one another. So does a government. The mind will go into disarray unless it has a greater purpose and a greater set of priorities to serve. So will a government. The mind has tremendous power and affects the quality of your life. So does a government. The mind needs a wise ruler. So does a government. The mind has different voices and different aspects, which must be recognized and brought together into an efficient working relationship. So does a government. The similarities go on and on. Therefore, if you become wise in your relationship with your mind and in working with your mind, you become a wise leader, a wise governor, so to speak. This means that you have compassion and respect for that which you govern. You try to take into account all aspects of that which you govern and serve everything to the greatest degree possible. This means that you must balance things constantly, that you cannot be too radical regarding one or two ideas while neglecting everything else. That is why following The Greater Community Way of Knowledge creates leadership, both internally and externally. It creates balance and Wisdom, a wise government internally and a wise government externally. That is why it is the path of resolution and the path of fulfillment.

Many people want to govern their outer lives more effectively, but their inner lives are chaotic. That is like saying, "We'll leave the government alone, but we will make the city look more beautiful. We'll plant trees." People try to make their outer life look more benign or more pleasurable or more harmonious, but unless they regovern themselves and assume responsibility for the government of their minds, nothing will change. They will have nicer scenery perhaps, but the real state of things will be the same.

As I speak of these things, perhaps you will say, "My God! This is too enormous for me! How can I possibly do all this?" Well, the truth is that you do part of it and Knowledge does part of it. Day by day, moment to moment, you learn to address the mind and work with the mind, and you give it things to focus on that are productive, just like you learn to do with your physical body. Yet part of the mind is governed by something greater. So, you have a range of responsibilities and Knowledge has a range of responsibilities. You are responsible for what you think and what you do with what you think, but Knowledge is responsible for giving the mind its purpose, meaning and direction. Here you are like a wise manager, but you do not govern the state. Recognizing this enables you to have a greater resource of Wisdom to carry out your range of responsibilities, which is quite enormous. The fact that people cannot manage their lives or their minds is evident, and so anyone who can do it to any degree has progressed and has a great advantage in life.

You are given the means for your development. We provide The Greater Community Way. It is effective if people learn to follow it and are patient and wise. When people begin preparation, oh, they want big results right now. They are jumping up and down to have things resolved and accomplished in their lives, but in reality things happen in a more slow and progressive manner. This assures substantial and lasting results and true progress. If you jump ahead, you can fall back just as easily. When you jump up in the air, you come down right away. But when you follow a plan and a means that is more slow, gradual and constructive, then you truly advance, and you will not fall away or fall back so easily.

To prepare you to work with the mind and to have a genuine relationship with the mind as well as with the Greater Power within you, The Greater Community Way of Knowledge is being provided. Without this kind of preparation, you could not do it. Try as you may to have good behavior and positive thoughts, you would not be able to escape your dilemmas because you could not establish yourself outside of your mind effectively. You could not establish a new foundation, a new vantage point, a new position. This requires assistance beyond yourself, not just friendly encouragement from those who appreciate you, but real assistance from those who possess a greater spiritual power. They provide their presence, their inspiration and the practical means for your accomplishment.

You either choose to prepare or you do not. If you do not, you can only think about it and contemplate it. Here you are still staying within your own ideas. When you prepare, you encounter new ideas, which requires rethinking, readjustment and a new position with your mind. This gives your internal state direction and momentum to move forward. Without preparation, you are walking around but are going in circles. You cannot go anywhere new. Trying to teach yourself things is very slow, and the prospects for success are quite remote. You will tend to recycle old ideas. When people walk in a wide circle rapidly, it looks to them like they are going somewhere. Yet, they are just making themselves dizzy and are not covering any new territory. The mind is not rethinking. Rethinking doesn't simply mean re-evaluating a position you have had or ideas with which you are familiar. Rethinking requires new information, new experiences and new challenges. These must come from beyond you. This activates your relationship with God and with your Spiritual Family. This provides an upward and outward movement for you.

The transition from being governed by your mind to adhering to something greater is one that must happen slowly to enable you to maintain your stability. At a certain point, formal preparation is absolutely necessary. If it is avoided or neglected, you cannot proceed. It represents a commitment to change and to rearrange your relationship with your mind and your body and with everything around you. This requires courage. This requires openness. This requires a recognition of genuine need within you. Life will teach you this need. If you are being honest with yourself, you will realize how great it is. You can only do so much for yourself. Beyond this, things have to be done for you and given to you and shown to you. That is why it is necessary to seek a preparation that you did not invent for yourself. This is what takes you into new territory, allows genuine rethinking to occur and opens you up to greater possibilities, which would not be available to you otherwise.

Those who have undertaken the preparation in The Greater Community Way of Knowledge must exercise great perseverance and patience. People generally want things to move along quickly, to get to the resolution, to get to the realization, right now! Or they want to slow things down because things are moving too fast. "Oh, my God! I can't handle it!" Over time you will realize that you have a certain pace that you can follow, for your mind must rethink and also restabilize itself. So, there is growth and there is integration and there is restabilizing yourself. Day to day, moment to moment, this can make things look very slow, but this is how growth is accomplished and how stability is achieved. Some people want to shoot out like a rocket. However, when the rocket lands, it blows itself to bits. If you do not want to be blown to bits, then do not shoot out like a rocket. Climb like the man or woman on the mountain who must move very slowly, who must understand each move and have great respect and consideration for the mountain itself. This is a good image and one that is worthwhile.

If you begin the preparation that has been provided for you and follow it faithfully and patiently, if you allow rearrangement to happen in your outer life and rethinking to occur in your inner life, if you learn to recognize your range of responsibilities, which the preparation itself will make evident to you, and if you allow the greater range of responsibilities to exist for Knowledge to guide you, then you can proceed. Then you will learn not only to work with the mind but to appreciate its great benefits as well.

The truth
of any relationship
can be known
at the outset.

Six

Discernment

THERE IS A LESSON in *Steps to Knowledge* that concentrates on the idea, "The quality of my relationships determines the quality of my life." Spend some time now and consider this idea. As you think about it, do not only think of the people with whom you are now engaged in relationship. Include, as well, your relationship with your mind, your relationship with your body, your relationship with the place you live, your relationship to the general physical environment, and so forth. If you do this honestly, without trying to exclude anything, you will see that everything is included in this idea and that this idea applies to all aspects of your life. If you have been out in the world a little bit and have become somewhat observant of others, you will indeed begin to see the utter truth of this statement.

So, where is the best place to investigate the quality of your relationships? The best place to start to investigate is in looking at how you start relationships—who do you start them with, what are your motives, what are you looking for, what are your criteria, how quickly do you move, how do you gauge your progress, what qualifies a person to be in relationship with you and what disqualifies someone? This investigation is one that you are encouraged to undertake for yourself, but it will only be fruitful if you engage yourself in it with as much objectivity as possible. Your experience and your observations of others will prove very valuable here. Yet, the opportunity for deception is very great because you will still protect certain motives and goals in relationships from this scrutiny, wanting to make sure that they are still genuine goals for you, keeping them from being questioned and examined honestly.

Developing discernment is absolutely fundamental in raising the quality of your relationships and, indeed, the quality of your life. How you start a relationship will determine the direction that it goes in and will establish its activity both now and in the future. Discernment or the lack of it will determine who you are with, what you will do and what you will have to learn as a result. So, clearly, how you start a relationship is the best place to begin. All the relationships that you have now were started at some point, and, indeed, you are looking for new relationships even at this moment. Perhaps you will think, "Well, I am not looking for a husband or a wife," but you are looking for other people for other purposes.

To emphasize the importance of discernment, we shall give you a very fundamental idea in The Greater Community Way of Knowledge. It is an idea that will require considerable thought and investigation. The idea is this: "The truth of any relationship can be known at the outset." This means that relationships are not as much of a gamble as they might seem. Is this possible? Not everything that will happen in a relationship can be seen at the outset, but the appropriateness of this relationship for you can be known. In fact, it is known already. But do you have access to this Knowledge? Are you available to it? It is certainly available to you. If you are not available to it, what is preventing you from having access to it? Here, indeed, you begin to ask some very important questions about your approach to life and the degree to which you can engage with life objectively and honestly.

Indeed, you might even ask these questions regarding me: "Who is this speaker who is giving me this discourse? Can this speaker be trusted? Does this speaker possess true Wisdom? I have been fooled before. Maybe I will be fooled again." Indeed, I can only be known. You can speculate a great deal about me and paint any picture you want. But my value can only be known. If you are with Knowledge, you will know who I am and you will understand the depth of my Wisdom. The question of trust will not be necessary if Knowledge is your guide. However, Knowledge is not really the guide for most people in an active sense, for people trust their assumptions until their assumptions prove to be false, which can take a very long time.

Consider how it is possible that the appropriateness of a relationship can be known at the outset. How do you know these things and how do you proceed? If you are open to experiencing other people's purpose, their temperament, how far they have progressed, their maturity, and their thinking and behavior—if you are open to knowing these things without trying to assign value and without trying to fit others into your ideals, then, indeed, you can know if they are an appropriate prospect for relationship for you. How can you know this? Because Knowledge within you will say "yes" or "no." If Knowledge does not say "yes," then it is "no." "No" can mean that this person is not appropriate, or it can mean that you must wait and not become engaged. "No" can also mean look away or pass on by. Here you must look beyond all appearances and not be swayed by charm, beauty, wealth, power and all the allurements that trap people. Here you look without bitterness and without distrust. You are just open. To have this openness, you must learn over time to have no illusions about yourself. You must not live according to cherished ideas or grand images. You must become a person who is simple, direct, open and discerning—a man or woman of Knowledge.

You see, at this moment you do not yet have this discernment. How can I say this about you, you ask. "He doesn't even know me. How can he say this about me?" I can say this because true discernment is rare in the world. It is only cultivated in a mind that has shed its illusions, that is living with life as it is and that is adhering to a Greater Power that includes what is seen and transcends what is seen as well. Discernment is not asking the right questions or having the right checklist. It is the ability to *know*. It is the ability to experience another, not critically but directly. It is the ability to restrain yourself until the moment of action is called for, however long that may be. If you are without illusions about yourself, then you will be without illusions about others.

Discernment, then, is the product of a great development. This great development must occur for discernment to have a real foundation and to be truly effective in life. The great development is called The Way of Knowledge. Here you regain the True Mind and with it, the true life. Let me give you an example. If you interact with someone and they charm you, confuse you, intrigue you or disappoint you, and you want to know them and comprehend them, how can this be achieved if you do not become engaged with them in any way? One of the first requirements here is that you cannot want anything from the situation. Whatever you want will determine the criteria that you will use. Even wanting Knowledge can be deceptive here because you will try to think and act according to your ideas of what Knowledge is and how Knowledge would think or what Knowledge would have you do.

The essence of discernment is stillness. If you can be still with another, without trying to make them good or bad, or divine or evil, then you can begin to experience him or her very directly. This is why we teach the path of stillness. This produces the necessary condition of mind for Knowledge to emerge. Indeed, we speak of stillness throughout our discourses and refer to it often. Many people think discernment is about becoming more critical, having higher standards, being more judgmental, being more careful, asking more questions or being more guarded about oneself and one's possessions. While it is true that as you become more discerning, you become more guarded, this is not the essence of what I am talking about. The essence of what I am talking about is the ability to experience others as they truly are, recognizing their higher qualities but also taking into account their position in life. This does not require a long analysis or a detailed study because a long analysis can only determine a person's thinking and behavior and may not at all account for his or her deeper aspects. Here you need to be present. Be still and you will know. This sounds so simple, and yet it requires a truly refined approach.

There are some very fundamental questions that you can ask in the process of getting to know someone. To begin with, ask yourself: "Should I get to know this person?" Second question: "Should I become involved with this person?" These are two different questions. You can know someone without getting involved with them, maintaining a respectful distance. Beyond these two questions, then, be still. Do not rush ahead. Become aware of what you want in the relationship and all of the images that illustrate what you want. Then separate yourself from these images. They are not necessarily bad, but they can destroy your ability to exercise real discernment in the situation.

Because the quality of your relationships determines the quality of your life, whom you become engaged with and for what purpose are all important. There is no escape from this, for you live in a mental environment as well as a physical environment, and the mental environment is made up of your thinking and the thinking of those with whom you are most directly engaged. This describes your physical environment as well. Relationship is the essence of your environment, the environment in which you live. What you decide to do in your relationships will determine the kind of life you will have and the kind of problems you will have to solve. This is so important; it cannot be overlooked. There is so much at stake if you make a wrong decision. And it is difficult to undo something that never should have been done in the first place. Your experience will illustrate this for you.

Therefore, you begin with caution, but you must also have a commitment to develop stillness, objectivity and the ability to experience another's reality, not in an analytical sense but in a direct way. Knowledge can be your guide, if you can be with Knowledge. To be with Knowledge you cannot be governed by your personal wishes, goals, wants and dislikes. For, indeed, the person who may make the greatest difference to you may be someone who does not meet your criteria. And the person who will do you the most harm could well be someone who is totally enchanting to you and who seems to fit the absolute picture of what you are trying to acquire for yourself. Once again return to Knowledge and to stillness. If you learn The Greater Community Way of Knowledge according to the preparation that has been provided, then discernment will be a by-product of your achievement and will grow with your achievement. Because everything represents relationship, your involvement with everything will be determined by the degree to which you have cultivated real discernment.

Discernment must always be based upon what you value. Let me speak about this now. If you value beauty and charm, wealth and power, comfort and pleasure, this will be the basis of your discernment. If you value any one of them or any combination of them, that will be the basis of your discernment. It is only reality that will bring you back to what is really true and to what could have been known at the outset.

Therefore, question yourself—what do you value? Ask yourself, "What do I value? What am I looking for?" It is easy to want things.

You can give yourself permission to want anything, but what do you really value? In this, you only have two real choices: You either value the truth and what the truth yields or you value the things that compete with the truth. If you have never tasted the truth, it will be very hard for you to value it. It will seem to be an ideal. You can say, "I want someone who speaks the truth, who reminds me of the truth." But if you do not know what the truth is, this is just another image and another personal goal.

If you value Knowledge as a living reality within yourself, then you will want Knowledge to be emphasized and you will want to stay close to Knowledge, for it is the most fundamental relationship that you have. It is so fundamental that if you re-establish your relationship with Knowledge, it will set you in right order with everyone around you. Knowledge cannot be deceived. It does not have conflicting goals. It lives with the truth because it *is* the truth. Truth is its only emphasis—a truth far greater than the truth that people concentrate on or acknowledge to be real. That is why when we come back to the most fundamental things to emphasize about discernment, we must emphasize your relationship to Knowledge, which represents your love of the truth, your experience of the truth, and all of its resonating qualities and life-affirming gifts.

Coming back to Knowledge is like coming home. Here you shed much unneeded baggage along the way. With false goals go false relationships; with illusions about yourself go illusions about others. When Knowledge is developed, it will be increasingly difficult for you to make a mistake in relationships.

Your life is precious; your time is short. You have come into the world to yield something very significant and to work with other people in a cooperative venture in a specific area. The only way that this can be discovered and fulfilled is to engage with the right people for the right purpose. You will need Knowledge to do this, and you will need all of the qualities that are required for Knowledge to emerge—such as stillness, patience, discernment, openness, restraint, compassion and affinity. These are great virtues, and they are fundamental to living a genuine life.

Developing discernment is becoming sober. It is shaking off the clouds that shroud your vision and make it difficult for you to think clearly. It is like coming out of a stupor. It is getting yourself straight, like a person who is intoxicated and must wash his face with ice-cold water in order to bring himself back, to get himself straight. People are intoxicated with romance. They are intoxicated with power in their business relationships; they are driven by things that only yield pain and misery. They are intoxicated. Discernment is beyond them. They only want to keep their indulgences, so they seek out others who share their indulgences and who show promise of fulfilling them within these indulgences. Meanwhile, there is a great need to know and a great need to be known, and these are neglected.

Lack of discernment is a great problem in human relationships. And real discernment cannot be acquired by the usual methods that people ascribe to it. To become truly discerning, you must become wise—nothing less. Knowledge must be your guide, nothing else. It will take time to achieve this and you must prepare, but the rewards are so great and so complete, the freedom from error so genuine and in such contrast to what you see around you, that the effort required is a small price to pay for such a great reward.

If you can discern what to do, then you can do what you know, and you will know what to do, and certainty will be yours. If you can discern what relationships to give yourself to and what relationships to deny, then your life will have the opportunity to have real depth and harmony, which are necessary for self-love and true achievement to take place.

Studying The Greater Community Way of Knowledge requires discernment. It doesn't merely encourage it; it requires it. Your progress here can only truly be thwarted by your misapplication in relationships—relationships with others, relationship with yourself, with your mind, with your body, and with the world. You may ask, "How can someone fail in learning The Way of Knowledge?" And I say: "Seek out or protect an inappropriate relationship, and you will fail, and your failure will be a difficult learning process." You have failed enough in this regard. Do not keep paying the price. Others are paying heavily. You can learn from them. Pay a small price for a great reward instead of a great price for a small reward. If you choose to learn The Greater Community Way of Knowledge, then discernment is a requirement. Life will give you the challenges that you need. And they will be genuine and your opportunity for success will be great. What you will have to deny, pass by or withhold within yourself will be great as well.

You know, people often ask, "How can I be successful?" And I answer by giving them something great to do, something really great to do. Learn to become still. Learn discernment. Learn The Greater Community Way of Knowledge. Do you want to be successful? Learn these things. My answer to your question will challenge you and challenge your discernment in this moment, for if you can discern my answer, then you will be able to discern your real request and understand that a real answer is being given to you.

Knowledge
will move you
to speak
to certain people
and will remain
silent with
everyone else.

Seven

DISCRETION

W HAT DOES DISCRETION MEAN? It means the ability to know when to speak and when not to speak. Can you recall a time when you said something and then regretted saying it? Can you recall a time when you said something to someone and then realized that it was the wrong thing to say? Perhaps it was wrong for them, or perhaps it revealed too much about you. Can you recall a time when you revealed something to another, but it was not appropriate? Or perhaps it was a time when you said something and it fell into the wrong hands or was misinterpreted, and it came back to haunt you later?

If you think about these things, you will see that they present a great problem in communication. Generally, there are three different stages of development in communication. The first stage is the inability to express yourself. The second stage is when you feel you have to express yourself. And the third stage is when you do not need to express yourself except on rare occasions to certain people. These three stages represent the three stages of development in a human being: the stages of dependence, independence and interdependence.

In the first stage, you are barely aware of what your own experience is, and you have great difficulty in expressing this to another. Either you do not have the skills to express this or you do not have the awareness of what you need to express, and you are so fearful that you cannot bridge the gap and pull it out of yourself. This first stage, then, is one of self-repression. It is not a stage where discernment and discretion are exercised much at all.

In the second stage, you are experiencing some freedom, which means you are experiencing your own ideas and are able to think more freely and independently. It is during this stage that you feel almost compelled to express yourself. You want to exercise your freedom. You do not want to restrain yourself, for you are trying to escape all of the self-restraint that had bound you previously.

Then we enter the third stage, which is a stage where you interact with others in a very responsible way. Here discretion becomes very important because you realize that everything you say has an impact on others, and in everything you say you declare yourself in a very permanent way. Certainly, anyone who has a position of responsibility or leadership realizes that everything they say will be taken to heart by someone. They must be much more judicious in what they say and in what they want to emphasize. Here communication carries with it great responsibility, not just responsibility to yourself and your desire to express yourself, but responsibility for what happens as a result of your self-expression.

Therefore, we have dependence, independence and interdependence — the three great stages of human development. Most people are in the first two stages. Actually, most people are in the first stage; many are working their way into the second stage, and very few have reached the third stage at all. In the first stage, people cannot speak. In the second stage, they must speak as an expression of their freedom and independence. In the third stage, they speak rarely to certain people for certain purposes, for they realize here the great responsibility that goes with self-expression. If you think about this, you will realize that within these three stages you are developing a thorough understanding of your own experience, and you are learning Wisdom and how it can be expressed most effectively in the world.

In the first stage of dependence, you cannot express yourself because you are not aware of your own experience sufficiently and you do not have the skills or courage yet to break the bonds that hold you. In the second stage of independence, you are breaking the bonds, and your desire to communicate is more a desire to release energy and to unburden yourself than it is to effectively change or impact others. Here self-expression becomes very chaotic. You do not yet realize the consequences of what you say. You are enjoying the freedom of saying it instead.

The third stage of interdependence, where you begin to interact in relationships from a position of responsibility and self-awareness, is the stage where your discretion becomes ever more important because without it you produce unwanted and often disastrous results, for yourself and other people. Here you must learn restraint. And here you must learn discernment in order to determine when and where you must express yourself. Restraint is important here because you must often withhold what you want to say. People who are involved in the second stage of independence often cannot tolerate withholding anything. They think withholding anything is a violation of their nature and their freedom. They think they have a right to express anything to anyone. Well, they will eventually find out that this produces un-wanted results and conflict. It produces great trouble in the world. So if they are smart, they will begin to realize that they have to be more careful who they communicate to and what they say.

Those individuals who have become wise have had to realize that they have to be careful of what they say to anyone, anywhere, at any time. They are careful because they realize that all self-expression affects relationships and generates a response in others. They want to cultivate genuine relationships, and they want to nurture a genuine response. They do not want the tribulation that goes with irresponsible self-expression. To the wise, then, this restraint is not seen as self-repression. They are able to fully express themselves. They are able to express their feelings, their anger, their sadness, their joy, their inspiration, their disappointment, and so forth. They have developed this skill. Now they know they must use it wisely.

People in the first stage of dependence cannot express their feelings effectively, for they cannot experience them fully. People in the second stage of independence are beginning to experience their own range of emotions and their own ideas, and their desire to express these is great. However, this desire is not yet born of Wisdom. The wise person must exercise discretion at all times. Here there will be feelings of loneliness and exclusion because the wise cannot express the depth of their experience effectively to many people. They must hold their experience within themselves and let it grow there. This generates focus and energy, which is power. It also develops respect for other people's experience and position in life and respect for one's own experience and position as well.

Responsibility must accompany power in order for power to be used wisely and to have a beneficial effect. How true this is in self-expression. Here Knowledge is your guide, for Knowledge will move you to speak to certain people and will remain silent with everyone else. As you progress towards Knowledge, and as you cultivate your relationship with Knowledge and learn to receive Knowledge, you too will express potent things to certain people and will be silent with everyone else. This will be done without judgment or condemnation. You will not judge one person as worthy and another as unworthy. It has nothing to do with that. It is just that you are called to express certain things to certain people whom you sense can understand and receive your self-expression in a constructive and beneficial way. With everyone else, you hold that self-expression within yourself and let its potency grow.

It is interesting that people in the second stage of development, independence, who feel so powerful as they begin to spread their own wings to some degree, dissipate their power and focus all the time through irresponsible self-expression. For them, self-expression is more about unburdening themselves, getting their experience out of their system. They do not want to hold it. They think holding back is a form of self-repression. Because they are trying to escape from dependency, they are afraid of withholding anything and tend to feel very affronted when they have to. This is an adolescent stage of development. Adolescence is highlighted by new expressions and experiences of power, but without the Wisdom and responsibility to carry power or use it wisely.

The second stage of development is like immature adulthood. Many people are trying to get into the second stage because you must go through it. Many people even teach it. They are very critical of anything that denies a person's right to self-expression or a person's right to have, to do and to be whatever they want. People teach this because they are trying to learn it, but they have not yet realized that there is a vast stage beyond this. In fact, the third stage, the stage of interdependence, is so much greater than the first two that there is no comparison between them. You will never graduate from the third stage of development, for there is so much growth and progress to be made here.

Many people want power and all that they associate with power, but few want the responsibility that must go with it. Responsibility requires discernment, discretion and restraint. Can people who are relishing their independence exercise this restraint without seeing it as a form of self-repression? They can only if they realize that their power carries a responsibility and that if they do not want to create chaos around them, they must use their abilities more carefully and more judiciously. This prepares them to have discretion.

Now, many people think discretion is simply keeping your mouth shut. "Don't say it. Don't say that thing. Hold it back. Don't say anything to anybody. You are safer when you keep your mouth shut." That is how people think of discretion, but this is not discretion. Discretion is knowing when to speak and when not to speak and being able to follow this faithfully. That is discretion. It requires that you have power, ability and a high level of self-acceptance. If you have a contentious relationship with yourself, then you will not be able to approach anything with Wisdom. The man and woman of Knowledge can withhold their self-expression without any sense of self-violation, and they can take the risk of telling someone something important, perhaps something that is deemed risky, without any sense of self-violation. Indeed, the only real self-violation comes when you are going against Knowledge. Yet, you must have a sufficient experience of Knowledge to know when you are going towards it and when you are going away from it.

Discretion, then, is the ability to speak and to not speak. Now, many people cannot express themselves, while others talk incessantly, saying everything to whomever will listen and to whomever they feel comfortable with. This represents two early stages of development, but neither represents a stage of maturity. Neither of these approaches is effective in nurturing genuine relationship or in accomplishing things harmoniously in the world. So, you may ask, "How do I know when to speak and when not to speak?" You will know because Knowledge will motivate you. If you want to say something to someone and you feel restraint, don't say it. If the feeling of restraint is deep within you, do not say anything. However, if the restraint is at the surface of your mind and deep within you, you know you must communicate something, then you have to take the risk and find the words, without apology.

How can you discern what is deep within you and what is at the surface? Without Knowledge you cannot do this. You can think any impulse is true or any impulse is to be feared. To become a student of Knowledge is to cultivate your relationship with Knowledge, which is your most primary relationship. This will teach you the real meaning of discretion, for you will find that Knowledge only speaks at certain times. It is waiting for the moments of readiness, when the conditions are right, the audience is right and the need is there.

When people begin to study The Greater Community Way of Knowledge and to follow its practices according to the Ancient Tradition that is being given here, they are always asking Knowledge incessant questions: "Tell me my purpose. Tell me what I should do. Should I take this job or should I take that job? Should I go with this person or should I not go with this person? Should I open up or should I close down? How can I have peace? How can I have equanimity? How can I get out of this situation? How can I get into that situation?" There is this incessant questioning, and what do they experience receiving ninety percent of the time? They experience silence, or they just hear their own mind — their own preferences and their own confusion. They hear yes and no, do this or don't do that — they hear all of these things. Yet, this is all at the surface of the mind. Down deep there is stillness.

This points to Knowledge. Knowledge is fulfilled within itself, so it is able to restrain itself for a very long time. Indeed, there may be a very long time between the experience of knowing and the expression of knowing. Usually this is the case. You may know something, and yet it may take years for it to come about. You may know something about another, and yet it may take years for you to express it to them effectively, if you ever do. Is this self-repression? No. This is Knowledge.

Your relationship with Knowledge must be developed in order to function at this level. For the vast majority of people who are struggling with dependencies, this is not meaningful. They are not experiencing discretion to any great degree. They are experiencing self-repression. They cannot speak. They often do not know what they have to say, and if they do, often they cannot say it. Why? Because it would threaten their dependencies. If you begin to make claims of independence and to assert yourself, you begin to threaten your dependencies. If you are not ready to do that, then you will not do it. If you are ready to that, then you will begin to enter the second stage of development, which is independence, where you will begin to enjoy its freedoms and to experience its liabilities.

I am giving you the idea of discretion in a larger context here. It is tied to learning everything else in The Greater Community Way of Knowledge. To be able to speak when it is appropriate and to not speak when it is not appropriate requires a greater de-velopment—a greater understanding of yourself, your nature, the dynamics of your relationships and a strong allegiance to your own inner life. All this represents the larger realm of your development.

Now you may ask, "How can I develop discretion? I realize that I need to use it." I say, "Become a student of Knowledge." If you experience an affinity with Knowledge and with the Greater Community, which represents life beyond this world, then The Greater Community Way of Knowledge is *your* way. How do you know it is your way? Because you *know* it. That is the only thing that will keep you with it and enable you to progress. After all, it is not promising you wealth, power, love, comfort, pleasures, glories, divine interventions, angelic contacts, and all this sort of thing. You follow The Greater Community Way of Knowledge because you *know* you must follow it. This is what carries you forth.

All other ambitions and motivations fall away sooner or later. As they fall away, you realize that most conversation is unnecessary. Most of what you think of as your need to express yourself is to merely offset your insecurity. Here you realize that everything you say has value or should have value. Even when you are being light hearted, you want it to be a meaningful experience without trying to create the meaning. Here you become more natural. You become more like the natural world, which is silent and still except when things are happening. The person who is still and silent has great depth and often evokes respect from others, particularly if his or her silence is born of Wisdom.

Individuals who are engaged in the reclamation of Knowledge are beginning to experience the Mystery of life and are experiencing carrying the Mystery within themselves. The presence of this Mystery affects others, even if nothing is said. The man and woman of Knowledge have a great impact upon others. They are not frittering away their energy with meaningless conversation, analysis or speculation. Because they are holding their communication within themselves, it is growing and becoming more potent. They are not constantly dissipating it by running off to their friends, telling everything that is going on with them and sharing all their deepest experiences in order to get it out of their system. No. The man and woman of Knowledge are holding it in their system so that it can grow in power and become more focused. They want to hold their energy now — to harness it and focus it — rather than expending it as soon as it is experienced.

People who are wise have experienced the need for discretion and are practicing it effectively. They practice it because they know it is essential. That is their motivation. They are not motivated by fear of reprisal, fear of repercussion or anxiety about the loss of love or money. That is not their motivation. Their motivation is realizing that their self-expression is valuable and must be given to the right people in order for it to be fulfilled. They realize that it is incumbent upon them to learn ways to express themselves effectively, using the right words and often using as few words as possible. For when you have something important to say, the more words you use, the weaker the communication is.

Their motivation is that they want success without betraying themselves. In fact, they want to honor themselves. So, they learn The Greater Community Way of Knowledge, which leads them to say certain things to certain people at the right time, and the rest of the time they maintain stillness and silence, carrying on conversations only to negotiate the necessities of life.

Students of The Greater Community Way of Knowledge realize they need to practice stillness all the time. Perhaps stillness seems like self-restraint or self-repression to you, for you keep wanting to get away from all your thoughts—your fantasies, little dramas, speculations, analyses, past recollections and projections into the future. Practice stillness. Stillness is necessary if you are to have discretion. It is necessary if you are to experience discernment. It is necessary if you are to see what is really occurring and to know how to respond. Stillness is necessary if you are to choose the right relationships and proceed in the correct way where there is no self-violation. It is necessary if you wish to speak and act with Wisdom. Stillness is necessary.

How do you develop real discretion? I will give you some guidelines now. First of all, begin as a student of The Greater Community Way of Knowledge if you have an affinity for the Greater Community. If not, choose another path, another form of development, but always choose a preparation that you did not make up for yourself. Do not take the eclectic approach, choosing a little of this and a little of that, the part of this you like, the part of that you like and add it all together. For you know what you will have? You will have just what you like, and what you like will not take you anywhere. It will just comfort you and affirm you where you are now. Indeed, in The Greater Community Way of Knowledge you learn to transcend your preferences rather than to live by them. The Way of Knowledge takes you beyond preferences to what is known. People who choose the eclectic approach to development only reinforce their preferences and never escape them. Their sense that they are unfree and unfulfilled will continue to haunt them, with little relief in sight.

Therefore, choose a preparation not of your own making. Choose something that can take you beyond where you are now into new territory. This is education and this is development. Yes, there is some need for self-reinforcement, but you must still go beyond where you are now. If you choose an eclectic approach, you will not go beyond where you are now. You will only emphasize where you are now. You will invest yourself more in it. That is why it is the great path of going nowhere. If you are to be a real student of The Way, then you must choose a preparation that is correct for you but which is not governed by your preferences and your feelings moment to moment. Then you will practice on days when you feel like it and on days when you don't feel like it. Then you will be able to entertain ideas when they please you and when they don't please you. And you will be able to learn skills when they seem to meet your goals and when they don't seem to meet your goals. This is what it means to be a student — to learn something new, to go where you have not gone before, to entertain ideas that are new, to rethink, to renew, to rejuvenate and to rediscover.

If you feel that you are ready to undertake preparation, you should begin to prepare yourself in The Way of Knowledge. This will cultivate all aspects of you and will make true discretion possible. In the interim, I will give you a few guidelines. These are only guidelines, which means that you must learn to use them wisely in different ways and in different situations. They are not rules that never vary and that are the same in all situations. Indeed, the person who is wise is very mutable and can change and apply Wisdom in different situations and in different ways. This represents maturity and advancement.

The beginning student wants to know the black and white of everything, so when the preparation says, "Do this," they try to do it in all circumstances without discerning how those circumstances vary or how the application must be different in different circumstances. So, given this propensity in most people, I say, "Say as little as possible." Communicate to people whom you trust, whom you sense regard you highly and who have a respect for your spiritual life without trying to impose their vantage point upon you. When you do have to say something, say it simply. You do not need to explain everything, to give a myriad of examples and to talk until there is nothing left to say. Let people spend time with what you have said rather than trying to make it totally palatable to them. If you feel the need to express something, but the opportunity is not there or the right people are not there, then hold this within yourself. Let the fires burn hotter within you. It is all right to have this pressure. Hold this energy. It is like sex. Some people think that whenever they feel sexual, they must go out and have sex immediately to relieve themselves. This is madness. Think about this, and you will see that it is madness.

Likewise, if you have something you need to say to someone in particular or to everyone or to the universe and the opportunity is not there or the opportunity is not correct or the time is not right, hold it within yourself. Let it grow. This is how you develop depth, potency, insight and self-awareness within yourself. If there is pressure, let the pressure be there. Then, when there is an opportunity to express whatever that is, it will be expressed with tremendous power. Like pulling back the bow, that pressure is what projects the arrow forward into the world. That is what gives your self-expression power. People who talk, talk, talk all the time have no potency in their self-expression. Nothing has built up within them.

The arrow just drops on the ground in front of them. It does not go anywhere. But if you let your communication grow within you, it has power, and when it is expressed, there is potency to it.

So, feel the pressure. Let the fires grow. If you do this wisely, it will develop insight and the ability to restrain yourself, which you must do if you are to become a mature human being. Only adolescents are wild and extravagant, going around having to say anything to anyone whenever the feeling strikes them. And they do not understand why their life is so fraught with conflict and enmity.

It is true that the Wise remain silent most of the time. Knowledge is like that. When Knowledge releases its arrow, however, it can change a life entirely. It can alter the course of the world. Yet, those who are struggling with dependencies cannot see this. This looks like a darkening and deepening of their dilemma, though it is entirely different. And to those who are enjoying the newfound freedom of independence in the second stage of development, these ideas may seem like they will take them backwards, back to a state of dependency. They don't want anything curtailing their new freedoms. This is because independence is a very adolescent stage. Adolescents don't want to be held back or limited by anything. That's why in adolescence there is very little Wisdom—a great deal of exploration and experimentation and a lot of disasters, disappointments and terrible mistakes, but very little Wisdom.

If you seek Wisdom, then you must exercise discretion, and you must learn the ways of discretion. To learn the ways of discretion, you must learn The Way of Knowledge. That is why instead of learning one skill, you must learn them all. Instead of learning one virtue, you must become virtuous. Instead of learning to acquire one power, you must become powerful. To learn discretion in its true sense is to become a whole and united person, a person who feels the presence of Knowledge within, a presence which is self-generating.

Here you realize that your life and everything you do is intrinsically expressed through a network of relationships, which you will want to develop slowly with the right people and with the right purpose. You are an individual, but your individuality only has meaning within the context of relationships. It only has meaning in terms of what you can contribute.

Here I am describing the third stage of development, the stage of interdependence, where you re-enter relationship as a responsible individual. Here you are able to think for yourself. Here you can account for your own experience and realize that you must re-engage with life in a real and purposeful way in order to have any satisfaction. For indeed, independence, though thrilling and exciting in its newfound freedom, is essentially lonely and isolating. It is inefficient and incapable of producing great results. After all, you can only proclaim your independence for so long. Then you realize you have something to do in life, and you want to do it.

To do something important in life, you must enter into relationship with other people and learn to work with them harmoniously. You must learn to share power. You must learn to restrain yourself. You must learn compromise when compromise is appropriate. You must learn discernment. You must learn all these things, and this prepares you for the third stage of your development, which is the stage of dynamic and genuine interaction with others. Here the need for discretion becomes greater as you realize the importance of your own life and your own self-expression. Here you realize that most conversation is unnecessary and is merely a way to offset insecurity for people. Here silence is preferred because in silence you begin to experience your presence, the presence of others and the meaning of your relationships.

Here is the problem
with problems:
little problem,
big reaction;
big problem,
little reaction.

Eight

SOLVING PROBLEMS

OLVING PROBLEMS AND LEARNING to engage with Knowledge is a major component of learning The Greater Community Way of Knowledge and realizing its total application in your life. So complete is Knowledge and its application that as you progress, you realize that Knowledge is with you at all times. It is just very still and you are very noisy. To experience this Spiritual Presence abiding with you in its stillness begins to give you confidence that if all is quiet with Knowledge, then it is time for you to be quiet too, while you take care of the mundane activities of your life and meet your normal range of responsibilities.

Problems large and small emerge, and here Knowledge plays a very important part. It is confusing to the recipient because Knowledge works very differently from the personal mind. It is quiet a good deal of the time. It must be activated by something beyond itself in order to fully reveal itself. How different this is from the way you think — always pondering, comparing, wondering, creating little scenarios, recalling former ones, working away at certain troublesome issues and reacting negatively against things that are taking your time and energy. Work, work, work. Busy, busy, busy. It is like a meeting that never ends.

Your personal mind always has the engine running. It is only when you go somewhere else while it's running that you begin to realize that there is something else within you. There is a very different kind of mind there. This is an important discovery, and it will come slowly because to go from living in your personal mind to living in the mind of Knowledge is such a complete and total transition that it will require a completely different perspective and approach to life, a different sense of identity and a different foundation for relationships and activities in the world.

So, how do you solve problems? To begin with, let's talk about the kind of problems you are trying to solve. Now, there is the big problem, there are intermediate problems and there are little problems. Occasionally, Knowledge will help you with little problems, but often it won't, so you must simply work them out. This is usually easier than people realize, but because they often don't accept that the problem exists or they have some sort of complaint about its appearance, to them a little problem can seem very big. So, instead of simply fixing the situation or discerning how the situation can be improved, there is often confusion with a great deal of upset and lots of conversation with the personal mind charging along, working overtime. This is a big reaction to a little problem.

Here is the problem with problems: little problem, big reaction; big problem, little reaction. This is the problem. This is the *big* problem. If you lose your car keys, or if your tires are flat, or if you made some kind of mistake or if you neglected something or if you forgot something or if some mechanical thing that you own breaks down, or if somebody else's mechanical thing breaks down—all these are little problems, but often they incite big reactions. The fact that they incite a big reaction is part of the bigger problem. So, rather than just charging into solving problems, right and left, big and small, let us delineate the problems that Knowledge is working on and the different problems that you are working on.

Trying to make more money, whether it is a necessity or a preference, is always a little problem. Asking "How can I make more money?" might take ninety-eight percent of your energy, but it is still a little problem. Even if the solution requires time and effort, it is a little problem.

Little problems comprise most of the problems that people are engaged in trying to either solve or avoid. Actually, there are only three possible responses you can have to a problem, big or small. You can avoid it, and there are many avenues for doing that, for human beings are very clever at avoidance. You can complain about it, which means you cannot avoid it, but you are not yet committed to resolving it either, so you complain about it. Or, you can solve it. In the first two, there is a great deal of response to a little problem. There is a great deal of effort extended in avoiding problems and in complaining about them.

Now, a little problem becomes a bigger problem, or let us say it becomes an intermediate problem, if it is neglected. Then the consequences of avoiding it or not solving it become more troublesome, more difficult and perhaps more expensive. A little problem usually can only become an intermediate problem. A big problem is something else.

If a problem is neglected for too long, it can become a bigger problem, but in and of itself, it is not a big problem. The bigger problem is that the little problem was not solved, or there was too much energy expended. That is a bigger problem. If a little problem over time becomes a bigger problem, it in itself is not a big problem. It is a problem, but the bigger problem is that it was not recognized in the first place.

The *big* problem is that people do not respond to Knowledge. Knowledge is waving flags, giving indicators, doing everything to warn the person, but the person is not aware or is avoiding something. That is the big problem. The way people respond to life—by not participating with life, by not being in relationship with life, by forging ahead for their own ambitions, trying to live out their own ideas and ideals — this is a big problem, and it gives birth to most little problems as well.

So, let me talk about problems in general a little more, and then we shall explore solving little problems, intermediate problems and then the big problem. First of all, do not try to not have problems. That is not intelligent. Because you are dealing with the physical world, there are many practical problems to solve. Because you have a personal mind that is disassociated from life, it has lots of problems. Because you are not fully engaged with Knowledge, you have problems. So, we have lots of problems. Trying not to have problems or trying to have fun instead of solving problems creates bigger problems or, should I say, emphasizes the big problem. Knowledge is solving problems all the time, but it solves only intermediate problems and the big problem. Why? Because the other problems are meant to be solved with your personal mind.

Many people say, "I can solve this problem. I'll use common sense." For instance, if you don't brush your teeth, they rot away and that becomes a big nuisance. This is common sense. Common sense is like kindergarten Knowledge. It is like Knowledge at a very rudimentary level. That's when something is obvious and it keeps bumping into you. If you don't pay your bills, you will lose things. If you lie to people, trouble will come after you. This is all common sense, or kindergarten Knowledge. In other words, most people know these things, but they choose not to pay attention because it is not expedient in the moment to do so, or perhaps it will cost some money, or they will have to deal with some kind of discomfort in regard to it, or it will just be more effort in the daily living of life.

So, you are going to have problems, and they are going to be at all three levels because they already exist at all three levels. Little problems are problematic because you live in a physical universe. Intermediate problems are little problems that are not taken care of. And the big problem is that you are disassociated from Knowledge and from other living things as a result. This is everyone's condition, so obviously learning to solve problems is very important.

Most little problems can be solved with your personal mind. That doesn't mean they are all simple. It just means they can be figured out. In other words, if you started to turn on your car and the motor wouldn't start, that is not a big problem. It may be a big nuisance, but it is not a big problem. Very rarely is it life threatening. So, should you go meditate on what to do? Perhaps. But it is common sense that will help you. Sometimes if you lose your keys, it will come to you where they are, but other times you may have to search the whole house. It is a little problem. You become more effective, more competent and more able in the physical world by solving these little problems, over and over and over again.

Most education is learning how to solve problems. So, why are people trying to get rid of their problems in order to be comfortable? That is like saying you don't want to be educated. Now, if little problems are attended to without so much avoidance, denial and complaint, they don't take up much of your life, and they enable you to become more aware, more conscientious and more capable in practical ways. This frees you to take on the big problem of life.

The big problem poses these questions: Who are you? Why are you here? What are you here to accomplish? How do you re-engage yourself with your deeper mind? This requires asking the same questions in different ways. It requires examining the big problem from many different angles. In fact, the problem is so big that people observe it in different ways and have very different interpretations. It is like looking at a huge thing, but you can't see all of it. You can only see part of it. So, someone over here is looking at this part, and someone over there is looking at that part. And if they happen to communicate, they have entirely different stories about what they are experiencing. In this case, you may say the big problem is trying to become spiritually aware or the big problem is trying to become really honest with yourself or the big problem is discernment in relationships. This is all the same problem, but you are experiencing and observing it from different vantage points. This is the big problem. Even if you solve all of the little ones and have made yourself very comfortable in life, if the big problem is not attended to, you will not feel any relief and the little ones will still preoccupy you.

In an ideal or pure state living in the world, there are no intermediate problems. There are only little problems and the big problem, and most little problems can be solved by common sense. If they are neglected or avoided or if you are not aware of them, they become intermediate problems, and then Knowledge will help you. For instance, if you feel the need to go to the doctor because you have an ache and you don't get the message and say to yourself, "Oh, I can't afford it. I will deal with it some other way," or something like this, eventually it becomes an intermediate problem, and Knowledge will start to prompt you to do something. You will start to feel that you *must* do something. You will feel the inner prompting of Knowledge. Why isn't Knowledge more concerned with day-to-day kinds of problems, even the aggravating ones? Why? Because Knowledge is engaged in solving the big problem. The big problem is very big and affects every aspect of your life. If you are moving towards a resolution there, you are entering a new life. Here little problems continue, but they stay little.

What takes the place of problems? Freedom. If your little problems remain large and contentious and absorb all of your energy, you cannot attain freedom. What is freedom? Freedom is responding to the truth within yourself and following it. Your freedom is to be able to do this. This solves the big problem and enables you to experience your worth and purpose in the world. When that is happening, self-love is natural. When self-love is happening, your relationships fall into the right order. This is freedom. People think freedom is being able to do anything they want with a minimum of hindrances or obstructions. That is not freedom. Lack of hindrance is necessary up to a point, but it is not freedom. Think of someone living in a country where there is very little political freedom and take someone living in a country where there is a great deal of political freedom. The person in the latter case would have more advantages and opportunities, but it does not mean that they are solving the big problem in life any more effectively than the other person. It just means that their little problems are different.

Remember that Knowledge is involved in solving the big problem and in keeping little problems little by enabling you to solve them at the level at which they occur. Because everyone has the big problem, it generates a lot of little ones that wouldn't be there otherwise. For example, consider the idea of solving problems at the level at which they happen. This makes sense, but very few people can do it. Let me give you an example. If you lose your keys and go searching all over the house madly and you think, "This must have some spiritual significance for me," or "This must represent some aspect of my psychology," and you start getting involved in various kinds of speculation, then your little problem begins to represent something much bigger, and you get all caught up in the significance of this. Meanwhile, your keys are not found. They are waiting there somewhere for you to find them, but you are off in your mind doing something else.

When people get involved in their own personal development in a conscious and active way, often they inflate things tremendously. Everything that happens is significant to them. Everything they feel must be significant. All of their problems represent greater truths or greater disabilities in life. Losing your keys is normal. It will happen to you regardless of who you are. Even the man and woman of Knowledge will lose their keys. The man and woman of Knowledge will get sick and die. The difference is in their experience of Knowledge and where they are devoting their energy. Most of the things in the world that are engaging people and overtaking them are little problems that have become bigger. Either they have been neglected or given too much significance.

Knowledge is engaged in the big things, but it keeps track of everything else. So, you lose your keys and you go to Knowledge and you say, "Where are my keys? I will meditate." Sometimes it comes to you to look in a certain place, and you say, "Ah, wonderful! Knowledge is so good!" Other times you try to focus and there is nothing there and you end up having to look all over the house anyway. And then you think, "Well, maybe Knowledge doesn't work." Knowledge is involved in something much bigger than these kinds of things.

Often when people are beginning to learn The Greater Community Way of Knowledge, they pester themselves incessantly with questions about what they should do about this and what they should do about that and how they can earn more money and how they can find true love and how they can get rid of aches and pains and on and on and on. There is no inner response and they say, "Either I am too stupid to get Knowledge, or maybe Knowledge doesn't exist." Knowledge is involved in something much bigger than these questions. It is like a scientist working on an important discovery.

You must solve ninety percent of your problems. Be resourceful. Seek help. Learn things. This is your education in being a human being. This is how you mature as a human being: by accepting these problems, by learning to become resourceful and by solving them. But you do not want intermediate problems, for they will rob you of your time, energy and focus in life.

Now let us talk about the big problem. The big problem is

so big that you can't put it all into a single definition. If you have
learned to solve little problems sufficiently or can keep track of them
as they arise, then perhaps you will cross another threshold and enter
a greater dimension of your life. Here there is a greater problem,
and here there are rewards that wouldn't be available to you unless
you had sought this greater resolution in your life. Not only is there
resolution, there is accomplishment and with it all of the things that
you have come into the world to serve. Knowledge is here. Meaning is here — the underlying meaning of how you do things and
who you are. Here the emphasis is not so much on little problems
but on the whole environment in which they exist. Alter this environment, and everything changes with it. Problems don't go away.
They are just minimized and become more interesting. Very few
people enter this level of problem solving. This is advancement.

In the Greater Community, much of the competition is for
intelligence. Intelligence is developed both within the context of an
individual's life and over the span of generations in his or her particular race by solving problems — little ones and in some cases, the
big one itself. Knowledge is there. Knowledge is working on the big
problem. Knowledge is guiding you to solve the intermediate ones.
And for the little ones Knowledge is saying to you, "Work it out.
Work it out. Work it out." You can see here why people cannot
comprehend Knowledge — its presence, its reality or its Wisdom.
They have little problems which have become big to them. They
are asking Knowledge to solve them and Knowledge is saying,
"Work it out. Work it out." They say, "I can't work it out! It is
too big! It is too difficult!" Knowledge says, "Work it out." Knowledge is not understood here because people think little problems are
enormously huge.

When you solve problems and you get most of them out of
the way, what do you have left? You have emptiness. This is the
invitation to go into the mystery of your life, but many people do

not realize this. With no problems to solve, they become frustrated, anxiety sets in and then emptiness.

In the realm of the big problem, you work with Knowledge, you follow Knowledge and Knowledge teaches you how to address all the practical dilemmas involved. It teaches you how to address the adjustments you need to make in your own thinking and in your emotional life. When you work with Knowledge, you receive the greatness of Knowledge, the silence of Knowledge, the mystery of Knowledge, the discernment of Knowledge and the peace of Knowledge.

It is true that the wiser a person becomes, the fewer little problems they have and the more they treasure emptiness so that they can engage with Knowledge in a big way. At the outset, a person is overtaken by little problems and intermediate problems, so often the first thing that happens in following The Way of Knowledge is learning how to resolve these things so that you are free to go on to something greater. And the funny thing is, you have to do it yourself. You can get help, but *you* have to do it. It is when you cross that threshold and you enter the mystery of your life and you take on bigger problems without neglecting the little ones that you enter the realm of the big problem. That is when Knowledge becomes something very real. Over time, if you persist, you will feel its greatness, and you will begin to understand its intention. Before this, Knowledge is just a strange and intriguing idea but hardly useful in solving little problems, which are usually thought to be big problems.

Another way of saying this is when you learn to solve little problems efficiently so that you have very few of them with you at any given time, and you are able to deal with them as expediently as possible, then you graduate into a different kind of problem solving in life and a different kind of life altogether. Here you can begin to see the problem for beginning students of Knowledge. This includes

almost everyone in the world, since advanced students of Knowledge generally are not even on the physical plane here. So, be happy
to be a beginner. You can see the problem for beginning students
of Knowledge. They think their little problems are big; they think
their big problem is little or they don't think of it at all. And they
seek divine intervention or divine counsel on their behalf. They
seek Wisdom, but their whole approach is wrong. Their whole
evaluation is incorrect. So, what happens? Misunderstanding, confusion, anxiety and resentment. They don't understand. Knowledge
was supposed to come and help them out and reveal itself! Often
even common sense is beyond the reach of people. They can't even
engage with that, so what is the point of seeking something greater?

There are many issues here. For instance, when people are
getting engaged in exploring the possibility that they have a spiritual
life, they often think that if they are doing the right thing, everything works out great. Doors open for you. Nothing is that difficult.
If something is difficult, well, then something must be wrong in
your approach, or something like this. This is completely wrong!
When you are doing the right thing, sometimes things happen very
easily and wonderfully. Sometimes when you are doing the right
thing, things are very difficult with lots of obstacles and you have
to work very hard to overcome them. Sometimes when you are
doing the wrong thing, everything seems to work out and is easy
until you realize how wrong it is. Sometimes when you are doing
the wrong thing, it is very difficult and there are tons of obstacles to
overcome, except that here you cannot overcome them. So, do not
be fooled by the appearance of things. Because something is hard or
problematic doesn't necessarily mean it is incorrect for you to be engaged with it. The true way in life for you will be wonderfully easy
at times, and at other times it will be very difficult. The wrong way
will sometimes look easy but will always be difficult.

Therefore, the approach to building Wisdom is to learn to

solve little problems at the level at which they occur and to keep them from becoming intermediate problems or chronic problems. Keep them small, but don't neglect them, and then begin to engage with the real problem in your life, which is following a path towards realization and contribution. Both are necessary, not one without the other. If you go off towards a spiritual life and you forget about paying your bills or keeping track of your keys or maintaining your physical health, you will be in for many kinds of difficulties and you will not go very far. So, you must do both. Your little problems will lessen as you learn not to avoid them but to attend to them as soon as you are aware of them. Then you are free to save part of your time, focus and concentration for the big problem.

As you approach the big problem, you will realize that you cannot define it and your definitions will have to change. This will lead you to adhere to a Greater Power within you and within the world. You are called on to be cooperative with the Greater Power rather than be a recipient of it only. The big problem is not something you just solve and it's over with. It is something you live with, and as you learn to live with the problem in a conscious and effective way, you learn to live the resolution. You cannot escape the big problem. You either live it in its unsolved state or you live the resolution, but you are always with it. It is always there for you.

As you proceed along the way, many of your former conclusions, assumptions and beliefs fall away, and what takes their place is openness. Real openness, not a pretend openness. Real openness. This means you can be empty and open to a situation, carefully observant of it and responsible to what you know. Problems can be avoided if this is your approach. You will want to minimize your complaints about life because complaints disable you from resolving things that are within your grasp to resolve. What you can resolve alone are the little problems. What you cannot resolve alone is the big problem. For the little problems you need help from Knowledge periodically. For the big problem you will need Knowledge completely. Not only will you need Knowledge, you must join with Knowledge. You must unite with Knowledge. You must let Knowledge overtake you, teach you and prepare you. This is where your mental life and your spiritual life become joined, married and united. This completely transforms you as a person so that you can begin to live the big problem and to live its resolution.

To a casual observer perhaps you will not look any different. You will still have to find your keys; you will still have to fix your car; you will still have to get your physical aches attended to, and you will still have to make enough money to live. But here the similarities end, for we are dealing with a person living in a different universe, a different life with a different mind—so different that there is no comparison.

This is possible for you. Begin today to accept the presence of all the little problems in your life and accept that it is given to you, with the assistance of others, to resolve them and to minimize them so that you can take on the big problem that is calling for you, that is awaiting you, whose resolution is awaiting you with rewards that are beyond human estimation. Here you learn to support yourself. You learn about your nature, which is how you do things, your thinking and behavior. You learn about the nature of others and their similarities and differences from your own nature. You realize your inner strength. Your priorities begin to change and you seek greater things. To reach these greater things you will seek a Greater Power, for greater things can only be acquired or received with a Greater Power. Take on the big problem of your life, do not neglect the little ones and you will open doors that are waiting for you, for they are open already.

*Honesty
is knowing
what you are doing
and doing
what you know.*

Nine

HONESTY

WE WOULD LIKE TO GIVE YOU a new understanding of what honesty can do for you and what honesty means in your relationships with others and in your relationship with life altogether. When people think of honesty, they often think of telling the truth about what one knows, what one has or what one does. This is a useful definition, but like all useful definitions it becomes misappropriated and a new definition has to be given, even if the old one is still useful.

Because we are giving you a much larger view of what honesty means, let us say for our purposes here that honesty is knowing what you are doing and doing what you know, or if you like, the other way around — doing what you know and knowing what you are doing. This is a very useful definition, but because it is new, it requires some investigation and like all truths, it requires much consideration and contemplation in order for you to penetrate its real meaning and possible application.

Honesty is something people don't think of when they consider what they know within themselves and the value of what they do. Short of breaking the law or telling outright lies to others, honesty ceases to become something people consider in any depth, unless of course someone else is not speaking the truth. Then the issue of honesty is brought up with great emphasis. So, in your own life, think of what honesty means in terms of what you tell yourself and not only in terms of what you tell others. Let us start here. Tell yourself a lie, and you will lie to others. Alter the truth to yourself, and the representation of truth to you will be altered as well. Base your activities or plans on one thing that is false, and the outcome will disappoint you. This is where honesty must be considered anew and be given a greater application.

What do you tell yourself? This is a good starting point. If you tell yourself that what you want is what is true, then you will believe it and try to convince others as well. When you fail to do so, you can either be disappointed in them or you will enter confusion yourself. You are in conversation with yourself all the time. You are telling yourself things; you are explaining things to yourself; you are analyzing; you are coming to conclusions; you are changing your conclusions, and you are fortifying what you know already.

You see, your personal mind—as opposed to Knowledge, or your Spiritual Mind—is like a great tree that is growing. It is built upon the past. Like a great tree, the new leaves are budding towards the top, particularly if you are growing in a great forest. The part of the tree that most people see is not the part that is growing now. They must go all the way to the very top to find the freshest young shoots that are growing. This is like the personal mind. It is built upon the great structure of the past, which makes up the personal mind, and towards the very top it is developing new things and creating new experiences, ideas, and so forth. But the great mass of it is grounded in the past.

What happens when you are being truly honest is that you are engaging in the present with a present state of mind. This is markedly different from the normal state of mind, which seeks to integrate all new experiences, ideas, and so forth according to past wisdom or, in other words, to continue to build the past. You are always building the past unless you decide to develop the ability to engage with the present with a present state of mind. A present state of mind means that you are open to something and that you are withholding your past interpretations so that you can understand something more clearly. The truly profound present state of mind is the direct experience of Knowledge, where you have recognition and insight into something that is occurring now. This is where Knowledge can enable you to transcend present boundaries, reinterpret the past and forecast the future. Such is the power of Knowledge, your Spiritual Mind.

Honesty, then, is a present time experience. If you are not engaged in this, then you are simply rebuilding the past or adding to the past. Here you will add things that are familiar. And if something unfamiliar comes to you, you will either make it familiar or you will put it in the category of the unknown or the unwanted. To have a present state of mind requires preparation, practice, attention and a desire for truth. Consider this: When you are truly honest with someone else, it may well change the nature of things, both in that relationship and in your overall activities. Honesty brings change. Dishonesty fortifies the past.

The personal mind, unless it is guided properly, is by its very nature dishonest. It will continue to build the past, integrating all new experiences, ideas and concepts according to its past ideas in order to fortify its sense of identity. It is, therefore, inherently dishonest. It is not necessarily intentionally dishonest. It is inherently dishonest. It can become honest if it is guided by a Greater Power within you, which is your Knowledge.

Therefore, being truly honest and having a present state of mind require engagement with a Greater Power within you. Does this seem extreme to bring about an experience of honesty? It is actually fundamental, for you see, until this happens, people will only be honest to gain advantage, which will continue their dishonesty. "I will tell the truth if it helps me. If it does not help me, I will not tell the truth." This is how people think until they overtake their thinking mechanism and guide it in a new way. Honesty, then, is seen as a good thing as long as it is convenient. When it ceases to be convenient, then other ways are chosen. Perhaps the truth is altered or withheld partially. Perhaps the facts are altered. Perhaps the truth is dressed up to look a little bit different than it actually is.

New experiences, new ideas and new people bring change. And here, honesty is compromised again and again, even if honesty is valued and cherished. Many people think of themselves as being very honest and forthright, but they are only so within a given range of experiences. Beyond this, unless they are guided by a Greater Power and have an incentive for truth, they become increasingly dishonest. The greatest dishonesty is to act for self-benefit and self-gratification. Here the truth is used for other purposes rather than being valued for itself. The truth may confirm a past experience or idea or the truth may require a change on your part. Honesty and truth go together. Truth must be a greater virtue, a greater thing to value than your own comfort and security because, indeed, truth will take you beyond these — not to deny or destroy them, but to give you a greater foundation for Knowledge.

So, to be truly honest you must engage with a Greater Power within you. You must be able to consciously have a present state of mind, an open mind. You must be able to consciously deny or withhold judgment until a greater certainty is acquired through new experience. You must be open to change — not the kind of change that takes you in the direction that you would prefer to go, but the kind of change that your life needs to have regardless of your preferences.

In considering other people, you have to consider that there is a range of honesty possible. The limits to their honesty are aware-

ness, understanding and their overall development. Lack of awareness limits honesty because without awareness you tend to be dishonest in order to protect yourself. Preparation is necessary because
preparation engages you with a Greater Power and develops your
understanding so that you can use your mind and body responsibly.
Therefore, as awareness expands and preparation grows, a person's
range of honesty will grow as well. This means that one is able to be
aware of more things and able to have a more present state of mind
in all situations.

This question of honesty would seem to be hopelessly complex
and difficult if it were not for the presence of Knowledge within
you, for Knowledge is always honest, regardless of what it encounters. Knowledge is unafraid of anything. There is nothing in the
world that can harm Knowledge. Therefore, the more you are allied
with Knowledge, the more fearless you will become, the more secure you will become, the greater the sense of self and identity you
will have, and the greater the sense of direction and relationship you
will possess. This gives you the foundation upon which to expand
your range of honesty and to receive its rewards in new and unexpected ways.

Now some people think, "Well, I say what is on my mind.
That is honesty!" I say no. That is not honesty. Even if speaking
your mind is a form of confession, it is not yet honesty. It has the
potential for honesty, but speaking your mind can be destructive
and hurtful to others and can indeed endanger and imperil you. So,
do not cling to that definition, for it is far from complete.

Here we must have a new understanding: Want what you
know. Know what you want. Honesty does not require that you
say everything that you feel. It just requires that you not alter or
deny the facts of the matter or alter or deny your real experience
of things. It will often ask you to withhold your conclusions and to
hold back your speech until a greater understanding can be ac-

quired. So, speaking your mind, which is usually a form of reaction, is hardly honesty. The greater honesty is to be aware of what you really know and to follow what you know so that you can apply it everywhere. Therefore, truly honest people are really very rare in the world, and even they are limited by their awareness and preparation.

Many people are free with their ideas, but this really says nothing about them. Many people will express their opinions with great conviction to anyone who will listen, yet if it is something of a personal nature, they will give a very different story. Honesty is actually inside you, but it is first gained by awareness. If you are aware of your true feelings towards something, if you are aware of what must be done, then you can plan out your actions in a way that will have the greatest benefit with the least harm. On rare occasions Knowledge will override this, and you will be moved to do something very unexpected and very forceful. But this is quite the exception. Knowledge is silent most of the time. When you learn to follow Knowledge, you will become silent most of the time.

Honesty is not something you inflict upon the world. Honesty is something that you experience within yourself. Truly honest people, then, may not always speak, but every time they speak, they will speak the truth. In other words, much of what they know to be true they will not speak of, for it is not useful to do so. Here, discretion and discernment must be developed — two great developments in The Way of Knowledge. Then your words will have greater impact and more awareness will be carried with them.

At every stage of a person's development, there is a particular experience of what honesty is. As people progress, their experience of what honesty is changes again and again accordingly. Therefore, one person may say, "Honesty is saying what you think." Another person may say, "Honesty is being aware of your feelings." Another person may say, "Honesty is not telling any lies or untruths." These are all correct but incomplete because we must go back to the beginning, which is what you tell yourself. If you lie to yourself and then tell those lies to others, you may think you are being very honest with yourself. You are speaking your mind. You are sharing your convictions. You may think there is nothing wrong with this.

Therefore, go back to what you tell yourself. What do you tell yourself about the latest new experience you had? What do you tell yourself about the person you just met? What do you tell yourself while you are reading this book? What do you tell yourself? If you judge this book immediately, you are reinforcing the past. If you say, "Well, I like what is being said here. This is wonderful. I have read this elsewhere. I think it is quite good," you are reinforcing the past. On the other hand, if you say, "I don't like this information. I don't understand it. It is not logical. It is not reasonable. It does not fit with my experience," you are reinforcing the past. To learn something new, you must have an open mind. An open mind means you are not trying to confirm what you know already. You open yourself to new information. Your guide here is your own deeper sense, which can override your prejudices, your fears and your insecurities. Then you are in contact with something great in your life. Therefore, honesty starts with what you tell yourself.

Knowledge is there for you. It will be silent most of the time. Yet, it will counsel you wisely if you listen. To learn of Knowledge you must be silent a great deal of the time and then learn to detect and to apply what is spoken to you or what you feel is a result of what is spoken to you. This is the beginning of honesty. This is why The Way of Knowledge is essential. Otherwise, people are always reinforcing the past and protecting their personal minds against the present. This determines their behavior and their actions and yields confusion, disappointment and misery as a result.

Honesty in the real sense is truly beneficial and illuminating, but it carries with it a great responsibility. It carries with it a responsibility to open yourself to life, to follow Knowledge within yourself and to become aware of how you are constantly reinforcing the past by your reactions to things, by the ideas that you maintain and by your prejudices and preferences. Life constantly gives you the opportunity to break through these. The opportunities are with you now.

Follow what you know, and you will learn how to be open. Follow what you know, and you will learn how to think constructively. Follow what you know, and you will be able to enter new territory in life and experience life in a new way. This, then, prepares you for honesty, which is an experience of realizing who you are.

In the context of relationship, there are times when you say something or when someone else says something that is a remarkable truth and you both respond to it as if it came unexpectedly from nowhere. It was a revelation. How different this kind of experience is from the usual kinds of truths that people attempt to pass on. This is moving in the direction that I am talking about. It is a different kind of honesty. You cannot just have it like that. You must work for it. You must cultivate it. You must value it. And you must apply it. This involves becoming aware of how you misuse it, forget it or alter it for some personal advantage. This requires that you learn to listen to what you say to yourself rather than respond to your ideas and feelings like a mindless servant.

As you engage with Knowledge, it will give you the opportunity to do all of this. Allow my words to penetrate and over time see what emerges as a result. If you claim right away that you like these ideas or you claim that you don't like these ideas or you make some other evaluations, you are not being honest with yourself. Following an old pattern of thinking and behavior is not honesty; it is a form of servitude.

Knowledge is with you. Seek Knowledge. Learn to identify Knowledge. Learn to give Knowledge the greater place in your life. Learn to see what your responsibilities are and claim them for yourself. This requires time, preparation and supportive relationships. It requires a program of development that you did not invent for yourself. This will create a new kind of conversation within yourself and will generate a new kind of response as well. I am being honest with my words because of my intent. My intent is more powerful than my words. Perhaps you might think a more eloquent or rational presentation would be better. I say, "Do not be dishonest with yourself." My words are adequate to convey my message, for those who can hear and for those who desire something greater.

It is very important here that you not condemn others for their dishonesty. It is part of the human condition to be dishonest. This is not to say that is your true nature; it is simply part of the condition of being a human being. It is part of the condition of being intelligent in the physical world, where you are aware of your own motivations and vulnerability.

To be intelligent in physical life requires a spiritual emergence. Otherwise, the most intelligent creature will be the most miserable and the most self-destructive. Surely, this is born out in human relationships. Intelligence requires Wisdom. Otherwise, it is dangerous and destructive and will turn against itself. To expand intelligence requires a spiritual motive, where spirituality is seen as your greater identity. If you are to have more power, you will need greater guidance. You will need larger definitions, new models and new ways of developing yourself and receiving Knowledge.

Do not condemn dishonesty. Dishonesty is what you can expect unless the person has made a real effort to counteract it. Much of what you hear, whether it is agreeable or disagreeable, is inherently dishonest. We do not consider this with any condemnation; we look upon it with compassion. It is expected. In other words, people will lie until they stumble upon some kind of truth or until, by their sheer devotion and desire, they break free of the old patterns they created in the past. This is when the great tree spreads its seeds and something new grows which has its own being in the world. It has new life.

Now, when I say honesty is being in a present state of mind, do not think that you should not know about the past. What I am saying is to not let your past determine how you will respond and what you will conclude as a result.

Be very compassionate. If you are to be wiser and more aware, compassion is essential. You will be far more aware as a man or woman of Knowledge. But this can lead to greater condemnation unless that awareness is tempered by a greater understanding.

When I speak of the Greater Community and provide this greater perception and perspective and provide information on the Greater Community, keep track of what you tell yourself. Suspend judgment. Do not react. This is a discipline. New information requires a present state of mind. New information requires this, and evaluation of everything that has occurred in the past requires this as well. If you want to have great insight into your past activities, engage with them in a present state of mind. Give up the need to have conclusions. Do not fortify your personal mind by building more and more bricks of judgment upon which to stand. The eagle that soars will always soar higher than he or she who builds a tower from which to look. The higher the tower, the more it is a prison for you — a prison from which you cannot escape. Better to develop wings than to build towers towards the sky.

Honesty is something you can practice every day in every situation. Here are two questions to ask yourself when engaging with new experiences which, regardless of your state of mind, you are having continuously: "What do I know about this?" and "What should I do?" If you ask these questions, you must be willing to have no answers. Remember that Knowledge is silent most of the time. It is silent and observant. Therefore, to learn from Knowledge, you too must become silent and observant.

Think of it like this: Imagine for a moment that Knowledge is a very wise, saintly person—enlightened, if you like that idea. This person is available to you, so you go to him or to her with all of your questions and you say, "Teacher—or Master, or Saint—tell me what I should do here. Tell me where I should go. Tell me if I should make this decision. Explain what happened to me yesterday. What is the significance of my dream? Will I be loved in the future? Will I have money? Will I be successful?"

Yet, when you go to your teacher, you find that in most cases your teacher is silent. At first, you leave very disappointed. Perhaps you are irritated by this silence. You may say, "That was an honest question. I have a right to ask this. This is a sincere question, and all I get is silence." Well, if you go back again and again and keep going back, even if all you get is silence, then after awhile you will start to think that maybe you should contemplate what you are asking and consider if you are really prepared to have an answer. As you consider this, you will need to question if you are willing to change and how flexible you are. Do you want more answers simply to give your mind the fuel with which to think its old thoughts?

Silence is an appropriate answer for most of the questions that people ask because most of these questions are mindless. It is when someone asks a question with real motivation, a real desire for truth and a willingness to change that an answer has real merit and impact. So, if you keep going to your wise, saintly person, one day he or she will say, "Listen, try this," or "Think about this," or "Give up doing that," and you are shocked because finally, after all this time, you have an answer. After hundreds of questions and all kinds of disappointments and reactions, you finally get an answer. But you don't know what to do with the answer, so you return and you say, "Well, what should I do? What should I do?" Silence.

The answer is a problem to solve. *You* must solve it. It could be a series of problems which you must learn to solve. Learning to solve them develops you as a person, matures your mind and gives you greater understanding. A wise answer is always a procedure of development. That is why it must be infrequent. Often people are not committed to any kind of development. They simply want new ideas to keep their minds going and to keep up their fascination.

Knowledge within you is like this wise saintly person. So, you go with questions and you don't get anything, and you are disgruntled and disappointed. You doubt yourself and you doubt Knowledge and you say to yourself, "Well, maybe this is all self-deception anyway. I'll just do what I want. Maybe I'll read a new book and get new ideas and do that." But if you continue to come back again and again and do not accept any idea your mind gives you that parades as Knowledge, then you will develop awareness and discernment. And eventually you will even see the necessity and merit of discretion.

Therefore, true honesty brings about the ability to wait, the ability to evaluate oneself constructively, the ability to discern, the ability to not speak when it is appropriate, the ability to speak when that is appropriate, the ability to follow a Greater Power within you, the ability to abide with what is known and the ability to avoid or step away from that which is harmful or untrue.

So, in proceeding towards honesty, consider what your range of honesty is now. Under what circumstances would you tell the truth? Under what circumstances would you commit yourself to a form of action, sensing it was the right thing to do without knowing the consequences or what it would require of you or even if it was ultimately the correct thing? Under what circumstances would you not speak even if you were certain of something? These are very important questions to contemplate.

Do not say that you require honesty from other people as if it were a right, your right to honesty. Indeed, honesty is a privilege, something rare and wonderful in the world. If a greater truth is being spoken, without personal investment or seeking personal advantage, that is a rare thing. It is not your right to have honesty. Do not demand it of someone if they cannot deliver it in this particular situation. Remember, everyone has limits here. You have limits. What are your limits? Know your own limits, and you will be able to see others with greater compassion. Recognize what a great and difficult thing it is to gain real honesty, and you will not demand it of others.

How do you achieve honesty? You achieve honesty through the reclamation of Knowledge and through the development of real Wisdom — easily said but difficult to do. The most direct path is the steep climb. The fastest way to the top of the mountain is straight up. Therefore, take your zigzag road to truth. Patience, development, silence and discernment — learn to digest these slowly and carefully. Have a present mind.

*Do not react
with hope.
Do not react
with fear.
Respond with
Knowledge.*

Ten

GREATER COMMUNITY
VISITATIONS

GREATER COMMUNITY VISITATIONS TO THE WORLD is a very important subject, but it is difficult to describe because it accounts for so many different things. Let us say at the beginning that the world is certainly being visited by different groups for different purposes. There are some groups who wish to assess your technology, to learn about your nature and to determine your biological codes, which will tell them about your temperament and predispositions. Others are coming here to determine whether you are capable of engaging in commerce and trade. Still others are coming here to look for the ancient depositories and to utilize and recruit those who show some skill and knowledge of the physical environment to help them do so.

The fact that your world is being scrutinized is now becoming undeniable, although many people still deny it. The evidence is mounting everyday. Some of the people's accounts are not accurate, while some are outright false. Yet, many are true although their descriptions are subjective and incomplete.

The world is being visited. The world is being scrutinized. Meanwhile, human beings as a whole go about their lives as if nothing else were happening. And, indeed, in many parts of the world, the difficulty of life and the conflicts occurring within cultures and between cultures are quite sufficient to dominate people's attention. Yet, in the midst of all of the normal occurrences in human life, the Greater Community is emerging. You could say humanity is emerging into the Greater Community, but humanity is not going anywhere. So, for practical reasons, let us say that the Greater Community is emerging into humanity.

The effect of this will be tremendous and will take generations in order to have its full impact. The implications for human thought, human institutions and human ideologies are so vast and so total that it is difficult for people now to even imagine what this might mean. Human beings live in a very subjective universe according to their own understanding, which means that the universe is governed primarily by human impulses, human sentiments and human motivations. The fact that this is not true and will demonstrate itself to be untrue will have a great impact on the way people think and the kinds of assumptions they will make about themselves and the world around them. Surely, this must change what people consider to be true. Interaction with other intelligent life that does not share human motivations, human morals or human sentiments will have a very great impact.

Who is visiting you? You have allies, you have observers and you have enemies. Your enemies are not what you usually consider to be an enemy, for they do not wish to conquer you directly; they only wish to use you for their own designs, which, in effect, will conquer you. They know about the mental environment, and that is why they are so effective in controlling people's experiences, or at least in limiting people's awareness.

We have provided *Steps to Knowledge* in order that people might develop their experience and understanding of the mental environment. Not only does this further people spiritually and provide the foundation for them to lead more fulfilling and more rewarding lives, it also gives them first-hand experience in the mental environment, for here you must have development, and here you must make progress in order to engage with other intelligent life in the Greater Community.

Remember that other intelligent life has made the journey to the world, so clearly they are superior in their technological achievements. Also, they must deal with other races in the Greater Community to a certain extent, and so they have become very clever in their understanding of the mental environment, or the realm of thought. The more objective human beings can become regarding themselves and their environment, the greater will be their ability to discern and eventually to control the mental environment in which they live. This is not meant to be used as a weapon, but it can be very important in terms of defense.

Some of the more lurid accounts of extraterrestrial encounters clearly point to the fact that the mental environment is being largely controlled by them. People are mystified as to how others could have this impact upon them, how they could be so manipulated and how they could be so helpless in the presence of another intelligence. Clearly, human beings interacting with one another need only have very limited development in terms of the mental environment. People are still very much engaged in brute force and subterfuge with one another. The greater, yet more subtle, mechanism by which human thought can be directed has not yet been discovered by human beings. Human beings are still very primitive in this regard, using force, intimidation or various forms of emotional persuasion. Yet, these are very gross and fundamental. Beyond them lies a greater range of involvement in the mental environment.

Here human ethics will play an important part in human development, but the proper skills must be developed as well. That is why people must study the preparation that we have provided.

Many people think that this preparation is basically a form of healing therapy, a form of medicine for their disturbed past. Others think that it is a pathway to God. The truth is that *Steps to Knowledge* serves in both of these capacities. Yet, it serves in another capacity as well. It begins to prepare people to understand the mental environment. This is necessary for you to be able to successfully encounter extraterrestrial life — other forms of intelligence — to counteract those forces that do not hold good intentions for humanity, to be able to utilize the assistance of those who do, and to be able to tell the difference. This requires a well-trained and prepared mind, a superior form of intelligence, which human beings are capable of achieving under the right circumstances and with the proper assistance.

The fact that Knowledge is present in each person is the essential factor. Yet, Knowledge alone is not enough; a person's personal mind must be cultivated and developed to become a vehicle for Knowledge, and a person's attributes and qualities must be cultivated as well. Otherwise, Knowledge is still only a potential. Knowledge is speaking to people all the time, but they cannot hear it. It takes a great deal of development on the personal level in order for Knowledge to have true efficacy.

Therefore, we are most emphatic in encouraging you to engage in the development of Knowledge according to the methods that are being provided. Do not alter these methods in any way. You must simply accept them, use them and practice them to the very best of your ability. If you alter them, they lose their effectiveness. The error here is that people think that they understand what *Steps to Knowledge* is for. It is either seen as a form of psychotherapy or as a spiritual path alone. Any spiritual path contains elements of psychotherapy, and anything that is truly therapeutic engages people in their spiritual life. Yet, we present this curriculum at a very important time. We present it, and this Teaching as well, to prepare human beings to engage with other intelligent life successfully. To do this, you must be developed spiritually and have attained greater understanding and abilities.

If for a moment you were outside the world observing it from a distance, you would indeed see how vulnerable human beings are and how little they know about the mental environment. Though human beings think they are wonderfully complex and very unpredictable, the truth is that they are very predictable and are not really that complex at all. Once you understood their behavior through observation and learned enough about them genetically, then you would have a good idea of what they would do given certain kinds of influences or circumstances.

This investigation is currently going on. Certain people are chosen given their predispositions and their vulnerabilities. They are used like laboratory animals, so to speak. The will of the investigators is not malicious; it just does not have human ethics. You are regarded as interesting, potentially dangerous and possibly useful subjects for study. In much the same way human beings study the behavior of animals, without a great deal of regard for the animal's well-being, human beings are being studied in the same way. There are human traits that are valued and human traits that cannot yet be understood by those who are undertaking these experiments. Those forces that are determined to assist humanity are not carrying out these experiments.

Now, many people do not want to hear this information. They want to stay in the realm of psychotherapy, which is all about thinking better, acting better and feeling better. Others want to engage in the quest for God. To them, all of these kinds of things are distractions from a greater journey they feel they must take. Still others are fascinated by the things that I am speaking of but are not interested in the spiritual or the psychotherapeutic aspects. They want to understand why these things are going on, what it means and how they can become involved or how they can keep from becoming involved. Different kinds of intentions are found here and different kinds of conclusions as a result. Yet, life goes on and the fact of the matter is that human beings are being scrutinized and studied.

Many of the demonstrations that are made and the evidence that is left behind are to enable those who are studying human beings to have a greater understanding of how humans may respond to actual encounters. This is testing the waters, so to speak. There are only a few people who are aware of these circumstances and who, through their own insight and self-restraint, are coming to realize that this situation is indeed very difficult. Though perhaps many people think that there is other life and intelligence in the universe besides themselves, very few people in the world are aware of what is occurring.

The Greater Community Way of Knowledge is now being introduced. People don't know what to make of it. It is not only a spiritual preparation. It is not only a form of therapy. It speaks of all these other things, which seem so troubling in a way and so mysterious. Some people encounter this information, and they are somewhat startled by it all. "What does it mean that the world is being visited? Should I run for cover? Should I lay out the welcome mat? Should I live in fear? Should I live in joyful expectation?" The answer is to develop a superior intelligence and to gain access to Knowledge, which is your spiritual mind, for it contains the Wisdom and the guidance that you will need to negotiate life successfully, both within the context of human interactions and in the context of interaction with other intelligent life as well.

The answer is found by learning about the mental environment and by bringing your life into harmony and balance so that you can engage in a greater form of preparation. This is what is called for. Clearly, living in joyful expectation is not adequate, for there are indeed forces at hand that are not benevolent and are using human beings for purposes that do not support the well-being of humanity. What is called for is responsibility, Wisdom, certain forms of empowerment and a greater understanding of what intelligence is and how it interacts in its different forms.

The world is emerging into the Greater Community of Worlds. The Greater Community is here now, but human beings are unprepared. Human beings are vulnerable. Human beings are so self-preoccupied and have such a subjective view of life that when something encounters them or is in their environment that is not part of their inventory of ideas or does not meet with their expectations, there is either denial or there is partial awareness — either of which can be dangerous.

The Greater Community Way of Knowledge is a spiritual preparation for those who realize they are living in a Greater Community. It is a form of psychotherapy for those who realize they must gain full access to what they know and to all of their mental and physical resources as they exist at this moment. The Greater Community Way of Knowledge is a preparation for living in a more intelligent and in some ways more complicated universe. To react to the presence of other intelligent life using the current thinking of humanity would lead to unwarranted and unfortunate conclusions, whether the approach be positive or negative. What is required here is objectivity, discernment and restraint, the kinds of qualities that are difficult to attain but which are so important, both within the normal range of life here and under extraordinary circumstances as well.

This is The Greater Community Way of Knowledge. It is meant to prepare people to live in a Greater Community of life. You do not need to go aboard a spaceship and fly to a distant planet to live in the Greater Community. You live in the Greater Community right now. You have always lived in the Greater Community. You are not isolated. There is no isolation for the world. The

Greater Community is emerging for you. There are forces here to help you and forces that will hinder you. How do you tell the difference? How do you discern this? How can you respond? How do you protect yourself? How do you establish lines of constructive communication? How do you break lines of destructive communication?

The answer to all of these questions requires a greater preparation for the mind. It requires people to become uniform within themselves, balanced, sensitive, capable, responsible, able to act effectively and able to restrain their actions. It requires extraordinary development for extraordinary circumstances. Without this preparation, people will respond in predictable ways and their responses will largely be governed by their own personal needs. Even if evidence is collected and events are correlated, there must still be the question, "Why is this happening?" Science cannot answer that. Reason cannot answer that. Wishful thinking cannot answer that. Fearful self-protection cannot answer that. What can answer that? You must ask this question with a different kind of mind, see with different kinds of eyes and have a different experience here. This will unravel a great deal of the mystery about your life.

It is what is happening beyond humanity that is the context for humanity's understanding of itself. This is an important idea. Until recent times, most of the people who asked deeper questions only thought in terms of people's interactions with one another and with the natural forces of the world. Much speculation has also been generated regarding humanity's relationship with the Divine. There has actually been more progress made in this last category than in the other two. But the fact is that humanity lives in a larger context.

Humanity is not the centerpiece of the Creation, only one of its developing aspects. This represents a tremendous breakthrough in understanding. This represents a great threshold in self-realization and the ability to effectively engage with the world. This is what

Steps to Knowledge is preparing you for, should you have the opportunity and the inclination to study it first hand. This preparation has come from beyond the world because it has come from a Greater Power, the Greater Power that knows the ways of humanity and also the ways of the Greater Community, of which humanity is a small part.

Do not react with hope. Do not react with fear. Respond with Knowledge. This requires preparation. Where will you find this preparation? From the religions of humanity? From the various psychotherapies? From the various philosophies? With few exceptions, even the greatest discoveries in these arenas were made only with the understanding that human beings were accountable to one other and to a distant and far-removed Divine presence. Yet, you live in a bigger arena, and you are now becoming a participant in that arena. This was always your destiny. When it would happen and how it would happen were the only uncertainties.

This Teaching comes from the Creator. It comes at the right time. Indeed, the circumstances of your times have called it forth. Some people will call it their religion. Some people will call it their form of psychotherapy. Many won't know what to call it, for it is beyond their categories. It is a wise answer to a grave problem. It is an answer to the spiritual needs of humanity; it is an answer to many of the therapeutic needs of humanity. But it is being presented now in response to a practical need, for this is the time that human beings must begin to account for the presence of other intelligent life.

This is no fantasy. In fact, its reality will call upon people to become more real, more objective, more observant, and certainly more compassionate. It calls for Wisdom. This Wisdom must come from beyond the world, for within the world, Wisdom has only progressed so far. What does this mean? This means that there is Wisdom beyond the world that can serve the world. You cannot hop in a spacecraft and go find it. Therefore, it is being sent to you.

The Wise amongst you will have the opportunity to witness in the course of your lifetime a remarkable series of events, not only within human societies, but within the whole world as well. The predicament that you are in regarding the Greater Community will call for Wisdom and will require it. That is why the preparation has been sent. Many people, of course, will not be able to undertake the preparation, and many of those who do will fail or get lost along the way. But the preparation is here.

It is important in this discussion that I am presenting that you begin to realize certain basic realities and the need for your development that this calls upon. Without this development, you will be a helpless participant in a larger interaction and the will and the intent of others will prevail over you. As you have recognized in the history of your world, competition for land, wealth and power has had many unwanted results. In the Greater Community, there is competition for land, wealth and power, but there is also competition for intelligence — intelligence being a highly-valued commodity. The greater the intelligence, the greater the acquisition of wealth and power by those who seek it with this intent.

Intelligence is also sought after by the Wise, for with intelligence there can be education. With education there can be advancement, and with advancement there can be new understanding and new behavior. We are here, then, to promote this. The gravity of the circumstances and situations that I have alluded to only serves to point to the necessity that this information be taken seriously and that true preparation be undertaken by those who are prepared to do it.

All that we are sharing with you is to lay the foundation for a greater understanding. A greater understanding is necessary if you are to engage in a greater life. The Greater Community represents a greater life. It requires that you be prepared for the future, for your future will be quite unlike your past. Contact with the Greater

Community will certainly determine this to be true. To make this transition successfully requires your development. It requires a greater understanding of life and of the motives which determine the direction of intelligent life in its own development and in its interaction with others. This happens within the context of your own personal relationships as well as within the context of your relationships with those beyond the human family. This includes your relationship with the natural world, to plants and animals—all forms of life. A greater experience here will give you greater abilities, which are being called for now.

Amongst the Wise in many places in the Greater Community there is the idea that Wisdom requires a form of retreat. What does this mean? It means that the more powerful that one becomes—the greater one's discernment, vision and understanding—the more one must withdraw from life. This means that as the Wise progress, their gifts become more refined and more intrusive on the lives of others. The providers here must be more discerning and more careful as to when, where and how their gifts are given. Because intelligence is a wanted commodity in the Greater Community, the Wise must retreat in order to protect themselves and their gifts, for they would indeed be regarded as highly useful and desirable by those who seek to use these commodities. So, a natural progression of events leads the Wise to withdraw.

This enables the Wise to have greater effectiveness, but it is quite confusing to human beings who feel that all power must be used as expediently as possible. Yet, in the mental environment, this is disastrous, just like the expedient use of power has proven disastrous in the way that people interact with their physical environment. Indeed, the more technically capable your race becomes, the more restraint you must exercise in using this capability in the physical world. The more potent you may become in affecting others within the context of your personal relationships, the more restraint you will need to exercise and the greater must be your discretion.

That is why we say the Wise remain hidden. That does not mean that they have escaped from life or do not wish to contribute to life or are unable to bear the vicissitudes of life. This means that they must withdraw to a vantage point where their gifts can be preserved and where the recipients of their gifts can be identified and most effectively served.

This presentation of Wisdom is an invitation for you to learn the ways of Wisdom. Wisdom cannot be enunciated or elaborated in a discourse. For one fire to ignite another, the sparks must jump. I offer sparks, not fire. The fire is the Fire of Knowledge, the Fire of Wisdom.

Many will think, "What is the use of all this? Why undertake all of this preparation? It is so difficult! There are many more fun and pleasurable things to do. Why be so aggravated? Why take on these kinds of challenges?" Many will go on their way with these conclusions. But the complexities of human life — the difficulties in the interactions within the human family, as well as the growing encounters with the Greater Community — must once again remind you that you have a responsibility in life to learn to recognize and to engage with life as it is truly happening, not as you want it to be. This understanding yields a great sense of self and inner value without demeaning anything else. In fact, it is the foundation for a truly satisfying life.

Satisfying lives are the result of meeting great challenges successfully. A great challenge is upon you now. Is it a blessing or is it a tribulation? Is it a means for redemption or a great nuisance? How you answer these questions will determine how you position yourself with life, with yourself and with the Greater Community in which you live now and in which you have always lived.

I leave these questions with you to contemplate. Do not be

satisfied with familiar answers. Instead, think of what this is asking of you. Consider this deeply. This is my invitation. This is the invitation to learn of the Greater Community. While human beings are struggling to have Wisdom with one another, now they must have Wisdom to engage with life on a larger scale. Any advancement made in this direction will enable each person who is so developed and so engaged to enjoy the most minute aspects of life more completely with greater fullness.

*Knowledge
is a great mountain.
You climb it slowly,
and you learn
to live at its
higher altitudes.*

Eleven

SPIRITUAL PRACTICE

*I*N ORDER TO PROGRESS and to begin to fully comprehend all that is being revealed to you in these pages, you must at some point undertake spiritual practice. This cannot be just any form of spiritual practice but a specific kind of spiritual practice that prepares you to engage with and discern intelligent life from beyond your human boundaries. This is essential if you are to truly understand the nature of human evolution at this particular time and the greater opportunities for yourself and for humanity that are now arising as a result of the world's emergence into the Greater Community.

I can illustrate over and over again the magnificent results when one begins to engage with Knowledge and learns to follow Knowledge. The rewards are so great and so pervasive that they indeed establish a new foundation for life and a new life as a result. But as much as I may extol the virtues of this undertaking and its great achievements, I must emphasize that you have to prepare in order to reach this new vantage point. It does not come in a streak of lightening. It does not come in a dream. It is not magically bestowed upon you one day. You must prepare. You must train your mind. You must undergo a process of preparation that you did not invent for yourself.

Consider for a moment those who demonstrate any great skill that you admire. Did not the individuals who demonstrate this skill have to prepare, perhaps arduously, over a long period of time? And did they not have to make some sacrifices along the way in order to devote the necessary time, energy and focus to their preparation? If you look closer, you will see that their preparation was guided and enhanced by the presence of individuals who trained and prepared them and was also accompanied by tremendous support from those in their immediate range of relationships.

The proper form of preparation, the proper form of teaching and adequate support all add up to a guaranteed accomplishment. Think of any great skill and certainly all of these must apply. It is no different in the preparation in The Greater Community Way of Knowledge. There is training, instruction and support. This is important because in The Way of Knowledge you are not merely adding something on to your life or simply perfecting some aspect of yourself; you are indeed engaging yourself with your entire life. This takes far more willingness and courage than, say, learning to play a musical instrument well or learning to climb a mountain. Here you must face yourself again and again; here you must face all of your deficiencies and errors with courage and a desire for resolution. You must in a sense go far beyond what most people are willing to do.

Your incentive for this must come from within you, from Knowledge, for only Knowledge can take you to Knowledge. All other goals and ambitions sooner or later will fall away. What carries you on beyond them is the desire for truth, the need to know your purpose, the need to find genuine relationships and the need to answer the fundamental questions and solve the greater problems of life. It is within you to do this.

This preparation is not reserved for one or two unique individuals. Though it will not be claimed by the majority of people, it is meant to be received by individuals who realize and sense that they have a spiritual calling in the world, a mission and an important contribution that exceeds their normal boundaries. Preparation in The Greater Community Way of Knowledge is specifically designed for those who realize that they have a Greater Community aspect to their nature and who feel an allegiance with life beyond the normal spectrum of human interaction. It is specifically designed for people who have a sense of life and affinity with life beyond the world and who are drawn to the reality that intelligent life is now entering the world from beyond. It is for these people that The Greater Community Way of Knowledge and its specific preparation in *Steps to Knowledge* are being provided.

Very few people are really trained or developed to be able to practice something repetitively over a long period of time. Other than the simple manual tasks that people learn in childhood, there is not a great deal of emphasis on practice and training. In your schooling, you learn something temporarily to pass the test, and once you pass the test, it is forgotten and discarded. Only in those situations or those avenues of learning where there is a real incentive for progress do training and ongoing preparation have any emphasis at all. So, not very many people are prepared to practice something diligently, consistently and on an ongoing basis. It is not that people are incapable of doing this; it has simply not been a large emphasis in their education. Certain mundane activities are learned in childhood, and these are repeated over and over until they become habitual. But when I speak of preparation, I am not speaking of habits. I am speaking of following a greater incentive for learning, choosing a method of learning and staying with it, progressing through many stages of development and staying with it whether you feel like it or not on a particular day.

To prepare correctly, one must have proper instruction and the correct methods. The methods are being provided now. The instruction is available when it is necessary. Support and assistance will gather as you learn to exercise discernment in relationships and seek out individuals who share your sense of mission and purpose in life. Here old relationships must often be abandoned or altered significantly. Here old attachments and alliances fall away in time, and you are faced with the need to establish a different kind of foundation for choosing whom to engage with and what purpose your relationship must serve. This change in emphasis is very natural because it is the result of a deepening commitment within yourself to realizing your purpose and mission in life. Naturally, then, your values and priorities will change and what you seek to experience in relationships will change accordingly.

The Greater Community Way of Knowledge is not something you learn in a weekend. It is not something you learn as a result of reading a book. It is not something you learn by following ten easy steps. It is a much higher mountain to climb. To climb this mountain, you must understand how high it is in order to prepare accordingly and to set your expectations of yourself in such a way that they will serve you rather than discourage you. The Greater Community Way of Knowledge is a great mountain to climb. It is not an easy stroll up a hillside one day. It is not a casual pursuit when you have the free time. It is not something you will be able to do without preparation, without the proper incentive and without the proper companionship.

It is not correct to say that the way is difficult, for this is relative to what you are used to. Indeed, the way may seem very easy to those who are used to trying to accomplish things that do not represent their deeper needs and motives. What could be more difficult than attempting the impossible by attempting to like something you don't really want or need or by attempting to be somebody else in order to fulfill other people's expectations? What could be more arduous and difficult than this? Therefore, it is not correct to say that The Greater Community Way of Knowledge is difficult. Different, yes. Difficult? At times. At other times, wonderfully easy. But whether you consider it to be difficult or not at any given moment, it does require a great deal of effort and focus. Indeed, it requires ongoing and consistent concentration. For some, this will be easy; for others, it will be hard; for everyone, it will be difficult at certain junctures when you must face something within yourself that is challenging or when you are having a new range of experiences that perhaps are difficult to integrate.

So, hard and easy are not the appropriate terms here. The appropriate emphasis is that The Greater Community Way of Knowledge will take a great deal of focus and a certain amount of time. Focus and time. This will be true in all cases. Nobody glides past you easily learning The Way of Knowledge. Everyone must undertake the preparation. If people alter the preparation to make it more palatable to themselves or to make it more comfortable or appealing, they will not move forward.

The Way of Knowledge has been given very specifically. Everyone has the same preparation. It is only in the future at more advanced stages that the preparation itself becomes highly individualized. Everyone must learn certain basic things. People must learn discernment; they must learn to engage with inner knowing and to realize how Knowledge expresses itself through them individually; they must learn to remain silent when silence is necessary; they must learn to speak when speech is necessary; they must learn to conserve their energy; they must learn to accept Mystery in their lives; they must learn to develop emptiness or openness; they must face relinquishing many ambitions and goals as these clearly become obstacles to their progress. These are things that everyone must face.

Therefore, everyone has the same challenges though individuals may experience them at different junctures along the way. One person may be feeling, "This is wonderful. I love this!" Another may be feeling, "Oh, God. This is so difficult. I don't understand it." Comparisons from one person to another are never helpful here, for you cannot see the overall development of other people. Perhaps they are enjoying it in the moment while you are not, or vice versa. Can you make an adequate evaluation of how well they are doing and how well you are doing? Some people think that if they are not enjoying it, something is wrong. Either they are wrong or the preparation is wrong, so as soon as it becomes difficult, they go find some other kind of preparation that is new and exciting. There are so many fallacies here to be revealed, so many errors to be corrected and so many false assumptions to be disappointed and recognized.

All of this takes time, patience, persistence, openness and the willingness to change one's thinking and behavior. All of this takes time. How long will it take? Well, if you are serious about this, then consider that it will take the rest of your life to learn it and to master it effectively and sufficiently. Having this understanding draws an important line that must be emphasized: Do not undertake The Greater Community Way of Knowledge unless you intend to carry it through. If you are walking across a long footbridge over a deep chasm in the earth, it is important once you embark to make sure that you are going to reach the other side. If you stand still, falter and look down, you will lose heart. You must keep going. There are times when you will love the experience. There are times when you will be deeply concerned about it, for it is not meeting your expectations or you are experiencing something you cannot yet understand. You must press on to the other side. This is most important.

Knowledge is a great and abiding power within you. If you begin to tap into its resources, then please continue on. If you tap into its resources and then quit or try to escape, you will leave yourself in a state of much confusion, and there will be very little relief here. If you are going to engage with Knowledge and release its tremendous power into your life, then go all the way with it. Don't dabble with it. Don't play with it. It is too potent, too powerful and too important to treat in this manner.

Practice, then, is a foundation upon which you build. Though you may be having a wide variety of experiences studying The Greater Community Way of Knowledge, your practice keeps you anchored and focused. One day you may feel this way; another day you may feel that way. But both days you practice. This assures that you will continue onward and progress. Like walking across the long footbridge, if you keep talking steps and keep focused on your goal, you will reach the other side and you will spare yourself much anxiety and aggravation. This is how you surpass self-doubt; this is how you continue forward and transcend those things that obstructed you previously.

Practice, then, is a gift that gives itself every day. It renews you every day. It reinforces you every day. On some days you will understand and appreciate it; on other days you will not understand it and won't know whether you should appreciate it at all. But the fact that you continue will guarantee your progress. Likewise, if you are prepared to climb the mountain, then you must keep going. Even if it gets hard or confusing, you must keep going. And, as you proceed, many of your expectations will prove to be wrong, and you will need to establish new expectations and new evaluations.

Knowledge is a great mountain. You climb it slowly, and you learn to live at its higher altitudes. You cannot simply run up this mountain eagerly. You must progress in such a way that you can integrate all of the steps of learning as you go. This requires an extremely wise form of preparation. It also requires the presence of wise companions who can help you to understand what you are doing and can give you a good perspective on yourself.

As you begin the ascent of Knowledge, you will realize the

way that you learn — your predispositions for learning, your limitations and your disabilities as a learner, all things that must be fully revealed to you. So, at the outset, understand that you will have to contend with these things as you become aware of them. Do not resist or avoid them. You must become aware of them. They will show you your current state and ability. This must be the starting point; otherwise, your expectations of yourself will far exceed your capabilities. You learn your abilities, your limits, and your current state of effectiveness by proceeding on. Holding back and trying to judge yourself are never successful here. Following the way will illustrate this to you very clearly. It will also show you a great deal about the way your mind works and how you are designed.

Let us talk a little bit now about design. Everyone is specially designed to fulfill a certain purpose. This design is perfect to serve this purpose if it is wisely developed and appropriated. The difficulty here is that people do not know what they are designed for, so they do not understand their design or their nature. Often they try to change themselves to look like others whom they hold to be more valuable or whose virtues they want to claim for themselves. But you cannot climb the mountain of Knowledge like anyone else, though your preparation will be shared to a large extent. The way that you learn and the way that you integrate new experiences are very unique to you. Your uniqueness here is important to realize and to accept. One of the great rewards of following The Way of Knowledge is learning to objectively discern your nature. Here you learn how to work with your nature effectively rather than denying it, criticizing it or trying to alter it to be like someone else.

Your uniqueness has to do with your contribution in the world. Uniqueness in any other regard will limit you and hold you back and create a great deal of misery and suffering. Your real uniqueness has to do with the kind of contribution you make. Here people have fantastic notions of who they could be or should be or would be if only conditions were right or if only they had no conflict within themselves. This is all foolishness. One discerns one's nature by engaging in life in a very conscious and determined way. Here you find your natural attributes and you find ways to balance them with your overall nature. Here you learn and balance, learn and balance, learn and balance. Like walking across a great tightrope, you take a step and then balance. You take the next step and then balance. Learning The Way of Knowledge is like this too. It is not about running, and it is not about stopping. It is a step and then balance, a step and then balance. This is a good analogy for understanding the stages of learning in your life. You take a great stride forward, have new experiences, and then you must integrate it.

How does this relate to practice? You practice while you are stepping and you practice while you are balancing. The preparation that has been given in The Greater Community Way of Knowledge is perfectly suited to learning in this way. Here you are able to advance in a very direct way, and you are able to integrate your learning effectively, which provides safety and security and enables you to utilize what you are learning to the best advantage. Here you progress slowly and consistently.

Whenever people begin a formal preparation, especially something that is more long term, through the early stages of their practice they must realize what to expect from themselves and what not to expect. Many of their expectations will be clearly disappointed in that they will not be able to achieve great heights or great levels of ability in short periods of time. As they proceed, they will also realize that the journey is greater and requires a great deal more than they had previously considered. Only real participation can reveal this correctly.

As you learn to learn, you learn to teach and to impart this to others. As you advance, you will be able to do this with increasing patience, compassion and understanding. Beginning teachers, like beginning students, all expect tremendous advancement with a minimum of investment. Only a wise practitioner realizes that the greater rewards come as a result of a more prolonged and consistent practice. The rewards are what one discovers along the way. It is not like reaching a pot of gold where the entire reward is given at the end of the journey. In the reclamation of Knowledge, which is the discovery of purpose in life, all of the rewards are given along the way. Therefore, you must pass along the way to receive them. You cannot take a detour, there are no shortcuts and you cannot rocket yourself to the top of the mountain. You must journey up. Here is where the rewards are discerned, received and accepted.

People often ask, "How can I find my purpose in life? What is my purpose in life? How can I gain access to my spiritual nature? How can I discover why I am in the world and what I am here to do?" All of these are important questions, but they call for a form of preparation and not simply an answer. In fact, the form of preparation *is* the answer. How could there be any other kind of answer? What other answer could there be? If you told people the truth about their lives, it would not help them unless they were in a position to receive it, accept it, and put it into practice. How could they be in this position unless they had advanced through the stages of development that await them? So, the correct answer is a process of development.

The questions that I have just mentioned are very great. They represent great achievements in life. They are not small pursuits. Their rewards are enormous. The rewards are life giving and life changing. The preparation, then, must be commensurate with the rewards. Achievement here is far more difficult than simply learning a particular skill. It involves the re-establishment of one's life and an entirely new experience of life and what life is. Therefore, the preparation is great. Do not set out on it unless you intend to complete it. Do not dabble with it. That will not give you anything. You will not understand it, and you will not be in a position to evaluate it.

The Greater Community Way of Knowledge is an answer to a great set of questions. It is given at a time to prepare humanity for its destined encounter with other intelligent life. This represents the greatest threshold of learning that humanity has yet faced, for this interaction will change the way that people think of themselves, each other and the world around them. What they consider to be their practical life and their spiritual life change tremendously. That is why The Greater Community Way of Knowledge is being introduced. It is not the only way for everyone. It is a special way for certain people. I am speaking to you now and encouraging you to receive the answer that has been given to your sincere request for purpose, meaning and direction in life. This is a genuine answer. Now the challenge is to learn to receive it. To receive it, you must welcome it, accept it and embark upon it.

Your commitment to the answer is reinforced every day as you choose to practice. This takes you through thresholds of learning where you have to find a deeper motivation for continuing. All of the false motives for beginning this journey will be disappointed. These disappointments represent thresholds of learning where, if you choose to continue, you do so because something greater and deeper is urging you on. Perhaps the journey will not give you the things you wanted. Perhaps it will not relieve all of your anxieties as quickly as you want. But something inside of you is saying, "Continue, continue, continue."

These are called thresholds of learning, where you choose again to go on. And your decision carries you forward. You do not have these experiences every day. You can experience self-doubt every day; you can struggle with yourself every day, but a real threshold of learning does not come every day. This is very important. Here you choose a Greater Power to follow within yourself, an with it, a greater reason for proceeding and a greater motivation. This is what enables true advancement to occur. You will have to do this even if your beloved companion falls away or chooses another way. It is when you have to go back and question yourself, "Why am I doing this? Why?" that you find Knowledge.

Knowledge is not a bolt of lightning. Knowledge is not the pot of gold at the end of the rainbow. Knowledge is an inner voice and a prompting, and it becomes real in your experience as you attempt something of the utmost importance. Do not seek to experience Knowledge in things that are not essential to you or in things that are not primary to your life and your fulfillment. Seek Knowledge within those things that are primary. Then you will begin to experience the power, the presence and the grace of Knowledge. This will renew your faith in yourself, and this will provide a real basis for self-love and appreciation and a real basis for respect and regard for others.

After you have advanced to a certain degree, you will begin to see the basis upon which people succeed and the basis upon which they fail. You will see failure and success within your own experience, and you will see it in others who share this undertaking with you. This, then, is where you learn to become wise, as real experience replaces expectations, ambitions, beliefs and assumptions. This leads to real Wisdom.

Wisdom always has compassion, patience and regard, for it represents a state of mind attained by one who has proceeded onward past the normal places where people quit, give up or lose heart. Only as you advance up the mountain will you understand this and understand what it offers you. Move onward and upward. Those who quit early will quit in disgust, thinking it is not the right pursuit. Yet, they cannot make this evaluation because they have not proceeded far enough to realize what they are attempting.

Learning even a mundane skill and taking it to a highly developed state takes you through certain thresholds of understanding and self awareness. How much greater, then, is learning The Greater Community Way of Knowledge. And how much greater the rewards, the thresholds of learning and the Wisdom and maturity that are acquired along the way. And as you go, you practice.

The forms of practice will change. Your practices will be repetitive and then they will change. Here you practice until practice becomes a way of life, something that is integrated into your experience and is part of your overall approach. This is when practice becomes easy and natural. This is when your mind practices to learn rather than simply learns to practice. This is when your skills begin to emanate from you naturally rather than you trying to express them or demonstrate them. This is when Knowledge speaks through you and its silence abides within you. Things which before were difficult to comprehend and seemingly impossible to experience now become natural and effervescent within you, flowing from you like a fragrance from a great bouquet.

Practice. Have your questions. Seek for answers. But practice. That will take you where you need to go. Practice is not the only thing that you must engage with, and it is not the only element in your learning to discover purpose, meaning and direction in life. But without it, nothing proceeds and everything remains only in a state of potential.

Practice is a gift to be given every day. When you come to practice, come to give yourself. Do not come just wanting something, saying, "Give me, give me, give me!" Practice is a form of devotion. It is where you give yourself. Then what is given in return can be experienced. People often start with a desire to receive, so they begin practice with great expectations about all that they will acquire and how quickly it will come to them. Of course, it does not come quickly, and they must re-evaluate their motives.

Here they must seek for deeper reasons for their participation. This leads to self-awareness, and this leads to self-inquiry. This is part of learning and is essential.

At a certain point, you realize that you must come to practice to give something, not just to get something. Something in you wants to give, and this yearning to give can be expressed in practice. Here you give yourself, your experience deepens, your understanding ripens and you begin to see and know things you could not see and know before.

Think of spiritual practice as a form of ongoing devotion. It is giving yourself to life; it is giving yourself to the mystery and the wonderment of your life; it is giving yourself to the Divine Presence that is beckoning you onward and is infusing you with itself through your Knowledge. Then your practice will fulfill itself and will become a natural expression of life.

*Do not underestimate
the power of the world.
The Wise do not do this.*

Twelve

SELF–EXPRESSION & THE MENTAL ENVIRONMENT

*E*VERYTHING YOU SAY AND EVERYTHING YOU DO represent you in the world. They represent what you think and what you value, what you are contemplating and what you are avoiding. Your actions speak very loudly, louder than your words. Here you are making a demonstration of what you value and what you feel you are every day, in a myriad of ways. This is your self-expression. Only a small part of it is conscious on your part. The rest you are not aware of. To a certain degree, you cannot be aware of it objectively until you are quite advanced because how can you observe yourself every moment of every day?

Even in your dreams you are expressing yourself. Though you may not see the physical evidence of this, in the mental environment you are producing an effect. The mental environment is stimulating you, and you are stimulating it, every moment of every day, whether you are awake or asleep. As you learn to become more aware of the mental environment, you will see this in effect, and it will open your eyes to the great interaction that occurs between human beings and between human beings and their environment. It is occurring at all times. Here, indeed, you are entering a larger arena of life. This arena will demonstrate a greater interaction and will reveal the influences that are producing it throughout the world.

Becoming aware of the mental environment represents a necessary part of your education in learning to recognize and to receive the Greater Community. You will not be able to share language with intelligent life from beyond. Your values will be different; your behavior will be different; your physical appearance will be different; perhaps your motives will be very different. But in the mental environment you will be able to comprehend their self-expression. They are seeking to comprehend yours, even at this moment. So, the study of the mental environment is essential, not only for successful living in the world, but also to encounter intelligent life from beyond, which is a necessary part of your education as the world now prepares to emerge into a larger arena of life.

Therefore, when you consider your self-expression, consider it in a very complete sense. And remember, you are only aware of a small percentage of what you are communicating to the world around you. Perhaps those things you want to say or intend to say and want to do or intend to do represent this small percentage of your overall self-expression. Your self-expression has a great impact on your relationships with other people and will determine in large measure how they perceive you and how they respond to you as well.

Becoming aware of your thinking and behavior leads you to become aware of your self-expression in the world and opens many new avenues for this expression to be given in a conscious way rather than demonstrated automatically. Here there are real breakthroughs in learning, for here people realize they can have a much greater impact upon the world than they had previously considered. They realize they can have a much greater impact upon their relationships. This affirms their power and the opportunities for this power to be expressed constructively. This is a large part of the greater education which is being presented in The Greater Community Way of Knowledge. Like all forms of great education, it has many stages of development, many thresholds of learning and many opportunities to gain new insights and to re-evaluate old ones.

You are expressing yourself continuously. Your thoughts are affecting the mental environment, and your actions are affecting the physical environment. You live in both environments. They co-exist together. You are becoming more aware of your physical environment, but the mental environment is still a great mystery to you. Everyone else is living in these environments as well, and they too are expressing themselves every moment of every day. The interaction between human beings, then, becomes quite complex. It is complex because people are unaware of their self-expression. They interact with each other, but then they have their interpretations of the interaction, which can be quite different from the interaction itself. When you are unaware of something, you make judgments in order to give yourself explanations upon which you build your assumptions about life and your sense of self.

This complexity between human beings is not natural. In other words, it is not meant to be that way. It is complicated by the fact that people are unaware of their self-expression and because they are unaware of their self-expression, they base their actions and thinking upon assumptions, which may have little to do with reality as it is occurring moment to moment. This is what makes things complex between people.

Indeed, if you think about this and consider it, it may seem hopelessly complex. How can one gain a real experience of self-expression and the interaction with other human beings without being governed by personal fear or personal preference, by judgments and beliefs? How can one have a real and direct experience that is not colored by these things or distorted by them? Indeed, because people are so minimally aware of the mental environment in which they live and have such little recognition of their self-expression, this problem can seem enormous and the solution can seem far in the future, if it is possible to accomplish at all.

The answer to a hopeless question is to appeal to a Greater Power, to abide with the Greater Power and to learn from the Greater Power. The Greater Power is within you. It is with you now. It is not far away; it is not a great god on a great throne who is so distant and so grand that you cannot approach it. The power is given you in the power of Knowledge that you possess. Following Knowledge engages you in real interaction between people, teaches you the subtle forms of communication that are occurring and brings you into an awareness of your own behavior and thinking so that you can come to realize what your self-expression is, what it is expressing and the avenues in which it renders its communication most effectively.

Following Knowledge also teaches you how others respond to you and how you respond to them. It gives you this view and this understanding because it reveals what is happening, without interpretation. It simply brings into your awareness the dynamics of your interaction with other people. The opportunities for success here and the benefits that can be derived from it are so vast and so great that you cannot imagine the impact this will have on your relationships and on your sense of well-being. Beyond learning this, there are essential skills to cultivate over time in order to enable you to engage with the Greater Community Forces that are in the world at this time and who will be part of your life in the future in an increasing way.

What you think and what you do are guided by what you value and by what you feel is essential. Therefore, to learn of your self-expression you must learn what these things mean for you. Here, in order to begin to develop a truly objective view of yourself, you must first recognize the way you want to see yourself, the way you want to see the world and the way you want to see other people. Here you must face your pain and error, not to condemn yourself but with the desire to see and to understand. Here you learn to view others with this greater objectivity, not to condemn them but to see and to understand.

The ability to gain this objectivity and this self-awareness comes by following the means that are provided in The Greater Community Way of Knowledge, for you cannot teach yourself these skills. You cannot lift yourself up. You must engage your personal mind in specific forms of education that enable it to come into harmony with your greater life and your greater mind, which are represented by your Knowledge.

Therefore, the answer to how this can be done is to follow a means of preparation. How could there be any other kind of answer? Even if I said, "Do this," and "Do that," it would seem beyond your reach. The requirements would seem too great. That is why you need a slow and progressive form of development. Your learning is always conditioned by your desire for it and your capacity for it. You can increase your desire intentionally, but your capacity must be increased over time through progressive levels of learning and reintegration. You cannot simply expand your capacity because you want to have it expanded. This takes time and preparation. The desire to learn must have your increasing willingness and intention to explore, to discover and to understand. And it must be accompanied by tremendous perseverance and patience in order for your capacity for learning to be recognized as it exists now and then for it to be slowly and safely expanded.

Let me give an example. If all of a sudden you became aware of all of the communication that is occurring in the mental environment around you, you would likely go insane. It would be too much stimulation for you. It would be too confusing. You would not be able to escape from it. This awareness would be very damaging to you because you do not yet have the capacity to participate in this communication consciously or to understand it or to integrate its meaning. This requires a very developed mind to be able to do this—a mind that is capable of experiencing prolonged periods of stillness and observation without judgment, a mind that is not driven by ambition and desire, a mind that can be calm and observant, a mind that can wait for answers to emerge rather than inventing them for its own self-satisfaction or sense of security. You do not have this mind currently, though it is possible for you to attain it over time.

Therefore, you cannot leap into a state of so-called "super-consciousness" without destroying your ability to interact with yourself, with others and with the world. Once you realize that you have limits and that these limits should not be transgressed, then you will appreciate the preparation that has been given to you. You will accept the fact that it takes a good deal of time. And you will feel more confident and secure knowing that you can proceed slowly and carefully without sending yourself into great discord or upheaval or producing an instability that you yourself could not arrest.

Learning about your self-expression is a natural by-product of learning what you know and how you interact with the world. It is taking full account of your mind. It is taking full account of your experience. It is taking full account of the experiences of those who are having a direct influence upon you. This is not acquired instantaneously or by taking a few simple steps. This, indeed, is having an entirely new experience of yourself and the world around you. With this comes a tremendous sense of power because you realize that you are an influence in the world rather than someone who is just being influenced. You are having an impact upon the world.

With this power comes the great requirement for responsibility. Without this responsibility, your power would be damaging to you and to the world. It would be used to fulfill your ambitions, to fortify your needs and to amplify your fears. The responsibility here is that you realize you have a contribution to make to the world. You realize you are committed to following a Higher Power in order to learn of this contribution and how it can be carried, wisely expressed and made manifest within your life. Patience, perseverance, stillness, objectivity, observation, the willingness to learn, the willingness to revise your beliefs, the willingness to overturn former assumptions, the willingness not to know, the willingness to be confused, the willingness to take charge when that is necessary and the willingness to step back and yield to others when that is necessary — all these things must accompany your development.

It is not expected that you will have this willingness at the outset. Of course you won't. But it is essential that you accept it as you proceed along. Then, you will have an opportunity to understand the power of your thinking, the power of other people's thinking and the incredible interaction that occurs between you and others. You will also have an opportunity to learn that you have a certain protected mental space, a protected mental position in life. Unless you yield yourself inappropriately, others cannot penetrate this. You could call it your personal space or location.

What is inviolable within you is your Knowledge. Your personal mind can be influenced, dominated, persuaded, overtaken, tricked, commanded, and so forth. So, when we talk about something that cannot be violated within you, we are speaking of Knowledge. It is the only truly safe place you have.

When you begin to learn about the mental environment, you will see how conditioned you are by the things that you accept, the things that you think, the ideas you share with others, the impact you allow others to have upon you, the weakness you have in attempting to acquire things from the world, your vulnerability, and so forth. Indeed, if you are developing and undertaking any kind of psychological re-evaluation of yourself, you must come to terms with how conditioned you are. This is a difficult part of the preparation process because here you discover your weakness and your vulnerability. Yet, you must proceed beyond this discovery to realize your strength. Otherwise, you can become discouraged and as a result decide to live in greater self-protection and isolation, sealing yourself off from everyone and everything out of fear that they will overtake you or dominate you. This is, perhaps, an understandable reaction to the discovery of your own vulnerability, but it does not lead to Wisdom and will engender misery for you and for others who have come to serve and assist you. You must go beyond this.

The mental environment is the environment in which you think. The physical environment is the environment in which you act. The physical influences the mental, but the mental influences the physical to a greater degree. Unless the physical environment is directly infringing itself upon you or controlling your actions or behavior, the influence of the mental environment on you is greater and more consistent. Therefore, the greater your awareness and understanding of your own mental condition and how others influence you and how you influence them, the greater the impact you can have intentionally upon the world.

Here your mind will become much more concentrated than others, which will give you power, for power is concentration of mind. This concentration can be for good or for ill, but it will exert a greater influence to the degree to which it is concentrated. The person who thinks only of a few things that draw all of his or her emotional intensity will exert a greater influence on the mental environment than someone who casually believes in something or considers something only periodically. The person who has a deep conviction and a deep sense of belief will exert a greater influence than someone who is only entertaining or considering an idea. People with conviction will be able to do far more and will have much greater impact in the world. They will be able to influence other minds. This does not mean that what they believe in or are convinced of is necessarily good, for power is neutral. Power used for good and power used for ill represents concentration of mind. Therefore, for you to have a greater influence upon the world, which is necessary if you wish to make a contribution to the world, you must understand your mental resources and the influences that affect them every day.

To give you an example of what this might look like, I will speak of The Greater Community Way of Knowledge here because it emphasizes development in the mental environment to a very large degree. In a Greater Community context, development in the mental environment is essential for success, for in the future you will be dealing with intelligences that are far more concentrated than you are and have a much greater perspective, having lived with a much broader viewpoint and experience. A more concentrated mind will exert a greater influence upon you than you will upon it. In order for you to engage successfully with a Greater Community intelligence, not only to comprehend it but to offset its influence, you must have a much greater concentration of mind.

People who undertake the reclamation of Knowledge often find themselves withdrawing from life in certain ways in order to minimize or limit the influences of society upon them. This gives them the freedom to re-evaluate themselves without feeling bombarded by the world's influences and images. This is why many people who begin to study The Greater Community Way of Knowledge seek escape from television, radio and even music — not because these things are inherently bad but because they are so influential. They withdraw from individuals who influence them in ways that are counterproductive to their well-being and to their ability to refocus their mind. This withdrawal is necessary for people to rethink their thoughts, to have the freedom of evaluation, to gain control of their own mental forces, to deepen their awareness of themselves and to become more sensitive to the things that are influencing them.

Now, there are gross influences and there are subtle influences. Initially, in The Greater Community Way of Knowledge people will want to withdraw from the gross influences. This will enable them to develop the sensitivity to comprehend and effectively engage with the subtle influences. Subtle influences include the thoughts of other people who are not in your immediate environment but with whom you are in relationship. Subtle influences include the presence of extraterrestrial life that may be in your vicinity. Perhaps this extraterrestrial presence is not affecting you directly or focusing on you at all, but its presence will exert a certain influence upon you. This influence is subtle, but this does not mean that it has no power or does not affect you.

Indeed, many of your depressing moods have nothing to do with you at all. Many of them are the result of you engaging with something in the mental environment that you are not aware of. Often it is something that is not even in your visual range. Here people can go through tremendous mood swings frequently, being affected by things that are not even part of their own lives. In other cases, their own thinking is governing their emotional responses to a very great degree. Yet, often people who are engaged in therapeutic processes make the mistake of thinking that all of their experiences are determined by their own conditioning, their own thinking and their own activities. This false assumption is made because people think they are isolated in life. They are not aware of the mental environment.

The mental environment is like living in a sea of consciousness. You are swimming in a great ocean of consciousness. When I say consciousness, it does not mean that it is self-conscious. It simply means that it is actively thinking. Active thinking is not necessarily conscious thinking. The mind is working all the time, whether you are aware of it or not. It is exerting an influence and being influenced all the time, whether you are aware of it or not. Gaining awareness of the mind, controlling its influence on others and controlling what influences it, or at least determining how much this influence can affect you, represents achievement and advancement in education. The result of this will give you greater empowerment, greater certainty and the ability to affect, nurture and support others in ways that are effective and appropriate for them. This is a very great achievement.

If you look about in the world, you will see that many people feel that they are the victims of life, that life is controlling them, that they have no power to change it, that it is too big for them. This is so common. You can see it everywhere. You can hear it in so many conversations. It is demonstrated in people's activities. It is demonstrated in their forms of escape, which are often destructive. It is demonstrated in the ineffectiveness that people feel in meeting real problems in the world. It is omnipresent. Why is this?

If your experience of being influenced is greater than your experience of influencing others, clearly you are not aware of the mental environment and do not have an awareness of your own thinking and its impact upon others. Indeed, the prevalent belief that people are governed by circumstances and are totally conditioned by them is reinforced by the people who believe in it, and so this belief becomes stronger and seemingly more impermeable. Thus, unconsciousness fortifies itself. You fortify anything you believe in. You add to it. Anything you value you fortify. If you value truth, you add to truth in the world. If you value the escape from truth, you add to the escape from truth in the world. The mental environment you live in, the human mental environment, is a result of all of this put together.

Here you can begin to understand why the Wise withdraw so

completely from the influences of the world. They realize that the mental environment in which they live will dominate them unless they take great and significant steps in insulating themselves from it. They have also learned over time that they can influence the mental environment of the world through the forms of spiritual practice that they have learned and that they reinforce. They withdraw from the gross influences to a very great degree. Then they are able to discern the subtle influences, and they are able to establish their own foundation and then contribute from this foundation. If they are wise, they do this without condemnation because when you condemn something, you enter into relationship with it. Your condemnation bonds you to it. Condemn evil and you will be bonded to evil. Condemn a form of ignorance and you will be bonded to it. If you do not want to be bonded to those influences that are holding you back or clouding your vision or disabling you from gaining access to your own inner resources, then do not use condemnation.

Emotion, whether it be love or hate or avoidance, always bonds you to the thing you are responding to. If you hate another person, hate will bond you to that person. If you love a person, love will bond you to that person. Love is the preferred bond, but in many cases you may not want to be bonded to the person at all. That is why condemnation is so inappropriate. Condemnation also disables you from gaining access to what you know, so it has a double liability. It bonds you to that from which you are trying to separate yourself, and it clouds your vision and disables you from gaining access to what you know. It is not only for moral reasons that we say, "Do not condemn others." It is for practical reasons as well because it creates injury and harm and prevents your progress. Therefore, it is for practical reasons that this must be discouraged.

So, you see, self-expression isn't simply what you say and how well you say it. It isn't only what you do and how well you do it. It is your entire being in the world. Consider this: A man and woman of Knowledge may do very little in the world. They may have a very simple job. Their activities may not be magnanimous or unique. Ah, but what an influence they will cast. Others will feel renewed and replenished being in their presence. Yet, others will avoid them because they cannot tolerate this influence. The man or woman of Knowledge who is developed and prepared will cast, in most cases, a greater influence upon the environment than the environment can cast upon them. Indeed, they create their own environment. They do not do this by furnishing their house and putting up pretty wallpaper. They create an environment mentally. They create their own mental environment.

In order for you to create your own mental environment, you must withdraw from the world and the gross influences of the world, at least for a period of time. Then, with as much objectivity as possible, you must come to learn of the subtle influences which affect you. This is not easy to do. You must prepare according to The Greater Community Way of Knowledge. You must cultivate yourself—your mental abilities, your awareness, your discernment and your discretion. You must separate yourself from people who cannot help you in this, even if they love you. You must engage with those few individuals who will play a part in your advancement. You must take risks.

You must develop the necessary approach. Then you can begin to establish your own mental environment. You still will have to protect it in the world because your mental environment is less powerful than the combined mental environment of everyone else. But as your mental environment becomes more formed and more established within you, it will begin to exert an influence upon others naturally. Here you will not have to determine the influence at every moment, for the more you are engaged with Knowledge, the more Knowledge can flow through you and speak through you. Its essence can surround you. Here you become a witness to your own influence upon others. You do not dominate, you do not command and you do not overtake others. You simply share with them that which you have discovered.

In relationship with anyone, you can only share that which you have discovered. The relationship can only demonstrate what you and another value and what you have discovered. It can also demonstrate conflict between you and another. Essentially, it cannot go further than you have gone yourself. That is why it is not appropriate to be in relationship with people all the time, particularly primary relationships. That is actually a rare thing, though people try to have it all the time.

You need time alone; you need the assistance of one or two people; you need an appropriate form of development and curriculum for development. Then you can begin to develop your own mental environment, an environment that can co-exist with life and cast an influence upon it. Very few people have been able to do this, so you do not have many models for success. Perhaps you will need to have faith in what I am telling you. If you look around, you can see that everyone seems to be overtaken by the world. In fact, you might not know anyone who has gained any real independence from the influences that are governing everyone. The demonstrations of this are rare, but very significant.

The reclamation of Knowledge is not a popular movement. It is not a bandwagon. It is not something where you can take all your friends along with you. It is not something where you become a very popular person because you are studying The Way of Knowledge. Perhaps you will have to set out all alone and go in a different direction from everyone else. Everyone else is being swayed and pulled by forces that they are not even aware of. Most people will simply go along with whatever is being determined. Perhaps they will go along with it complaining all the way. Perhaps they will go along even sensing something is amiss, but they are not yet developed enough to exert an influence upon their lives sufficiently, to be able to reclaim their own sense of self and to have a sense of contribution in the world.

Remember: Do not underestimate the power of the world. The Wise do not do this. The Wise do not claim omnipotent powers for themselves. Knowledge is silent in the world a great deal. It recognizes the power of the world. It casts its influence in ways that the world cannot obstruct. Like the flower giving fragrance, Knowledge exerts its influence. You can walk by the flower in an angry mood or in a happy mood, but it is exerting its fragrance nonetheless. Knowledge is hidden, so it cannot be removed or destroyed. It is silent because it permeates things. It is not in constant conversation with itself because it has no conflict and does not need to reassure itself.

To come into contact with Knowledge means you are beginning to develop a sense of true self-assurance. You are beginning to become more silent, more still. You are beginning to talk less and to observe more. You are beginning to take on the qualities of Knowledge. You are beginning to realize that your influence on others is pervasive. Here you begin to take on a different set of attributes which are in keeping with your nature. Here you begin to realize that the greater influences are actually the ones which are more subtle, more pervasive and more permeating and that many of the gross influences, though they are perhaps loud, obnoxious and visible, are actually weaker than the subtle ones. Coming to this recognition is part of the great transformation that I am indicating, a transformation that is calling upon you now to prepare, to learn, to re-evaluate and to reclaim that which is truly yours.

*When the
Mystery is present,
then you will know
that God
is in the world.*

Thirteen

RELIGION AS MYSTERY

F YOU PARTICIPATE FULLY IN LIFE, there are two domains you will be involved in. One is the manifestation of life, which is the world of physical things; the other is the Mystery of your life, which is the realm of deep experience. One is objective; the other is subjective. These are two different realms, and it is very important that you not confuse them. By this time, you know a fair amount about the world of manifestation — the physical world. But you do not know much about the world of profound experience. It is a different realm.

With religion, no one wants to think they are being superstitious. That indicates you are believing in something that does not exist, which makes you look very foolish. And indeed, if you persist in doing this, you will feel that you are wasting your life. When religion disappoints, it is felt to be superstitious. The controversy of whether something is religion or superstition cannot be ended in the conscious, intellectual part of your mind which thrives on doubt and is afraid to get involved in anything very seriously. The controversy is resolved in another state of mind called Knowledge.

Therefore, do not try and understand all the things that we say from your personal mind because you cannot do that. It is fruitless to try. We want to take you to a greater state of mind where things can be known. In that state everything makes sense, though it is quite difficult to describe the experience once it is over because it sounds very fanciful.

The physical world is involved in the movement and interaction of things. The realm of Knowledge emphasizes the nature of true relationship, how things are truly related. Why is it important to know this? It is important because this is where your meaning comes from. Any sense of purpose in life that is genuine comes from this mysterious part of your life. In order to enjoy life, there must be Mystery. In order to grow in life, there must be Mystery. This means that there is a part of your life you participate in but do not understand.

Therefore, if you are to be a person who is evolving, do not allow yourself to have an understanding of life that is conclusive. As soon as you begin to think that you know what all things mean and are for, you begin to stop in your development. Your security must come from something greater than your own thought system and beliefs. If beliefs are what you establish your identity upon, well, you will not want to investigate life very much because if you do, you will begin to challenge and question the very ideas that you have accepted without question.

For students of Knowledge, all of their assumptions will be questioned at various points until they find a greater foundation in life, a foundation that does not change and is not based upon popular opinion or social trends. Here they gain access to something that is beyond the world but which they can bring here. Wherever you can contribute Knowledge, it has a lasting and resonating effect. It is different from building something for the good of the people, something which they can use for a while until it is used up and discarded. When you give Knowledge, it continues to move from person to person.

Why is Jesus still alive in the world? Because people are still giving Jesus, like a current running from person to person. You are all conduits for spiritual power. It will resonate naturally, but it will not pass through those who are not well prepared or who are not willing to think deeply about things. This leads to some unhappy consequences and, in a way, cannot be helped. The ignorant will attempt to use the truth foolishly. Those who do not want to question or investigate the Mystery of their lives will be happy only with assumptions that are comforting to them. These individuals, even though they were perhaps well meaning at the beginning, can become agents of destruction, as your history has so often indicated.

Religion is not the church. It is not a theological system of thought. Let me make a new definition for religion so that you can understand what I am talking about: Religion is profound experience. Out of this experience churches and theological systems arise, but they are not where you will find God. You must be in a different state of mind to comprehend the Creator, or you will merely create beliefs that will become superstitions.

Our purpose is to bring people to true experience and to minimize the possibility of erroneous conclusions, inappropriate approaches, and so forth. This is not easy to achieve. You cannot do this with all people. You can only do this with a few, but the few can then give everything they have learned to others, and this creates a resonating effect.

Why can you enjoy the comforts of what you have all around you? Because of what other people gave. I am talking about the people who invented electricity and all of your conveniences — everything! If anything, this is a world of gratitude. If you could experience that genuinely, well, it would be very difficult to be unhappy here. Unknowingly, you are enjoying the fruits of the labors of your ancestors every moment, every day. You are experiencing some of the liabilities of your ancestors, too, but the benefits far outweigh the liabilities.

Therefore, religion is also practical because it deals with the meaning of things, and meaning is what determines what you will want to do with your life and what you will value. What you value determines your behavior and communication with others. What you value is absolutely essential to your experience here.

Now, I want to make an important distinction which will require some thought. Do not confuse Mystery and manifestation. This means that when you are dealing with physical things, deal with them physically. Understand the process of how they work. This becomes very obvious when you think about it, but it is incredible how people do not do this very much and how ineffectual they are as a result. If your car breaks down, do not deal with it spiritually. Do not make it a religious experience! You may have a religious experience that is related to the car breaking down, but it does not fix the car. If you break your arm, do not deal with it as a religious experience. It is a mechanical problem. Perhaps your reasons for breaking your arm go much further, but in terms of repair, do the repair. Do not think of mechanical things as mysterious things. This gives them a value and a meaning that they do not have because the Mystery is much greater and goes beyond the manifestation of things.

Do you know what happens when people confuse manifestation with Mystery? They become entranced with marvelous things and they miss the obvious. Their imagination takes over. Likewise, it is very important not to deal with Mystery in a logical way. Do not treat Mystery objectively. It requires a different approach. Each realm requires a different approach. If you become scientific about God, well, you will create a great deal of thought about God, but you will still be far removed from the experience, and you will go off in the wrong direction. This is not the realm of scientific approach, and you cannot deal with it logically. God is illogical.

There is so much Mystery in your life! How much bearing

does this have on your everyday decisions and experience? A great deal. So, the important distinction to make is: Do not deal with manifestation mysteriously and do not deal with Mystery logically. They require different approaches. When you make everything mysterious, you lose touch with what is obvious and you will live in fantasy about everything. That is both pathetic and dangerous for you and your race.

Your true state of mind, Knowledge, generally deals with material things in a very down-to-earth fashion and deals with things that are beyond the material in a wholly different way, naturally. There is no confusion of levels or different realms here.

God is like a place you go where you experience something extraordinary, and the result of this experience affects the direction of your life, the expression of your life and what you value. God is everywhere. God is a constant Presence, constantly giving, giving, giving.

Is religion superstition? Is it people fooling themselves because they are insecure? Are they looking for escape? Do they just want to believe in something because their lives have no meaning? No matter how devout you may feel you are, you will have times when you have these questions. Yes, you will, and it is okay. You can say, "Go to Hell, God! I've had it with you! I'm going to go out and make money and get smart." You see, you love God so much that sometimes when you reject God, you get closer because when you reject God, nothing happens in return. You always go back to God because it is the only thing to go back to and because the world of manifestation is temporary, and the world of Mystery is permanent.

While you are in the world, you can only know so much about the Mystery, but it is enough to receive its benefits. If you had the capacity to fully understand the Mystery, you would not be in the world. Your mind would be too broad and great. You could not deal with specific things. Therefore, I am not saying you must understand the Mystery. I want you to become aware of it and allow it to have a place in your life.

Your Teachers know about everything you want—all your preferences, everything. You don't need to say, "I want to find my husband or wife." They know this already. Perhaps you need to say it to convince yourself that you are finally willing to do something about it or that you want something else. Here you may be enlisting yourself into active duty, but the Teachers know already.

You know, when people begin their spiritual development, in the early stages they are like children. They want everything, but they have very little capacity for anything that they want. "I want God! I want a holy marriage! I want spiritual powers and discernment and freedom from conflict now—or by the end of this year at least." But the capacity for these things has not yet been developed. When the capacity is developed, well, things happen of themselves. Better, then, to develop people's capacity so that they can actually experience these things.

Why am I here? Because I remind you of where you have come from, which is not the world of manifestation. Why does it take human beings so long to become functional in the world if they are so intelligent? Why is that? After all, other animals are moving about doing things in a day or two days or a week. You may call it instinct, but it is much more intelligent. Why does it take people so long to learn the basics? The world is a very unnatural place for a being who has a conscience. You are all visitors here. It was necessary that you forget where you came from in order to be here. That is part of the process of being here. But you are obviously visitors. You are here a very short time. You will continue on after you leave here. You have no choice about that. You have a choice about what state you will continue on in, but the fact that you will continue is beyond your control.

I represent the Mystery of your life. You do not necessarily need to understand me, but you can experience me, and if you experience me enough, perhaps you will learn to trust me. The only way you can trust me is by seeing that I am good and by having this demonstrated in your life. This is very important because this opens you up to a whole level of support, assistance and direction that you could not provide for yourself. Now you have a great asset, and the Mystery of your life can serve to direct your life in the world in a meaningful way. The Mystery will give you a new way of dealing with the world you see and sense. It is extremely practical and effective.

There are many people who talk about religion and think they are religious, but they have only accepted religious assumptions and have not entered into the real experience. For them, it is self-comfort they are seeking, and they will build their sense of themselves upon these assumptions and will be terrified when these assumptions are challenged by anyone or anything. That is why it is very important that you have exposure to things and learn to discern things and allow your assumptions about life to be questioned. That is how you progress. After all, if I am real, many of your assumptions are not.

You cannot find a way to use the Mystery to help the world because you are not in control of the Mystery. You can only control your exposure to the Mystery and your acceptance of it. You cannot make it do what you want it to do for the world. The world needs a great deal, but you can only give to it according to what capacities you have. Therefore, if you develop a greater capacity and a greater wealth of experience, you will have more to contribute. The greatest contribution that can be rendered into the world is Knowledge. Here something greater is giving itself through you. It is not you trying to improve the situation according to what you like or dislike. Something greater is moving you naturally to do this or do that. Something greater is then given and transmitted from person to person. Whether you are building a hospital or feeding a sick person, something greater is being transmitted. The current is now flowing through you. You are a witness to it. You are still doing practical things to help the world, but there is a Spiritual Presence that is moving through you. You are conducting its current. This is very mysterious. Your understanding of it can only go so far. It is profound and your questions will remain.

That is why in The Greater Community Way of Knowledge, we take people to a certain state of mind, and then something inside of them takes over. It is the very heart of them, the very center of them that begins to become manifest. The preparation is to make their outer life free enough to allow this to happen and to make their mind clear enough so that the light can shine through. This requires both an inner and an outer preparation.

Your ability to be practical in life is very important here because you do not want your outer activities to interfere with what is happening on the inside. Inner and outer development are related, but I tell you, the influence is only one way. The manifestation does not influence the Mystery. The manifestation of things — the course of events, your history, all that happens here — cannot influence the Mystery.

The Mystery influences the manifestation. God influences the world. The world does not influence God. The world influences you a great deal, so it is very hard for you to understand that the world does not influence God. Yet, as you become closer to God in your thinking, the world will influence you less and you will influence it more. That is when your ability to contribute becomes greater, and you are able to transmit something beyond your actions. Beyond what you can do physically, you can transmit a profound quality of love that has a great bearing on the lives of others. Indeed, it can kindle the spark of Knowledge in another. There is no idea I can give you that can initiate you into

Knowledge. Only the power of my own Knowledge can do that. I can do all manner of things for you, but Knowledge can only be ignited and transferred. You must be prepared for this.

Now, you must give great thought to these things that I am telling you. Do not say, "Well, I believe in this, but I don't believe in that," or "I think this is real, but I reject that." When you do that, you are merely defending your assumptions. That is being mindless. You have a good mind. You must use it now to do a little investigating. When you investigate, avoid the temptation to come to conclusions. If you were digging in the ground for buried treasure or a hidden city on an archaeological dig, you wouldn't jump to conclusions. You would carry on the investigation—until you came to the conclusion of the investigation.

People who are happy always have Mystery in their lives because they are always excited about learning new things. Life for them is an adventure. It is difficult, but it is magical as well.

Religion must be mysterious. If you are to have a religious life, you must allow Mystery to exist. It is like a great well in the ground, a well that is so deep that you cannot see the bottom, but from its depth come things that are important. If you have Mystery in your life, you can still be a rational person who deals with the world in a practical way. There need not be any conflict here, if you understand that you need to deal with tangible things tangibly. Yet, there is simply another part of your life that represents the religion of your life, which is the source of your meaning, purpose and direction.

It is important for you to be practical because this enables you to get things done. You are here to do things. This is a place where things are done. This place is not where you have come from. You don't do here what you did there, because "there" is not a place of doing. It is a place of being. This is a place of doing. That is why you have a body, and that is why you have a personal mind to direct the body. So, doing things is the emphasis here. The more competent you are, the more you can bring things about. But if you are merely competent and nothing else, your life will be empty and desolate, and you will find little comfort in the world of manifestation because its offerings are very limited compared to what the Mystery of life has to yield for you.

You only have to wonder about where you have come from and where you are going to see how much Mystery is a part of your life. You actually know very little about anything, except perhaps the mechanical things that are right in front of you. That is okay, because there is a great deal of Mystery. Mystery can be known. You know something because you are in relationship with it. You understand something when you are separate from it. When you understand something, you may figure out its process, how it works, its stages of development and how it influences other things. Yet, when something is known, it is because you are experiencing a relationship with it. This is a different kind of interaction and involvement.

There are people who understand a great deal about their relationships — their influences, the other person's influences, how they interact, their tendencies, their fears, their compulsions, their strengths, their weaknesses. Perhaps they've gone through ten years of analysis to understand everything about their relationship. Yet they do not *know* each other. You can know someone without knowing anything about his or her life. That does not mean you should marry this person. Don't do that! People often get married because they have this experience of recognition with another. That is because they are confusing Mystery with manifestation. "Well, if I have this profound recognition with another, he (or she) must be my partner." That is not a correct assumption, but many people make it and do not question it. Then they find out later if there is any relationship there.

There is no reason why a man or woman of science cannot

have profound Mystery in life. There is no reason why a person with great involvement in Mystery cannot be a competent and effective person. In this way, you can give to the world what is the world's, and you give to God what is God's. There is no problem, unless you try to make them the same. Then all manner of contradictions and dilemmas arise.

It is not a problem with God that there is pain and misery in the world. That does not mean that God is not helping you with it, but it is not a problem for God. Does that not sound heartless? It does not mean that God does not care. God is God no matter what is going on here because God is that big. But God also brings resolution, balance and harmony to everything that is within God. Why, then, is there conflict in the world if God is all powerful, or seemingly so? If God brings resolution to all things, why is there not resolution here? The answer to that question lies in your relationship with God. If you only want God to be in your life ten percent, what is the other ninety percent of your life? If there is ten percent God in your life, there is ninety percent something else. In the world, God is about two percent. I am talking about God as a mysterious, profound, direct experience.

God cannot take away from you what you want to do here, but God can influence you to return to Knowledge. Knowledge is a very different state of mind. I want to make this very clear so that you will then think, "How can I attain this state of mind?" instead of "How can I use this to make things happen in the world?" From your personal mind, the world cannot be known. The source, nature and resolution of conflict cannot be known.

People become students of Knowledge because it is natural for them to do so. There is little other incentive. I do not promise people, "If you study this, you shall have wealth, love, greater powers or be better than others." That is not the incentive. The incentive is beyond all this. You come to Knowledge because Knowledge brings you, because you are moved by something greater.

In the beginning, people doubt and fight this great inclination because it will change their lives. It seems so impractical, and they can't understand it. My God! If you had to fully understand what you were doing, you would never be able to do anything new! Understanding is always associated with the past. It is always an attempt to understand the present from the past. All scientific advancement and all true advancement on any level occurred because certain individuals moved forward without understanding what they were doing and then found something new.

It is very important to be honest enough with yourself to say, "In that situation, I do not know what I am doing, but in this situation I do know what I am doing." If you do not know what you are doing over there, it does not mean that you do not know what you are doing somewhere else. Because you are developing in the world, you will always have a large part of your life that cannot be explained or is not yet discovered. So, why come to grand conclusions about anything? You'll just have to give them up! There is no comfort in thinking, "I finally understand the way things are!" You finally understand the way things are only for a little while.

Enlightenment is not a one-time thing, you know. You will become enlightened again and again. There are major breakthroughs. One leads to the next. When you have broken through one, you are now a beginner in a new realm. It is so exciting! I very much enjoy this! But after all, I don't have the practical burdens you do. Not now, anyway. Yet, I have responsibilities that would be crushing to you, but you know, I'm not worried about it. That is why I'm so effective. If I were worried about you, what could I do for you? I'd become desperate, and then you would have two desperate people! But I am very interested in your finding your treasure and not wasting your time in life. Your treasure is what you came here to give, but to find this, you must establish your foundation in the Mystery, and you must become competent in the world.

What you are looking for is not an answer. It is a discovery and a set of abilities that are related to that discovery. Don't think that I will come along and say, "You are going to be this!" and that takes care of the problem. When people think like that, they are being lazy; they are being passive. To do what you must do in the future, you will have to be a greater person than you are now. You will have to be stronger and more open.

By the way, don't worry about the world blowing up. What is happening in the world is that humanity is in the process of becoming one race, and my God, it will go through terrible things to do this. But this is its evolution, and it must come to pass. As the adolescent must become an adult, painfully or not, the evolution of your race cannot be stopped. Conflict can be moderated and in many cases eliminated, but it takes a person who has a very great awareness to be able to give this perspective to other people.

In the future, everyone will have to be in relationship with everyone. That will be terrible for some people because when that happens, people begin to sacrifice their national identity, their class consciousness and all these other distinguishing factors, some of which they may never have thought of. "Rub shoulders with these people? Oh, my God, no!" But everyone will have to confront everyone. Here, the distinctions will begin to break down. It is not that everyone will become equal because that will never happen, not at this level, anyway. But people will need to develop a greater capacity for relationship with one another. They will also need to develop a greater level of discernment as well because with greater exposure to anything, you must have greater discernment and greater education.

So, there are conflicts and they will continue, but the world will not blow up. There are forces in the world to keep this from happening. It is possible these forces can fail, but it hasn't happened yet. Do not think the fate of the world is up to people alone.

God is always there. Yet, in the realm of worldly existence, you can either have God or not. You are free to not be in this relationship. When you are not being in this relationship, you are lost in your thinking. You are living in your thoughts and in other people's thoughts. After all, to not be yourself you must be something else, yes? To not serve God, you must serve something else. You must serve something, but that does not mean that what is real has changed. What does not change is the greatest foundation you can have, but you must experience it repeatedly, and you must refrain from making conclusions about it. This leaves the door to God wide open.

Even the manifestation is a Mystery, but for the sake of practicality, we don't make everything religious. There are problems in doing that. There is a distinction between the influence and the manifestation, and the manifestation rarely completely demonstrates the Mystery because it is a physical thing.

If Knowledge moved you to invent something, you would invent it, and you would go through a physical process to do that. What you would invent could be understood, but what moved you to do it is mysterious. This must be thought about because what moves people to do things and the things that they do are related, as cause and effect, but they are not the same. The pure experience that moved individuals to create a new manifestation in life may be something that those individuals could never describe in words, but it is something that they can transmit through their creations. Whatever they were moved to do is a temporary thing, but it was moved by something permanent. What is permanent seems very difficult to distinguish from anything in the world because everything here is moving and is impermanent.

So, what is constant in the world? What is constant has an influence, and it brings about good results, but the results that it brings about still do not identify or exemplify the full power of the Mystery. With Mystery you will contribute to the world because you are happy and not because you are terrified. If you think that the world is about to blow up and you are desperate to do something about it, your contribution will be violent. You will be forced to take sides, and you will have enemies. The Mystery does not think like this. It does not have enemies. It merely has people who are not willing to move, so it works around them. It is like the air that comes in through all the cracks.

The problem with religions is that they are at war with each other's manifestations and assumptions. That is not a problem for individuals who are grounded in religious experience. But people who are relating only to the manifestation will compete with one another and threaten one another because at this level of existence there is only identification with ideas. Here they will not want to challenge their own ideas because then the whole foundation of their identity will be threatened. That is a very mindless state and many people live there. If you think of religion only in terms of its manifestations — which are the behaviors exhibited by those who profess to believe in it, its tenets and its impact on people's lives — then you are only dealing with religion as a political force.

Now, I know that everything that happens in the world will eventually have a political expression and that anything good that is given to the world will be used by someone to produce harm. I know that. I know that even The Greater Community Way of Knowledge that I am presenting will be misused by many people. Does that mean I should not give it? No, it is simply the liability of giving in the world. I know that and I am prepared for it. Jesus Christ was prepared for it. How many people have slaughtered other people in the name of Jesus Christ? How much violence has been wrought in the name of Jesus Christ? How would you like it if your name were slandered like that? Does that mean that Jesus

Christ should not have given his gift? I assure you he was aware of the price that would be paid. That is the conflict.

If the level of a few individuals can be raised, everyone will benefit. Humanity has always moved forward because of the work of a handful of people. They bring the Mystery into the world and everyone else manifests it and uses it, but where it comes from very few know.

It is not a problem for me if people do not grow, even though it makes my job harder. I only want to make life easier for them, but I will say that sometimes working with people is very frustrating because they keep going back to the old thing that does not work and they don't try the new thing. So, sometimes I need reinforcement from my friends and from my Teachers as well. My Teachers operate on a different scale, let us say. I am their manifestation. This is very hard to understand here in the world, and it is not even important. After all, what mystical cosmology has ever gotten anyone through the day? Therefore, God does not need to be understood, but God can be experienced. That is enough.

Most people want God to be someone around in case something goes wrong, like Mommy at home. Well, when you go out and play, you don't want anything to do with Mommy, but you want to make sure that if you fall down and hurt yourself, you can always go home to Mom. Mom is always there.

So, you must see religion in a new way. I want to talk about what it really is and not what people have made out of it. What people have made out of it is not what it really is. Therefore, if you want to carry a new vision into life, you must be prepared for what people will do with it. That is why there must be very little personal investment involved because someone will use it for harm. That does not mean that you have failed. It just means that you must not tamper with the gift once it has been given.

Achievement has two different realms: There is achievement in the Mystery, and there is achievement in the manifestation. Achievement in the Mystery is always enhancing the quality of relationships. It is always a greater experience of communication or shared identity. That in itself has tremendous bearing on achievement in the manifest world, because Mystery is always influencing the manifestation.

Most people are concentrated on achievement in the manifest world, and that is good because that needs to happen, too. They carry out whatever has happened in their realm of relationship. Whenever you are inspired by anything, you are experiencing a greater capacity for relationship in that moment.

If you want to stop experiencing Mystery, create a definition for it. Hold to that definition and the door will shut. Then you will experience your definition and not the Mystery, and you will defend your position and the Mystery will be lost to you. The problem here is that people base their identity on their assumptions and not on real experience. Knowledge is always taking you beyond your assumptions, but if your identity is based upon your assumptions, that is too frightening.

Why do people not want to experience God? Why is there that profound resistance? It is because they are afraid to challenge their idea of themselves. Maybe they are not who they think they are. Can they live with that? God gives something much better, but people are afraid to give up what they have created for themselves. I'm not talking about your giving up your car and living like a monk. That's ridiculous! What people are afraid of giving up is their ideas about themselves. That is true renunciation! True renunciation is not giving up worldly things. It is giving up *ideas*. They are the bars on your prison.

To give up ideas you must be willing to be without ideas for awhile until you can find something new. Your security must be based upon something else. Knowledge is your foundation no matter what you believe. What you believe will determine how much you can experience your foundation, but Knowledge is still your foundation. When you know that this is your foundation, then you will progress very rapidly because you will not be afraid of new information. You will not be afraid of new experiences. You will not be afraid to find out new things. And the more you find out, the more you will give because that is natural.

I will tell you something. Because I have been talking about Mystery, I will tell you something that throws you back into Mystery: The way it really is, it's even beyond love. It's even better than that!

We talk about God as an attraction, as a force that is moving you and stimulating your Knowledge. Think about the Mystery in your life in this way. Mystery is a living Spiritual Presence. It is something you are either aware of in your life or not. Think of religion as a Mystery and not as a philosophy or a political movement so that you can gain access to it within yourself. People create churches because they want to create an opportunity to have an experience. When the Mystery is present, then you will know that God is in the world.

*In the
Greater Community,
intelligence is the desire,
the willingness and
the capacity
to learn and to adapt.*

Fourteen

INTELLIGENCE

IN ORDER TO LEARN The Greater Community Way of Knowledge, one must face the fact that one's intelligence is very limited and needs to be expanded. Intelligence in the Greater Community is highly regarded, not only for what it can produce physically, but for what it can know and perceive. That is why intelligence is considered to be a commodity, something that can be exchanged, acquired, controlled, used, and so forth. In fact, intelligence is considered even more valuable than technology. This is a very important fact and represents a new understanding for the human community, where due to a lack of competition with other intelligent life, intelligence has not been developed sufficiently, especially when one considers the capabilities that humans really have and how these can be used for good and for greater accomplishment.

When you do not compete with others, you tend to rest upon your own abilities and make great assumptions about them. You seek comfort, complacency and confirmation. These things are not appropriate in an environment where competition is active. Indeed, it is true that you will be competing in intelligence with those who are now visiting your world. It is not just their technology that is superior; it is their understanding of the mental environment and their ability to manipulate it for their own ends. Here you are at a great disadvantage, for you have not cultivated your mental abilities and are not aware of how your mind can be controlled by other minds that are more concentrated, less diffused and less conflicted than your own.

This is a very great and perhaps sobering fact of engaging with life in the Greater Community. All of a sudden competition becomes very real. It is not merely competition amongst yourselves, for the differences between you are not great enough to stimulate a truly competitive environment. Interacting with other intelligent life — intelligent life that has a very different orientation and a very different set of assumptions about the universe, intelligent life that is seeking you out for purposes that are unknown to you — you are suddenly thrust into a situation where you must rise to meet many different kinds of occasions, occasions for which you have no preparation and no understanding. The Greater Community Way of Knowledge provides a way to meet this great need. Many people need this preparation, though perhaps few will undertake it at this time.

With such a great disadvantage regarding competition for intelligence, you must accept this recognition with great seriousness. Since you are not used to being in a competitive situation regarding intelligence, you are ill prepared for this and will want to fall back on your old accomplishments and assumptions, for they have been adequate in many respects to carry you this far. In the future, they will prove to be very inadequate.

Regarding the visitors that are in the world now, they are much more concentrated on their mission than you are. They are much more focused on achievement than you are. They are less compromised by conflicting desires, wishes and beliefs than you are. Perhaps they will seem mechanical to you and one-dimensional. This is not the case. When you think these things, you are reacting to being in the presence of someone who is very focused, very concentrated and very determined. Having this sense of contrast is necessary for you to recognize the need for intelligence and to prompt you forward in a practical form of development.

Let me now give a helpful definition of intelligence: Intelligence is the desire, the willingness and the capacity to learn and to adapt. It is the desire and the willingness, which means you are willing to undergo the preparation, and the capacity, which means you are able to go through the preparation. This is a very great thing to consider. Here you must abandon many ideas you hold about yourself and the accomplishments and attributes of your race. Here you must go through a tremendous process of re-evaluation, part of which may seem very painful in the starkness of the recognition that you will have of your limitations.

In the Greater Community, the weak are overtaken by the strong, just as in your world. In your world, you have the distinct advantage of being the predominant species of intelligent life. You have undertaken to dominate the world, but in the Greater Community you would not be considered strong or advanced. This must give you a very sober view of yourself, but a view that can engender a desire for greater intelligence and perhaps even the willingness to undertake the preparation. Your capacity varies amongst you individually, but it is still relatively small. However, human beings are capable of achieving great things if the incentive, the desire and the freedom are all present. That is why a greater intelligence than your own is bestowing this preparation upon you and with it the understanding of its importance, its relevance to your time and its possible application in the future where it will be called upon again and again.

Along with the preparation for greater intelligence comes the development of a larger perspective on life, which you may call a Greater Community perspective. The Greater Community perspective sees humanity as a growing, evolving race in a larger arena where there are other forces of intelligent life interacting and competing with one another. Humanity is not yet competitive in the Greater Community. It is not that unified, developed or focused. This must not be seen as a repudiation of humanity's potential, talents or achievements. It is simply that in a larger environment you cannot yet compete with other forms of intelligent life. Yet, they are entering your world, and you are faced with the prospect of having to encounter these intelligences in situations where you will recognize your limitations. These situations can be very frightening, but they call upon you to rise above your sense of vulnerability and helplessness and cultivate yourself in ways that call forth the greater possibilities that you now have.

This requires a very unique form of education. It must be a form of education that is presented to humanity from beyond the world, for humanity cannot prepare itself for the Greater Community. Though people will prepare other people in The Way of Knowledge, its source is from beyond the world. It emanates from a greater intelligence and a greater race. You must recognize the need to have the willingness to undergo the preparation in The Greater Community Way of Knowledge. You must feel this need; you must see it in the world; you must consider it deeply. Your desire for truth, for the resolution of conflict and for self-realization is essential here. Here your own desires and needs are not sufficient, for you need to recognize that your abilities and understanding are needed in the world. This, then, will call forth what is possible within you. This can stimulate the development of intelligence.

Now, people already consider that they are very intelligent. This is generally assumed because they do not live in a competitive environment in this regard. Compared to plants and animals, you do seem very intelligent. You are also very troubled in comparison to these life forms. Yet, now you are emerging into a new arena with new requirements, new possibilities and new dangers. Clearly, it is a danger when human beings will not respond to what is occurring in their lives and will not seriously consider the implications. That is a risk.

The desire to learn, the desire to understand and the desire to overcome are all inherent within you. These all add up to a great motivation that is being accelerated in the human race. As larger and more complex problems arise, they call upon human beings to concentrate, to learn, to adapt and to rethink their current positions—all these things. It is wise, then, to consider that you are a developing intelligence.

Intelligence requires development on many levels and in many different arenas of activity. It requires clear thinking, objectivity, inner perception, highly cultivated intuition, the ability to understand mechanical things and the ability to identify and discern behavior. In practical matters and in the mysteries themselves, greater intelligence must find a larger view and a larger application. After all, if you evaluate your own intelligence, you can only do so in contrast to something else that you consider to be intelligent. Indeed, there are life forms that are more intelligent than you and, obviously, life forms that are less intelligent. It is the life forms that are more intelligent that can advance you. They will reveal your limitations and emphasize the need for these limitations to be overcome, and they will demonstrate to you that you live in a competitive environment as far as intelligence is concerned.

Following The Greater Community Way of Knowledge requires a much higher level of thinking, evaluation, recognition, insight and decision making. It also stimulates your greater virtues and requires them to be developed and to be expressed. To undertake this you must be willing to go beyond your former understanding of yourself and of the world. This is essential. From a greater viewpoint, you will see the same things that you saw before, but you will have a different perception and will draw different conclusions.

The presence of alien life here in the world demonstrates this clearly. Perhaps you have not had an encounter with other intelligent life, but you are feeling the effects of their presence here. Your inclinations, your emotional states and your sense of things are all affected. You don't need to be face to face with someone from beyond in order to experience their presence in your life. Yet, how is it possible to ascertain these things and to distinguish them from your own emotional instability? Only a Higher Power within you can make these distinctions and reveal them to you. Only a Greater Mind, which is beyond the influences of the Greater Community, can lead you to discern the influences in your life and how they are affecting you. That is why The Greater Community Way of Knowledge must be emphasized and not merely the phenomenon of things that are occurring, no matter how intriguing they may be. Human beings need to learn to think, to deliberate, to concentrate and to focus on one thing at a time. It is not expected that you would have the incentive to do this unless you were in a competitive environment and a competitive situation. You are in a competitive situation.

Humanity is also at a great disadvantage in that people here are surface dwellers and are easily scrutinized and observed. In many more advanced worlds, races have taken to living underground, both for the many environmental advantages it offers and for the protection it affords as well. Human beings are numerous and yet have not made this important discovery. In fact, human beings look at underground living with great disdain, whereas in the Greater Community it is recognized to be a tremendous advantage. Being surface dwellers your actions, gestures and forms of communication can be easily observed and deciphered. You are out in the open where eyes from beyond can watch you carefully.

Your minds can be read. Though you may not be understood by those who observe you, your actions are nonetheless predictable and, therefore, many correct assumptions can be made about human behavior without a great deal of inquiry.

Part of the problem here is that human beings tend to be very superstitious. Superstition is when you are responding to something you cannot understand and you make false assumptions and conclusions about the nature of what is stimulating you. In the presence of a greater intelligence, human beings will make many erroneous conclusions. That is because you do not understand the mental environment. Indeed, from a practical standpoint, should an alien power want to take greater control of human affairs, they certainly would not need weapons to do it.

Therefore, in order to understand what this means, to successfully encounter other intelligent life and even to move towards competing with it in a favorable manner, you must develop your mental abilities. You must find the Greater Power within you, and you must transcend a purely human viewpoint, which cannot account for these things. You must free yourself from old beliefs, associations and relationships because learning requires the willingness to change, to entertain new things and to rethink old positions and assumptions. It is choosing a path of change, not knowing what the result will be, but having faith in a favorable outcome. You will have to do this with very little assistance from others, for only a very few are ready to undertake a preparation such as this. It is important that you find them and develop relationships based upon mutual need and mutual understanding.

You need greater intelligence. You are capable of cultivating this and developing it, but it is not an easy thing to do. Because human beings are very insecure, they are always prone to go backwards and not forwards in this regard, seeking validation rather than understanding and seeking to have old views confirmed instead of entertaining new ideas and new requirements. The cultivation of intelligence takes a great deal of time.

Inherent in intelligence is the need for Wisdom in the recognition and application of power. You have a certain amount of power over your physical environment now. In a Greater Community context, however, your power is very limited. How you use it, for what purpose you use it and how you manage its consequences are determined by the degree to which you have acquired Wisdom. There actually is some Wisdom in the world in this regard. There is Wisdom regarding human affairs and humanity's relationship with the physical world, even if this Wisdom goes unheeded.

Wisdom in the Greater Community, however, is something else and requires an entirely different perception and approach and a great desire to learn. This learning will set you apart from others. It will seem difficult and mysterious simply because you are traveling a way that few have traveled, but you are not undertaking this alone, and the way you will travel has been traveled before. To undertake everything that is being spoken of in this book requires a greater intelligence and adherence to a Greater Power. Adhering to a Greater Power can generate greater intelligence on your part. This is essential.

You cannot yet compete in the Greater Community, primarily because you do not understand the mental environment. It is not your technology that is limiting you. Those who are capable in the mental environment can cast a great deal of influence upon a more technically advanced race because minds persuade other minds, minds influence other minds and minds can dominate other minds. Therefore, it is not your technology that is the limiting factor here. It is your lack of understanding of the mental environment. It is your inability to be truly objective. It is your inability to have a Greater Power guide and direct you in the face of new experiences and difficult situations. This develops intelligence. This development

provides protection for you and the ability to bring about constructive change. It also can establish humanity as a formidable race rather
than a weak and pathetic one.

This development carries a blessing and a difficulty. The
blessing is that the privacy of your world will be more respected,
and you will be able to defend your mental and physical resources
far more effectively. You will also be able to undertake the resolution of many of your world's problems in a far more expedient
and effective manner. The difficulty is that the more you develop
your intelligence, the more you will become engaged in the Greater
Community. Your mental resources will become more valuable.
With all accomplishments, there are risks. There is a risk in gaining
greater intelligence. The requirements of your life become much
more demanding. The consequences of your mistakes are greater.
Only the man or woman of Knowledge can successfully undertake
this and remain relatively unburdened by the disadvantages that
greater intelligence will bring about. The fact that you live in the
Greater Community is a beneficial aspect here, for it will temper
any arrogance that might arise. It will tend to hold these things in
check to a certain degree. This is the blessing of realizing that you
live in a larger arena of life.

A greater intelligence is called for; a greater intelligence can be
stimulated; a greater intelligence can be developed over time and
with it humility, self-restraint, discernment and discretion — all of
the necessary qualities with which a greater intelligence can be beneficial unto itself and unto others.

Think not that *Steps to Knowledge* is merely a form of therapy
or a spiritual path to God. Yes, it includes these, but its primary
function is to prepare you to enter the mental environment in
a conscious and conscientious manner, to participate effectively
with one another and to discern the presences from the Greater
Community that are now infiltrating the world. Such is the great

opportunity that has now arisen for you, an opportunity whose rewards are not only great and meaningful but essential as well.

To meet
a great need,
you need
great incentive,
you need
great preparation
and you need
great companions.

Fifteen

RESPONDING TO THE GREATER COMMUNITY

T IS NECESSARY when speaking about Greater Community influences to talk about how the mind responds. The mind is designed to act and to interact with the environment. It is both a generator of information and stimulation and a receiver of these as well. The mind naturally engages with the mental and physical environments in such a way that it is constantly sending and receiving information. The mind is not the master of the environment, nor is the environment the master of the mind in a truly balanced and harmonious state. When this state is disturbed, however, imbalances result, which create distortions in experience, in recognition, in processes of thinking and in the conclusions that are derived.

In order for your mind to function naturally and harmoniously, it must have a dynamic and harmonious relationship with the environment. This, of course, is an ideal state and is not achieved when the mind is not in harmony with itself. When the mind is not in harmony with itself, it experiences its own imbalance and the imbalances in its environment as well. Here it will produce imbalance and discord and respond to what it produces. This creates a vicious cycle in which the mind produces experiences and then responds to its own creations. Rarely is it aware of what it is producing.

This discordance generates a force in the world, a force of dissonance. For instance, if you are troubled, concerned or very fearful about something, or if you are very angry or resentful, you will create a dissonance in your environment. Once this dissonance leaves your own mind, it becomes a force in the environment. Now, if only one person is generating this, it will be a very weak force and easily dissipated. However, if many people are generating these kinds of experiences, they will create a force that is more lasting and much more potent and effective. This force, then, can influence other minds in such a way that it seems to overtake them. A mental force in the environment can become very concentrated and quite strong and can have, so to speak, a whirlwind effect on other minds. Indeed, if you recall the times that you have entered somebody's personal domain and you walked into a discordant state, you will recall how powerful this can be and how it can affect you emotionally and determine your responses.

Therefore, a discordant mind has an impact on the environment. Once this discordance enters the environment, especially if it is shared by others, it creates a force that has an impact on other minds. Human beings are not aware of the power of their own emotions or the effect of their thinking upon others. Though there are some obvious examples of this, its overall effect and the kinds of interactions that can be generated as a result are rarely, if ever, consciously accounted for.

Cultivating a good mental environment around you personally is very, very important. You generate this environment and you live within it. If you generate a hostile, discordant environment, you will live within that. So focused can this environment become and so effective in determining your own experience that it is like living in a shell, where the rain seems to fall upon you and no one else. But the effect on others can be very great as well, especially if you are in close proximity to them. When you are out of doors, the effect of your thinking is more generally dissipated, and the reaction of those who feel its effects will not be as great. That is because it represents a large mental environment that is subject to many other forces beyond human forces alone. But if you are indoors with another or in very close proximity, then the impact can be tremendous. That is why, if you are engaging with someone who is in a very discordant state and it is having a damaging effect upon you or making it difficult for you to think clearly, it is always a good idea to try to get them out of doors so that their mental projections can be dissipated more effectively. This will lessen the impact upon you to a certain degree.

So powerful is your interaction with others that you must be very careful with whom you associate. If you are to associate intentionally with someone who is in a very discordant state or who is very disturbed or conflicted, you must be well prepared for this because the impact upon you will be great. People will naturally gravitate to those who can help them experience a positive mental environment. This is especially true for people who are undertaking the reclamation of Knowledge and are attempting to become aware of their own mental state and its impact on the environment as well as the environment's impact upon them.

Many people fear that the environment has ultimate power over them, and others believe, but rarely experience, that they have ultimate power over the environment. Neither, of course, is true because you are in dynamic relationship with the environment. Just as your body thrives on the resources of your environment and interacts with these resources continuously, your mind—your brain and all of its functions—and Knowledge, the mind beyond the brain which accounts for more refined qualities of thinking and evaluation, exist within the mental environment, thrive upon its resources and interact with it continuously as well.

Individuals who are in the process of reclaiming their Knowledge will seek to create a positive mental environment. They will naturally do this to create an upward spiral instead of a downward spiral. They will become much more sensitive to those with whom they are engaged and to what transpires in these interactions. They will want to seek freedom and reprieve from stressful situations unless these situations are necessary. They will seek greater equanimity and more quiet times. All of their values and inclinations will change accordingly.

Before this happens, people seek to create an environment that is agreeable to their beliefs, so they surround themselves with people who generally will accept their viewpoint and will confirm their prejudices. But when you are entering a more conscious state, a state more committed to education and revelation, then you will seek an environment that is more conducive to the experience of awareness and knowing. This is a natural process, and it will become greatly accelerated as you become aware of it and can make conscious decisions in order to enhance your mental environment and to create greater opportunities for insight.

Many people seek to be out of doors because it is a freer mental environment than when they are confined with other people. Here people seek communion with nature because nature provides a freer and often more conducive mental environment for introspection and for insight into the behavior and interaction of others. Some seek nature purely as a relief.

When you begin to concentrate on the mental environment, you realize how absolutely it impacts your sense of well-being and how important it is for your development. This is the beginning of becoming aware of the mental environment. As this is undertaken in a conscious and intentional way, you begin to become aware of the influences that are affecting your emotional states and your thinking. Should you undertake the reclamation of

Knowledge according to the Greater Community Tradition, then you will need to develop stillness, focused thinking, objectivity, discernment and observation—all things that generate a more focused and powerful mind, a mind that has a greater impact on its environment and upon the experiences of others as well.

With Knowledge as your guide, your personal mind will have the environment and the stimulation for true development, which will produce great benefits for you and for others. Here you can make a positive overall contribution to the mental environment. This is quite true. Knowledge is a very pervasive kind of influence. You cannot trace its impact on others, nor can you follow the direction in which it will travel, whom it will contact and how they will respond. But perhaps you can accept on faith that the world is progressing because of the contribution of many concentrated individuals who are dedicated to the well-being of humanity and to its advancement as a race. The benefits you see in the world are the result of this contribution, not just practical and physical benefits, but the concentration of many minds on the well-being and equanimity of human function and interaction. They are caring for the mental environment like one who cares for a great forest, looking after it with loving attention, giving it a remedy when that is possible and protecting it from outside influences.

Now I must speak of the Greater Community influences that are affecting humanity at this time. If you can begin, at least conceptually, to see that you live in the mental environment and that you are in continuous and dynamic interaction with it, it is then necessary for you to think of the kinds of influences that exist in that environment—influences that you may welcome, accept and promote and influences that are in your life inadvertently, without your invitation, as part of the environment in which you function. The impact of television, music and radio is very, very great on the human mind, so great that students of Knowledge will seek to limit these influences and screen them conscientiously. These are influences that are part of the environment in which you function. You don't necessarily welcome them, but they are a part of your environment and will have an impact upon you nonetheless.

There are influences that you are barely aware of that are also casting a strong influence upon you, particularly if you are sensitive to the Greater Community. Your sensitivity to the Greater Community is determined by your background—not simply your history as a human being in this life, but your background far beyond that as well. You carry your accumulated learning with you into the experience of life that you are having now as a single human being. If this accumulated learning accounts for the Greater Community, then you will be especially sensitive to Greater Community influences. This is part of your make-up. You cannot change this, but you can learn to become aware of it and to deal with it effectively so that in time, as your mind becomes stronger and more focused through preparation and right association with others, you can learn not only to offset damaging or discordant influences, either within human situations or from influences that extend beyond human awareness, but in time to have a positive influence on them as well.

Consider this: A strong mind will always influence a weaker mind. A strong mind can to a certain degree control a weaker mind. This happens even if the stronger person is not trying to cast an influence or persuade anyone to do anything. The fact that his or her mind is more concentrated and less conflicted, with greater intention and self-determination, will have an impact upon other minds that are less focused and less concentrated. This is a fact of life and cannot be avoided. When people begin to compete with each other, they realize in time that they must have an increased level of concentration and focus and very specific forms of preparation, which are determined by what they are attempting to undertake. Clearly, in all cases they must become stronger, more focused and wiser in their decisions. This is stimulated because human beings compete with each other for certain advantages in life. This competition can be healthy, but it can be damaging as well.

Now that Greater Community presences are active in the world, you are dealing with a set of influences with which you cannot effectively compete, and that is why the preparation in The Greater Community Way of Knowledge is being presented. Only a preparation from beyond the world can be effective in teaching you to engage with influences from beyond the world.

Now let me speak about how the Greater Community influences can affect the human mind. First of all, if there is a visitation occurring, those who are undertaking the visitation will want to create a force field around their presence which will hopefully have a predetermined effect on human beings. Human beings have been studied for a very long time — at least in terms of their behavior and their predispositions. Therefore, the visitors will want to create a certain influence in the environment in order to have a desired impact upon anyone whom they might encounter, either intentionally or inadvertently. Should they wish to investigate individuals directly, the visitors will, in a sense, hypnotize them. That is perhaps the best word that can be used in this situation. They will suspend people's conscious minds and then suggest things to them that they will then tend to accept as their own. People will then forget where the suggestions came from. This makes it easier to affect people's behavior and to bring about a desired, predetermined set of actions. Human beings have been doing this to one another since the beginning of their existence in the world, but they are not masterful at this.

There are Forces of Dissonance from beyond the world that are visiting the world. They are not coming here on your behalf. They are adept in certain ways at manipulating the mental environment. To affect and influence the behavior and the recognition of those whom they might encounter, particularly if they wish to study the thinking, behavior or biology of their subjects, they will use these skills to whatever extent they feel it is possible. There are increasing numbers of individuals who have been affected by these Forces directly, and they are deeply disturbed and distressed by the encounters that they have had, if they are aware of them at all. They wonder how their memory could be so suspended, how their evaluations could be so blotted out and how their recollections can seem so vague. Think, then, of the idea of hypnosis and remember that a more concentrated mind will by nature have a greater impact on a weaker mind than the weaker mind can have on the more concentrated mind.

Therefore, understand that human beings are being studied, even examined, by Forces of Dissonance from beyond the world. This is unfortunate because humanity is ill prepared for this. Yet, it does hold certain opportunities for development if the situation can be clearly understood. Competition can engender creativity, responsibility, resourcefulness and self-determination. You are competing in your mental environment now with intelligent forces from beyond the world. This is a fact; you cannot avoid it. It would be foolish to deny it or pretend that it is not occurring. This, then, is a form of competition. You are competing for control of your world; you are competing for control of your own life; you are competing for who in the future will dominate the world. Does this sound too grave? Does this sound too foreboding or too ominous to consider? Perhaps at first it might seem like this, but if you think about it carefully and are willing to consider it further, you will see that this is the kind of involvement that humanity needs in order to generate harmony within the human family and to create a greater focus and incentive for learning. That is not to say the Forces of Dissonance are intentionally helping you by their interference in human affairs, but it is to say that the situation does offer some extremely important opportunities and incentives for development.

You cannot change the events that are occurring, but you can interpret them wisely and learn to use them to your advantage. To do this, you must reconsider where you stand in life, what you have accomplished and what you have not accomplished. You must consider the impact of your own thinking and consider as well the environments in which you place yourself, either intentionally or inadvertently. This creates greater self-awareness, discernment and conscientiousness — all of which are necessary if you are to progress as a human being.

Consider this: If you come in proximity to a force from the Greater Community, you will begin to react very strongly. Usually people feel a tremendous sense of avoidance, a desire to leave, to get away, to find refuge. There is often a tremendous sense of anxiety. This is a normal response, but other responses are possible depending upon the temperament and nature of the person involved. There are places in the world where people do not want to go. They feel uncomfortable there. There are places in nature that people pass by or avoid intentionally. They feel uncomfortable there. This is not to say that all these places contain Greater Community influences, but you can see how easy it is for those from the Greater Community to establish themselves in the world and to be relatively free of human scrutiny. So powerful can manipulation of the mental environment be here that even the curious or the adventuresome can easily be dissuaded.

Until individuals gain an objective overview of their experience, which they can only do with Knowledge as their counsel, guide and foundation, they will be influenced. They will follow their own feelings and will be governed by the predominant ideas that they hold. Ideas can be injected into other minds. Feelings can be motivated by certain kinds of stimulation. Human beings are not so terribly complex that these things cannot be planned and executed with great intention and effectiveness. People will not know why they are responding the way they are. Perhaps they will give themselves reasons, but having reasons does not mean that one understands the situation or the influences at hand.

If people are unstable psychologically, they will become more unstable around a Greater Community influence. They can even be driven to insanity. This is not because the Greater Community influence seeks to make them so. It is simply that when you are around a more powerful mind, it will accentuate your present state. In other words, you will become more extreme in your own behavior. This is one of the reasons why the man and woman of Knowledge must remain hidden from the world and must be very judicious about whom they encounter and what they communicate because they will have a great impact on everyone they meet. The unwise will become more unwise around them, and those seeking Wisdom will become wiser, for the more concentrated mind will accentuate the present state of every other mind that it comes in contact with. That is one reason why the Wise withdraw. This is very necessary.

Our emphasis here is to reinforce your understanding that you live in a mental environment and that you are subject to influences within that environment. Influences from the Greater Community are present here. They are not everywhere, but they are in certain places and their numbers are not small. Not only are they having an influence on human thinking and behavior, they are using human thinking and behavior, testing it, experimenting with it, learning how it functions and practicing in its manipulation. This is occurring, like it or not, accept it or not. It is occurring. It is better to accept it, to face it and to learn how to counteract it and to affect it yourself, for if you do not affect it, it will in time affect you increasingly.

There are some people in the world who have such a strong Greater Community background that they feel the influence of Greater Community forces, even those forces that are far away and not in their immediate proximity. They react emotionally to these things and they cannot account for their own experiences. They say to themselves, "My God! Why am I feeling the way I am feeling?" Perhaps they have unexplained feelings of dread or anxiety that cannot be explained in terms of their current circumstances. Sometimes these people blame themselves greatly for these experiences and try to repress them or escape from them. Others blame society at large or the political climate in which they live, but still they cannot account for their range of experience. This certainly does not happen with every person, but with certain people it is quite pronounced. These people will need to learn The Greater Community Way of Knowledge if they are to gain access to the source of their own experience.

To learn the source of your experience, you must learn the influences that are stimulating it, affecting it and in some cases even generating it. You must learn to engage with the environment responsibly and consciously. This means you recognize the nature and the effects of your own thinking and learn to discern those influences that are affecting you directly. To a certain extent, you can control your exposure to influences in the mental environment. And certainly as your skill and awareness grow, you will become more effective in this. This is a requirement for education.

There have always been problems in the mental environment with human beings because their mental and spiritual lives are not united. But there are greater problems now because of the Greater Community presence in the world. These problems can generate important solutions, but they are problems that are very difficult for people to recognize and to accept. Let us give you this idea to consider: The Forces of Dissonance in the world, which by the way are not the only Greater Community forces in the world, are able to move about quite effectively without human recognition in many cases, not because they are invisible, not because they are spiritual forces—they are physical forces—but because they can influence the mind that perceives them. How can this be, you ask? Well, if a more concentrated mind wills or wishes that the less concentrated not recognize it, then in most cases the person with the weaker mind will not recognize the presence of the more concentrated mind.

Remember, thoughts affect minds. Thoughts affect thinking. Thinking affects thinking. When thinking is affected, certain responses can be predetermined. Because you are only used to interacting with other human beings, these things can sound quite phenomenal, even impossible. But in your mental environment now there are intelligent forces that are not human beings. They are here to collect information. They are here to practice their skills on you for future uses and advantages. This is an unusual and difficult situation that requires an unusual and effective resolution. You cannot use the normal range of human explanation or human response in order to deal effectively with these influences. That is why The Greater Community Way of Knowledge is being presented.

I have mentioned several times in these discourses that there are forces for good in the world as well. They are here for the protection and the benefit of humanity. Therefore, you are not left helpless in the face of a seemingly more powerful adversary. Not only are there Greater Community forces in the world here to assist you and to educate you, there is the power and presence of Knowledge, which must become activated to enable you to effectively deal not only with the problems and dilemmas of human affairs, but the problems and dilemmas that exist in the Greater Community as well.

Consider this: Human thinking can be directly influenced. Human perception can be directly influenced. Things can be done to people without any forewarning. People can be overtaken and manipulated, and, in fact, this is occurring already. I realize that this is not a popular idea that I am presenting. It is a very sobering one. And yet, because it is a fact in the world now, it is something you must accept. Acceptance is the beginning of education — accepting a deficiency, accepting a problem that needs resolution, accepting your own desire for advancement and accepting that your current state is inadequate for you. These things all provide the incentive for greater education and development.

Incentive is necessary in order to bring about any accomplishment, yet it must be driven by need. Human beings need to become stronger mentally and more balanced and harmonious within themselves. This is not merely a preference. It cannot merely be some form of entertainment or a pastime or a hobby. It must become central in your priorities. What will make it central in your priorities? The recognition of what is influencing you in your life and your own need for development, resolution and greater equanimity. Need drives progress. Your needs are great. Even if there were no Greater Community influences in the world at this time, your needs are great and are growing greater every day. To meet a great need, you need great incentive. You need great preparation and you need great companions.

The Forces of Dissonance are not trained in the ways of Knowledge. Here you have a possible advantage, should you choose to prepare and should you take your preparation seriously and undertake it with great patience and perseverance. Here is your advantage. That is why we emphasize the development of Knowledge. We do not emphasize it merely so that you will feel better or have a greater sense of purpose in the world or will feel more self-loving and self-accepting. No. Though these are the great rewards in following The Greater Community Way of Knowledge, this teaching and preparation are being called upon now for other real and pressing needs. The Forces for Good from the Greater Community are here to emphasize Knowledge, for this is what will save the human race. The Forces of Dissonance are not educated in The Way of Knowledge or they would not be Forces of Dissonance, for Knowledge cannot oppose itself and must contribute to the welfare and benefit of life everywhere.

You may feel powerless in the presence of Greater Community influences, but you have the greater advantage. If you can be prepared in The Greater Community Way of Knowledge, then you will have a greater prospect for success. That is why the emphasis is on Knowledge. That is why it is being called upon. It is necessary for your well-being, and it is necessary for your advancement as well.

There will always be minds more clever and cunning than yours. There will always be technologies more advanced than yours. There will always be minds more concentrated than yours, in the Greater Community that is. But should you undertake and progress in the reclamation of Knowledge, then you will establish a foundation within yourself that cannot be influenced and cannot be corrupted, for Knowledge cannot be influenced by thinking minds. Knowledge cannot be corrupted by the inducements of physical life. Knowledge is without fear, for it is immortal. It cannot be penetrated by the outside world. Only Knowledge can influence Knowledge because it is a spiritual reality which exists within each person in the world. Though it is latent in the vast majority of people, it is there nonetheless to be cultivated and developed. Though the requirements in this cultivation and development are great, it is possible that many may advance. Not everyone has to advance in The Way of Knowledge, but it is vital for certain people, and it is vital for the human race that a sufficient number of people advance in this regard.

I am speaking now of the future and of the present. No one will take over the human race any time soon. That is not desired, even by those who are studying you now, those who have come from the Greater Community. That is not their mission, but they will study you, influence you and affect you. They will learn how you think, how you behave and how you respond. They will ascertain your weaknesses and limitations, and they will capitalize upon them for their own purposes. This is a detriment to humanity now and will be a detriment in the future.

What can counteract this? The development of the mind and the reclamation of Knowledge. The development of the mind will enable you to perceive, to counteract and to affect the influences which now affect you. But the reclamation of Knowledge will give you Wisdom and true safety, so much so that in time you will have the greater influence, for nothing is a greater influence than Knowledge itself. This is difficult to account for in the world because there are very few individuals who have developed in The Way of Knowledge. Those who have, have had a great influence and a great bearing on the well-being and destiny of humanity. Their examples may be few, but they are very pronounced. You have only to look into your own life and do an objective review to see who has influenced virtue in you. You will find that they are not only people with whom you were directly engaged, but that there are many who have lived long before whose contribution continues to reverberate through human minds everywhere.

Such is the power of Knowledge. This is your advantage. Claim it for your well-being, and claim it for the well-being of humanity. Claim it for your ability to interact with the Greater Community because it is part of your life now and will become increasingly so, for the world is emerging into the Greater Community and must learn to account for its influences, its powers, its motives and its existence. This means that humanity is emerging into a larger arena of life where there are many forms of influence and many opportunities for development that were unavailable to people before.

Greater problems bring greater resolutions and greater achievements. You have a greater problem; now you must find a greater achievement. You cannot do this on your own, for you will need mighty companions to help you. It is possible to accomplish this, but you will have to rethink many things that you hold dear, many ideas and ideals that you cherish, and you will have to undertake a form of preparation that is quite mysterious, for it comes from the Greater Community. We emphasize truths that human beings hold to be universal and which have been emphasized in all of the great religions of this world. But you will also learn of things that have never been taught in the world, and you will have to become more effective in your discernment and in your interaction with others to a degree that was rarely called for before. Such is your burden. Such is your gift. Such is your opportunity.

This is not simply to create harmony within you, but to enable you to give the contribution you have brought with you from beyond the world. If your contribution is to serve humanity's emergence into the Greater Community, then all that I am telling you is relevant and extremely important for you to accept and to learn to comprehend.

I offer these ideas with the confidence that Knowledge within you will stimulate your acceptance and your understanding, for Knowledge is what engenders and nourishes life everywhere. Its mystery and its certainty represent the revelation that is awaiting you, to be discovered and contributed. This holds true here and beyond the world as well in the Greater Community. Knowledge is the universal language, the universal mind, the universal recognition and the universal redemption. It is great enough to meet the demands of your life, both here and in the Greater Community.

To have a greater life,
to have a greater mind
and to have a greater
set of relationships,
you must pass through
the great thresholds.

Sixteen

THRESHOLDS

WHEN WE SPEAK OF SPIRITUAL PURPOSE, Knowledge and the world's emergence into the Greater Community, it is necessary to realize that you will go through some very important thresholds as you progress and develop. Indeed, you now have the opportunity to develop to an extent that few have had in human history. Life is calling upon this development not just for one or two individuals in the human family, but for many because many are needed now to cultivate and nourish a Greater Community perspective and understanding. Many are needed to lead humanity forward, and many are needed to contribute their Knowledge so that humanity can join together, unite itself and reach a greater level of cooperation and integration. Evolution calls for this. Many people are being called into service now. Many people have come to the world to give and to assist in this great emergence — at all levels of society and human interaction.

So, let us talk about these thresholds and what you can expect at the outset. This is an important discussion because even though you cannot see where the road will take you or what will happen as a result, it is important when you are undertaking a journey or, to use our analogy, climbing the great mountain that you are prepared. You must be prepared for certain eventualities. You must have the right attitude. You must have the right equipment. You must have an understanding of what will be needed and what will not be needed. This is important and enables you to embark. Then, when you come upon difficulty or adversity, you will not have to turn back. You will be able to proceed forward because you will already have the necessary understanding to enable you to begin to climb the mountain, to begin to develop your inner life and to develop a greater objectivity about life around you.

There are minor thresholds, and people often attribute great significance to these. That is because people experience the minor ones more immediately when they are occurring than the major ones. The major ones take longer to approach, longer to experience and longer to pass through. Yet, their effect is far more pervasive and complete. Minor thresholds may engender tremendous emotional responses and great expectations or anxiety, but this is more the up and down quality of living in life, especially when you do not yet have the foundation of Knowledge with which to balance your internal forces and attributes.

The great thresholds are much larger. When you are undergoing passage through these thresholds, it is very hard to know where you are. You cannot accurately say, "Today I am at this stage of passing through the threshold, and yesterday I was at another stage." You cannot know where you are in it. But you will know that something great is transpiring because you will feel very differently about yourself and other people. You will have a different perception of life around you. Your values have changed; your emphasis has changed. Things that yesterday or last year were important perhaps are not important now. Other things have arisen to take their place. Your whole foundation has shifted. It takes only a very small shift in your foundation in order to yield a different experience and perception. This represents a great threshold.

As I speak of great thresholds, let me remind you that you

cannot determine when you will pass through them. You can only know that in hindsight, and your hindsight must be very great and very objective because people attribute tremendous significance to things which actually prove to be very minor in the larger scheme of things.

There are three stages of development: dependence, independence and interdependence. The first great threshold in human development enables the individual to become independent. Everyone is working on this to a certain degree, and a few people have attained independence and have even transcended it. Because entering independence is a great threshold, it takes a great deal of time and has many steps. Rarely will people think they are entering a threshold at all because the experience is not necessarily immediate and the resolution is not immediate. Independence here is not complete, for there is no such thing as complete independence. That is why independence is an intermediate stage. It must lead to something else, for in itself it is not complete. You cannot be completely independent, for you are joined with all life. You live in the mental environment; you live in the physical environment; you live in the world; you live in the Greater Community of Worlds. So, how can you be independent of all of that? Obviously, you cannot and when you think about this objectively, you see that independence is really a very relative thing.

What independence means within the context that I am illustrating is that individuals are able to begin to think for themselves. To win this freedom, one must make some very difficult decisions, honor these decisions, trust them and abide by them. These decisions can be difficult because one might have to relinquish some degree of love or financial advantage or social acceptance to do something that is recognized to be correct. One must be willing to make these sacrifices and take these risks in order to gain a greater sense of well-being, inner certainty and correctness about life. It is making these decisions and abiding by them that establishes the ability to think with relative independence.

By relative independence, I mean that you are able to create your own thoughts rather than simply borrowing someone else's. You are able to begin to discern your own direction rather than simply following along where everyone else seems to be going. You are able to have your own feelings in the moment rather than living in the past. You are able to say "no" to wealth, love and pleasure when that is the correct thing to do. For you must say "no" to these things in order to say "yes" to them at a later time and have an affirmative inner response that is genuine and beneficial. You must take responsibility for your own suffering, accept your own suffering and learn from your own suffering without blame or a feeling of revenge upon others or life in general. These are all trademarks of becoming independent, becoming a person, becoming an individual.

Now, in much of the study of human psychology, becoming independent is considered the absolute hallmark of development, the end point, the ideal state, and many models are illustrated to draw a picture of what an independent person looks like. But independence is an intermediate stage. It is, therefore, unstable. As individuals gain true independence by taking the great steps forward that enable this to occur and by making the sacrifices and taking the risks, whatever they may be, after awhile, after congratulating themselves and receiving the great rewards and benefits of acquiring and achieving independence, they then begin to realize that they need other people to do anything meaningful in life. Being independent, though it is far greater and more rewarding than their former life, must lead to something, for it presents new problems that require resolution. Achieving independence represents a great threshold of learning. It has many steps and many challenges. It does not happen overnight. It takes a long time to recognize, a long time to accept and a long time to achieve. And there are many risks and dangers along the way.

Another great threshold in life is when you begin the slow approach to a life of interdependence where you consciously and responsibly choose to give your life to something. Now, there are very few human beings who have achieved genuine independence and far fewer still who have achieved genuine interdependence. So, this is a threshold that few have passed through. Of course, just because one acquires a functional state of independence, it does not mean that one will necessarily go on. You can get stalled by the side of the road anywhere in the journey of life. And the reasons to become stalled can always seem to be very compelling and self-satisfying.

To become truly interdependent means that you have realized the limits of being an individual. You have accepted the assets of being an individual, you have experienced them and you would not betray them. But you realize that they are limited and that you need others, not simply to accommodate your needs or to be companions for a time, but to engage in a greater union. You need community; you need relationships of a very, very special and great nature. You need deep understanding; you need devotion; you need compassion; you need commitment; you need compatibility. Why? Because you are here to do something in life. Your independence is to enable you and to empower you to do something in life. It is not simply a reward; it is preparation. It is hardly an end point.

The threshold of becoming interdependent is tremendous. Here there are many steps and many opportunities to become stalled or waylaid by the side of the road and many places where people give up. This is a great threshold. This is where you recognize the need to give your life to something. This can be very difficult because perhaps you have taken great pains to secure your own life, to establish your own boundaries and you do not want to go back into the state of dependence, either emotionally or physically, that illustrated your early life from the time you were born until the turning point in your life when you became your own person.

Many people never achieve independence, so it is a rare and valuable thing, but now you have to give it up! You have the power to do this consciously and intentionally because you are independent. No one is going to take it away from you. Here you consciously say, "I will share my life. I will give over what I have earned in order to have a greater reward." Then comes the challenge of actually meeting someone, a set of circumstances, a community or a great cause that involves intimate and cooperative relationships. Here your prayers have been answered, and the opportunity is being given to you. You now have to make the decision, take the risks and make the sacrifices. This is a great threshold.

Another great threshold that few people have passed through is the threshold of realizing the presence of Knowledge in their life. Here Knowledge has nurtured their quest for independence and should they acquire it or achieve it, it will nurture their desire to go on, to achieve union with others and to find purpose in life. Realizing the presence of Knowledge is a great threshold, for this is what initiates your inner life and gives you a sense of spiritual presence and purpose, a sense of origin and destiny. This is what enables you to transcend mundane life.

This is a great threshold with many steps. It takes a long time—a long time to recognize, a long time to accept and a long time to achieve and secure. It is a great threshold. Only an independent person can make this decision because you must *have* your life in order to give it over. You must be a person who can make very sound and important decisions based upon what is known within you. Only an independent person can do this.

Then you will realize that Knowledge is not only intuition or certain kinds of urges or feelings or sensations or insights or recollections or premonitions—it is a living Spiritual Presence within you, the Mind behind the mind, the Spirit within the mind, a Spirit that is not an individual, but a Spirit that is flowing through you as an individual, a Greater Power expressing itself. It is not yours to own and claim, it is not your private domain or private property, and it is not your little section of Heaven. Instead, it is a great and abiding Spiritual Presence that passes through you and abides with you. Recognizing its existence in your life and joining yourself with it is a very great threshold through which to pass.

Here you not only make room in your life for other relationships, but you give your life in service. Now, you do not necessarily have to be a religious person to do this, for this happens to people who think they are religious and to people who think they are not religious. Yet, a sense of reverence will enter your life, a sense of greater destiny, greater origin and greater relationship. This is a spiritual emergence, a great spiritual threshold. Few have passed through it; few even recognize that it is awaiting them; few are ready for it. Like traversing a gigantic mountain range, the pathway is narrow and winding. It is not a great thoroughfare through which hoards of people crowd. It is a tiny walkway, not recognizable to many but traveled enough so that it can be discerned.

This is a very great threshold. You do not simply pass through it. You live in this threshold. You do not pass through it and go on to something else. You live in it. When you leave this life, then you will pass through this threshold. Living in this threshold takes you to great heights, if you don't come down again. Many people claim they have passed through this threshold or feel that today they are passing through it or yesterday they passed through it, but it is not like that. You live in it and with it, and the degree to which you live in it and with it determines your advancement.

To ascertain this advancement, you would have to stand outside your life completely. But it is not expected that you will be able to do that and rarely will you have glimpses of your life like this. This is not necessary for advancement. Independence, interdependence and spiritual emergence — or said another way, uniting with Knowledge, becoming interdependent with Knowledge and being Knowledge. These are three very great thresholds.

There is one other threshold that I would like to mention, and that is emerging into the Greater Community. You already live in the Greater Community. The world is not an isolated place. It does not exist in a separate reality from the rest of the universe. To emerge into the Greater Community as an individual, however, is a very great threshold. Here you must accept your humanity, learn to recognize it with greater objectivity and, to a certain degree, transcend it. This is necessary for your spiritual life to have full self-expression through you.

Here you become not simply a citizen of your town, state or nation. You realize you are functioning in a greater context of life. You do not claim identity with all life because that is too big. But in a practical way you claim a larger association with life that includes your humanity and transcends it. Here your idea of God, or a Greater Power, your idea of life, your idea of destiny, your idea of your origin, your idea of individuality, your idea of race, consciousness, community, culture — everything begins to change. It is not simply that you say to yourself or others, "I am a citizen of the universe." We are speaking of a different state of mind, not simply a self-proclamation.

The rewards of passing through this threshold are immense. They are so important for your greater understanding and your greater participation in life and for your ability to contribute to the world's emergence into the Greater Community. You do not necessarily have to be a visionary or a philosophical person to have this experience of being part of the Greater Community. You can be a very practical person with very specific skills within the context of the mundane world. It is this larger understanding that matters. Like all the thresholds that I have mentioned, it is but another way to transcend your former understanding of yourself. It is not only something that you do intentionally. It is something that happens to you that you learn to accept and to receive, to join with and to participate in.

Passing through this threshold gives you greater capacity as a person — a greater range of vision, comprehension and discernment, a greater capacity for feeling and experience and a greater motivation to develop your mental abilities. Here you begin to understand what the mental environment really is and the forces that are functioning within it. You also begin to understand more fully the physical environment that you live in and how it can be enhanced and supported. Indeed, here you transcend the limits of human identity in a very practical way. This is a very great threshold and very few people have passed through it. Very few people even recognize that it is a threshold or that it is something valuable to approach.

Only the great and the Wise travel these roads, but do not think that the great and the Wise are a different species than you are. They are men and women who have passed through great thresholds in life and have kept their sense of themselves and their sense of balance. They have kept their life in proportion and have undertaken these great changes and re-evaluations — initiations, if you wish to call them that. They have kept themselves intact and acquired the benefits of each of these great thresholds. That is why they become great and that is why they become wise.

Now, each of these thresholds is approached because something inside of you is forcing you on. They are not approached through ambition or the desire to have great power, wealth and advantage. You must have intention to pass through them, but the intention is not the initiating factor here. The initiating factor is the emergence of a deep inner need which cannot be satisfied through normal means. This need, should it be accepted and honored by you, will carry you into a new range of experience. Here you are approaching a new threshold. Here you will feel alone, doubtful and disassociated from people around you to a great degree. While everyone else seems to be passing through a great corridor on an easy path, you are choosing a different way.

What confirms your approach is that you know it must be done. Along the way you meet certain individuals who point the way, and then you meet certain individuals who will join you. Some will join you temporarily; some will join you more permanently. They all provide encouragement, contrast, demonstration — all the things you need to recognize and to experience in order to proceed forward.

Passing through each threshold forges tremendous self-trust and self-respect, as well as the recognition of your own limitations as an individual. Each is brought about by a very natural process within you. Each has great risks. Failure is possible in each. Each sets you apart from others to a certain degree. Each requires greater ability and self-application. Each requires greater self-trust, greater humility and greater recognition of the importance of true relationship. In this, they all share attributes.

The emergence into the state of independence will encourage a lesser dependence upon relationships, for becoming independent is a temporary recognition that you do not need people so much, that you can do things on your own, and that you want to do them on your own. But you will soon realize that you need important people to help you, to nurture you and to show you what independence is. So, even here dependence on important relationships is very great, but it is not as predominant as it is in the other great thresholds of life.

The requirement for true relationship is very great in order to enter the state of interdependence. It is very great in order to undertake a spiritual emergence. It is very great in order to enter the Greater Community. These can all be understood as great steps in the reclamation of relationships, great steps in entering an interdependent relationship with life, where life depends on you and you depend on life.

The inner experience of passing through these thresholds is so great and so unique. It will make you feel different and think differently. It changes you. It changes people around you. The more you have progressed in passing through the great thresholds, the greater an agent for change you will be and the greater will be your ability to serve, nurture and represent genuine progress for others. Here you become a living example of what the truth can be if it is honored and followed without distortion and ambition. Here you will give without trying to give because your life is a demonstration. Your life is a demonstration of what you are and what you value. This is true at all stages of development. The ability to pass through a great threshold is what will mature you and what will give you depth and character. What is character? The ability to have a natural and unique expression of a greater understanding and a greater life. That is what character means within this context.

Passing through these great thresholds brings you into a new arena of life that is greater than the arena of life you were in before. Many of your former assumptions, beliefs and ideals will not be appropriate here. You must start from the beginning. This is what gives you a greater sense of yourself and life. This is what enables you to acknowledge the Spiritual Presence in your life, which is abiding with you and assisting you, both through Knowledge within you and through the spiritual benefactors who are contributing to your overall advancement.

Passing through these great thresholds engenders a great deal of change. Change is a process of giving something up and acquiring something new. It has stages. Change begins with the recognition of a need and is then followed by a recognition that change must occur both in your inner and outer life. Then there is undergoing the change itself, which leaves you in a state of unknowing and confusion because you are entering into a new arena, and you don't know what you are doing, why you are doing it, where you are, and so forth. Next, there is abiding with the change without certainty of the result. Then, there is the confirmation of the change once the change has truly been made and you have reached a point of no return where you cannot go back.

For better or for worse, you must go on. It is at that point that the reward begins to become available to you. Many people give up before they reach this point. They will not go on unless the rewards are guaranteed, unless the rewards are identified and unless the rewards are confirmed. But true change is a process of giving something up and acquiring something new. Between giving something up and acquiring something new you are empty. Here is where the mind is enabled to grow because it relinquishes its former understanding and is willing to abide without an understanding, which makes it available to acquire and to cultivate a greater understanding. For many people, this is a greater risk than giving up all their money or saying farewell to all of their loved ones. It is a greater risk to them because their ideas about themselves and the world are more important to them.

In order to have a greater life, to have a greater mind and to have a greater set of relationships, you must pass through the great thresholds. What you will need in all the thresholds is the desire to go on, which is built upon the recognition of genuine need. You will need a great preparation and you will need great companionship. You will need these in order to become independent; you will need these in order to become interdependent; you will need these in order to emerge into your inner life and to reclaim your relationship with Knowledge. And you will need these in order to enter the Greater Community.

Each threshold brings about a tremendous change in your

experience of being in the world. There is a loss associated with all change because you must give something up. There is faith associated with all change because you must abide with not having anything. Self-trust and self-love are required in all change because you must be open to receiving something else. There is a genuine regard for life in all change because you must be willing to welcome what life presents to you. And in all change there is a sense of allegiance to a Greater Power because you realize that in the process of real change something greater must help you. You yourself cannot do it all. This is the Mystery that brings about change. This produces reverence towards life and faith in the presence and activity of a Greater Power with which you are becoming increasingly engaged.

Now, as I say these things you may wonder, "Well, how does this relate to emerging into the Greater Community?" Emerging into the Greater Community does not mean getting on a spacecraft and going on a tour of the stars. It means that you are beginning to have a sense of relationship with all life. With relationship comes the requirement for discernment and the ability to participate. Here you can serve not only the needs of people but the evolution of life in the world because evolution always recognizes a greater context for existence. For example, it would be pointless to discuss the evolution of the world unless you considered the greater environment in which the world exists and its relationship with that environment. Evolution, by its very definition, affirms an origin and a destiny. What is the origin of intelligent life here in the world and what is its destiny? These are genuine questions for a person who is beginning to emerge into the Greater Community. These are questions that call for spiritual sensitivity, a practical approach and a tremendous willingness to relinquish your former ideas and assumptions. They require the willingness to go through a perhaps prolonged period of uncertainty and to be open to receiving the greater comprehension that is born of a greater sense of yourself and your relationship with life.

You do not need to see spaceships or have encounters with extraterrestrial influences in order to become a Greater Community person. Becoming a Greater Community person is a great threshold. Achievement here is partially dependent upon your intention to continue. It is partially dependent upon the circumstances in which you live, which includes the quality of your relationships and their ability to support you. However, achievement here largely depends upon the nature of the preparation itself, for who in the world can teach you of the Greater Community? You need a preparation from beyond the world to learn of the Greater Community.

If you wish to go beyond human speculation and human fantasy, you must receive something that will enable you to do this. You cannot invent the way for yourself. Here is where you need help of a very special kind. This is true for all the thresholds that I have mentioned, which represent the great thresholds in life. You need mentors to become independent, to learn to become interdependent, to undergo a spiritual emergence and to enter the Greater Community. You will need independent people to help you become independent. You will need interdependent people to help you learn interdependence. You will need spiritually evolved people to undertake a spiritual emergence. And you will need allies in the Greater Community to become a Greater Community person. You cannot do this yourself. To think that you can is to misconstrue your abilities and to underestimate the greatness of what you are undertaking.

Regardless of how you perceive yourself or where you think you are in the development of life and regardless of how cultivated and advanced you may consider yourself, it is important to recognize that there are great thresholds and that each will change your ideas about yourself, about others and about life. Because you have a spiritual nature, you can undertake the transformation that occurs in each of these great turning points, for you are not your ideas and you are not your associations. Though you abide with them and use them and rely upon them to a certain extent, you are greater than they are.

Your greatness can only be known by taking the steps that will require this recognition and this willingness to go beyond. Life will take you there. In this, you learn to become fearless. You learn to recognize your range of responsibilities. You learn your limits and your greatness. And you learn the greatness of the Greater Power that abides with you and that enables all individuals — in the past, now and in the future — to undertake a great change and preparation in order to render a great contribution in the world.

Learning how
others view you
gives you a
reference point
and an idea of
how you must
cultivate your abilities
and what you
must achieve.

Seventeen

VISITORS' PERCEPTIONS
OF HUMANITY

T IS ALWAYS HELPFUL to understand how others view you. In the context of the world's emergence into the Greater Community, it is most beneficial that you have some idea of how your neighbors perceive you. This is important to give you a new understanding of how to relate to intelligent life around you and to give you a greater vantage point to view yourself from a larger and perhaps very different viewpoint. This is a rare opportunity, for though people may attempt to have a more objective viewpoint of each other, they are still far too subjective in their evaluations, and they do not have a reference point that is significantly unique or different in order to develop a truly new perspective. You see each other according to a standard set of values.

Let me then give you an idea of how others who have visited your world and who are visiting it even now perceive you. Because the visitations in the world are being made by several varied groups with divergent interests, I will give you some different viewpoints, for they are certainly not all the same. These viewpoints vary according to the purpose that these groups are serving, but together they can give you an idea of the kind of relationship you already have with other intelligent life. Though you are not yet a conscious participant and cannot participate directly or intentionally, you are in relationship already simply because you are part of the Greater Community.

The discrepancies between the various viewpoints of your visitors serve also to give you a larger perception of yourself and to indicate something about their nature and motives as well. Indeed, in any relationship, learning how individuals or groups observe and interpret each other is essential to establish a bond and to establish a true understanding, even where a bond is not important or appropriate.

You may, of course, discount what I am saying, but it would be far wiser for you to consider it seriously. Since some of my remarks will seem very critical or perhaps humbling to your evaluation of yourself, still it is important to receive them with the intention to learn and to understand rather than to criticize or defend current viewpoints or sets of preferences. Therefore, I invite you and encourage you to be as open-minded as possible.

Let us, then, begin with the Forces of Dissonance — those groups that are allied with each other and are attempting to exploit the world to discover its secrets and its wealth and who are testing human beings, both directly and indirectly, to learn of their nature and predispositions for possible future alliances. I can understand their perception because their minds can be easily read, for in the mental environment, only the very adept can shield their own thoughts effectively from both mental and technological scrutiny. The Forces of Dissonance are not adept, though they are clever and cunning in the ways of espionage and observation. They seem far more advanced than you in this regard and can easily observe you and are learning ways to manipulate you very effectively. But they are not adept, in that they cannot control the mental environment and they cannot shield their own minds effectively. Therefore, those who are wise and more advanced than they are in influencing the mental environment can not only comprehend their motives, but in time can learn to affect them as well. The Forces of Dissonance are, indeed, being controlled by others who are far more powerful but who are not present in the world.

Their perception of you is that you are very curious and very strange. They find you simple and very fundamental, but they do not comprehend your emotional nature at all, and your religious propensities and devotions are completely mysterious to them. They find you easy to manipulate but difficult to understand, which to them makes you unpredictable. That is why they are taking a long time to learn about you. Not only are they learning about you, they are learning from you, for you are setting certain examples which are having an impact upon them.

They are not evil; they are simply misled. They are not guided by Knowledge, so they cannot gain access to the Greater Spiritual Power within them. They are part of a larger alliance where the mental influence upon them is strong. They are serving that power, so they are not here for their own interests, though their own interests seem to be served by their presence here, according to the directives that are given to them by those whom they serve. They do not look upon you with scorn or enmity; they do not look upon you as if you were stupid and ignorant. They are learning to exploit your weaknesses but are having great difficulty understanding your psychology. This makes you a greater challenge to them than you would be otherwise. Your technology is understandable to them, but it is your unusual nature and how you can use your growing technology that concerns them. Indeed, this is holding them at bay to a certain extent, which is beneficial for you.

Your affections for one another are equally mysterious to them, for they do not have this experience with one another. Your emotional nature is confusing to them and as such is exerting an influence upon them, though at this point your influence upon them cannot offset their influence upon you. The very few amongst humanity who are advanced in Knowledge not only pose the greatest puzzle to these observers but also the greatest possibility to influence them. That is why we advocate the reclamation of Knowledge, so that you may not only offset unwarranted or inappropriate interferences in your life, but so that you may exert a positive and important influence here as well.

These observers consider you to be very weak minded and indeed you are in comparison to them. In fact, human beings are very weak minded in contrast to all of the visitors here. What does it mean to be weak minded? It means that your minds are not concentrated or focused and are therefore easily distracted, easily disturbed, easily distressed, and so forth. You are not concentrated in contrast to your visitors.

The Forces of Dissonance, then, find you remarkably easy to influence. Yet, they are having difficulty in understanding your motives and your behavior. For example, they cannot comprehend your experience of love. They can understand why you respond with anger or defensiveness when you are threatened. They can understand your sense of confusion when they are manipulating you. But your devotion to love as well as your religious fervor are completely mysterious to them. Here you are more advanced than they are, for this capacity is only latent within them. So, in this you are influencing them; you are confusing them. You are not as easy to manipulate if you are given to these greater spiritual incentives, these mysterious impulses. The fact that human beings devote their lives and all of their time and resources to their affections for one another is inexplicable to this group of visitors.

Therefore, the ease with which you can be influenced or affected is being offset by your complex nature. Indeed, it is also being offset to a certain degree by your religious development, for here humanity has actually made some significant progress in comparison with other intelligent life in the Greater Community. For example, in some advanced societies there is no religion at all. In others, technology is the religion. That is not to say that you are the only race that has religion—of course not. But you cannot assume that all advanced races have a developed religious life or a set of religious traditions. Many societies have rites by which an individual is perfected in their intellectual ability or in their virtuous behavior. But worshipping a Greater Power or a greater force or identity in life is not an emphasis that is shared by all intelligent life, even within the vicinity of your world.

So, there are some offsetting influences that you are exerting upon these visitors. However, do not take great comfort in this, for religious fervor can easily be manipulated once it is understood. In fact, it does not even have to be understood. Religious fervor can simply be studied and then it can be controlled. As an example of this, the Forces of Dissonance are able to project images in the mental environment. Here they can project an image of a preferred religious symbol or personality. The people being affected by this can have this experience in their dreams or in an altered state. They will then think that they are having a religious experience, and they will want to give themselves to this experience.

Humanity does have a rich spiritual life and set of traditions, but there is not the commensurate understanding of the mental environment in order to balance this and to offset unwarranted and inappropriate influences upon it. When you think of this, you will realize that whole groups of people, even nations of people and whole cultures of people, can be influenced by the projection of religious images. An example of this would be the idea of The Second Coming of Christ. This could be well orchestrated by the Forces of Dissonance. Indeed, they could create this great drama which would divide humanity into the so-called believers and non-believers.

This could cast brother against brother, family against family, nation against nation.

At the present time, it is not the intention of the Forces of Dissonance to create global warfare or to establish a state of complete breakdown in human society. It is possible that they can influence this. Though it would not happen immediately, it could certainly take place. It is for this reason that there are spiritual forces as well as beneficial Greater Community presences in the world to offset the presence of the Forces of Dissonance.

Humanity has great promise, though it has great difficulties and some important liabilities. Here you must understand that you are very vulnerable. Though you are casting an influence upon the Forces of Dissonance, their commitment to their purpose is such that it will override any fascination they may have with you and will enable them to learn ways to manipulate you, even if they cannot comprehend your behavior. For example, in your world scientists can manipulate animals in order to study their behavior by making them do things they would not do otherwise and by controlling their responses by controlling the stimulation. This does not mean that they understand the way these animals think or feel. It is not necessary to understand someone to control them. It is not necessary to empathize with them in order to learn ways of stimulating them and manipulating their response. Therefore, you are very vulnerable here.

The perception of you by the Forces of Dissonance, generally speaking, is that you are weak minded, foolish, inexplicable and somewhat fascinating. They are also quite fascinated by your physical environment, for many of these individuals were born in space, and they have lived aboard spacecraft their entire lives. Here they are visiting this lush and marvelously diverse world with a seemingly infinite variety of life forms. This is fascinating to them. This, too, has the power to somewhat offset their mission, for they are quite taken with this place. Nonetheless, the power that is controlling them will continue to reassert itself and reaffirm the purpose that these groups are trained and prepared to serve.

It is possible, however, that should enough individuals in the human family cultivate Knowledge and be able to exert a greater influence while offsetting unwarranted influences through wise discernment and self-control, then they could turn the tide in time. To give an example, imagine that you were sent out to make someone else do something and to engage with this other person whom you had to control or manipulate in some way. Then you meet that person and become fascinated with them, and this fascination begins to change your ideas and your motive. In time, if the attraction is great enough, it can overcome your initial purpose. This happens on rare occasions between human beings. It can happen as well in the Greater Community.

Therefore, though human beings appear foolish to this group of visitors, they hold an attraction as well. These observers have never seen flowers, have never seen birds, have never seen insects, have never seen foliage such as your world possesses. What a marvel it is to them! This is important in diffusing their initial purpose, the purpose they were sent here to fulfill, which is to gain information about this world and to acquire all of its technological and mental powers — especially the mental powers that advanced human beings have been able to cultivate. Their quest is for power. Their quest is for possible domination in the future.

Now let us speak of another group that is here. I shall not mention their names because that is not important at this time. They are here to observe you because they live in your district. They are more numerous than the Forces of Dissonance because the Forces of Dissonance always travel in concealment, attempting to hide their presence and to make their investigations as secret as possible. Many of the more obvious demonstrations of extraterrestrial presence in the world have been from your neighbors who are here to observe you. Why are they observing you? Because you are an emerging world and you are gaining access to important forms of technology. It is well known to them that you are very warlike and seek conquest and dominion. This makes it very likely that you will carry out this motive once you learn to escape the boundaries of your world.

Therefore, your neighbors are here to learn of your technology, your capabilities and your predispositions. Many of the sightings of craft have been of these individuals. They are not so concerned with being secretive, out of sight or hidden. In fact, many of their presentations have been quite intentional in order to gauge your response. They do find you fascinating and somewhat unpredictable, but their regard for you is not very high, for they consider you brutish and uncivilized. Though they have studied many individuals in the world and have been impressed by them, they recognize overall that the race of humanity is not yet united and represents many divergent views and interests. This makes you potentially very dangerous, for it is clear that you will turn upon one another for even trivial reasons. Because devotion is such an important virtue in the Greater Community, it is assumed by this group, who is studying you for their own self-protection, that you are a race that cannot be trusted and that you will wield your newfound powers and abilities in ways that are very harmful to yourselves and to other races who potentially could be your neighbors in the distant future. They have come at a time in keeping with humanity's development of atomic power because this represents an ability to affect life beyond your world.

This group is not advanced in the ways of the mental environment, though like all groups that travel in the Greater Community, they are aware of this power. It is evident to them that humanity has the potential for cultivating this power, but humanity's liabilities are so great, in this group's estimation, that it is unlikely that humanity as a whole will mentally advance much at all. Human technology will advance, but that does not mean that people here will advance in the ways of influence.

Therefore, they are studying you, and they are also learning about the biology of the world, for their world is far more barren. This has engendered their need for advanced technology. They are taking many samples of plants and animals away from the world for their own cultivation needs. They have no intention of dominating the world, conquering it or influencing it. They are studying it, and they are learning some things about you. Your agriculture, for example, is very fascinating to them. Your domestication of animals is very fascinating to them. Though they grow food, they have no domestication of animals. As a matter of fact, this particular group does not even eat flesh, so they are somewhat shocked and fascinated by human consumption of animal flesh. The mutilation of animals has been conducted by this group, for example, because they want to understand what these animals are, why you feed upon them and how they can be developed for possible food resources for themselves.

This group is on a learning mission, but their involvement in the world has grown over recent years. They do not pose any threat to you, and in fact, their visitations here show promise for the possibility of establishing future relations. They are concerned, however, that you are raping and diminishing the world's resources, which will eventually force you, once your technology can accommodate it, to seek resources beyond your world. This group does not inhabit your solar system, but your solar system will not meet your resource requirements, which will force you to explore beyond it once you learn how to travel at appropriate speeds. This will bring you into your neighbor's territories.

They are on a fact-finding mission here — learning a great

deal about you. They are also learning a great deal about your plant and animal life, taking many samples, doing much evaluation, going back and forth, and so forth. They are learning from you. But they are also learning how to defend themselves against you. Your relationships with one another are not as inexplicable as they are to the Forces of Dissonance, but your erratic behavior, your compulsions and your fascination with trivial things are things that they do not understand. To them, you are unpredictable and somewhat chaotic, which makes the opportunity for establishing meaningful relationships, except with small groups of people here, extremely remote.

Let us now speak of a third group. I am talking about three primary groups. Though there have been visitations by others — resource explorers, for example, who are looking to see what the world contains and to see if there is a possibility for trade with the culture of humanity — I am talking about three main groups that comprise those who are visiting the world.

The third group is here for very different purposes. They are a small contingency of individuals who are monitoring the presence of the Forces of Dissonance, for they have come to monitor this presence. They, too, are learning about humanity, but for a very different purpose. They wish for humanity to thrive and to progress. They are driven by a greater incentive. They have spiritual alliances that are serving them. They are not here for commerce; they are not here for conquest or manipulation; they are not here to learn about you for their own self-defense. They are here to cultivate humanity's education, to support humanity without direct interference. They, too, are studying individuals, for they must learn not only your psychology, but your physiology as well. They are providing education. They are stimulating certain individuals who have the real potential to receive a Greater Community understanding. They are supporting the introduction of The Greater Community

Way of Knowledge. They are wise enough not to interfere with you directly, and they maintain their surveillance in such a way that their physical presence is not made manifest.

Overall, this group represents the Forces of Good for humanity. In your own vernacular, they could be called "the good guys." They are more advanced than your neighbors who are studying you. In fact, they are also studying your neighbors. They are studying everyone here to learn about the condition of humanity and to learn how you are going to respond to the Greater Community. They are in contact with several individuals around the world, attempting to cultivate a greater spiritual knowledge and understanding. They are establishing relationships with these individuals in the mental environment. This does not mean that these people are aware that they are in relationship or that they necessarily accept the relationship. It just means that the relationship is already there and that should these individuals accept it and learn to participate in a conscious and responsible manner, they will be the beneficiaries of a greater Wisdom.

This third group is very concerned that the Forces of Dissonance not discover the secrets of this world. We are not speaking of the secrets of humanity here because humanity does not have many secrets. We are speaking of the secrets of the world—what has been put into this world, what has been kept in this world for a long, long time, far longer than human civilization. They are here to protect these things. They do not want humans to discover them either, for humanity is not ready to wield great power, and they do not want them to be discovered by any other alien force.

Their presence, then, overall, is to protect humanity and to protect the secrets of the world. Perhaps this seems incomprehensible to you. This is only because you hold a viewpoint that is so limited it does not account for other intelligent life. There is a general assumption amongst people that their world is the center of the universe, that it is a place that is isolated from everything else because of vast distances, and that it has come into being with human society. But the world has been here far longer than human civilization, far longer than human beings have been here. Much has transpired in your world. This world has been considered a valuable place to visit, to conduct experiments and to develop the depositories where secret things could be kept hidden from the Greater Community.

Now, there is another influence here — a spiritual influence, a spiritual group, if you will. They hold you to be very, very promising though still quite adolescent in your development. Their commitment is for you to learn The Greater Community Way of Knowledge, to enable your sense of spirituality and your spiritual traditions to evolve into a larger arena of life and be applicable there, in order to give you a more universal sense of the Greater Power in life and to engender the cultivation of intelligence, responsibility and cooperation. These are the three fundamental pillars upon which any race or society must develop and advance. This group is not here to protect you; they are here to educate you and to lift you up. They are working in an alliance with the Forces of Good that I have just described. Their viewpoint of you is very commensurate with the Forces of Good, though their comprehension of you is greater. The Forces of Good consider you to be fascinating, childlike, irresponsible, mentally weak, foolish, predisposed to do things for ridiculous reasons, yet nonetheless worthy of their assistance and support. They are particularly impressed by your ability to love and to be devoted, to whatever extent this has been developed.

You are a race that has developed in isolation. You are unique in this respect in that you have not been tampered with by the Greater Community until very recently. The Forces of Good are particularly impressed by many of your religions, particularly those that emphasize the development of virtue in the individual, for these are values that they hold dear as well. They are a highly cultured group of individuals, representing several races that are working in cooperation for a particular mission here.

Spiritual forces are present, but you will not be aware of them until you undertake the preparation that they have provided and are supporting. They will enhance true development, the commitment to serve others and the cultivation of virtue and intelligence, which is the willingness and the capacity to learn. Unless you are undertaking the preparation for the great threshold of emerging into a Greater Community identity and awareness, you will be unlikely to experience their presence. They work in conjunction with other spiritual forces that have been in the world all along, cultivating and nurturing human advancement.

Given my very simple descriptions of your visitors, which I might say are rudimentary and leave out many important aspects and complexities, you will begin to see that you have a great responsibility here to cultivate Knowledge and Wisdom, which will allow for the wise expression and application of Knowledge. You must cultivate the ability to learn to cooperate with others, which you will be able to do more effectively once you gain a Greater Community perspective. Here you will see that the differences between people are slight instead of great and that cooperation is not only possible but necessary in light of your growing relationships and involvement with the Greater Community itself. Here you will realize that there is a tremendous emphasis on the human family becoming mature, developing a greater viewpoint about themselves and life and learning over time to accept their relationship with other intelligent life and the very fact that they are living in a Greater Community of Worlds.

Human advancement will be greatly furthered by individuals becoming educated in The Way of Knowledge according to the Greater Community traditions, for now you need to learn the

Greater Community traditions in order to surpass what human beings have attempted to accomplish on their own. You need education from beyond; you need a mentor from beyond; you need forms of preparation from beyond, for in isolation you cannot prepare yourself. You must be prepared. This will offset the destructive and conflicting incentives on your part. It will enable you to support the emergence of a greater understanding and will allow you to utilize your mental and physical resources far more harmoniously and effectively. All of these are necessary for the evolution and advancement of humanity.

Here you must see that you are not yet mature, that you are not yet adults in the real sense. You are adolescent in that you are experiencing new power and newfound freedoms and abilities, but you do not yet have the maturity, the sense of responsibility or the interdependence in relationships necessary in order to use these powers constructively. Human beings, for example, must learn to live for the welfare of their human family, not simply their blood family, but for their society and world. They must learn to do this in such a way that their individuality is enhanced through contribution and is not denied. Human society has not established this ability yet, though it has been proposed by many visionaries and wise individuals throughout the ages. Humanity has not developed sufficiently to enable this to find a firm and complete expression. Many people even consider it impossible, given their understanding of human nature. But human nature is not something that has been completely explored or developed, and human beings have not been prepared by a greater and more intelligent power.

Consider this fact: It is far more time consuming and far less effective to learn something on your own than it is to prepare with someone who is more advanced in that skill than you are. Human beings have been trying to prepare themselves on their own, yet what has allowed the greatest advancement is that information has been given to certain gifted individuals who were capable of actually producing a tangible result or carrying out a tangible demonstration in the world. Your technological advancement has been sparked and furthered through this contribution; your spiritual comprehension has been sparked and furthered through this contribution. It is outside influences that keep nurturing your advancement, and though these influences are rarely accounted for, rarely acknowledged and sometimes cruelly considered, they nonetheless have been responsible for your advancement and your increasing freedom and ability, both mentally and physically.

Therefore, humanity overall requires tremendous preparation. The world now is supporting this by calling upon people everywhere to join and to unite to fulfill common needs and common purposes—to salvage your environment, to equalize the distribution of your wealth, to learn the wise use of your resources, to cease incessant conflict and warfare and to learn to see beyond tribal and regional identities in order to develop an identity as world citizens. All this is happening at a remarkably quick pace, so fast in fact that most people cannot keep up with it. This is all part of your emergence into the Greater Community. It is all part of living in an accelerated evolutionary period. This is a very difficult period and will incite and bring forth much of the inbred human resentment and conflict that already exist here. This acceleration can lead to new achievements and understanding or it can lead to tremendous breakdown and destruction for humanity.

Present in this acceleration are the Forces of Good and the Forces of Dissonance. Present here is a great opportunity for a quantum leap in spiritual development and understanding and a quantum leap in humanity's cultural integration and establishment. These are necessary because in order for humanity to begin to effectively engage with the Greater Community in a conscious way and to establish relationships, it must be a unified community. It cannot be a set of divided and conflicting societies. In the future, this will require some form of world government—one that perhaps will allow for tremendous regional diversity. But there must be a world government. This is slowly developing. In fact, it is developing very quickly when you consider how slowly these things normally develop. You are in an evolutionary fast-forward right now. The Greater Community presences here are stimulating this. The growth of the human family and its changing interaction with one another and with the natural environment here are also contributing to this tremendous acceleration in development.

Humanity is in an adolescent period in its development. You have newfound powers and abilities; you have greater freedoms; you are learning new things; you are entertaining greater insights; you are becoming more aware of the environment around you. But adolescents are still self-seeking and self-serving and are still committed to their own personal priorities. You have not yet significantly developed a social consciousness. You are not aware of other races' experience significantly, especially in the Greater Community. Adolescents cannot yet account for the forces that are shaping their lives, though they are beginning to be sensitive to them.

In this difficult period, you are developing a Greater Community awareness at the very, very beginning stages. You are not necessarily adolescent with each other, but you are adolescent within the context of the Greater Community and in your ability to be in relationship to the Greater Community—to accept its presence and its reality, to discern its influences and to learn to participate with the degree of Wisdom that will be necessary for you to have in order to survive as an independent race in the future.

Here, then, is your great calling and your great requirement. The call and the need for advancement is tremendous. Even if you do not accept your life in the Greater Community or if you discount the Greater Community influences that are present in the world today, you must still realize that human society needs to grow, to become integrated and to become wiser and more cooperative even in order to meet your environmental and economic needs.

Everything that I am presenting here is absolutely essential for your success and well-being, even if you remained an isolated race. Yet, I paint a greater picture and illustrate the larger range of your relationships and the influences that are being cast upon the world at this time from beyond the world. How much greater this is! This is your life. If you learn to respond to your life, you will be able to participate in a way that is both effective and satisfying. If you cannot respond, then you will feel infringed upon by the changes and influences that are shaping you, both from within your world and from beyond. And you will find no relief from the miseries that attend you until this responsibility is recognized and is accepted. This is true within your own individual life. This is true within your life as a community, within your life as a nation, and within your life as a world in the Greater Community. As it is above, so it is below, for the truth exists everywhere. The denial of truth and the acceptance of truth is a process that is going on wherever intelligent life has emerged.

Learning how others view you gives you a reference point and an idea of how you must cultivate your abilities and what you must achieve. You start with your individual life by bringing greater harmony, balance, responsibility and accountability to it. You do this because you recognize a deeper need within you, and you are willing to take the risks and make the sacrifices. Here you gain access to Knowledge, the Greater Mind within you, the Mind that knows, the Mind that can guide and direct you and give you the strength and the confidence to undertake the transformation of your life. As you do this, you will be able to contribute things of greater value, greater magnitude and greater influence in the world around you. This will draw to you individuals who will help you in your own development and in your capacity to serve and to assist others.

*Compassion
is choosing
a greater response
to a greater problem.*

Eighteen

COMPASSION

GIVEN THE ENORMITY OF THE CHANGE AT HAND and the great requirements being placed on humanity at this time to meet its own internal needs and to meet the challenges of emerging into the Greater Community, it is quite essential to emphasize the importance of developing great compassion. Change is difficult, even under more normal circumstances. It is often resisted and usually feared. It involves uncertainty and often generates blame and condemnation. People rarely undertake change willingly or intentionally and even when they do, it proves to be a greater challenge than they often had anticipated.

It is for this reason that great care must be taken now and that people realize that they must treat themselves with compassion. They must develop a foundation for self-trust and self-appreciation, even when they are uncertain or fearful or greatly doubt their motives. This is especially true when you realize you must do things ahead of other people, when you don't have the certainty and reassurance of everyone doing something with you. Indeed, many of you who read these words will be the forerunners for your race, which means that you will be undergoing a profound internal change, far ahead of humanity at large.

This is the price of awareness; this is the price of advancement; this is the price of being in tune with the evolution of the world—

that you will know things, see things, feel things, realize things and take steps ahead of other people. This requires tremendous courage. You must trust these deeper inclinations, and yet with this trust there must be discernment and Wisdom in their application. You cannot be casual or complacent. You cannot give away your responsibilities to a Greater Power, for they are yours to assume and to carry out. You cannot run away and hide, for you know too much already. You cannot say, "Someone else will do it and I will applaud them," for it is given to you to assume your unique role. You cannot stand by the sidelines and say, "I don't want to get involved." You are involved. You need to be involved. You want to be involved. You are only afraid.

So, this requires great care and understanding of yourself and of others. This is especially true because people's disabilities — their negative imagination and their unhealthy dispositions — will become greatly accentuated during times of stress and change. Times of stress and change bring out the best and the worst in people. Here people will do things that are very damaging to their well-being and to the well-being of others. People will take ridiculous positions in the face of great change. People will attempt to go backwards and to reclaim an earlier time, which now seems much more pleasing than it did before. People will try to relive earlier epics that are long past. People will deny their experience. They will deny the world's emergence into the Greater Community. They will deny what they know. They will deny their truthful associations. They will blame others for their difficulties.

All of this will happen and happen in very intense ways. Why? Because in the face of great change, people are helpless and this brings out their worst tendencies as well as their courage and their ability to be devoted. You will see in the next decade tremendous discord as tribal societies, ethnic groups and people of different religious persuasions clash with one another, competing for their own identity, which is rapidly being changed. Some of the events to come will be very appalling; some will be magnificent and encouraging.

For you, the participant, the observer and the student of Knowledge, this is a time that calls for great self-restraint, great patience and great compassion. Self-restraint means you must hold in abeyance many of your own reactions to allow a deeper and more pervasive response to emerge and to guide you. You must hold back your angry speech and your frustrated words on many occasions. Exercising this forbearance enables you to realize something you know that is at a deeper level. This requires great patience, for you must wait for things to come about. You must wait for certainty. You must wait for confirmation. You must wait for companionship. You must wait for the results that you want now. And in many cases, you must realize that some of the goals that you have set for yourself will never be obtained. So, there is disappointment.

As I have said, change requires letting go of something and then receiving and developing something new, with a period in between where you do not have anything. What you may be missing are possessions, financial security or the emotional security of having close companions. You may be missing the intellectual security of being certain of what you are doing and having a clear view of your life and priorities.

There will be disappointment. Ideals will fail. Great expectations will go unanswered. Longings will be seen as hopeless. This brings you back to the truth within yourself and to the requirement that you must learn to wait, to observe and not to judge and to use this self-restraint in order to gain a deeper insight born of a deeper experience. Here you must abandon self-comforting ideas and live close to life, in touch with life and vulnerable to life in many situations. Here you are re-engaged in direct relationship with life, instead of merely playing it safe on the sidelines and watching while life takes its course and then feeling angry and resentful because things happen that are not of your choosing.

This is a time to directly participate, and this will require a special preparation, great companions and a decision on your part to participate in the world's emergence into the Greater Community, to participate in the unification of human society and to participate in the reclamation of your physical environment in ways that are specific to your nature and deeper inclinations. Here you are not to be only an observer but to be a participant, for you are a participant. If you want to find purpose in life and realize your greater resources and your true inner strength, you must make this decision, fortify this decision and live this decision. It is not up to someone else; it is up to you. You are the one who is reading these words. You are the one who has the power to respond.

For this, you must learn to be compassionate with yourself. This means that you observe yourself, give yourself time to undergo development and re-evaluation, gain a sense of where you have been and what you have concluded from your earlier experiences and accept the fact that in many cases you will have to change your evaluations and become vulnerable, without explanations. You will have to redefine your life, your purpose and your destiny.

This openness and this vulnerability speak of an inner self-trust. It is not a self-trust that one day you just have or that someone gives to you. It is a self-trust that you yourself must forge. It is forged by making decisions that perhaps seem incompatible with other people's decisions, or which seem costly in terms of the advantages which you were formerly seeking for yourself. It is forged by being true to what you know without adding any assumptions or con-clusions of your own. It is letting yourself feel the pain of loss and uncertainty without inflicting this pain upon others. It is developing a greater capacity for experience within yourself, rather than at-tempting to live through the experience of others.

Compassion is observing yourself without judgment, aligning yourself with the truth to the extent that you can experience it, being a direct participant in life, choosing what is true over what seems comfortable or accommodating to others and seeking truth over advantage. While others are repositioning themselves for advantage in times of change, you can abide with the truth and thus be free of the many adversities and calamities which befall those who seek to outwit life for their own personal advantage. Here you choose to follow the truth rather than seek gain and acquisition. Your reward will be lasting while others will fail, without seeming recourse or redress for their needs and their disappointments.

Compassion means you look upon the world from a greater viewpoint and you do not give yourself the seeming luxury of condemnation, which validates your idea of yourself by demeaning others. Here you are willing to be wrong; you are willing to be confused; you are willing to be uncertain; you are willing to appear foolish; you are willing to recognize your mistakes; you are willing to accept disgrace if disgrace must be accepted. This is coming home to the truth within yourself.

Great change brings people to a great threshold and forces them through it. Great change is where great people emerge. Great change is when great things are contributed to the world. What greater change could there be for humanity than to emerge into the Greater Community of Worlds, to engage in meaningful relationships with other intelligent life and to discern a greater interaction in a larger arena, which you can neither understand nor control? What greater change could there be than for human civilizations to finally unite, recognizing common needs and seeking cooperation and solutions which provide mutual benefit and development? This must accompany humanity's emergence into the Greater Community.

Humanity's emergence into the Greater Community will

bring about greater change for every person. This will change their circumstances, their position in society, their sense of themselves, their opportunities, their risks, their friendships, their acquaintances, their priorities, their values, their religion and their God. And though this seems cataclysmic when it is seen all together, it is the opportunity for you to finally rise above the littleness of your preferences and preoccupations, to live a greater life — a life that is bonded to the world and to the true needs and aspirations of people, a life that can accommodate genuine relationships, deep satisfaction and full re-engagement with your spiritual life. People do not reach these heights without great circumstances prompting them and without passing through great thresholds.

Why complain that the world is changing when this gives you your only true hope of advancement? When the world changes, you cannot stay where you are. Whether you are comfortable or uncomfortable at this moment, you cannot stay where you are. You have to move with life. Life is moving. Your ideas, your opinions, your prejudices and your beliefs now are overshadowed by a greater series of events, a greater requirement upon you and a greater opportunity for advancement.

With compassion comes Wisdom, for compassion establishes the conditions for Wisdom to emerge. Be compassionate with yourself and others. Be open. Seek a deeper understanding. Do not fortify your former ideas by judging others and trying to live according to a set of standards which may not be appropriate anymore.

Indeed, in the years to come, people rich and poor, people of all religious persuasions, of all social orders and representing all personal interests, will be increasingly involved with one another. This will tend to neutralize the extreme tendencies of humanity and will create a more common sense of identity. Though cultural diversity will certainly continue as will individual expression, people will be forced to integrate with others in ways that they prefer and in ways that they do not prefer. There will be more people; there will be fewer resources; there will be less personal freedom, and there will be a larger general consensus upon which things must be decided. Here it is not merely a matter of what serves one group over another; it is what serves everyone, for common needs will grow and become far more intense.

You cannot stay where you are—mentally and, in some cases, physically. You must rise or fall in the face of a great change. Many people will fall. They will not be able to cope with it; they will not be able to accept it; they will not be able to integrate themselves with it. They will not be a part of the change. They will be part of the obstruction to change, for change must happen. The question is, how can change happen in the most beneficial way? You cannot alter the fate of humanity, but you can determine the quality of its outcome.

Compassion is choosing a greater response to a greater problem. It is choosing a greater response than the one that you may automatically feel as a result of a new or demanding experience. Learning not to judge here is very important. So are learning observation, learning stillness of mind, learning to listen within yourself as you listen to others, learning to be patient, learning to forego self-comforting ideas, learning to forego early conclusions while you wait for a greater realization, learning to live without so many self-definitions and learning to accept your problems and to work with them constructively. This involves giving other people the benefit of the doubt and learning to understand why they are reacting the way they are, for many people are poorly equipped to be a part of a world that is emerging into the Greater Community. Challenging times can bring forth either condemnation and hatred or compassion and Wisdom. You must consciously choose and choose again and again and again which response you will exercise, for both are possible within you.

Therefore, when I speak of the change at hand and of the challenges at this great turning point in humanity's existence, do not slink away; do not become overwhelmed; do not seek escape or denial. Instead, consider that everything that is being presented here is but a calling for you to rise to meet the occasion. You do not know what this will look like or how it will come to pass. Perhaps your ideas of what you will contribute are incorrect, and other things will be contributed by you when the situations require it. Here you realize you must be a bigger person, have a greater capacity for Wisdom and understanding and have a greater ability to give.

How do you achieve these things? First, you must accept the condition of your life as a starting point. Then you must undertake certain forms of preparation, many of which are quite specific, and be certain that you are not inventing them or changing them to meet your current preferences, for this will not enable you to elevate yourself. You must re-evaluate your relationships, both now and at many junctures in the future, to see if they can support your undertaking, however ill defined it may seem to you at that moment.

Many people at this time are thinking and asking, "What is my calling in life? What is my spiritual purpose?" Often they think of some wonderful thing, like being a healer, or being a priest or a priestess and having marvelous experiences of joyfulness and spiritual ecstasy. Perhaps they see themselves healing the sick, being magnificent, living in beautiful places, living a beautiful life or all of these. Well, it is very important that you recognize that this is a fairy tale and with few exceptions, all of this must be relinquished.

To find your calling in life and spiritual purpose, you must learn to prepare. Here you learn to make decisions based upon what you know rather than what you think or want. Here you roll up your sleeves and become involved with life. Here you become basic, honest, simple and straightforward. Your glory will come from this, not from living out fantasies. This is the reality of living a truly spiritual life. The rewards are deep and pervasive, but they are rarely recognized by those who seek to have glory and ecstasy be the foundation of their experience. There are the doers and the dreamers. Be a doer. Dreams are merely a waste of your life unless they can be done, and they must be done to a certain extent by you.

Therefore, regarding your expectations about what your spiritual calling or spiritual purpose may be, you must clean the slate, erase all of the images and put away the fantasies. Be open, compassionate, patient, observant, and ready to act. Wait for the moment when action is truly called for and resist all of the premature motivations for you to act. Be committed to learning and to unlearning and to discovering the truth no matter what you may have to confront within yourself and no matter what you may have to do. It is this commitment abiding with compassion and all that compassion requires that will enable you to progress in your development and to keep pace with the movement of the world so that your real gifts may find their emergence through you.

You cannot pull your real gifts out of yourself; you cannot bring them forth through dialogue or spiritual practice; you cannot squeeze yourself to wring them out of you. You must be in the right frame of mind, in the right situation, with the right people. Then they will issue forth, and issue forth with such potency that you will not be able to deny them or mistake them. Yet, reaching the place where you are in the right state of mind with the right people and the right circumstances requires preparation. It requires compassion and all that I have spoken of.

Be patient then. You are growing slowly because you are growing something important. Things that grow quickly die quickly. Things that happen just like that are gone in the next moment. Great accomplishments are born of great preparation. When you ask yourself, "What can I do to support the evolution of life here? What can I do to find the foundation of my purpose? What can I do to develop the state of mind that is necessary?" I say prepare, observe and be honest. You will know the form of preparation when it comes to you, though you may resist it and attempt to deny it. It will be the right thing at the right time for you. Perhaps you will begin your preparation by thinking, "It is only for a short time. It won't ask too much of me. I will only give a little bit until I am sure." Yet, if it is the right preparation, it will ask more of you than you had planned to give, and you will find you had more to give by giving it. Giving is the emphasis here.

You may ask, "How can I possibly undertake all of these things you are saying?" I say, become honest, become simple and become patient. Prepare. Accept the preparation that is made for you. Do not invent one for yourself. Get involved. No one can do this for you; you must do it. If you seek to know what real purpose is, then contribute to someone who has found purpose for themselves, and they will help you find your own way. If you feel you have greatness in your life, read about, learn about, and if possible associate with great people. If you wish to know The Greater Community Way of Knowledge, then you must study it, integrate it, digest it and live it. You cannot dabble with it, play with it, try it on for size. You must take it on! If you do that, then it will yield its rewards to you. It is the same with your relationship with life. You take it on; don't play with it or sample it. You take it on! Your relationship with your mind and with your body, your relationship with Knowledge — you take them on!

This is not a time for indecision. This is not a time for ambivalence. This is a time for commitment, a time for inner resolution, a time to move forward. There are many things you know already you must do. It is time to do them. That is your starting point. Do what you know today and then you will know something tomorrow. Do what you know tomorrow and then you will know something the next day. This is how Knowledge is reclaimed.

Whatever you do, whether it is a wise decision or a foolish one, whether you act nobly or in ways that are not beneficial, return to patience, forgiveness, forbearance, observation and re-evaluation — all of the things that make up compassion. Look upon others not with criticism or with self-righteousness, but with the understanding that they, too, are struggling to come to terms with living in a changing world. They, too, are coming to terms with their own failures and their own possibilities for success. The more you see yourself struggling, the more you will understand them and will not be so ready to condemn them or dismiss them.

Those who are wise and compassionate have faced their own suffering and have passed through it. Now they can face the suffering of the world and contribute to its resolution — not simply because they have good ideas, but because they have traveled the way and have found resolution and the way out.

It is facing the world
rather than
seeking escape.
That is what generates
courage.

Nineteen

COURAGE

*I*T TAKES GREAT COURAGE TO CHANGE, even under normal circumstances. One must recognize and accept the truth, trust one's deeper inclinations and in many cases give up a preferred advantage, relationship or situation. One must face the unknown and entertain new possibilities. This all requires courage. Yet, when change is required on a greater scale — indeed when humanity itself is changing and you are in the center of this — an even greater courage is required. It is built upon trust, recognition, preparation and compassion. You cannot muster this courage up within yourself if you do not have these pillars upon which to stand.

Perhaps you do not think of yourself as a courageous person, thinking that courage is something that some are endowed with and not others. But in truth, courage is something that everyone must forge and develop in his or her own experience. This happens through making difficult decisions. This also happens through making important mistakes, learning through these mistakes and taking the necessary steps to set things right.

This is what generates courage. Courage is the result here, though it can be the cause and the motivation for later action. In other words, you must generate courage. It is not something that is bestowed on some and not on others as people enter life. It is something that must be forged. Difficulty, adversity, changing circumstances, changing relationships and changing priorities all create the great opportunity for real courage to be cultivated and applied.

Therefore, do not think of courage as a divine bestowal. If you feel you are lacking in courage or perhaps lack sufficient courage, then remember that it is something you must generate within yourself. You have the power to do this because Knowledge is with you. You have the opportunity to do this because of the time in which you live. You have the requirement to do this because you have come here to serve a greater purpose, which you are yearning to discover and to carry out. All of the ingredients are within you; all of the ingredients are in the world. Conditions are right. Knowledge and courage go together, for without courage you will not undertake the reclamation of Knowledge and without Knowledge you will not trust in the courage you have developed thus far.

If your well-being, your fulfillment and your inner resolution are important to you, then courage is something you must accept as a necessary requirement. It is not something I can give to you. It is not something you can purchase. It is not something you can learn from a book alone. It is something that you must use and apply. Otherwise, it is like a muscle in your body that is never used and thus is never strong and reliable.

Everything that you enjoy in life — the benefits, the creations, the objects, the opportunities for education and self-expression, the fun and the recreational things that you enjoy — are all the products of other people's contribution. In all cases, it required courage and belief in one's self and one's deeper inclinations in order to bring these things about. You are literally living on a foundation built by the contribution of others.

That is why it is important to understand that your contribution will serve people who are yet to come. You don't know who invented all the objects that you use every day. You don't know the names of those who secured for you your political freedom. You don't know the names of those who created your educational system and made it possible for you to take advantage of it. It is not expected that you would know them, for they are far too numerous and their names stretch back in time. However, it is important for you to understand that your contribution in life is something that will have a bearing on the future of humanity, for the future well-being of humanity is dependent upon what you and your generation contribute today. This is the essence of nature — that the future is secured by contribution in the present time. This happens in the plant world, in the animal world and in human existence as well. It is a law of nature.

Therefore, if you are prone to lose faith in yourself, consider the courage it took for others to create all of these things and how everyone benefits, either directly or indirectly. They, too, had to forge courage. They, too, had to take risks. They, too, had to have confidence in their deeper inclinations. They, too, had to face their own errors and be willing to risk making more of them. They, too, had to learn from their mistakes and bring about the appropriate corrections. To whatever extent any of them did this, they were able to contribute something of lasting value — both things of a tangible nature and things of an intangible nature. They have served to create both the physical and the mental environment in which you live.

Take heart, then. It is not you alone who are called to do this, but you are not excluded from the necessity of this, either. You are given an equal opportunity to carry out what is known within you to be correct. Start with what you know today so that you may know something tomorrow. Already you know things you must do that you are not doing. Already you realize there are changes you must make in your behavior and perhaps in your thinking as well, and you are either not doing them or you have not fully carried them out yet. Do not wait for greater certainty to come. Do not wait for new insights. Carry out what you know to do today. That takes courage; that takes faith in yourself; that takes a reliance upon Knowledge, even if you do not know what Knowledge is. That requires the conviction that what is prompting you from deep within yourself will bring about good for you and good for others, if it can be wisely discerned and applied. How can it be wisely discerned and applied? By your taking chances and by your learning the ways of Wisdom, for Wisdom, like courage, cannot simply be bestowed upon you. You cannot get it from a book, although a book can stimulate Wisdom in you or show you how Wisdom can be applied. You cannot gain it from me, although you can consider everything I say, which would be wise for you to do.

Wisdom, like courage, must be cultivated by direct engagement with life, by making important decisions and abiding with them, by facing error, by facing pain, by accepting help, and by rearranging your life whenever this becomes necessary. In all cases, it requires giving greater priority to truth over your personal wishes or preferences. And it requires that you change your goals and objectives in life, should they prove to be unhealthy for you.

All the great qualities and virtues of the man and woman of Knowledge are not things that are simply given. Yet, the seeds for their expression are within each person. Those who cultivate the seeds, who grow them and who abide with them will be the ones who will receive the great rewards. They will be the ones who will build a better future for humanity and make it possible for people in the future to undertake the reclamation of Knowledge and to discover a greater purpose in life. As those in the past, unknown to you, have given you this opportunity and this advantage, so will you secure this for people in the future, people as yet unborn.

The world is requiring all of the change that I have spoken of so far. Do not think this does not involve you directly. Do not think you can step aside and say, "Well, I think I will just watch how it turns out." This is your opportunity to give. In giving you will find your courage. Its possibility is within you, and its success is assured if you exercise it sufficiently.

It is very important to distinguish courage from much of the rash and compulsive behavior that people demonstrate in a myriad of ways. Sometimes people rush into things without any forethought. Sometimes people rush away from things without any forethought. There are many compelling factors that lead people to do dangerous and unwarranted things. Sometimes they think they are being courageous. People even do some very dangerous things to test their own sense of courage, taking great personal risks for some thrill or momentary experience of superiority or self-control. This is not courage. Risking one's life to prove something to one's self is not courage. You may call it recklessness, foolishness, ambition, compulsion, or many other things. But it is not courage. It is not the courage that I speak of.

The courage that I speak of is the willingness and the developed ability to recognize something that must be done and to play your part in doing it, if it calls upon you specifically. It is the courage to open yourself to the suffering of the world. It is the courage to make yourself available to it so that it can pull out of you that which you have to give. So, do not only sit in meditation or try to figure it out or squeeze it out of yourself through some kind of psychological process. The needs of the world will call upon you to give your gifts. You do not need to lie about the condition of the world. You do not need to paint a pretty picture of it. You do not need to deny or discount what actually exists. You do not need to falsify your understanding of yourself or others in order for this gift to be stimulated and rendered into the world.

Open yourself to the suffering of the world. You do not need to seek it out or immerse yourself in it. Simply be open to it when you perceive it. If you want to live a beatific life and have everything sweet and lovely around you, you will find escape temporarily from the difficulties of living in the world and many of its tragedies, but you will not find escape from your inner conflicts. And the Knowledge that you have not resolved your inner need for meaning, purpose and direction will go unanswered. Your escape from the world will only be temporary, for you are part of the suffering of the world and your suffering adds to it and contributes to it. This you cannot escape. Though other people attempt to find escape from their own inner dissension and conflict through a myriad of activities and involvements too numerous even to list here, do not make the decision to do this. Face life and life will face you. Give to life and life will give to you, for you are in relationship with life.

Face life. Face yourself. This takes courage. This is real courage. Thrill seeking and risking your health or well-being for wild, exotic experiences to prove to others how strong you are do not qualify as real courage. These things do not require as much of you as telling the truth about your life, living the truth, following the truth, expressing the truth, and learning how to do all of these things by trial and error and by gaining Wisdom and assistance from others. What courage does it take to say no to financial rewards when they are inappropriate or require something that is not correct for you? What courage does it take to turn away from love or a loving person when that involvement is not correct for you? Those who seek advantage and who take advantage of others and their affections and who seek only to fill their own coffers of wealth and personal self-esteem will find only misery as their reward, for what they try to secure can be easily lost. They have not met their inner need; they have not answered their greater questions. So, their sense of stress and lack of well-being will persist and grow deeper and darker over time.

Let this not be your destiny, though many choose it and express its glories and its benefits. Do not let this be your decision. It takes little courage to follow in the ways of the world. It takes great courage to follow in the ways of Knowledge. It takes little courage to accept the pleasures and to deny the pains of life around you. It takes little courage to try to live a beatific life while the rest of the world goes on without you. It takes great courage to face the world, to face yourself and to face the possibility of living a greater life here — a life of service, a life of meaning and a life of meaningful engagement with others. It takes courage to face what this may mean, not knowing how it will turn out or what it will look like when it finds its true expression.

It takes great courage to undertake The Greater Community Way of Knowledge, for here you are preparing for something you can barely understand. Here your personal ambitions will fail you or it will seem that they cannot be fulfilled by undertaking the Greater Community preparation. But you go on because Knowledge prompts you. This requires courage. This is choosing truth over pleasure.

How secure and how powerful the man or woman of Knowledge is who would not give up their mission for love or money. Are they fanatical? Perhaps. But they are committed because they have realized that truth is a source of meaning for them. Their ability to join in relationship far surpasses that of other people. What they will experience and what they will give will far surpass the goals and ambitions of others around them. They will make life possible for humanity in the future. They will strengthen humanity.

This is needed now as the world is preparing to emerge into the Greater Community. Humanity must become stronger, more unified, more capable of cooperation, with greater self-care, greater support and assistance and greater cultural integration. All of these things, many of which you hold dear as great virtues already, must be founded upon a stronger humanity — physically, mentally, emotionally and spiritually stronger.

Who will bring about these great advances? It is up to you. Do not look over your shoulder. It is you. Though your part may be small and not require a great deal of recognition, what you can give playing a small part is very great. Only very few will gain notoriety and recognition, and this is as much a curse as it is an advantage. For many it will be their undoing, so do not seek this for yourself. Truth is a greater reward and a greater vehicle for service and accomplishment than success and fulfillment. When the eyes of the world are upon you, there is much you must conceal. Truth will live like a prisoner within you, even if you are committed to its expression. It is better to be invisible and to render your gifts without the world's recognition. This, too, requires greater courage, for here you must forsake self-gratification for something that acknowledges the deeper truth within you, something that is far more fulfilling and important.

In fact, you could say that the reclamation of Knowledge is coming to terms with what is truly important and what is truly not important, committing yourself to the resolution of big problems and devoting only a small amount of your time to the small ones. It is facing the world rather than seeking escape. This is what generates courage. Do not be disheartened that few choose this path. Though courage is possible for each person, it takes extraordinary circumstances to bring it forth. It takes great challenges and great change to provide the opportunity for courage, for Knowledge and for true love to genuinely emerge. You see, then, how foolish it is to resist or avoid or condemn the needs or the condition of the world when they are actually the very things that can redeem you, show you your strength and give you the foundation of certainty that you so desperately seek in other things that have no promise.

The greatness of life should never overwhelm you, unless you are approaching it with personal ambition or great expectations for yourself. Instead, let the greatness of life give you the opportunity to find your greatness and your expression of greatness, keeping in mind that true greatness in the vast majority of cases goes unacknowledged by the world. Yet, you will find support and supportive relationships as you find your purpose. In fact, your purpose will join you and bind you with those who are destined to help you and with those whom you are destined to help. Here you must relinquish all of the images of spiritual greatness — priestesses, priests, kings, queens, angels, gods, masters and mastery. Leave this all behind. It will only confound you and make your way far more difficult.

The simplest act can express the Wisdom of the universe. When Knowledge is working through you, you will be as much in marvel of it as anyone else could be and perhaps more so because it is happening through your mind and body. For this to take place, ambitions must be left aside. Goals and desires for a happy, unfettered and uncomplicated life will either have to be abandoned completely or greatly altered. That is not to say you are choosing difficulty and duress. You are simply saying, "I must do this and I will accept what comes." Say this. Know this. Mean this. And you will have an opportunity to know what courage is and what courage can do. Then you will find that you have an advantage in life that few others have claimed. Though the rewards of your contribution and the recognition of your contribution may be far in the future, you have secured to a large degree their expression by taking this great step within yourself. This declaration will be challenged and will be tested, not because life tests you as when you go through school and you get tested. God does not test anyone. The test is meeting the requirements of your life. What greater test could there be?

Do you want to find out what you know? Do you want to know what Knowledge is? Do you want to experience courage? Do you want to find out what self-confidence really means? Do not ask God for a test. Do not think God is giving you a test.

Do not think that God is doing something to you because God doesn't believe you. Meet the requirements of your life, the mundane requirements and the greater requirements. Open your mind to consider where the world is really going and what is really happening. Be patient and open. If your mind is racing a hundred miles an hour, trying to find the answers, trying to resolve questions or trying to secure a place in the future for yourself as you reconsider your life, you will not go forward. The approach is stillness, openness and discernment — all qualities that must be cultivated and developed through practice and application.

Does all of this sound too great for you? If so, you have underestimated yourself. Do not underestimate what Knowledge can do for you, but let Knowledge do it. Abide with Knowledge. If Knowledge is silent, you can be silent. If Knowledge is not moving, then you do not need to move. Maintain the outer requirements of your life, but hold fast to your allegiance to the truth within you, which is represented by Knowledge. This requires the courage to act when action is necessary and to not act when action is not necessary. Both require great courage.

Great courage is forged and developed through this kind of application. Exercising forbearance and exercising the will to act when it is necessary require courage and develop courage. Until you do this in a significant way, courage is only a potential within you; you do not yet have it. Knowledge is only a potential; you do not yet have it. Love is only a potential; you do not yet have it. You can claim them for yourself. You can declare their presence in your life. You can even claim that you have achieved great things with them, but real courage, real Knowledge and real love emanate from you when they are being expressed every moment. They are a demonstration of your life. You do not need to do magnificent things. Just meet the requirements of your life. Meet the requirements of change. Let the world teach you what you must give.

It takes courage to even hear these words without judging them, altering them or denying them. It takes courage to receive them without trying to change them in some way to make them more palatable, more acceptable, easier or more pleasant. Courage. I cannot tell you something you do not already know. Your reaction, then, is determined by your association with, understanding and experience of what you know. Start from where you are. Perhaps you know something very small today that you must do or that needed to be done yesterday and you have not done it yet. Do that. When learning to play a musical instrument, you start with very, very simple exercises. You do not begin by taking on a difficult piece or a great challenge requiring much skill. You start with simple exercises and you do them over and over again. Such is true in cultivating courage, Knowledge and love. The exercises are meeting the requirements of your life, learning to be still, learning to be able to respond to Knowledge within yourself and accepting that you do not understand Knowledge even though you know it is there. You start today with what you know.

At a certain point, you will realize that you have to prepare according to a certain preparation that you did not invent for yourself. It will play an important part in your overall development and will save you a great deal of time as well. Do not think you need to orchestrate your own education. Meeting the requirements of your life, learning of the reality of Knowledge and learning to follow the required preparation will give you all the education you need. Your part will be great, but you do not control everything. Learning what your part is and what Knowledge's part is, is part of the overall education of which I am speaking.

Sometimes the way will seem easy and delightful; other times it will seem difficult and inexplicable. These are merely different reactions to an ongoing process of development and contribution. Courage has brought you this far. It can certainly meet the demands of the world. Though you have limits as a person, and you certainly do, you do not know what these real limits are. Take courage, then. When in doubt, be still and listen, unless action is required. Practice forbearance, for you will find that Knowledge is silent ninety percent of the time, which means that it does not appear to be doing anything. Thus, you must become silent ninety percent of the time, even as you carry out your mundane activities. This takes courage — as much courage as it takes to do a very difficult thing, to follow a very important decision you have made and to face the results of this decision with confidence and determination.

Do you want to know what it means that the world is emerging into the Greater Community? Then be very patient and do not make early conclusions. Be a student of Knowledge, for you are certainly not its master. Then courage will grow in you like the seed grows in the ground and like life grows in the world — slowly, deeply and with a firm foundation. Then your experience of courage will grow and change, and your definitions will change as well. But as you meet each new requirement in your life and discern and follow each new certainty, you will not only be able to receive courage, but you will be able to bestow it upon the world.

In order to learn,
you must
associate with those
more advanced
and with those
less advanced
than you.

Twenty

Learning from Others

To advance in The Way of Knowledge, to learn of the world and to find your contribution, you must be able to learn from others. So, let us now explore this together.

Positioning yourself as a student offers you a great advantage and can in many ways protect you from your own destructive tendencies. Claiming and reinforcing your studenthood gives you the opportunity to learn in a very maximal way and tends to prevent you from making premature conclusions or identifying with self-comforting ideas. It allows you to be open, vulnerable, perceptive, observant and can in many ways restrain you from coming to conclusions that do not represent a deeper understanding. By the very nature of studenthood, one must wait to learn. Yet, during this time of waiting, one must apply oneself. One must seek a curriculum of preparation, and one must become very observant of others.

This seems so obvious in order to learn anything of great importance. Surely, if you think of any skill that you value, you realize that you will need instruction; you will need some kind of curriculum; you will need help from others. And you will need many examples. This is universally true and has so many applications. Yet, people do not consider this when they view their progress in life. They stumble along, learning things unwittingly and often unwillingly, trying to hold onto old ideas, trying to protect themselves and trying to buffer themselves against change, new interactions and opportunities, and so forth.

If you take this active student approach to life, you are able then to proceed in a way that is very conscientious, and you are able to engender the necessary responsibility for your learning. If you are honest in this approach, you will realize that you will make mistakes and that some mistakes are necessary. You will realize that many things will have to be accomplished through trial and error, that you will have to expose yourself to the different viewpoints of other people and that you will have to try things out and test them. This is a very different approach from trying to prove yourself or validate your ideas or defend your position, which is a very common approach and does not engender real learning. A real student approaches disappointment and confusion in a very different way, seeing it all as a necessary part of learning and preparation.

To be part of the world and to discover your place and your purpose in it requires that you take a position as an active and intentional student. Here, if you can take the position that you do not know anything and that you want to learn as much as possible, this gives you the great advantage. This allows you to move with life in the direction in which life is going and to learn of the things that I have spoken of in these discourses. You need not take my word for it. I invite you and encourage you to explore these things for yourself, for though I am very correct in what I am saying, that will not help you unless you can find this realization for yourself.

Become a student. Become a student of Knowledge because the discovery of Knowledge, the emergence of Knowledge and the guidance of Knowledge is what you will need to negotiate a rapidly-changing world. In fact, you will need to realize and experience Knowledge to become a complete human being, to find a Greater Power in your life, to develop a relationship with this Greater Power and to realign yourself with people in such a way that meaningful relationships can arise and find their full expression.

Therefore, given the normal requirements of life and the greater opportunities that the world is presenting you now, Knowledge is your foundation because it is the greater mind within you. It is your resource for truth. It is your resource for meaning and direction. You will stumble blindly without it. You will live by ridiculous assumptions without it. You will seek comfort and avoid pain without it. The results of this latter approach have generated the confusion, the ambivalence, the uncertainty, the misery and the self-denial that you see all about you. All advancements in life that are meaningful and genuine have been prompted by Knowledge and, in most cases, individuals did not even know that Knowledge was their guide and the source of their inspiration, their strength, their courage and their motivation. But those few individuals who did realize this and aligned themselves with Knowledge consciously were able to give so much more, for they positioned themselves in life in such a way that life could become the recipient and the motivation for a great contribution to be given in the world.

A necessary part, and a very big part, of being a genuine student is learning from others. This involves many things. First of all, you will need those more advanced than you to serve in your preparation and even at some points along the way, particularly as you become more advanced, to provide direct instruction. Here you must accept yourself as a student and accept all that you do not know. If you try to teach yourself, in most things and especially in learning The Way of Knowledge, your progress will be slow, frustrating and inefficient. You will not progress. You do not have time to wander blindly about, trying this and trying that, taking a little bit of this and a little bit of that, following an eclectic approach. That is like picking up scraps from beneath the table when in fact a great feast is being presented to you. Why pick up scraps when you can sit at the table and receive the gifts of Knowledge? Do not be a beggar. Be a recipient. Be a student.

You will need instruction. You will need to accept that other people are more advanced than you are and, without glorifying them, deifying them or making them your sole focus, you can learn to receive from them and to support them. Learning from a teacher involves several things. It involves receiving, evaluation and application. It also involves supporting that individual, which is your form of giving to them. Particularly in The Way of Knowledge, real teachers of Knowledge rely upon this, for they are giving their life to this service and they are worthy of generous support. Do not bargain with your support, but give what you know you have to give. Then there will be no inequality and no uncertainty in the relationship.

In order to learn, you must associate with those more advanced and with those less advanced than you. Certainly, this is a given fact in the world. Yet, many people are trying to have equal recognition, equal skills and equal opportunities, when in fact, they are in very different stages of development. When you have a specific focus in learning, this becomes very apparent. If you do not have a specific focus in learning, it is hard to tell. In this situation, people make ridiculous proclamations about their skills, their awareness and their abilities. And other people who are more skilled often deny their own abilities. So, it becomes very confusing, and there is a tremendous amount of self-deception. But when you are attempting something specific, such as becoming an athlete or a musician or a scientist or an engineer or a physician, you don't simply wander about trying to pick up pieces of information. You commit yourself to a training and preparation. Because you have a specific focus here, you realize that you need this preparation. You realize that you do not have the skill, the experience or the understanding necessary to carry out this form of service or contribution.

Therefore, accept that you are a student. Accept that you need instruction and accept that you must learn from others. You can accept all of these things because they are obvious. This holds true in learning The Way of Knowledge. Learning The Way of Knowledge is more difficult than becoming a physician or an engineer or an athlete. Why? Because it is more personally challenging. It requires more change and re-evaluation. Rather than simply adding something on to yourself, learning The Way of Knowledge will change your whole viewpoint of life. This requires greater courage. I do not demean these other pursuits, for they can indeed be very special. But The Way of Knowledge is greater and requires even a more focused studenthood with more openness and fewer assumptions.

The Way of Knowledge is more difficult because you are not sure what the result will look like. If you go to medical school, you know that if you can pass the examinations, you will come out as a physician. You know that if you undertake preparation to become a musician, if you persist and pass your tests, you will at least be competent at your skill. Following The Way of Knowledge, however, you are not sure what you will look like. Obviously, you will not have a career and be a professional person of Knowledge. Therefore, it is more difficult here because you must proceed with greater uncertainty. Rather than being motivated by wealth, fame, recognition or achievement, you must be motivated by something deeper within you that says that you must do this. And you go forth not knowing what it means, what it will require or what advantages you will have.

Being a student of Knowledge is a very focused form of studenthood. You will need instruction. You cannot learn The Way of Knowledge yourself. You cannot learn it from going to seminars or reading books or carrying on an eclectic approach. This keeps you on the outside where you cannot enter the inner courtyard. This keeps you as an observer. You can collect all kinds of examples of other people's preparation and other people's achievements. You can even become a scholar studying how others in various religious traditions have attained a greater understanding. But unless you can travel the way yourself, you are simply a fan up in the grandstand waving a flag—interested but not willing to take the journey yourself.

Being a student of Knowledge is being a student of the Mystery, but this does not mean that all of the preparation is mysterious. Much of it is very tangible. Here you must become a person who is consistent, balanced, functional, responsible and very capable. This all requires a very practical form of development. You cannot be a dreamer and enter into The Way of Knowledge because, in fact, many of your dreams will prove to be ineffective and even unwanted as you proceed. What, then, will you have to turn to as your greater resource and motivation? You can't follow The Way of Knowledge wanting to escape the vicissitudes of life. The Way of Knowledge will turn you to face them, to meet them and to understand them. You can't follow The Way of Knowledge to fulfill your ideals because most of them will prove to be the real obstacles that are holding you back.

Therefore, there must be a stronger motivation because there will be these disappointments. Rather than trying to have what you want from life, you are able to follow what you know and to give something of greater meaning. This will give you greater meaning, and you will see greater meaning in others. Here compassion is necessary. You will need it in your approach to yourself because you will go through periods of tremendous confusion and at some points disappointment.

As you learn to re-evaluate your motives and your current understanding, you will learn to recognize your limits. You will not progress unless these limits are identified. Many people do not want to have their limits pointed out to them. They feel this is an affront to their sense of pride and accomplishment. Yet, real learning requires that you discern where you are. And where you are at the outset is being a beginner who wants to learn but who doesn't know much. How obvious this is in other forms of education that you are aware of, yet how difficult it is for people to accept that the same thing holds true in learning of the Mystery. Here many people become very proud of all that they have read in books and all of their little experiences. "Oh, yes, I know about this!" and "Oh, yes, I know about that!" and "Oh, I have read about this teacher" and "I know about this school." They are beginners. But they cannot even be beginners because they won't accept it.

Be a beginner. Not only be a student of Knowledge, but be a beginner! This gives you the greatest motivation, opportunity and ability to learn. This enables you to receive instruction and to give to others without self-glorification, for indeed your sense of pride will be humbled in contrast to the presence of Wisdom and Knowledge. In fact, in The Way of Knowledge, one of the first things that students learn is that they know very little and that they are basing their life on all kinds of assumptions, many of which are unquestioned. In fact, they generally are not even aware of many of their assumptions. They have just followed others and made this assumption and that assumption, and they have wondered why in life they have felt so insecure, so uncertain, so troubled and why their happiness and pleasure were so easily assaulted by changing circumstances and the opinions of others.

If you base your life on assumptions, if you base your identity and your meaning on assumptions, you will feel weak and vulnerable, easily assaulted, defensive, resentful, uncertain and angry. And you will fear dishonesty because you are being dishonest. This is the result of not having a foundation. Becoming a student of Knowledge is to build a real foundation, not an imaginary one, not a fanciful one, not one that you simply pick up inadvertently by growing up in the world, but one that you consciously forge that represents the truth of what you know and what you realize can be practically demonstrated in the world. For this, you must examine yourself and your own experience and learn to evaluate yourself objectively. This also requires learning from others.

People are teaching you everything not to do in life. Why condemn them? They are a necessary part of your education. They are saving you time. Why condemn them? Every form of self-violation, every expression of fantasy and every blind assumption being acted out are being presented to you if you can see them — not with criticism or condemnation, for criticism and condemnation are easy. They are for people who are protecting their pride and guarding their own assumptions. But if you are able to see with gratitude, compassion and understanding, you will be able to receive this part of your education, which is absolutely fundamental.

Why spend your life making all of the common mistakes when you can accelerate your learning by observing others? You will still make some mistakes. You will still have to try some things out. And to some degree, you will still have to taste romance and personal power and all of these kinds of things that are so glorified in the world in order to find out how absolutely hollow and lacking they are.

Do not simply rely upon your own incentives and values. Observe others. Do not think that you are so different from them. You could make the same mistakes they are making. Perhaps you will think, "Oh, that would never happen to me. I would never do that." But given the same circumstances and the same inducements, yes, you probably would do that. Yet, why go through it all? Why reinvent what other people are demonstrating to you? You can only learn from them, however, if you observe them objectively, with compassion and without judgment. They are part of the hand that is feeding you, but only if you take a position as a real student can you benefit from their demonstration. Otherwise, you will say these people are good and those people are bad, these people are stupid and those people are smart. A person who is not committed to education will make these kinds of assumptions because they are easy to make and because they are self-congratulating. A student, however, will take a different approach and a far wiser one.

Observing people is very important, but only with this approach. It is easy to condemn; it is difficult to discern. It is easy to categorize; it is more difficult to leave things unexplained. It is easy to assert your opinions; it is more difficult to alter them. People who do not want to learn choose what is easy; those who want to learn choose what is right, whether it is easy or not.

How can you not have gratitude for the world when it is teaching you the results and the outcome of all of your dispositions that are not guided by Knowledge? Even when people are extreme in their expressions of self-violation, it is about you! This engenders compassion and gratitude, for they are teaching you. They are showing you the outcome of choosing this way over that way, the outcome of believing in this idea or following these compulsions or seeking this form of escape or trying to lose yourself in this interest. They are teaching you, if you can observe them, what it is like to be in this vocation, to assume this role, to have this job or to be in this relationship. If you can learn from life's great bounty of demonstrations, it will refine your vision and your idea of yourself, leaving you to discover the essence of who you are and what you must do.

Sometimes you will respond to others with revulsion, but this does not necessarily mean that you are condemning them. It might mean that at the level of Knowledge you are withdrawing from the situation. This does not mean that you have to be loving and happy and open and accepting of everything. It means that you let yourself respond, but you do not judge. There is a very great difference here. You can withdraw from something because you know it is very dangerous or harmful without condemning anyone that you are observing. Likewise, you can feel a natural inclination to move towards some people without glorifying them or placing a higher value upon them over others.

This represents a natural attraction and resistance that you can feel. This gives you a sense of the instinct of Knowledge. There need not be any judgment or condemnation. It is yes or no, not right or wrong. Right or wrong is what people say when they cannot experience the reality of something or when they feel they must justify their own responses. Instead, just respond. Do not react. You will be motivated to go towards some things and away from others. Towards many other things you will just feel neutral. Stepping back and letting yourself feel this response is very important in learning how to discern others and in finding your way. This gives you an experience of what Knowledge is like.

Give yourself this freedom. Become observant and objective and you will be able to feel your deeper inclinations. In time, you will be able to learn from these inclinations—what they mean, where they are trying to take you, and so forth. It is because you have come here for a purpose and are trying to reach something that you have the need for direction. Your engagement with life, if you are facing life, will teach you your inclinations and your direction. Yet, if you are standing by the side of the road saying, "Well, I do not know what I want. I do not know where to go. I do not know anything," how can you have any direction? You must be moving to have some direction. If you are stalled by the side of the road, you are not going anywhere, so how can you experience direction? You must get up and do something and go somewhere and engage with life.

Perhaps you will feel foolish and stupid because you do not know what you are doing. Yet, anyone who is approaching Knowledge and has accepted his or her real studenthood must accept this experience. This will temper your pride and develop real openness of mind. If you are trying to be something, do something or have something and that is your overall focus, then how can you be discerning? Everything will be evaluated according to how it fits in with your idea and your image of what you must be, do and have.

Discernment requires objectivity. Objectivity requires openness. Openness requires an approach where you are focused on learning rather than acquiring. Here you are facing the world rather than simply trying to use it. Here you will need instruction, and you will need to recognize and profit from the demonstration of error.

You will also need some great companions. Here you will have to alter what you value in people because the wonderful, the beautiful, the charming, the exciting and the unusual are not what you will seek. Perhaps these represent your former interests in people and the criteria upon which you based your attractions. This will all have to change. Again, you will have to wait for a deeper response. You will have to evaluate people differently, which is different from judging them. You will want to learn what people are capable of and what their inclinations are if you are interested in being in relationship with them. Even with those with whom you feel a spiritual resonance, you must find out if they are able to participate with you and if you have a sufficient degree of compatibility. This requires objective observation. Remember, you are not here to condemn or to glorify them. You simply want to learn. You are going somewhere in life, and you want to know if they can go too. Potential is not enough here. Someone must actually be ready, willing and able to go with you. Trying to rehabilitate someone that you love in order for them to hopefully join you is fruitless. They must go on their own inner direction, not on your prompting. They must go because they realize they must go, not because they are doing it to stay with you.

Here, as in learning all things with Knowledge, there is a great process of re-evaluation and a new approach is developed. This is true in all education. All students must go through this. People begin their studenthood with grand expectations and all kinds of assumptions about what they can and cannot do and what it is like to learn and what they will learn and what it will look like. Much of this must be re-evaluated. Here, not only do you have to acquire new skills, you have to acquire a different state of mind.

This is even more true in becoming a student of Knowledge. Do you think you know how it is going to be? Well, it will be different. So, do not try to base your sense of worth upon whether you are correct in your assumptions. Rather, be open and ask for the truth to reveal to you that which you need to learn, that which you need to do, and that which you need to re-evaluate. If you do this, then you can become a person that has real direction, and you will be able to have a meaningful foundation for relationships with others.

Being a real student requires that you not have all the things that you think you want right now. Many people say, "I would love to undertake the study of Knowledge, but I really want to be married. I want to have a partner. And I want to be financially secure." They are not accepting their studenthood. You go on this journey whether you go alone or accompanied. You go with whatever financial resources you have. You begin where you are. If you add on demands and requirements, you will stop yourself. You go forth because you must go forth, whether or not you have marriage or financial security. Most people want these things, but you must go forth not knowing whether they will be for you or not. This requires courage. This is a demonstration of self-respect. This gives you real integrity. This opens up your ability to learn. If you have been listening and considering the many things that I am presenting in these discourses, you will recognize how important this is.

I am not saying that what you want is wrong. I am saying don't be committed to getting it. Only be committed to learning

Wisdom and reclaiming Knowledge. If you do that, then all that you need will be given to you — not necessarily all that you want, but all that you need. This is the basis for happiness and fulfillment.

Look about you in the world. Some people are getting what they want, and many others are not getting what they want. For those who are getting what they want, their happiness and satisfaction are momentary and fleeting. Those who are not getting what they want are in constant complaint and turmoil. The winners and the losers here are not that different in that neither have satisfied their real needs and requirements in life. Those who are committed to getting the money, getting the relationship, getting the position, securing the pleasures — they are investing very poorly. They are everywhere. You can observe them. Are they demonstrating the qualities that you hold to be most valuable? Are they demonstrating a life that is inspiring, that is based upon contribution? Are they discovering their own worth through the contribution of their gifts?

Do not condemn them; observe them. They are living in disappointment. They are having what other people are wanting and it is not enough. But it is difficult for them to break away because they have invested so much, and they are still hopeful that the next experience or the next acquisition will somehow relieve them of their disappointment and the sense that what they have given themselves to is without merit.

Students of Knowledge become attentive and observant within and without. They learn this because it is necessary. They seek a deeper direction, and they must patiently wait for this to emerge. In fact, it is often the waiting that is most important for their development. If you can learn to wait, you can learn to trust. If you can learn to trust, you can learn to observe. If you can learn to observe, you can learn to recognize things. This is a very important part of your education.

Much of what I am saying in these discourses is actually beyond your comprehension and your understanding. Do not try to merely understand it, for if you do that, you will think you understand it, but you will not. Or if you cannot understand it, you may tend to dismiss it or condemn it or condemn yourself. I am not asking you to understand what I mean when I say that the world is emerging into the Greater Community. I am not asking you to understand what I mean when I speak of the Forces of Dissonance and the Forces of Good, The Way of Knowledge or the development of discernment and discretion, courage and compassion. Given where you are, you cannot fully understand these things.

Accept this. If you do, you will have a real starting point in your learning. I am not asking you to understand. I am asking you to learn. Become a student. If you really want to learn what these things mean, for the world and for yourself, if you want to learn and discover who sent you here and what you were given to provide, if you want to learn to discern your nature and to learn to work with it wisely and effectively, then become a student. I offer a greater body of Wisdom and a greater challenge. An observer or a critic or a dabbler will not be able to benefit from this. But those who accept their studenthood in life and take this position constantly and maintain it will be the ones who will be able to achieve the state of mind where all of these things become obvious.

To see what I see and to know what I know you must have my vantage point, and you must have the clarity of mind that I have had to acquire. To do this you must become a student. Even I am a student. Mastery here is relative. Even the masters are students of greater mastery.

Be a student and you will learn and you will know and you will be able to act. Anything less than this will leave you outside the realm of true discovery. Yet the opportunity is yours, an opportunity that you can now receive.

When people
are devoted,
they give their
lives to things.
It is not a
sacrifice to do that.
It would be a
greater sacrifice
not to.

Twenty-one

DEVOTION & COMMITMENT

DEVOTION AND COMMITMENT can truly arise when you recognize that a relationship is intrinsic rather than created. You have done nothing to establish it. It is not based on a past life. It is based on recognition that was established before you entered this world, and now it has been regained through recognition with another person. This recognition fosters devotion, which is an expression of love and companionship. It fosters true commitment, which is an expression of your purpose together now.

You may well ask, "How can there be commitment without obligation? How can there be devotion without personal loss?" The answer to these questions is very basic but not obvious or easy to discern. You have devotion and commitment without loss because you are committed to Knowledge together. It is not your ideas about Knowledge. It is Knowledge itself. It is a shared experience. You cannot have this with whomever you like. It can only arise with certain individuals at certain stages of your development.

Appreciation of others is warranted, but devotion represents a far greater participation. It is the pinnacle of relationships between individuals. It is the highest expression of relationship with another person. It holds a great promise, yet it is feared by those who do not experience it. Devotion is not given by attempting to use another to fulfill your ambitions and desires. Devotion is a natural outpouring of your True Self. It cares not for success or loss.

Sooner or later you must discover devotion. It is inherent in the raising of children, yet it has a greater role than even this, for you may not be intrinsically related to your own offspring. That is one reason why parents and children fight. Intrinsic relationship is established beyond this world. It can only be recognized, and once recognized it is supported through your commitment to its purpose. We must bring devotion and commitment into the right order or you will not understand our meaning.

Devotion is not something you can try to have. It is something that moves you. It is not a virtue that you attempt. It is something that moves you. Knowledge is not ideas. It moves you. It is force within your life. Something is moving you. You do not know what it is. You are afraid of it perhaps because it has such tremendous power, and yet it is so natural to you. It is from the very heart of you, but it is moving you now. This is Knowledge expressing itself in your life. It will move you to devote yourself to another when the time is appropriate.

Your commitment, then, will simply be recognized. You do not *make* commitments. How can you make a commitment? You can only make agreements that are temporary in nature. True commitment emanates from within you. You find you must make a commitment because you *must*. It is not justified in terms of what it will give you in the immediate future. Perhaps it will raise more problems than it will solve. Perhaps temporarily it will be a tremendous inconvenience. But it is coming from within you. It is moving you. It is as if you were finding yourself and surrendering yourself all at once.

Here you are giving over your authority to a Greater Power within you. It is you, yet is greater than you. This seeming contradiction between what is you and what is greater than you must be clearly understood. I have said that your Higher Self is not a greater individual. It is part of the fabric and matrix of life operating in time and space. It is associated with a specific group, whom we call your Spiritual Family. Your Higher Self is not a greater individual. It is not a superego. It is intrinsically you, but it is you in intrinsic relationship with life. It is you without separation serving in time and space, for that is where you are. When relationship is understood at this level, devotion and commitment arise naturally. You do not need to attempt to have them, yet it may take great strength on your part to accept them.

Relationship is like life itself. You pretend until you find out what it really is. You operate on your own assumptions until you release them and discover something else. It is quite evident that people's attempts at relationship have not satisfied their difficulty with loneliness and isolation. Yet, these things can be resolved because it is God's Plan that they be undone.

People are very impatient because they are afraid, yet they want to make sure that they have everything now that they want before they decide anything important. People often ask, "Will I find a true partner for myself?" This is a very common and understandable question. "Will I have true companionship?" It is possible, but first you must seek something more important, for true companionship arises out of your purpose in life. People want everything that purpose can give but without the purpose. Therefore, they are content only with ideas. They hear our words as simply more ideas: "Now I have heard this teacher say this, but it is not the same as what that teacher says. I am very confused. I am more confused now. I do not know who to believe."

You must seek purpose first. It is intrinsic within you. That will give your relationships meaning and direction. That will produce the possibility for true union. You do not need to go looking for a partner. They will look for you, yet your activities involving your purpose will bring you to them. This is life operating now. You are working with life now and are not independent of it.

Fundamentally, it is your independence that is your problem. There is no freedom in independence. You are a castoff. What freedom is there then? You are bereft of your Spiritual Family. You are bereft of Knowledge, with only your wishes and fears to guide you. This gives rise to a very troubled world. Yet, this is not your Heritage. This is not why you have come here—to act out this lonely and barren existence. Everything you want, you know you will lose. But this is not what is intended for you.

You have within you the seed of Knowledge. It contains all of the Knowledge you have acquired or reclaimed so far. It also contains your specific calling in this life. It contains your ability to recognize those relationships that are intrinsic to your purpose. This is a gift. Yet, it is evident that there are not many who will seek for it. This *is* the Kingdom.

In your desire for community and partnership, you are seeking for your Spiritual Family, always. It is entirely natural for you to do this. Yet, you must seek in the ways that bring success. This happens in all worlds.

You have not come to the world only for learning. Learning is only a small part of why you are here. It is fun to be a student, but students have not yet joined with life. They are only studying things. They have not entered into the mainstream of human life. Your purpose here is to discover your Knowledge and contribute it. That is, in words, a most succinct definition. People are attempting the most dangerous and destructive involvements in the name of learning. They say, "It is a great learning experience, though tremendously painful," and so forth. That is not cause for involvement. You can only unlearn the false by accepting the true. The true is what you contain within you in your Knowledge. Knowledge is expressing itself through you in subtle ways. Periodically, it expresses itself through you in dramatic ways. It does not think like you think. It does not choose between ideas. It knows. It acts. Knowledge is instinct in intelligent life.

It is Knowledge that we advocate. It is central to all your success here. It is your greatest yearning and your greatest fear. Yet, it is so gracious in how it emanates. Its blessing to you is so evident. If you think back, you will realize how it has attempted to keep you from error and guide you towards your best option and towards your true application. It has even saved your life on occasion. It is a mysterious power, and many people attribute it to forces beyond themselves. "God came in and pulled me out of this terrible situation!" God did not do that. It is Knowledge that kept you moving forward. If you destroy your ability and your inclination to discern Knowledge, your life would begin to be over. Your Being would attempt to reach you at another time.

There are resolutions to make in relationship. That is evident. There are things to recognize. You must find out what is genuine and what is not. There are many attractions that appear to produce great stimulation but which have no content at all. There are other attractions that seem tasteless but have the power of God within them. Here learning discernment is very important. Do not attempt devotion and commitment until Knowledge directs it, or you will become dishonest. You will tell people that you are devoted and committed, but at the first test you will fall away. It is wiser then to make temporary agreements that can enable you to follow through in your plans. But devotion and commitment are far greater.

With devotion and commitment, you will be willing to do what few people will do, and you will be willing to do it with very little applause. Why? Because you must. It is this "must" that is the essence of life. People are very, very covetous of their freedom, but it has not given them anything except the opportunity to discern

Knowledge.

When we speak of Knowledge within the individual, we speak of this essential drive. It is not compulsive. It is not based on fear. It is deep. It is consistent. It does not discuss things. With this, you become alive. This is when life is active within you. This is where devotion and commitment come from. You do not devote yourself because it is a good thing to do or because you will look more spiritual or because if you don't do it, you won't get what you want. You do not devote yourself to keep others happy with you. You do not devote yourself for self-gratification of any kind. You devote yourself because you *must*. That is all. Explanations are secondary now. It is entirely natural. It would be unnatural not to do it. This is where recognition really begins.

As I have said, until you have this experience, do not play with commitment and devotion. Be a student. When people are devoted, they give their lives to things. It is not a sacrifice to do that. It would be a greater sacrifice not to. Therefore, this quality of devotion is quite unique. You will not see it expressed frequently. Where it exists, there will be great anxiety amongst observers. And there will be great inspiration as well.

Devotion is essential for you to be able to take your next step beyond this world. Then you will join your Spiritual Family, and your sense of devotion will enable you to carry on your next task. You see, this world is not a place where you join Ultimate Reality. It is a place where you prepare for the next step. That is why we do not advocate that you attempt to reach great heights in spiritual advancement. You do not know what this is. You are trying to perfect what needs to be set aside.

People who are able to be complete in this world have very simple lives. They are simple inside. Their lives may seem daring and bold to others, yet there is a gracious simplicity. They are now able to serve the world, for they do not need to take anything from it. Their desire for service and their nourishment from service enable them to join the Teachers who serve this world. They are in a position to receive the Knowledge and graciousness of the Unseen Ones, who oversee those who serve this world.

Life does not ask you to be perfect. There are no perfect personalities, no perfect bodies. These things are transitory. Life does not require this. Therefore, do not require this of yourself. That would be very unkind. It is not asked of you. You will have to make personal adjustments in your behavior and habits, of course, but only to accommodate a true ability that is beginning to emanate from you. Then personal change is not for pride. It is for usefulness. You simply must make changes in your life in order to have a greater experience of Knowledge and to find the right expression for it. It is that simple. There is no great fanfare about it. Things that are destructive are given up because they are destructive. It is not a matter of good and bad now. It is a matter of choosing support over obstruction. This brings you into life. Here you begin to see life operating in service to *you*, both in the visible realm and beyond. You begin to feel the Spiritual Presence with you and begin to discern Presence. Your life has not yet been defined, but it is moving.

You will not know your calling in life, in most cases, until your life is well underway in service to Knowledge. It is rare that individuals will have an experience of their calling prior to this. To accept a calling in life, you must be completely available.

People say, "Well, what is this devotion you talk about? What can it give to me? I seem to be just a servant now. What is the benefit to me?" There is benefit. There is great benefit—a sense of self, a sense of direction, a sense of true association with others, a sense of well-being, a sense of continuity of life—are these not all things you seek for? Are they not fundamental to your happiness here? Life will offer you what it is intended to offer you, and you will give life what you are intended to give it if you discover Knowledge. It will take you a lifetime to do this. There is no quick and easy path, yet there are direct ways that do save you time. Devotion, then, is what you want to receive, for this speaks of your intrinsic relationship with life, which ends the idea of separation altogether.

Knowledge is the most mysterious yet the most natural thing in the world. The world does not attest to it because the world is ignorant of Knowledge. Yet, Knowledge is the only reality that you bring with you from your Ancient Home, and it will be the only reality you take away. It is the light within you.

Your intrinsic needs in this life are for true relationship, true community, true purpose and true calling. Those are your intrinsic needs. You will have them no matter who you think you are, no matter what you are trying to do or who you are trying to be. You cannot extinguish them. They are central to you. When you have received the means for answering these needs, then you will be in a position to help others do the same. Knowledge ignites Knowledge. As Knowledge is more evident in you, it will ignite others. This is an entirely natural process.

Money
is a resource
that serves your motives.
It demonstrates
what you value.

Twenty-two

MONEY

ONEY IS A SUBJECT that is on most people's minds. It is a subject that will naturally arise when you consider attempting something of greater importance and magnitude in life. So, what about money?

First of all, as with everything else, you must gain a new relationship with this resource and learn to treat it as a resource. In order to have a new relationship with yourself and with life, you must re-evaluate your relationship with many important specific elements that make up your practical existence in the world — your relationship with love, your relationship with friends, your relationship with your mind and your body and your relationship with money.

Money is a fact of your life; you cannot escape it. You will have to contend with it at least to some degree, even if you assume a very ascetic existence. It is a practical necessity in your life. It presents its own problems, many of which you can avoid and some of which are unavoidable. Money is a resource to which people give great meaning and significance.

Money, then, is not the problem. It is the use of money. Here you must look at your motives, your nature and your preparation. Your motives with money will determine how you perceive it, what qualities you attribute to it, how you arrange it in the priorities of your life and what you attempt to do with it. Your nature will determine your predispositions and will color to a very great degree how you perceive money and what role you feel it will play and should play in your life. Your preparation is very important because this will determine how mature you are in your dealing with this resource and how and for what purpose you attempt to use it.

Therefore, there is your motive, there is your nature and there is your preparation. The more prepared you are and the further advanced you are in The Way of Knowledge, the more you will use money as a resource and not attempt to use it to build your survival or well-being, your position in society or any advantages you are seeking to claim over others.

Here we come back again to motive. To look at money, you must look at yourself and ask some very important questions. In fact, eventually you will have to ask the most important questions, which are, "Why am I here? What do I serve? What do I have to give?" and "What do I want to communicate?" Until you reach these fundamental questions about your life, you will use money for a mixture of reasons, which will make your perception and understanding of it very confusing, and at times even contradictory. You will use it for survival; you will use it for pleasure; you will use it to impress others; you will use it to acquire things; you will use it to get rid of things. Money is a resource that serves your motives. It demonstrates what you value.

Some people make great claims about the meaning and value of money. Others deny it altogether, thinking that it is an evil substance, something that corrupts or leads one astray, entangling one in dangerous and unfortunate circumstances. Money is given magical powers by some and demonic powers by others. Some consider it to be a divine substance; others consider it to be something that can only corrupt a person's well-being and integrity.

However, money is not the problem, for money is merely a

means of conveyance to carry out what one values and what one intends to do in life. Here it is the nature of the individuals and their own maturity that will determine their motives and what they value. Money will be used to serve this. It is wise, then, to consider money to be a neutral substance, at least as far as you are concerned. Here you must understand what values you place upon it. You cannot simply claim, "Money is neutral." You must understand how you view it presently and undertake to change this view by withdrawing the significance that was formerly given to it and by recognizing money as an important resource that can be used for a variety of purposes.

Now, an important thing to remember here is that other people will continue to give money an inordinate amount of significance and attribute great powers to it, either divine or demonic. Therefore, even if you consider money to be a neutral substance, you must recognize that the rest of the world does not, and you will have to deal with it with great care and consideration. Money represents power in the world. It is a power that has claimed many lives and will continue to do so. Therefore, even if you feel that your relationship with money has finally reached a basis of true understanding, you will still have to deal with it very carefully in the world.

Money is an important resource because it can fuel the accomplishment of many valuable things. Therefore, it is unwise to think that it is meaningless or without merit. Again, it is in whose hands it is placed, what purpose it serves and what values it demonstrates that are the important considerations. You will need it to accomplish anything. You will need it to provide for yourself because money is a means of conveyance for what is needed to live in the world. It is meant to be given and received.

Therefore, when we speak about money, we are addressing a very confused and entangled subject fraught with a great deal of significance that is attributed to it — tremendous fear, misunderstand-ing, desires and ambitions. Some of these associations are recognized and acknowledged while others are secretive and cast their influ-ence without an individual's recognition. It is not a simple subject. In many ways, money represents the confusion of mind that is the causative agent and the natural by-product of much of the suffering and misery in the world. It is the result of people living without Knowledge.

When we speak of your relationship with money, we are speaking about your condition of life. We are talking about your motives, which represent what you value and what you are try-ing to do. This is all based upon who you think you are and what you think you must do in life to secure well-being for yourself. So, when we speak of money, we speak of you in the deepest kind of way.

Re-evaluating your relationship with money is a process of introspection and self-analysis. If this can be carried out without condemnation and as objectively as possible, great insight can be derived and an important understanding can be established that will enable you to deal far more wisely with yourself, with the necessary resources in life, such as money, and with other people's approach to you.

Now I will give some general ideas about how to utilize money effectively. The starting point here is to recreate your rela-tionship with money. For this, you need to know where you stand with it currently. Your understanding of this must be based upon a very honest evaluation. In other words, you must recognize how you really stand with it — not how you want to stand with it or how you think you should stand with it, but how you really stand with it. If there is fear and anxiety surrounding money, this must be acknowledged. If you are greedy or selfish with money, this must be acknowledged. If you avoid money and do not want to deal with it, thinking it is too powerful or too confusing, this must be acknowledged. Here you must have a realistic starting point. Otherwise, you cannot proceed. You cannot re-evaluate anything unless you know your current position and use this as a starting point.

Now, for most people, too much or too little money is not good. Remember, money is a resource. If you have too little of it, you are always in need of it and it gains too much significance in your life. If you have too much of it, then you spend your life protecting it, managing it and keeping it away from other people. Indeed, in this situation, other people's approach to money is a constant interference and can endanger your life and make money far more of a burden than it would be otherwise. That is why the rich are generally dominated by their relationship with money. Yet, the poor are also dominated by their relationship with money.

Here it is important that one seek to develop a meaningful balance. How much is enough? What degree of ownership of money will enable it to be a useful resource without becoming a dominating influence? Here you must determine what you know rather than what you want. If you can follow what you know, this will give you real insight and will balance your relationship with money. What you want here will always exceed your needs. Much of what people want is based upon their present fear of loss, their past experience of loss and their anxieties about future loss. They want to buffer themselves against the harsh reality of life at the expense of their Knowledge, their sense of themselves and their honesty.

Therefore, the first fundamental question to ask yourself is, "Where do I stand in my relationship with money at this moment?" To answer this question, you need to review your past experiences and to view yourself with as much objectivity as possible. Here you will need to ask yourself, "What meaning do I give money? What purpose does money serve for me? How can I use money effectively to support myself and to contribute to the world?" This is all part of the question, "Where do I stand in my relationship with money at this moment?"

The second important question to ask yourself is, "How much money do I really need?" To be able to respond to this question effectively, you must have a deeper sense and experience of knowing within yourself. Otherwise, your wants will dictate the answer and once again you will be bound to try to fulfill your goals and expectations based upon your desires, which will once again set you in the wrong relationship with money.

How much is enough? If you seriously take on this question, you must go to the third important question, which is, "What am I trying to accomplish?" This, of course, is a very important question. In fact, it is one of the essential questions. "What am I trying to accomplish?" The answer to this question will determine how much money you need and what kind of relationship with money you will have to have. Some people need very little money to carry out their real contribution in the world, just enough to keep them alive — food, shelter, clothing, a little bit for recreation and a little bit for the future. They don't need a great deal. Others will need more. Perhaps they are going to raise a family. Perhaps they are going to start some kind of business enterprise. Perhaps they are going to become an advocate for something important in the world. Their need for money here is greater, for they must provide for other people. They must provide for their business establishment. Or they must provide for their advocacy in the world.

The range of need can vary considerably. If you are trying to raise money for an important activity in life to support a mission or an advocacy, then you may need far more than you would personally require, yet you do not want to be encumbered by money. Therefore, the personal requirement for money varies greatly, even for those who are learning to live a real and genuine life.

When you ask the question, "What am I trying to accomplish?" you must always realize that the answer to this question is something that will develop and change. But your answer must be solid enough that you can stand upon it and use it as a reference. It must be a foundation, even as it evolves and changes through the process of your life. It cannot merely be a form of speculation, a set of hopeful fantasies or some magnificent personal goals. It must be something very solid.

Again, you have to assess where you are now. If you establish that you are going to do something that is far beyond your reach and current preparation, then your assessment of what you are trying to accomplish will not be useful to you. Therefore, the answer to this question should reflect where you are now and what you are doing now. Perhaps you are working towards something greater that you understand or, as is often the case, something that you don't understand. But you still are where you are now, and you have a set of problems to solve in life now. The things you know you must do, some of which you are doing and some of which you are neglecting or denying, are what you have to do now. So, this is not an ultimate question that only the future can answer. It is a practical question for now.

Determining what you must accomplish will help you to determine what your motives are. If you recreate your motives based upon this understanding, then you will be able to recast your relationship with money. People always have motives, but they are rarely responsible for their creation. They just accept them from the environment around them. They absorb them from the cultural values that they share with others. They go along with what everyone else thinks and wants and what everyone else is trying to be, do and have, and so forth. Here you have an opportunity to re-establish your definition of yourself based upon what is known and what is real for you.

Money is a resource to serve a purpose. What is the purpose
it is serving? Well, you may say that money is necessary to live in
the world. You have to eat and have shelter and have clothes. Yes,
but this does not account for a great deal of people's investment and
involvement with earning, protecting and spending money. You
could live a very simple life, have enough to eat, have adequate
shelter, good clothing, and a little leftover. People around the world
are living on a fraction of what you are living on. And many of
them are not suffering for it. But when you want to be more than
you are, then it becomes an emphasis of constantly having more and
acquiring more, and then you feel that you have to protect what
you have already, and you have to maintain it. That requires more
and more money. So, having more becomes an ever-increasing emphasis, and money becomes a greater and darker burden and shadow
for you.

Even the rich sometimes feel they can barely keep up with
things financially. Their expenditures are so great that they have to
work harder and spend more time protecting their money, more
time investing it, securing it and preventing its loss or dissipation.
But for a purely subsistence, survival level, you need very little
money. This is obvious when you think about it, but then you may
say, "I would not be happy living such a simple life." Many people
will say that. But I say, why not? What are you trying to accomplish? Do you simply want to be more comfortable, have more
personal diversions, have more things to play with, always have a
bigger house or better house, more clothes? More, more, more.
Here money becomes a great burden for you, and you cannot use it
objectively. It is feeding a set of desires, ambitions and self-imposed
requirements that may have little to do with why you are in the
world or what you are really trying to accomplish.

Some people go hot and cold in their relationship with money.
They get hot with it, and they want to have it, and they are going

to earn it, and they are going to secure it, and they are going to make a lot of it, and it is going to work for them, and they have it all figured out. Then they begin to realize over time that the investment is consuming more and more of their attention, their energy, their focus, their well-being and their time. It is eroding their relationships. It is dominating their focus and priorities. Then, they turn away from money saying, "I am going to do something very different." So, they try to live without money or they deny it. But this is how a person tries to reposition himself or herself with something that has become an addiction. Look at the behavior of the person engaged in addiction. They are going hot and cold with their addiction. They are giving themselves to it with all kinds of explanations and justifications, and then they are denying it and claiming that they are going to free themselves. Then they say, "Oh, I can't do it. Why bother?" And they give in once again.

Money is a tool. Beyond meeting basic survival needs, it is a tool. What purpose does it serve? What are you trying to accomplish with it? Here you must not only look at your own goals, priorities and values, you must look at what the world is requiring. If you are sincerely seeking to realize a greater purpose in life, do not look to yourself alone. Look to yourself and to the world. The world says, "I need this, and I need this, and I need this." Which need can you fulfill? Indeed, it takes the recognition of real need and suffering in the world to bring people out of their intoxication with what they want and what they don't want — their self-absorption.

It sometimes takes a very rude awakening. Either something very powerful happens to you that shakes you out of this dream state you live in regarding what you want and what you must have and all this, or you become engaged with someone whose needs are so real and so much more genuine than yours that it shakes you out of this fog. This dream state is really a form of intoxication. For example, you might be considering buying your next pleasurable object or a new wardrobe of clothes or a new car, and then you meet someone who needs money for food or who has a medical problem that they cannot attend to because they do not have the financial resources. Their need is so much more legitimate and real and compelling than yours. You are spending a fortune on trivia, and they need money for basic and important things. It takes this kind of encounter with life to shake you out of your own self-absorption and to make you feel like you have something important to give.

People who are only committed to their self-gratification are so profoundly unhappy and so driven and so addicted that though they can demonstrate beauty, power, influence and sophistication, as human beings they are really pathetic. They have invested in that which cannot yield anything of real merit for them or for others.

The question here is not whether one has money or not. The question is, "Is money serving a real need? Is money being a useful resource?" Look at your society. The youth want money for fun and play. The elderly want money to meet their great medical needs and, if they can afford it, more fun and play. There is all this emphasis on fun and play.

So, when we deal with money, we deal with purpose. When we deal with purpose, we deal with what people value and what people are aware of. Bringing people back into a real engagement with life, renewing their sense that they are here to contribute something, to give something of value and to leave an important legacy — that is the emphasis. Unless that is the emphasis, money will be a problem and not a solution. Money will be a god or a demon, a curse or a benediction. It will be imbued with magical and mystical powers, and people will be profoundly confused about what it is and what can be done with it.

Your needs are small. The world's needs are great. When you come to this realization, then you will be in a position to give and to recognize what you have to give. It will be pulled out of you. Instead of going through life asking, "Who am I? What do I want? How can I be happy? What should I do? What shouldn't I do?" you become a person who looks into the world and says, "I can't do this, but I can do that. I feel I can help here. I can do something meaningful here."

Do you want to experience real spirituality? Do you want to have meaningful relationships? Do you want to have a sense of direction in life? Do you want to have a sense of your own value? Then contribution must be your emphasis. Sickness in the mind is born of self-absorption. It is born of selfishness. When money serves this, it is part of the affliction. You only have to look about you to see the myriad demonstrations of this. Everyone is trying to have more, and yet they are feeling miserable, afraid to be with themselves, afraid to be with anyone else, afraid of stillness, afraid of silence, afraid of intimacy, and driven to have more and more and more, far beyond their legitimate needs.

In many of the discourses in this book, I have spoken of the condition of the world—what is changing in the world and the greater influences that are at work in the world today, which are determining the world's evolution and are governing its overall direction. You cannot entertain these things if you are still entrenched in your own self—your wants, your needs, your fears. The answer is not there. The answer is to re-engage with life, with Wisdom, with Knowledge, with inner direction. Many people lose themselves in the affairs of the world, and this is common as well. This is not what I am speaking of. You must do your inner work and you must do your outer work. At a certain point, you cannot do any more inner work, so you must do your outer work. This means that you find a real need in the world and you work on meeting it.

As I have illustrated the greater movement of the world, you must come to realize that its needs are tremendous. People ask,

"What is my calling?" and I say, "Look at the world." They ask, "What is my purpose?" and I say, "Look at the world!" With big eyes! Not fearfully or fancifully, but with big eyes! Consider the world's emergence into the Greater Community. Consider the need to reclaim the environment. Consider the immersion of cultures into one another. Consider all of the great and compelling needs of society. Which calls to you?

If you want to lose yourself in luxuries and pleasures, you will find no relief. Along with this, there will be guilt because you are wasting a great resource in the world. It is all right to have pleasure; it is all right to do fun things. But keep your sense of responsibility. You are here to contribute to the world. The world is not here to pamper you and make you secure. You will die. So, what are you going to do to make this life a meaningful experience? Have more fun? Take more vacations? Buy more things? If you think that that will meet your need, then go spend time with people who have more than you do. If you do this, you will certainly be convinced that this is not the way.

In nature, everything is useful. Nothing is wasted. Everything contributes to everything else. Nothing is squandered. Learn from your natural world. Re-engage with it. You will see. All creatures need certain things for their survival and well-being. But you do not see them laying up great treasures for themselves. All creatures in the world are vulnerable in the world. Beyond their protective instincts and the shelters they may provide for themselves, they are vulnerable to the world. They are engaged in the world.

Do not get lost in the idea that money is good or money is bad or that pleasure is good or pleasure is bad. This will always lead you astray. Come back to ask, "What must I do?" Here you look at your natural inclinations. You assess your natural abilities, and you look at the needs of the world. You will need to do very simple specific things, perhaps not seemingly related but still contributing and necessary to the world's emergence into the Greater Community and the unification of human society. Find your role and fulfill it and you will find your fulfillment. There is no other way. If you want to know your value and your gift and your nature, this is the way. Trying to seek transcendental experiences to get out of the world, to get back to God, is not the way. God sent you here to do something, and yet you want to get back to God!

Being in the world is not simply being in a prison from which you must find an escape. You will not be in the world very long, so your escape is guaranteed. You are not sent here forever. You have come from someplace and are returning to someplace very different from the world. So, your escape is guaranteed. But can you have a sense of your Ancient Home while you are here?

The person who is healed is the one who gives and finds a place to give. If you know you have to give and have trouble finding a place to give, then start giving to something or someone that needs what you have. It does not have to be the ultimate place where you will give, but it is a starting point. You learn your gift by giving. You do not wait until the ultimate situation comes around, and then maybe you will give if it does not cost too much. You start giving now. There is no relief for neurosis or selfishness other than this. Here you do not give for your glory, even for your spiritual redemption. You give because you are needed. And you will find that place where you are genuinely needed and where you can genuinely give.

In the future, which will be your future, the needs of the world will become greater and more compelling and people will be forced to share the world's resources with each other far more than they do now. They will be forced to share their heritage and what they know with each other. The rich will become poorer and the poor will need a great deal more. Many of the great inequities that you see now concerning people's affluence will be balanced out because the resources will be diminished and the population will be greater. It will become increasingly inappropriate to have great personal wealth. Unless your role in life is to be a benefactor and you end up giving most of it away, it is inappropriate and will become increasingly so.

Remember, giving is not giving up. Giving is directing your resources and your attention to something that needs you. This is what produces well-being and advancement, and your giving will far exceed the specific need to which it is directed. It will enhance the mental environment. It will cast a wave of inspiration on others to give and to escape from their own tragedies.

The future that is your future will require more and more of you. This is good for you, though it will not be good for humanity if this need goes unmet. But it is good for you. It offers you the real possibility to redeem your true value, your true meaning and your true abilities. Your future means you will not be able to have all the things you want to have. If something you want is not appropriate, then you will know it. And if you commit yourself to it, you will carry with you a sense of guilt and irresponsibility that no one will be able to alleviate.

Having too much is as bad as having too little because you are out of balance and your relationship to life and the resources of life are not correct and require change. Being in the right relationship with money means being in the right relationship with your true objectives in life and being in the right relationship with the world around you. If you have too much, you will suffer. Likewise, if you have too little, you will suffer. Both situations require change and readjustment. Your Knowledge knows what is correct — in your relationship with money, with people and with life, and in all of the particulars that are involved within these categories. Being out of balance calls for readjustment, re-evaluation and a new application of yourself. In this light, the rich are as bad off as the poor. Yet, the poor have a greater possibility for happiness than the rich, for often the rich cannot be reached. They have given themselves much too much, and they are too indulged. Perhaps if they became extremely poor all of a sudden, they would be able to relive their life and to awaken and reassess their genuine needs.

Having too much or too little creates imbalance and requires a readjustment. Those who are wealthy and have realized the imbalance can commit themselves to giving their resources away, not to become poor but to become benefactors. The role of the rich is to be benefactors. There is no reason to become rich other than to become a benefactor. If it is your design and role in life to be a benefactor, then you will need a lot of financial resources, a small part of which you will need to carry on your own work and a small part of which you can assign to your pleasures and happiness. But the main focus in using this resource is to give to others and to enable others to give themselves. Why make those living in poverty more affluent? So that they can give! When the rich do not give, they do not set an example for this, and as a result their lives becomes decadent and self-destructive. Giving is what inspires people, and there must be many great examples here. For some, giving will require tremendous education. They must achieve a tremendous practical, academic education. For others, it will require a different kind of education, a different kind of sensitivity.

Money, like intelligence, is a resource. If it is used wisely and directed properly, it can be used for a greater spiritual purpose, which will give it real meaning and value. In reality, almost everyone in the world needs to adjust their relationship with money because they need to discover why they are here and what they are trying to accomplish. The answers to these questions are not static definitions; they are a growing realization. Even if you find the truth about your current situation, you will realize that the application of truth will need to be adjusted as you go along. Perhaps your need for money will become greater; perhaps it will become less — depending on what you are working on accomplishing. If you are building a hospital or replanting a forest, you will need quite a bit of money. Here you give others the opportunity to give and to assert true value both in their giving and in what they receive. Other people will simply need to care for the sick and the dying. They may not need as much money. Some will need to counsel. Some will need to build.

There are so many examples, too numerous to mention here. But it is necessary to reaffirm the idea that money is a useful tool to serve a real purpose. If it serves an unreal purpose, it will have an unreal meaning and will be a source of confusion and disability for people. The time for self-indulgent use of money is over. The time for contribution is now. Only this can establish for you a right relationship with money, with other people and with yourself.

Therefore, money is a vehicle to express a real purpose. In this, it finds its true value. Take this opportunity, then, to assess your current needs and determine as best you can what you are working on accomplishing now. Have this be based upon Knowledge and not simply upon your wish list. Then determine your real need for money. This will determine how much you must work in the world and what you must do to secure the resources that you need. If you ask for more than you need, you will work more than you need, and your life will be out of balance as a result. Sometimes you must make money for an important project, and you must work very hard for it for a period of time. But it is worth it. The question here is not whether it is hard or easy. It is whether it is correct. Here Knowledge is your guide, for within yourself you will know. When things are not right, you will feel it. You will know. When things are correct, you will feel it. You will know. And you need to be exposed both to things that are right and things that are not right in order to have this contrast. Then you can begin to sense or feel this greater part of yourself that *knows*, this vital reference point within yourself that we call Knowledge.

You will see much that is wrong in the world. Do not condemn it. Have it teach you to reflect on Knowledge within yourself. Have what is correct inspire you. Have what is incorrect reorient you to Knowledge and bring you back to Knowledge. The world contains both what is correct and what is not correct. Both can lead you to true relationship. Having a true relationship with money is the same as having a true relationship with another and having a true relationship with yourself. If it serves a real purpose and meets a real need, then its expression will be real and its value will be confirmed. Such is the truth in relationships of all kinds.

*Wisdom is
abiding with a
Spiritual Presence
and sharing
in its perception and
understanding of life.*

Twenty-three

BECOMING WISE

W HAT DOES IT MEAN TO BECOME WISE? How do you discern Wisdom in another? What are the results of achieving this state of mind and readiness? Of course, people have many images associated with Wisdom. It is often associated with asceticism or self-sacrifice, loneliness, suffering, mystery or an inexplicable quality in others. It is often held in very high regard, but in such a way that people feel that it is quite remote from them and quite beyond their reach or grasp.

Let us, then, not approach Wisdom as an ultimate state of mind or as what people generally think of as enlightenment, as if one reaches this great threshold and arrives at a complete and fulfilled state and after that everything takes care of itself. It is important to realize that enlightenment is relative to where you stand in the overall evolution of life. There are very great thresholds in all learning, and in learning the reality of life there are great thresholds as well. There are many of them, not just one. So, let us not consider Wisdom as an ultimate achievement, but as something that you cultivate as you go along.

Therefore, it is possible for you to be wise today, if perhaps only for a few moments. It is possible for you to be wise tomorrow, if perhaps only for a few moments. This is quite valid because it is okay if you are only wise for a few moments. In fact, that is magnificent! That is a great achievement, for if you are wise for a few moments today, then perhaps you will choose Wisdom tomorrow and be wise for a few more moments.

The experience of Wisdom builds upon itself. You must have this experience in order to value it and to see how much it is in contrast with your normal state of mind. Even though Wisdom is different from insight, it should be considered in the same way. If you have a moment of real insight today or tomorrow, it is for a moment. Don't expect yourself to have an insight every single moment.

The difference between insight and Wisdom is that with insight you have an understanding of something. You penetrate the mystery of something, and you have a very brief but significant understanding of it. Wisdom deals more with your approach to life. It is more a state of mind rather than any piece of information you might gain or any understanding that you might derive from a specific situation.

Therefore, do not discount Wisdom by holding it far above you or by reserving it only for rare individuals who, given great sacrifices and a superhuman will, have achieved a magnificent height. This is not a healthy approach. Wisdom is available to you. It is available to you because Knowledge, the Great Mind, lives within you. Being with Knowledge is Wisdom. Being without Knowledge is being without Wisdom. Both give a very different experience and account of life. Both create a very different perception. The Wise see a different world from everyone else, for however long they are experiencing Wisdom. Some people are wise only a few times in their entire life. Others are wise more frequently. Fewer still are wise on a consistent basis.

The question, then, is not whether you want to be wise or not, for most people would say, "Yes, that would be wonderful." However, they would say "yes" with great trepidation and doubt, considering all that they may associate with Wisdom. The question is how often do you want to be wise? That is the more useful and practical question. Your response will be conditioned by how you view Wisdom and what you think Wisdom will do for you. Many associate Wisdom with asceticism, so they think Wisdom will deprive them of all their little pleasures, to which they give such great devotion. Or they think Wisdom will lead them into some kind of dangerous set of encounters in the world where they will be persecuted and crucified, and that does not look like a very happy outcome. So, perhaps people will say, "Not today. Some other time."

Each person needs a very small experience of Wisdom in order to learn about it. You have to learn about Wisdom. You cannot just say, "Yes, I want Wisdom!" It does not mean anything to say that unless you really want it and value it, and you will value it when you have experienced it and have seen it to be gracious and redeeming. In fact, should you pursue the study of The Greater Community Way of Knowledge, you will find over time that it is only Wisdom that will give you what you want. It is only Wisdom that will provide a real sense of certainty, true self-respect and the ability to love. It is only Wisdom that will give you the resources and the approach necessary to live your life to the fullest and to give to others in such a way that your value is emphasized and theirs is as well.

So, let us talk about experiencing moments of Wisdom. This is possible for you. This is not beyond your reach. When I say Wisdom is being with Knowledge, what I mean is that Wisdom is abiding with a Spiritual Presence and sharing in its perception and understanding of life. People are afraid of Wisdom or are ambivalent about it because they are afraid that they will want to change, not that something will change them. When you are with Wisdom, you are perceiving something of greater magnitude in life. You are waiting for that spark of truth that runs like a current through humanity, and you are opening yourself so that it may run through you, so that you may conduct it and be a terminal for its expression.

The experience of Wisdom is far beyond any pleasure that you might try to acquire for yourself in the world. It supersedes your normal range of needs. It is ecstatic. It is energizing like great electricity. It is deep and penetrating. It dispels fear. It takes you beyond the ambivalence that permeates normal thinking. It is life changing indeed, even if it is experienced momentarily, because it creates such a contrast. You know now what is possible. It is possible to have this experience! And you will come back to it.

Sometimes people have an experience of Wisdom, and it is so different. It creates such contrast and brings up such issues and questions that they seek to avoid it. They may say, "Well, it was a magnificent experience, but I don't think I want to have it again." But in time they will come back because it is natural to do that and because they will realize that all they are seeking in their other endeavors can be attained or fulfilled in this state of mind.

The experience of Wisdom is profound. But it can be confusing because it creates a tremendous contrast. Here you realize that who you thought you were perhaps isn't who you really are. What you thought the world is perhaps isn't what the world really is. This calls for a tremendous re-evaluation. Often, people do not want to undertake this. It is too uncomfortable. They would rather be secure in their current assumptions, associations and beliefs. Yet, they will, in time, come back to this, for once the great door is open a crack, you will want to open it further. You will return because it is natural for you to do so. It is the yearning of the heart rather than the anxieties of the mind that will bring you back to open the great door a little further. You want to see. You want to know. You want to be secure. You want to feel included. You want to have purpose, meaning and direction. This brings you back to Knowledge and to the experience of Wisdom, which is being with Knowledge in the world.

So, what is the experience of Wisdom like? It is so great I

can only describe it in its various aspects. No definition in words can contain it, and any words which might be used would seem so magnanimous that you would perhaps think, "Nothing could be that good. Nothing could be that wonderful." But, indeed, it is. When you are experiencing Wisdom, you are like an empty vessel through which a great power or current can flow. The mind, then, instead of being filled with its own complexities, becomes, in a sense, empty. Here you become far more observant and aware of your surroundings because your mind is free to do this rather than being embroiled in its own wants and confusion. Here there is great potency because your mind can be completely focused, and it will naturally do this. Here you enter into present time because you are not living in anxiety about the future or trying to reconcile the past, which of course cannot be reconciled.

When you are in present time and your mind is being completely focused, you will have tremendous insight. Here you can penetrate the reality of things. Here you are not seeking for answers as much as you are seeking for experience. Here you are able to exercise real stillness, which allows the mind to concentrate, and the mind will concentrate because this is one of its natural functions. Here you will be able to be with each situation as a participant and an observer. You will feel a timeless quality as if you had known this state before, but it has been so long. You won't know who you are or where you are, but you will know that you are in the correct place.

Being able to give up the need for self-definition will allow you to experience the magnitude of life in a very concentrated way. In this state, perhaps you will have insights, perhaps you will not, but the experience itself will be important and memorable. You will recall it at a later time in terms of how it felt rather than what came into your mind.

Just because you have intuitive impulses or gain insights does not mean you are experiencing Wisdom. That is a very important distinction. Wisdom is being in a certain state of mind. Here insights will come to you if it is necessary. If it is not necessary, there will be no insights.

In this state of mind there is relief from the constant attempt to get things, to have things and to understand things. This striving, which is to offset fear and anxiety, is a chronic condition in people's normal state of mind. You are given a relief from this, and a tremendous relief it is! Even if your experience of Wisdom is only for a moment, the relief is so great that you will have an experience that will be unforgettable. Here you are not asking questions, and you don't need to ask questions. When Knowledge arises in the mind, all questions cease; when Knowledge is lost in the mind, or is hidden by the mind, all questions emerge.

The experience of Wisdom is necessary to give you true insight into everything that I have said in all of these discourses. As I have said before, you will not be able to understand these things from a normal state of mind. Though much that I have said will seem sensible and meaningful, a greater comprehension must come from a greater perception and a greater capacity. Having momentary or fragmentary experiences won't be enough.

Wisdom is not something that simply happens to you periodically, though this is how many people experience it. For example, they may wake up one morning and their mind is clear and they are just present—they hear sounds, and they experience being alive in a very poignant way. This is Wisdom. And then it passes or they shake it off and go on, saying, "I had such a wonderful moment this morning. I felt so good." They don't know why they had that experience. Why did it come? Why can't it come again?

Sometimes people have a profound experience of Wisdom and they try to regain it by going back to the same place and doing the same thing, by having the same conversation or the same stimulation. But they cannot get it back. Perhaps they have a moment like this in practicing meditation, so they practice again very hard, but they cannot get it back.

Perhaps these moments seem like they just happen to you out of the blue, but indeed something is stimulating you. It is not the normal things. It is not the lovely place you were. It is not the wonderful thing you ate. It is not the charming person you were with. It is a different kind of stimulation. It is Knowledge in another stimulating Knowledge in you. Perhaps the other is not a person in physical life. Could it be a Spiritual Presence? Could it be a person on the other side of the world who entered that state, and you entered it with him or her? How can you account for this influence? How can you recreate it? You cannot. It is a great mystery how minds affect minds. Stimulation in the mental environment in its more subtle manifestations is so pervasive and complex that no one in the world could understand it.

Think of the mental environment like this: a highly-charged field through which electricity flows in a myriad of ways. Though it appears to be random and confusing, it is following natural and significant patterns in life. Or, think of it as a great electronic circuit board through which electricity flows from one thing to another in ways that are pre-established but which would seem confounding to an observer.

To fully have the experience of Wisdom, momentary and random experiences will not be enough after awhile. You will want to return to the great door and have it open further for you — not opened all at once, for that would be too much. Just a little crack at a time. You will be nourished through this experience, so after awhile you will always want to come back to it. This will lead you to seek methods of practice and preparation which will enable you to cultivate the opportunity and the receptivity for this experience to return in an increasing manner and in ways that are relevant to your current life and needs.

Sooner or later you must come to practice. Just like people who dabble with a musical instrument and, though frustrated, have moments of delight with it, sooner or later they will say to themselves, "I really want to learn to play this instrument! I like playing this instrument, but I can't play it yet." And they will seek preparation. They will not try to teach themselves if they are smart. They will seek instruction. They will seek assistance. They will seek correction.

Should you be drawn to the great mystery and beneficence of life, you too will sooner or later seek real preparation because this will give you the greatest access to Wisdom and to Knowledge. Remember, I have said that having great insights is not Wisdom, even if the insights prove to be very accurate and true. Knowledge lives within you, whether you recognize it or not, whether you can experience it or not, and whether it has any avenue of expression through you or not. It is there. It does not come and go when you come and go. It does not fade away when you are blind or preoccupied. Wisdom is learning to identify Knowledge, to receive Knowledge and to ultimately become a vehicle for its expression. This is Wisdom.

Preparation is very important, not only to enable you to achieve the state of Wisdom and to increase its presence in your life, but also to realize and to learn all that prevents the recognition and the expression of Knowledge. Unlearning here is as important as learning. Do you want to unravel the restraints and the complexities that keep you preoccupied and lost in your own thoughts? This is how you do it. This is how you begin to unravel or take apart all that keeps you fused within yourself and unable to relate to anyone or anything directly on any kind of consistent basis.

In achieving the rewards of Wisdom, you learn the essential

virtues, and you learn to recognize what prevents Wisdom in others. This is so important. You will need to know this in order to work effectively with people and to relate to them in such a way that you will be able to contribute to them and to receive their contribution as well. Here your perception will change, your understanding will change and your abilities will emerge. You will learn how to adjust your behavior and gain control over your conscious mind. You will have insight and understanding, and with these compassion as well. Compassion will emerge because you will find that the preparation is far more difficult than you thought. It is not something you learn in a weekend.

Over time, you will have compassion because you will learn that you must be compassionate with yourself. Here you learn to become a good teacher for yourself, a trusted friend, instead of a constant critic — a demanding, irritable, harsh, judgmental critic. The critic within you is eventually replaced by an abiding coun- selor, as you learn to remind yourself of the important things — patience, perseverance, openness, acceptance and the return to Knowledge. All the things that a wise counselor or teacher would tell you as you proceed, you learn to tell yourself. Here you will learn restraint, forbearance and tenderness with yourself — com- passion. These are necessary qualities. They enable you to give in the world. They enable you to establish a meaningful and work- able relationship with yourself.

Preparation creates this. You will come to preparation because sooner or later you will want to find the source of your meaning, purpose and direction. You will return to Knowledge because, like a great instinctual homecoming, it will draw you back. You will increasingly find that the pleasures of the world are momentary and tasteless for you. There is something else emerging in your life that is drawing you and calling upon you. This is natural. This is the great spiritual emergence within you. It happens very slowly and gradually so that you can receive it within your own capacity and make the proper adjustments so that you can develop your capacity over time.

The great door of life is not thrown open. It is opened very, very gradually. Why is it gradual? Because it is governed by Wisdom and by the Wise. Consider how long it took them to learn and to unlearn, to evaluate and to re-evaluate, to receive, to accept and to give. They know something about learning here. They have learned to learn, and this is part of their Wisdom. Wisdom, then, is not only being with Knowledge; it is learning to become a vehicle for Knowledge — to abide with Knowledge, to allow Knowledge to express itself through you, to join in the stillness of Knowledge and to utilize the perception of Knowledge.

Learning to do this is the great education. It is what could wisely be called Higher Education. People learn this very fearfully and falteringly at first. They are not sure they even want to learn it. It seems so strange, yet so wonderful. They are perhaps afraid that they will lose interest in the things they have given themselves to, and they are afraid of the sense of guilt and waste that must surely arise as they realize that they had formerly invested themselves poorly and ignorantly, having given their life, time, energy and resources to pursuits that had little or no value or promise. This is a very difficult thing to face, yet you will face it because you must seek that which is truly meaningful.

The pursuit of Wisdom and Knowledge is relentless. If you do not make it in this tour of duty in the world, you will certainly return again because when you go home to your Spiritual Family, you will realize that this is the only thing that matters. Once you are there, you will say to yourself, "I completely forgot myself down there. I must go back." You will come back, and you will forget yourself and once again go through the process of self-reclamation within the context of your humanity. Without the great garment of humanity, this understanding is so clear, but you must have this perception while you are in the human experience for this understanding to be an effective means of contribution here.

Therefore, Wisdom and the approach to Knowledge constitute the great education. The journey here is the essential thing. Wisdom is not just a great final reward of life. It is the ability to be with life as it is occurring, to engage with it directly and meaningfully and to be able to draw upon Knowledge that you carry within you, which previously only seemed to be an idea or a potentiality.

At a certain juncture, approaching Wisdom requires a very formal preparation. For instance, people who are practicing in *Steps to Knowledge* are preparing for Wisdom. They enter this preparation perhaps thinking they are going to get some other things — love, wealth, recognition or security. They may hope to cavort with angels and to rise above the world and escape its difficulties. But they find that the preparation is really quite different. The Way leads them in a different direction. Perhaps the mountain that they are seeking to reach is the same one that Knowledge is taking them too, but the path leads a different way. And they say, "I thought we had to go this way," but the preparation is taking them in a different direction.

You could say that the approach to Knowledge is a series of great re-evaluations, born of necessity not curiosity. These re-evaluations are necessary because you have reached a juncture where you must re-evaluate or rethink your position and your assumptions. No one is forcing you to do this. You have simply reached a place where you must do this because it is clear that you need a new position in life. You will see it, you will feel it, you will know it and it will be demonstrated in your life. These are minor thresholds, though they will seem great in the moment. They might even seem cataclysmic, but they are minor. Even though they are minor, they are necessary and are very important for you to progress.

Learning to direct the mind rather than being dominated by the mind, to use the mental environment, to use your mental resources, to use the physical environment and your physical resources rather than simply being lost in them requires a great deal of preparation. Some aspects of the preparation make great sense, while other aspects seem very confusing and inexplicable.

For example, people wonder about the emphasis on stillness. They think, "I am trying to get something done! I am trying to learn something! I am trying to acquire Knowledge. I am trying to figure things out! Why deal with stillness? Well, all right, I'll practice stillness because if I practice stillness, I'll get the answers, yes?" No, you get stillness. People don't see that stillness in itself is the reward. They think stillness is being stupid and passive. The emphasis on stillness, then, seems inexplicable. Its only value to people is that maybe if they are still, they can get what they want. They are still into getting and having and acquiring. They bring their madness to the preparation and try to use the preparation to satisfy their madness and the demands of their madness. But the preparation is such that it will relieve you of your madness, not fulfill it, for madness cannot be fulfilled. That is why it is madness.

At the outset and for quite awhile in real preparation, the students are at variance with the preparation itself. Perhaps they will go along thinking it is wonderful, but at some point they will really begin to wonder. Here people will often abandon the preparation and go seek for something new. They will say, "I am not going anywhere with this. Things are not happening for me. I need results." Then they abandon the preparation and go seek something else. What they don't understand here is that their approach to themselves, to life and to their preparation, which is all the same, is at variance with the preparation itself.

The preparation is a cure for madness. *Steps to Knowledge* is a cure for madness, the madness that everyone in the world lives with to varying degrees. Do you want to have Wisdom? You must be relieved of madness. You don't know what that will mean, what it will require or what it will be like. Here is where people have images of asceticism. "Giving up madness is living in a hut with a bowl. I certainly don't want to live like that! So, rather than seeking Wisdom, I'll just be around someone who is wise and I will be able to get my answers from them." This is ridiculous. You have not the slightest idea what life will look like when Wisdom is abiding with you consistently. You are just ambivalent about whether you want to give up the madness. You still think the madness is going to work for you and give you what you want. People are actively participating in their madness. It is not something that takes them over, like a disease they cannot shake off. They have invested in it and continue to invest in it.

The preparation for Knowledge, which seems confusing, inexplicable and perhaps undesirable, will cultivate real Wisdom because it will teach you what Knowledge is and how to abide with it. It is not here to give you what you want. It is here to give you what you know. You are not sure that what you know is what you want, so this must be demonstrated and proven to you over time. This requires a long preparation.

Your madness is engendered by wanting something that you do not know and that you do not really want. This is the madness of the world. This is what keeps all of humanity in a state of prolonged misery. Part of the suffering of being in the world is in living a physical life where death and harm are very present and possible. Yet, the vast majority of human suffering is in the mind. This is madness. Facing this madness will lead you to ask greater questions and seek greater relief. Seeking relief is part of what motivates you towards Knowledge. But this cannot be your only motivation, for you must also seek, at least according to your current understanding, what Knowledge possesses.

You cannot escape into Knowledge because Knowledge will bring you back into life. You cannot seek only comfort in Knowledge because Knowledge requires change and work. You cannot seek only confirmation in Knowledge because Knowledge recognizes something else in you than that which you are seeking to have confirmed. Knowledge is not a holiday. Knowledge is bringing you into the world and teaching you how to be in the world wisely.

You learn to be still because stillness enables you to know things, to penetrate things through your perception and to assimilate things as well. It gives you the presence of mind to recognize that which is beneficial and that which is not, and it does this without condemnation. Stillness gives you the freedom to have peace, but it also gives you the potency for action. Here you are reserving your mental resources and energy. Knowledge is like the archer who exerts effort in pulling back the bow so that when the moment to release the arrow comes, it has real power and direction.

Therefore, as you learn how Knowledge functions, you are able to abide with it and to express it in the world. This is Wisdom. Wisdom is not having all the answers, like the wise man on top of the mountain. The man and woman of Knowledge at any moment may not have any answers for anyone, but they are having an experience that is beyond the seeming reach of everyone around them. Possessing Wisdom does not mean that you are happy all the time, for you will indeed experience the suffering of the world very sharply at times.

With Wisdom, you are always giving. You realize you do not understand how you give, although you do understand certain things you can do where giving can occur, and you will be inclined to do those things. But how giving functions through you is a mystery and a gracious experience.

Leisure and
pleasure are
the natural benefits
of a life
that is meaningful
and full of work.

Twenty-four

WORK

ORK IS THE ESSENTIAL ACTIVITY OF LIFE. What you do for work, who you work with and for what purpose you work determine the essential value that you will experience in life. Work is natural. It is necessary, and it is the foundation of your existence here. To think otherwise is to miss the point about life. It is to misunderstand your purpose for coming here, the value that you bring with you and the opportunity for relationship that your work provides for you.

Just because most people do not find value in their employment does not mean that it is not the source of great meaning in their lives. But to understand work, one must have a sense of having a greater purpose, and one must bring into right order many things that constitute the essential elements of living here.

There is much that you would be able to learn from your neighbors in the Greater Community since they have traveled far beyond the stage that humanity is in at this time. They could give you an idea of what is up ahead and what will be expected of you in the future.

Work, like most other things that are natural and fundamental, has been greatly misconstrued and, therefore, misapplied here. Work is seen in your culture primarily as a way of making money to provide for essential needs, and beyond the provision of essential needs, money is used for personal enhancements. But what is work really if it is merely a way of collecting income? Not much is expected of it here in terms of real value and meaning. Of course, people hope that their pursuit of money will be meaningful because it requires so much of their time and energy. But in essence work fulfills a greater purpose and a greater need as well.

Let us start at the beginning. The beginning is this: You were sent to the world to work. The world is a place of work. Work is the natural activity of life. Work is the focal point for your relationships. When I say work, I do not simply mean earning enough money to get by or earning enough money to enrich yourself with personal enhancements. I am talking about the essential activity of life that provides the meaning for your existence, the justification for your past learning and the foundation for your meaningful relationships. It would be accurate to say that purpose and work are the same. When you ask, "What is my purpose?" you are really asking, "What is my work?" If you do not include work in your idea of purpose, then your idea of purpose is pure speculation and won't yield anything of real value. People think that their purpose has to do with their identity, but this is not accurate either. Your true identity transcends your work activity in the world. Though your work activity will define your role in the world, your true identity is something beyond this altogether.

Therefore, we must place work in a larger sphere. Your work is not simply doing one thing. Your work is all of your productive activity in life. Everything that you enjoy and rely upon is a product of work. If work is done with a larger idea in mind and a greater purpose to serve, then its value will extend far beyond the products, services and results of the effort itself.

It is true to say that in recent generations people have been losing their ability to work. They are losing the value of work because there is so much pleasure and so much leisure time for so many people now. In this, there is a great misfortune. Because your work requires so much from you, it cultivates you. It enhances you. It demands things of you. It places responsibilities on your shoulders. It provides balance, structure and the opportunity for greater meaning. If these are avoided or neglected, the results will truly be pathetic — anger, depression, chronic confusion, self-denial and self-abuse. All these are the result of not responding to a call for work in the world and not fulfilling that response.

Many people do not work; others work and are very unhappy. Therefore, to gain a greater sense of what work means, we must put it in a larger context. Work is not simply what you do to get by to earn enough money to meet whatever needs you define to be necessary and important for yourself. Work is what you are here to do. It includes great activities, but it is largely made up of small activities — mundane things that have to be done every day, simple tasks that once fulfilled give you the opportunity to do greater things in service to humanity.

What is your real work in the world? Well, to find your real work you must go through a long process of refinement, for it is the same as asking, "What is my real purpose?" Can I tell you your purpose by a simple definition? Well, yes, I can, but it will not mean that much to you until you are in a position to experience it, apply it and live its reality.

To gain access to your real work, or your real purpose, you must begin to value work itself and to build upon what you do today in order to expand it and to broaden its scope and application. To simply go to a job and endure it and then come home to rest and recreate will not bring you to the great realization of what you are here to do and what you are equipped to contribute.

It is true that following The Greater Community Way of Knowledge brings you to your true work, but it does so gradually, stage by stage. Likewise, it brings you to your true purpose, but it does so stage by stage. You see, having a greater purpose or greater work is not simply taking on more work responsibilities. It is having a larger understanding of what your work is and what it can do and then being able to bring into balance all the important components of your life — your health, your financial responsibilities, your primary relationships and your spiritual development. These are the Four Pillars of successful existence here.

The fact that most people can only focus on one pillar to the exclusion of the others is quite evident. Occasionally, you will see someone who can do two of the four, but that seems rare. Beyond this, it is a rare individual indeed who can be competent in all four of these areas. By competent, I do not mean that they are expert. I mean that they are competent. Competent means that they can carry out things, progress and maintain something beyond their own personal needs. This is all the result of work. Relationships require work. Gaining financial stability requires work. Proper health maintenance requires work. Spiritual development requires work. If insufficient effort is expended in any of these areas, the results will fall far short of what they are intended to be.

You might ask now, "Does this mean I have to work all the time?" The answer is yes, you will be working all the time, with periods of rest and carefree enjoyment sprinkled here and there. The rest is all work. You have a long time to rest when you leave this world and return to your Spiritual Family. In the interim you are here to work, to accomplish tasks, to complete things and to develop as a worker and contributor to life.

If you think about what I am saying, you will realize that it is absolutely true. Everything that you see around you has been the product of people's efforts — the product of their work. Let us say here that work is a combination of effort, direction and determination. If you focus on achieving something, you aim yourself in a certain direction so that achievement can be made. You expend effort consistently. You learn, you make mistakes, you grow, you change and you re-evaluate all along the way. It is all a process of work.

A leisure society is a society that is dying. And, indeed, much of the decadence that you see in your culture here is directly attributable to the emphasis on leisure and pleasure. Leisure and pleasure are natural benefits of a life that is meaningful and filled with work. Work hard and you will enjoy your leisure. If you do not work hard, your leisure will seem like a weight upon you, something that you do not want to lose but which gives you little or no value within itself.

There is satisfaction with accomplishment. There is satisfaction in relationships that are geared towards accomplishment. The fact that these values have been eroded or are associated with earlier times or with old ideas is truly unfortunate. It means that people are requiring more from life but are diminishing the very thing that will give them what they want. People want more leisure and more pleasure, but they are cutting out the very thing that vitalizes them, that keeps them awake, aware and moving. You did not come to the world to fall asleep by the side of the road. Life is not a beach. Life is a project and a process with all the Mystery and manifestation built in.

When you think of work, think of what you must do to maintain financial stability, to maintain your primary relationships which require time and effort, to maintain adequate health so that your body can serve you and to further your spiritual growth. All of these require work. They require effort, direction and determination. This does not leave a lot of time for confusion or ambivalence or wandering around aimlessly. Now you do not have time for things that only frustrate and confuse you because you have a greater set of needs, and these provide definition for you and give your life direction.

Every activity that is meaningful is a form of work. Developing stillness is work. Here effort is extended to produce a state of mind where there is no effort, yet it is work nonetheless. We refer to having faith in Knowledge and the study of *Steps to Knowledge* as "the work." People say they are involved with the work because it *is* work. People have difficulty with practice and often give up far too soon because they are not accustomed to work. They think the work is to be a pleasure, a refuge and a retreat from life — time off. The Way of Knowledge is not a beach. It is not a refuge. It is work. It is choosing a direction to which you apply yourself with determination. In this, you become aware of what you need to work on in your life, and you begin to work on these things.

Now, let me give you a very important distinction. Many people think that they must work on themselves to change, correct or improve themselves. This idea is correct but only in a certain way. You must work on yourself but only insofar as it enables you to work on the Four Pillars that I have mentioned. To work on yourself for any other reason is meaningless. In fact, it is an escape from work. To be able to work on developing financial stability, adequate health, primary relationships and spiritual growth—that is the work! You make corrections within yourself and you analyze yourself only insofar as it enables you to participate actively in these areas.

The only value of personal retreat is so that you can learn to work better. But in fact, people use retreat in order to try to improve themselves. You cannot improve yourself. You can only give yourself to something. There is no self-improvement that can be the focus of your life. You will be improved as your work becomes better — more complete, more effective, more nurturing to others and more meaningful to you. The only work you do on yourself is to enable you to work in the world. Trying to improve your personality or arrest unwanted habits or behaviors will not lead to success.

Life will purify you if you involve yourself with it correctly. You do not purify yourself so that you can be involved in life, for in this you have taken yourself out of life and are attempting to do for yourself what only life itself can do for you.

Let us say that you receive what you give in life. This is a familiar idea, but if you apply it within this larger context, you will see how true it is. If you work very little and give very little of yourself, if there is very little devotion in your life to anything beyond fulfilling your own personal desires, you will feel empty, and no amount of new stimulation or pleasure or relationship or excitement will offset the terrible emptiness that haunts you. People who find meaning are people who find an engagement in the world where they are needed. When you realize you are needed for something, this provides meaning and value to your life. In the world, your life does not have meaning apart from your work. To proclaim that you have a universal meaning regardless of what you do is in fact a meaningless exercise because it does not enable you to justify why you have come into the world. To say, "I am a Divine Being no matter what I do or where I go," will not offset the gnawing sense that you must respond to something important and give yourself to it.

When we talk about our work, we talk about our shared endeavor. It is not only for your personal fulfillment; it is to enable you to give something to the world. Now, the world does not necessarily want what you may want to give. What the world wants is what the world needs from you. Let us say this in different words. People think that their great work is what they want to give, so then they try to figure out what they want to give. Here they get all tied up with themselves trying to figure out if they want this or if they want that, what will give more pleasure, what they really want.

This is not the way. Find out where you are needed and give there. And if you have found the right place, you will give more than you had planned to give, and you will receive more than you had planned to receive. What you may end up giving may not at all resemble what you thought you had wanted to do. That is why the path of personal fulfillment is the path of darkness. You will never be able to fulfill yourself. You will never be able to have enough pleasure, delight, sensation, recognition, appreciation, glory, fame — whatever you might want to call it. You will never have enough. In fact, this is really a desperate attempt to offset the pain of emptiness and the pain of isolation.

When you put yourself in a position to give, and it is the correct position and the correct situation, you will give. And you will find that you have to give much more than you had planned, without guarantees of fame, glory, love, pleasure or wealth — without any of these things. And in this, your work can become focused on the Four Pillars that I have mentioned. But this can only happen if you have the correct engagements and the correct understanding.

Let us make another important point. Many people think that everything they do is for their spiritual growth. This is not true. Spiritual growth is only one of the Four Pillars of life in the world. Most people will not want to admit that they do everything just to make money. Most people would not think that they do everything just to enhance their health. A few people think that they do everything for their primary relationships to the exclusion of everything else. So, why think that everything is for your spiritual growth?

Spiritual growth serves the other three Pillars as the other three Pillars serve spiritual growth. If you are financially unstable, you will not be able to begin your spiritual development because you will be so hampered by external problems and irresolutions. If your health is compromised and you are ill, it is very difficult to be wholeheartedly involved in a spiritual practice. If your primary relationships are chaotic and in disarray, how will you be able to approach your spiritual growth? All of these must work together.

Spiritual growth gives purpose and meaning to your work and to earning money. It gives purpose and meaning to your relationships. It gives purpose and meaning to your health. You cannot have good employment in the world if your health is compromised. You see, they are all interdependent. You don't choose one to the exclusion of the others. This is not to say that everyone has to maintain the same level of health, the same level of financial stability, the same kind of relationships or even the same pursuits in their spiritual growth. But it does mean that the Four Pillars all work together and must all be areas of work.

When you develop your relationships, you will experience spiritual growth. If you develop your work in the world, you will have greater health. Advancement in any one area, as long as it is in keeping with your overall purpose and focus, benefits all of the others. Now, if you neglect your relationships because you want to make a lot of money, or if you neglect making an adequate amount of money because you are consumed with your relationships, this will produce instability, and your work will become misappropriated. We are talking about achieving a balance, a balance that Knowledge will promote, a balance that you will naturally and instinctively feel. When imbalance exists, you will feel that imbalance. You will feel the urge to do something about it, particularly when the opportunity is at hand.

Commit yourself to work because everything that is important will be realized through the process of work and the results of work. The focus of your work, the understanding of your work, the application of your work and the engagement of your work — these are the things that are significant for you. You leave a little time for pleasure and time off for rest and introspection. If you are a student of *Steps to Knowledge*, you have time in your practices — quality time — to integrate all that you are doing and to learn how to feel the presence of Knowledge and to express Knowledge in different situations.

Most of your activities are work. You do not get the ultimate job right up front. You start out with a little job, and then you move on to something more complete. All of these steps help to shape you, to define you and to bring you in touch with your deeper needs.

Do not ever think that you are only going to work as much as is necessary and that the rest of your time is for fun. This is a great mistake, for you will lose the means for generating vitality and meaning, and your fun will be a burden — more like an addiction or an escape than something that is truly meaningful to you.

The world has tremendous needs, and these needs will grow. People are wandering around, not knowing what to do, not knowing how to find value in life. You see this everywhere. Do you see here where the connection is not being realized? Do you see here where the need and the response are not coming together, where the question and the answer are not meeting each other?

Your work is your purpose. It is who you are and what you do in the world. It is not your ultimate reality, but it is your purpose for coming here. All forms of work, most of which will be very mundane, all serve this. You build a foundation of work. You do not want to retire from work; you want to expand your work and rededicate your work. This keeps you vital; this keeps providing meaning. Do not believe that escape from work will lead to any kind of satisfaction. Though you may be tired of your current employment, think of expanding your work into new areas. Think, "Where could I be helpful to others, given what I know?"

In your society, you have many older people who have tremendous life experience and who are being put out to pasture. They are not needed anymore. Many of them put themselves out to pasture, and many others are simply neglected. This is a great misfortune because the Wisdom of life is not being passed on. When giving stops, meaning stops. You only find your gift through giving. And giving is work; it is what you give yourself to. The value of that work will be determined by your inner nature and by what the world is requiring from you. Where these two realities meet — the reality of your inner life and the reality of your outer life — is where purpose is found in the world.

Therefore, do not think about retirement. Do not think about escaping to a pleasurable, non-demanding life. Do not think about getting out from under your responsibilities. Instead, think about changing what you are doing and finding new opportunities to work and apply yourself. Always apply yourself. This will keep your battery recharged, and this will keep you advancing to meet your mundane responsibilities and your divine responsibilities, for they are inseparable.

*It is generally held
in the Greater Community
that should a race spoil its
natural environment,
then others are free
to intervene
and to displace them.*

Twenty-five

ENVIRONMENTS

HERE IS A GROWING CONCERN about the environment in which you live, the natural environment. This, of course, is important because this is the context in which you live. But the environment is far more important than most people realize. It is important not only for your well-being and your future, it is important in terms of understanding the Greater Community.

You see, in the Greater Community, environment is considered the most important thing. It is not something that you use, and then after it has been misused, you worry about it a little bit. Environment *is* the most important thing. It is seen as the absolute, fundamental context for survival and creation and a model for education itself.

In the Greater Community, there are few environments that are as lush and abundant as this world. This world is truly a gem in the universe. This place and places like it are highly valued and considered remarkable and unique. But humanity has been bound to this world for a long, long time and has taken for granted the great wealth and abundance of this garden world, this Garden of Eden, if you will. For this world is most surely a Garden of Eden in contrast to other environments where intelligent life has had to adapt and advance.

Environment is not simply the plants and animals that you see around you. It is the context in which you live. It is life. There are two kinds of environments we shall speak of—the physical environment and the mental environment. The physical environment you are acquainted with, and perhaps you have a certain amount of knowledge and understanding about it. Yet, the mental environment is something very new to human understanding. The mental and physical environments are not the same. They operate on different levels of existence and follow different laws. They overlap tremendously, but you cannot take the principles of one and apply them to the other.

Your concern for the physical environment is important, but it must grow. It must become the most important thing, not something that is simply present or taken for granted or considered as an afterthought. It *is* the most important thing. You do not want to find out the hard way that this is true, for then your prospects for survival would be much fewer than they are today. Do not wait for calamity to teach you what you needed to know in the first place.

How you preserve and manage your environment in many ways represents your level of development. This refers both to your understanding and perception as well as your behavior. A very advanced society will value the natural environment tremendously and will utilize it in such a way that its productivity can be continued far into the future. It is a sustainable relationship, a relationship that humanity at this point does not have with the natural world.

Should humanity fail, then others from the Greater Community will come to take over the world. They will take it over because they value the environment. The environment is more important than any one race or species. It is generally held in the Greater Community that should a race spoil its natural environment, then others are free to intervene and to displace them. This is an established principle in the Greater Community and is widely held, though not all societies subscribe to it. Being human, this is very difficult for you to understand because you feel that the environment is there for you—there for you to use and to throw away. And you think that humanity is the most important thing in the universe, and certainly the most important thing in this world.

But your neighbors in the Greater Community do not share this view. The reason that they are advanced is that they have had to develop a sustainable relationship with their natural environment. In some cases, their environment was greatly damaged, which required a tremendous advancement in their technology in order for them to survive. They know the risks, and they know the cost of neglect. They know the price of irresponsibility. But humanity has not learned this, for it has not yet paid this price. It has not seen the great cost involved. Should you ever have the great opportunity to learn of the history of another world, then perhaps you will gain the perspective that makes what I am saying absolutely obvious. Humanity is at risk, but so is your environment. You will not survive without your environment, but you can regain a new relationship with it based upon a new understanding.

In our discourses we have talked about work, contribution, conflict resolution, and so forth. Apply what has been said here to your relationship with the environment, and you will see that there is a great deal of work to be done to restore and to renew your environment and to establish a sustainable relationship with it. Here you take from it what you need and you give back to it what it requires. This balance can be attained and must be attained if humanity is to have a future, for certainly without this balance, your future is in great jeopardy. Either you will perish by your own poisoning of the environment or others will come to displace you.

The possibility for this latter prospect is very great. This is why tremendous experimentation is being done on plants, animals and human beings at this time because the risk to your environment has grown. The possibility of human failure has grown. The possibility of your damaging your physical environment beyond repair has grown, and as it has grown there has been intervention from the Greater Community. This is difficult to see because human beings still think and base their values and assumptions on the idea that they are alone in the universe, and that if there is anyone else in the universe, they are so far away that there cannot be any possibility of involvement. Here there is no accountability to anyone or anything else.

It is now becoming popular to be environmentally aware, but this is not enough. How you manage your personal life and how you relate to the natural world are fundamental. Knowledge will give you the right relationship here, as it will straighten out your relationship with everyone and everything else. But this takes time, and you do not have this kind of time to freely use. You must now become a student and become serious in this matter, for it is of very great importance.

If your children are to have a world to live in, a safe and healthy world, then environment must become the most important thing. If environment becomes the most important thing or the number one concern, then war will be ended because war is damaging to the environment. Pollution, poverty, strife and conflict between cultures and nations is antithetical to maintaining a healthy environment. If you think of this, you will see that as the environment becomes the most important thing, other things must fall into place. But if the environment is an afterthought and is not considered to be the most important thing to concern yourself with, it will constantly be compromised in order to meet other goals and objectives.

Let us talk now about the mental environment. This is a concept that we have presented in a number of our discourses, and we shall say more about it now. Unlike the physical environment, you cannot spoil the mental environment. It is an environment that is made up of thoughts and groups of thoughts, which are called forces. The mental environment cannot be destroyed, but it can become very polluted. It can become very destructive. Unlike the physical environment, the mental environment knows no boundaries in terms of time and space. For instance, if you have great emotional distress where you are, it affects someone on the other side of the world, and vice versa. Perhaps the effects seem to be very slight, but they are real nonetheless because minds are not connected simply by the recognition of another's physical presence. Minds are connected through a very subtle internal network. That is why we say that if a person discovers Knowledge and makes advancements in the reclamation of Knowledge, he or she will affect minds in many places simultaneously. Most of these individuals this person has never met and is not even aware of because minds are joined by a deeper fabric that extends far beyond the physical realm.

Here you can make a contribution to improve the mental environment. If this is done, people will function better, be more harmonious and less prone to conflict and be able to recognize opportunities as they arise with far greater ease. Everyone will be stimulated. Everyone will be encouraged to carry on what they were sent here to do. In this light, contribution is felt in many places by many people.

The mental environment is what you create for yourself. Nature has been created for you — a gift. The mental environment is something that you have to be responsible for because unless a foreign intelligence is in your midst, almost everything that you experience in the mental environment will come from other human beings. Plants and animals do not have a strong influence on the mental environment. In nature, as you may have noticed, there can be neutrality in the mental environment. That is why people seek refuge in nature — it is refreshingly open and free of dominating influences.

There are, however, influences in the mental environment even where people are not present. But for our discussion now, you need to be most concerned with your impact on other people and their impact on you. Here you can make a great difference, both in the quality of your own experience and in the possibility of having meaningful relationships with others. This represents a more refined participation in life. It represents advancement and intelligence. Humanity needs to cultivate these at this time if it is to engage effectively in the Greater Community, where the mental environment is considered very important, second only to the physical environment. If the physical environment is maintained, you have the possibility to survive. Yet, if the mental environment is enhanced, you have the possibility to develop and to advance your own intelligence and understanding.

Let us give some examples of the mental environment. People go to a university because it is a concentrated learning environment. It is a place where people are concentrating on their education. This is a mental environment. A library at a university has a very different feeling than a library in a city community. It is a concentrated and focused learning environment. It may be easier to study in the university than it is in a public place. These represent two different mental environments. Mental environments are made up of forces and stimulants. Each force has an effect upon you and you, in turn, have an effect upon it. If you go to a place where everyone is focused on a sports event, it can be much easier to enjoy it and participate in it than it would be watching it on the television. This represents a mental environment. People are together thinking about something in common. This creates a potency or a force in that environment, a force that will affect you greatly.

These represent two obvious examples, but understand that

the mental environment is far more subtle and pervasive than these. Its importance in the Greater Community is that it represents the ability of one race to influence another race and even to dominate the other race without the use of physical force. Human beings are still very primitive in this regard. They use physical force to control others. But even here you will find, such as in advertising, the basic understanding that people can be made to do what you want them to do if you give them certain kinds of stimulation and certain kinds of ideas.

This represents only a rudimentary understanding of the mental environment. For you, the mental environment represents the atmosphere in which you think and feel. If that mental environment is enhanced and positive, it will be easier for you to be creative, intelligent and aware of what is going on within you and around you. In turn, if the mental environment is adverse and filled with conflict, hostility, disturbance or distress, it will be more difficult for you to have clarity of mind. It will be more difficult for you to be aware of yourself and your surroundings. It will be more difficult for you to concentrate.

Human beings are the primary influence in the mental environment here, so long as a Greater Community intelligence is not present. In the physical world, you are only one of many, many races and species that are engaging in a dynamic network of life. The difference here is that human beings exert a greater influence in the mental environment, particularly on one another. In the natural world, everything influences everything else in a much more physical way. For instance, if a cat scratches you, that creates an impact on you in the physical environment. However, the cat's thoughts do not influence your thoughts, though you, in fact, may influence the cat's thoughts. Plants and animals have direct bearing on your physical well-being and sensory experience in the world, but plants and animals do not influence your thinking, unless you are able to respond to them on a very subtle level. On this level, you can communicate with them insofar as you can discern their present state, their nature and their needs.

In order to have a positive effect on the mental environment, you must become aware of the mental environment around you, learn how to establish your own mental environment and learn how to influence it and maintain it. Here you learn about your effect on others and their effect upon you. You learn this through many, many experiences and through objective observation. Surely, when you go into someone's home, you enter their mental environment, and you experience it first hand. If you were to go up and down your street and enter everyone's home, you would enter a different mental environment in every place and would have a different experience. Some places you would feel comfortable; some places you would feel uncomfortable. Some places it would be very easy for you to think clearly; other places it would be more difficult.

To have a positive influence on someone else's mental environment, you must first be able to influence your own mental environment. This requires the ability to control and direct your own thoughts. This requires the ability to be aware of Knowledge and to practice stillness. *Steps to Knowledge* teaches all of these things, and that is why it is an important foundation for gaining awareness and capability in the mental environment.

Human beings, then, have a tremendous amount of work to do. They have many conflicts to address. They have a great range of responsibilities, only a few of which they have claimed thus far. Again, let me give you an example from the Greater Community so that you can see through contrast where you stand and where you need to develop. All Greater Community races engaged in space travel interact with many other races who represent very different environments, different conditioning, different beliefs, and so forth. Their interaction with each other is far more challenging than your interaction with other people. Although you may highlight the individual differences between you and another person, the fact is you hold so much in common that the differences in personality or in temperament between you are very, very slight, particularly compared to the differences you will experience in encountering a Greater Community intelligence — someone from a different physical environment, with a completely different history and different biological and psychological make-up. The differences here are enormous.

In order to function in the Greater Community, you have to develop tremendous abilities of discernment and methods and avenues of communication. You also have to become aware of another race's impact upon you — the power of their thoughts, their concentration, their social cohesion, and so forth, in comparison and contrast to yours. One of the laws in the mental environment is that concentration is power. This has a corollary in the physical environment where physical force is power. In the mental environment, it is concentration. An individual more concentrated than you will have a greater influence on you than you will have on him or her. A group or race more concentrated than you will have a greater influence on you than you will have on them. How true this is in the Greater Community. That is why advancing societies must learn something about the mental environment if they are to effectively compete, relate and deal with other races.

You have not had this requirement yet in your learning, but you will have it soon. That is part of the reason that The Greater Community Way of Knowledge is being provided at this time. The need to address your physical environment and to begin learning about the mental environment is very great, and it is upon you now. It is not something you can neglect; it is something that must be addressed. We give this overview to substantiate the understanding that you have a great deal of work to do and a great deal of learning to do, learning far beyond your current boundaries and parameters.

In order to preserve your world and make it a habitable place for future generations, the physical environment must become your first priority. This will have a beneficial effect on your behavior, on your relationship with others and on every aspect of your culture and society.

Your second great focus for learning and application is the mental environment. Here you will be able to learn more about yourself and others and be able to eventually bring greater harmony and balance into your relationships. Even more importantly than this, your preparation in the mental environment will enable you to discern and interact with Greater Community presences, which represent societies of far greater concentration and social cohesion than you presently can enjoy.

The mental environment and the physical environment are the contexts in which you think and act respectively. Each requires a conscious approach; each requires enhancement and development. Your ability to advance in these two arenas is possible only because you have Knowledge within you to guide you, to motivate you and to lead you forward. Without Knowledge, you would continue to abuse your physical world until your race would begin to die out. Without Knowledge, you would be centuries away from learning anything about the mental environment. Without Knowledge, you would have neither the compassion nor the will and strength necessary to elevate yourself and your race to meet the challenges of life that exist now and that will surely arise to meet you in the future.

When you think about why you are in the world, what you are here to do, and what it means to be an individual, think about your work with the environment—your enhancement of the mental environment and your preservation of the physical environment.

Then think about all of the education and activity that this will require of you and of others. This will begin to give you an understanding of the great opportunities that life is giving you now.

If you minimize
conflict in the world
and in yourself,
conflict is minimized.
If you avoid
conflict in yourself
and in the world,
conflict grows.

Twenty-six

CONFLICT

*I*T IS A GRAVE DISAPPOINTMENT to many people that the world is so full of conflict. There is a general hope that when you came to the world it would be as peaceful, as wonderful and as inclusive as your Ancient Home. But what you find instead is conflict, dissension, turmoil, all manner of deception, attack, warfare, competition, alienation, estrangement and a host of other maladies experienced on an individual and collective level.

This is the world that you have come to serve. Why do you think it is supposed to be as wonderful as your Ancient Home? It can become more wonderful through your contribution, but as it stands today and as it will stand tomorrow, it is a place full of conflict. It is a place where people believe they are alone and compete with one another for any recognized satisfaction and benefit.

This competition for personal fulfillment occurs in relationships and on cultural and national levels as well. As nations compete to try to outdo each other or to undermine each other, peace is tenuous. Warfare can be expected sooner or later. This is the condition of the world. People are still very much in a tribal state of mind. There is no world community yet, though it is destined that humanity will have to establish one in order to survive in the centuries ahead.

So, here you are in the world of conflict. You have your own conflict—your own conflicting ideas, wishes and impulses. You struggle internally to realize and exercise a greater truth despite all of the selfish and fearful motivations which prompt you to do things against your better wishes and greater well-being.

This conflict is endemic here. It exists within each individual. It exists at the level of family, community, culture and nation. And it does not stop here, for the physical universe is also a place of conflict, though many civilizations have evolved to a point where they have been able to minimize conflict in order to stabilize their societies.

Do not think that perfection can be achieved on the physical plane, but great improvement can be, and this is the nature and purpose of your arrival here. People are unhappy because they are selfish. They think they are here only for their own personal protection and satisfaction, but that is not why they were sent to the world. Everyone was sent to the world to give something to the world so that the world could be a better place as a result of their participation. Many people never realize this and never find this in their lives, and tragedy occurs as a result. This tragedy exists everywhere.

But what does this mean for you who are responding to this message? What does this mean for you who sense that there is a greater spiritual reality and purpose that is infused in life and that permeates everything you see? What does this mean for you who feel a deeper calling that takes you away from the general activities of people to seek something more mysterious and complete, more engaging and more vital? It means that you have come to serve something and that your service in the world is vital to its improvement and to your ability to find meaning, purpose and value in life.

In a previous discourse we talked about work. Where is the work applied? It is applied in dealing with conflict primarily. Not everything that you work on is aimed at resolving conflict, for much of your activity is aimed at preserving or maintaining things of value, but even this is to avoid future conflict. For instance, you maintain your health because you do not want the conflict of illness or disability. You maintain your financial stability so that your ability to function in the world does not break down.

Conflict is ever present. When order breaks down, there is disorder. If disorder continues, there is chaos. With chaos comes disaster. To help maintain order, you must become orderly. To help maintain peace, you must become peaceful. All of these things are cultivated in you as you give to the world to minimize and in certain cases to eliminate conflict. As you do this, conflict within you becomes minimized and is eventually eliminated.

However, the resistance to conflict is considerable, and the prescription that I have just mentioned is not easily put into practice because there is more conflict than you can possibly face at any one time. So, where do you dedicate your energy? How do you approach conflict? How do you work towards resolution? What is the resolution? And how do you maintain the resolution in such a way that conflict can be minimized in the future? How do you deal with conflict that is beyond your control, such as natural calamities, cultural wars or great strife? How do you face this, and what is your responsibility here?

All of these questions are important. The response to them exists within a secret intelligence that lives within you, which we call Knowledge. Knowledge knows how to respond to situations in the moment, so you do not have to have definitions and guidelines for yourself regarding everything in the world. But Knowledge requires your participation and activity. In order for you to experience Knowledge, the Greater Mind within you, to follow its expression and to apply its Wisdom, you must become responsive to it and not try to use it, limit it or manipulate it for your own personal gains.

You bring your conflict to Knowledge by learning to establish your relationship with Knowledge, but Knowledge itself is not in conflict.

At the beginning in the reclamation of Knowledge, students always want to use Knowledge to get more of what they want. Part of what they want is to avoid conflict. Yet much of the conflict that they are trying to avoid represents things that they must learn to face. Some of the conflict they want to face they do not need to face, so it all becomes very confusing. If you have conflicting motives and you come into proximity to Knowledge, which is wholehearted, single minded and has one purpose and direction, how can you interact with it? Well, what happens is that Knowledge remains silent until you are ready. Even if you seek it honestly, Knowledge will wait until you become aware of some of your conflicts and irregularities. That will provide an opening for Knowledge to emerge within you. If you try to simply take Knowledge and say, "Well, I'm going to get more of everything for myself and everyone else with Knowledge," Knowledge will remain silent, and you will not be able to use it.

You see, Knowledge is more intelligent than you are. It is more complete. That is not to say it is different from you, for it represents the essential part of you and your life here. But the personal part of you, which is deeply conflicted, must be brought into focus. You must become aware of it and must make certain corrections in it in order for you to gain access to Knowledge.

Now, many people think that they must correct conflict within themselves before they can do anything to resolve conflict in the world, but this is not correct. Other people think that conflict within themselves is not important and that they only need to deal with conflict in the world. This too is not correct. The truth is that you must work in both arenas, and here your work in resolving conflict will require a great amount of time, energy and attention.

The Way of Knowledge is very complete. It does not give you the freedom to escape or to avoid things which are essential for you to resolve. At the beginning, many students become very frustrated with their preparation in *Steps to Knowledge* because they are trying to do something with it. They want the results now. Here they want the curriculum and the preparation to become as conflicted and as driven as they are. But in truth, the preparation is silent and certain. It will wait until you become more silent and certain. You must learn to go at its pace. It does not go at your pace.

Knowledge will continue to be latent within you until you begin to understand its nature and adjust yourself to it. It is here to lead you and to guide you, to prepare you and to enable you to do all the things you are meant to do in the world. How can it follow you in this case? Must you not learn to follow it? It is the leader. But even to follow it, you must learn what it is, and you must learn what your responsibilities are and how they can be applied, where they need to be applied, and so forth. You cannot relegate your own responsibilities to Knowledge, for Knowledge will require you to claim them and to apply them in a manner that is far more complete than anything you have ever done before. Here you become stronger with Knowledge and not weaker. You become a leader and not simply a follower.

Knowledge is here in the world to resolve conflict. It knows what to do. You live in a world of conflict, and this influences and affects you greatly. Without Knowledge, there would be no escape. There would be no other possibility.

People respond to conflict in different ways. Some people try to resolve conflict, but they do so without Knowledge, so their actions are fearful, erratic and often unproductive. Many people try to avoid conflict altogether and try to live in a peaceful, spiritual state of mind, but conflict is bombarding them at all times. Some people think that if they just change their thoughts, there would be no more conflict. "I will just not see the conflict. I will turn the conflict into something good. I shall make everything good, and then I will not have to feel the pain and the responsibility which is mine to feel." Some people retreat from life altogether. Many people retreat from themselves altogether and replace self-awareness with a host of other preoccupations.

Your society, with all of its pleasures and wonderful reprieves, offers a myriad of escapes from conflict. If you look about, you can see how varied and how intense this escape is. If you look at yourself, you will see your own forms of escape.

You were sent here to work, to give and to help resolve conflict. You were not sent to the world to work on yourself. You were sent to the world to work on the world and to work in the world. You work on yourself as you go along. The only work you need to do on yourself is to make adjustments along the way so that you can participate in life and maintain an open mind, freedom from judgment and adherence to Knowledge in yourself and in others. That will provide all of the personal growth you can ever imagine. In fact, that challenge exceeds what most people are even capable of at this moment. You will feel meaningful as you do something meaningful. You will feel valuable as you do something valuable. Do not deny this. It is natural. You have come to work. You are at work. You have come to help things out here. You have come from a better place, and you will return to a better place. But while you are here, this is a place to work. The world is like a hospital. There is a great deal of sickness and difficulty here. It is not a beach or a holiday resort. It is not a vacation land. It is the place where work needs to be done.

So, finding your work is essential. You cannot define your work in terms of what you want. You must define it within the context of the world. You will never find your work based only on what you want. You need to give something the world needs, and you must listen to the world to find out what that need is. People who only give what they want to give are still lost in what they want and cannot go beyond their shifting desires. They will remain in their personal hell as life goes on around them.

You have Knowledge. It is living within you. You cannot use it for selfish purposes, but you can open yourself to its grace and its power. Then gradually, step by step, it will help you overcome and control the conflict within yourself and will lead you into activities which serve others in vital ways, in ways that are in keeping with your nature and your design. *Steps to Knowledge* will teach you about your nature and your design if you stay with it and if you follow it faithfully. This takes you beyond conflict to see a greater possibility in life. This takes you beyond your wishes to the realm of what you know. This frees you from the endless conflict and internal debate about what you want and don't want in life, and it engages you in your work completely.

Why complain that the world is in conflict when this very conflict gives meaning and purpose to your life? Why complain that things are not better? Be aware that things are not better, but see what you can do about it. Idleness and boredom are a sign that people are not valuing their lives or responding to their environment. Please understand, you are not in the world for self-realization. You are in the world to help the world and to help your race. Self-realization is a by-product of giving something of meaning to the world.

If you study the lives of people who have made important contributions, you will see that they have many important things in common. Even though they suffered personal conflicts, difficulties and tribulation in the world to a certain extent, they were freed from much of the grave and debilitating anxieties which afflict most people.

Now, your contribution to the world does not need to be

grand or magnificent. In fact, except in very rare cases, it will go unheralded. You work quietly behind the scenes, doing something good for the world so that you can leave a legacy behind. To do this, you must be very patient and be very tolerant of the world. You must accept its conflict, not as an irreversible condition, but as a present reality. To begin to resolve conflict, the first step is awareness and acceptance. Until this occurs, there is nowhere to go. There is nothing to improve. Many people are not even at this starting point. They have great difficulty accepting the conflict within their own lives and their immediate circumstances. Tell the truth about this. Do not embellish it. Do not diminish it. Simply tell the truth about it. If things are not right, they are not right. If things do not work, they do not work. If people are not productive, they are not productive. If people do not get along, they do not get along. If you are not at peace, you are not at peace. That has to be your starting point.

In order for you to find your work, there must be a need. The world provides a sufficient set of compelling needs. There must be a genuine and compelling need to do greater work. It must be a need that transcends your personal wishes and anxieties, for these are not strong enough to generate devoted action, nor are they wholehearted. The person who is doing something only for himself or herself will be changeable and inconsistent. Dedication will not be possible. Certainty will not be possible. Knowledge will not be possible.

It is accurate to say that humanity has advanced through the efforts of a very small percentage of the population. This percentage must grow for humanity to be able to meet the great and global challenges that face humanity — problems that have been created here and problems in the Greater Community as well. Even the Greater Community is a place of conflict. There is no escaping conflict. You are here to work on conflict. Conflict provides the need and the impetus to work. Now, if you are paying attention to what I am telling you, you will begin to wonder how people can sit around asking themselves, "What is my purpose in life? I don't know what to do. What do I really want to do with my life?" Can you begin to see the problem here? The problem is that people are not responsive to the inner need or to the outer need. They feel a loss and they are wondering about it, but they are not responding to the very things that can lead them to a path of resolution.

To end separation in your own thinking, you must rejoin life in meaningful activities. To have real relationships with others, you must join them in meaningful activities. You must do something good for the world—together. That will do something good for you and for your relationships.

Now, the question arises, "Well, there is so much conflict and so many problems, where do I apply myself?" It is important here not to seek the ultimate answer but to get involved. Find something that you can do in your local community to help people and to help restore nature, something you can give yourself to. Here you are beginning to participate rather than sitting on the sidelines of life wondering and pondering while the world calls to you and you do not answer. It says, "We need your help! We need your help!" You have to find that calling and find where it is coming from and where to apply yourself.

Do not wait until conflict in the world becomes so great that everyone is reduced to desperation. Yes, this will engender action, but it may be too late. Why wait until your financial condition is so deteriorated that it takes all of your time and energy to repair it? You do not need to wait that long. You can respond now. You can respond to your needs and others' needs now. Your primary needs in life are to have sufficient resources and time available in order to give yourself in service to the world. For that, you may need a little money or a lot of money, depending on what your role is. For that you may need a little time or a lot of time, depending on your role. Your role will evolve as you participate. It cannot simply be known by you at the outset.

Donate part of your time now, beyond your job and relationships, to do something important in the world. You will feel drawn to certain things. Follow that. As you stay with your *Steps to Knowledge* preparation, your sense of purpose, the thing that is driving you forward, will become stronger and stronger. And as it becomes stronger, you will be able to perceive it, feel it and interpret it more correctly. Escape the dilemma of trying to have, do and be what you want. There is no hope there. People are lost when they devote themselves to that. You are not here for you. You have been sent to the world by your Spiritual Family to serve the world in specific ways with specific people. To find those ways, you must start giving now. This will lead you through a series of involvements, each focused on contribution. Through this, you will find that involvement which is most significant for you and where your talents, nature and design can be most fully employed in service to the world.

Now, being in service to the world does not mean that you are doing something for everyone. Maybe you will be helping an older person who lives next door. Maybe you are participating in enhancing the beauty of your community or in assisting people who are having difficulty. This is all serving the world. Do not be grandiose. Do not think you have to do something that affects everyone. Do something that affects one person, two people, or three, or five or ten or fifty or a hundred. Certain people are designed to help one person. Certain people are designed to help ten people. Certain people are designed to help ten thousand people. This is all serving the world.

The world will be good or bad depending on how much is given here. The future will be good or bad depending on what people give today. Your life is good now to the extent that others have given in the past. Your children and their children will benefit from what you give today. You will go home to a wonderful life when you leave this world, with your job done or undone. And you will feel good or not good about your participation here based on what you were able to contribute, for what else can you take with you beyond this world?

Giving brings you out of isolation. It provides a means of escape from many of your own personal dilemmas. This is not to say that you must work all the time, for you will need time for retreat and re-evaluation. But work will constitute most of your activity. The more this work can be of service, the more value and meaning it can give to others. As Knowledge becomes stronger in you, you will find those specific engagements that are needed. But first you must start somewhere. In learning a musical instrument, you do not simply walk out onto the concert stage and tell yourself, "Yes, I have arrived!" You have to go through many stages of development. You start out having great difficulty in learning. If you quit, you do not proceed. If you proceed, you advance. As you advance, you become more proficient and more well defined in your activity.

The value of conflict is that it calls to you to do something. The value of conflict within yourself is that it tells you that you *must* do something. The value of doing something is that you realize your value. Value must be earned in the world. This is true. Meaning must be earned. When you go home to your Spiritual Family, you will have all of the value and meaning you could possibly want, but while you are here you are on assignment to work and to bond with others in work. Therefore, work is the nature of fulfillment in the world. By work we do not simply mean going to a job every day, for there are things you must work on in your own life, as we have mentioned before, to resolve conflict and minimize the effects of conflict. They will make the world more free of conflict.

Perhaps you think that your contribution could not possibly

make a difference, but I assure you that it will make a difference because all that you give will continue to be given by those who receive your gift, and your gifts will continue to resonate through minds everywhere in the mental environment. Who are you to say where the limits of this exist? Every time Knowledge is strengthened in one person, it is strengthened in everyone. Every time a great act is done selflessly, it strengthens the possibility of good for every-one — even for those people who have no idea what has occurred.

In the mental environment, there are great forces of influence. There are forces of confirmation and there are forces of dissonance. If you contribute to the forces of confirmation, they become stron-ger. Here you affect the mental environment, both in your imme-diate circumstances and throughout the world. This is how import-ant this is, and this is why we emphasize the reality of conflict and the importance of contribution. We emphasize this because this is the means for resolution, fulfillment and value in the world. This confirms the world and this confirms you. And this takes away all justification for error, failure or neglect.

By doing something bigger in the world, you become big-ger. By doing less in the world, you become less. If you minimize conflict in the world and in yourself, conflict is minimized. If you avoid conflict in yourself and in the world, conflict grows. This can be easily seen, but it is a great challenge to apply. This will require courage, perseverance, rededication and the presence of Knowledge to prompt you onward.

Doubt what is doubtful.
Trust what is certain.
Doubt what is temporary.
Trust what is permanent.

Twenty-seven

SELF-DOUBT

ITH ALL THE WORK THAT THERE IS TO DO in the world and all the responsibilities to be assumed, surely this must generate self-doubt, so let us speak about self-doubt. Let us see how doubt can be faced and circumvented and what can be done when doubt cannot be escaped.

What is self-doubt? What does it mean to doubt yourself? And what is this self that you doubt? When you experience self-doubt, you just experience doubt. There is rarely ever any introspective questioning. You just feel doubt. You feel uncertain. You are concerned that you might fail or that you are unworthy or incapable of meeting the challenge or completing the task. And you shy away from yourself and from whatever is stimulating the doubt on the outside. Many people live with doubt almost continuously. They try to inure themselves from the discomfort of feeling this and try to escape all of those things that stimulate their doubt and bring it to the surface.

What is this doubt and what is this self that you doubt? This is an important question because it leads you to the discovery that there are really two aspects to you. There is the personal aspect and what we call the Impersonal aspect. The personal aspect is your personal mind, which includes your personality and all of your habits, interests and idiosyncrasies. It is the part of you that you have acquired during your time so far in the world. It is all the parts of your mind that are conditioned by the world around you and by your primary relationships. It is the part of your mind that is filled with memories and has patterns of thinking and behavior, some of which are very difficult to change. This is the self that you doubt because this self is frail, uncertain and inconsistent. It has failed you, and it has deceived you. It is fully capable of presenting lies and misusing real facts for personal gain. It is deceptive. It is often dishonest. It is weak. It is conniving. It is all these things, but it is not evil. It is simply protecting itself from a world that is too large and too incomprehensible for it to comprehend or understand. It does not feel safe in the world, and so it arms itself against all anticipated threats and possibilities of loss. It arms itself against embarrassment. It arms itself against anything which might threaten its social and physical survival.

This is the personal aspect of you, and this is the self that you doubt. You have good cause to doubt it, for until it comes into service and into relationship with a Greater Power, it is alone and afraid and will misuse reality and even its own experience to defend itself against the world and against any intrusions, real or imagined. This is the personal part of your mind, and this is the self that you doubt. It is foolish and reckless to say you should not doubt yourself, for if this is the self that you identify with and that you experience moment to moment, then you should doubt it, for it will let you down.

It is important here to know what to trust and what to doubt — not in a critical way, but in an analytical and an objective way. For example, you realize that your body has certain limitations. It has limitations in terms of what kind of environment it can survive in. It has thresholds for what is too hot, what is too cold and what is too painful. It has a myriad of sensations. It is vulnerable to pain and damage and can fairly easily be destroyed. You realize this. The body has limits.

The personal mind, given a greater purpose to serve and meaningful relationships with which to identify, can become a useful and productive aspect of yourself. But it too has its limits. It is not eternal. It is not wise. It cannot function at the level of Knowledge. It can only comprehend things to a certain extent. Its analytical skills are limited. And it is prone to fear and anxiety, given very slight or even nonexistent stimulation. Indeed, the personal mind frightens itself frequently where there is no real cause for fear at all. It has very serious limits, and when you know these limits, you can train it to function within its boundaries. Then it can become a useful and productive aspect of yourself. If you do not know its limits and its boundaries, however, you will expect things of it that it can never provide. You will expect peace, equanimity, strength, courage, openness, acceptance and unconditional love — all things that it alone cannot produce or provide. It can only be a vehicle of expression for these greater experiences as it comes to serve and to accept a Greater Power in your life.

While you have a self that you need to doubt and that you need to understand, you also have a Self that you can learn to trust — completely and wholeheartedly. This Greater Self is the source of certainty, guidance, strength, courage and Wisdom. It is what we call Knowledge. It represents the immortal part of yourself — the part of you that came into the world fully intact and fully prepared to carry out a mission in life. You carry it like a secret cargo. It is within you at this moment. You can doubt its existence. You can doubt its value. You can doubt the depth of its Wisdom and the limits of its strength, but until you know it, you will not understand what it can do or what it is for. You are not in a position to doubt it. You can join with it, become part of it and become united within yourself. Or you can avoid it, hide from it, resist it or demean it, but it is within you nonetheless. You cannot spoil it. You cannot use if for selfish ends. You can misinterpret it. You can misunderstand it. And you can wrongly apply its guidance and Wisdom to the extent that you have experienced it. But it remains pure within you.

This is the Self that you can trust. The more that you experience Knowledge and the greater your comprehension of Knowledge, the greater will be your foundation for self-trust. This is not merely theoretical. This is actual. You can experience it profoundly, and it will give you a sense that you have solid ground to stand upon while you are in the world. This is God's great gift to you. This is the answer to your prayers. This is the great comforter and reassurance, and it lives within you.

Knowledge lives within you, but you must find a way to it. You must become worthy of its grace. You must develop yourself to receive it and to follow it. To enable you to do that, you have been presented with The Greater Community Way of Knowledge. This is a means of regaining access to Knowledge that is unparalleled in the world. As you undertake this great journey with its many stages of development and its many opportunities for application, you will build a foundation for self-trust that will be unshakable in the world.

How different this is from trying to trust your personal mind and trying to eliminate doubt without finding this greater foundation within yourself. This trust has no falsity. It has no false excuses. It has no lies surrounding it. It has no fragile and thin justifications. It has no deception, no dishonesty and no deceit. With this inner certainty, there is humility, for you realize you are standing at the threshold of something very great within you. You realize as well that it is something that you personally cannot own, but that you are blessed to receive and blessed to have within you, to be with you and to be the center of you. You cannot claim it and use it to control or to dominate others. You can only follow its grace to find resolution in life and to build a foundation of relationships and a greater realization of purpose and contribution.

Now, what establishes a way to Knowledge and what secures your experience of Knowledge so that in the future you can learn to rely upon it and have faith in its presence? What establishes your connection to Knowledge and your relationship with it is making important decisions at important junctures of life, where you have to choose the truth over all other seeming conveniences and benefits, where you have to give up something that you had been clinging to in order to have freedom and a new opportunity for life. These are the great turning points where Knowledge reveals itself. It reveals itself because it is chosen in the hour of decision. Now it is no longer a hope or an idea or a theoretical possibility. It is now something real within you.

Can you trust that deeper inclination? Can you recognize its consistency and its depth and distinguish it from all the other impulses, compulsions, needs or anxieties that you might feel? It lives within you. Deep, silent, powerful. In contrast to a world of mad pursuits, frantic activities and dangerous involvements, what greater gift could you be given than a part of God to live within you? It is not a spirit that visits you occasionally when you are in dire straits. It is not a benediction given to you after fervent prayer. It is a living reality within you. As you learn over time to come to Knowledge and to take the steps to Knowledge, you will have a foundation for self-trust, and this will give you a basis for releasing self-doubt.

The personal aspect of your mind will continue to doubt. It will doubt and doubt and doubt, for it can only doubt or believe. It cannot *know*, for only Knowledge can know. It requires assurances, like a child, until it becomes a part of Knowledge itself, until the human and the Divine in you are joined together in meaningful and true matrimony—the real marriage of mind, body and soul that is possible and only possible with Knowledge. The personal mind will continue to be fretful, doubtful, anxious and prone to rash decisions and rash behavior.

But increasingly, as a student of Knowledge following in The Way of Knowledge, you will be able to step back from these impulses and anxieties and rest upon that which is much more sure and even within you. This is essential in order to become a contributor in life. To learn how to really work and to learn where your work needs to be placed, to resolve conflict, to enhance your mental and physical environment, you need this inner strength. Even if life did not place demands upon you, you would need this inner strength to justify your existence here and to realize with certainty that you have an Ancient Home from which you have come and to which you will surely return. You need this inner strength to experience that you have a life within the world and a life beyond the world and that they are joined by a purpose — a purpose for which you have come.

Life is not casual. Life is not ambivalent. Life is fully dedicated. Everywhere. To be part of life is to be fully dedicated, completely committed, completely involved, completely joined and completely whole. As Knowledge becomes stronger within you, your personal mind will have a greater foundation upon which to base itself, and increasingly its self-doubt will disappear. Then you will face a different kind of doubt, a doubt that is a warning sign within you to tell you that something may not be right and may require greater observation or verification of some kind. This is doubt born of Wisdom. This is when you sense something is not quite right or that the decision that you are about to make may not be the best decision and you feel a restraint inside. This is not self-doubt. This is doubting something on the outside. This is healthy and wise. This is part of your inner guidance system working for you to guide and protect you and to keep you from going astray. The more you are sensitive and responsive to this, the more difficult it will be for you to make a mistake. What a blessing this is.

Knowledge will hold you back until you find that place to which you can give yourself. It will hold you back in relationships with people. It will hold you back in many things. Why? Because it has not found its place to give. How can you give your life to something if Knowledge is not going with you? The personal aspect of you is too small and too bound to the world to take on greater things. In order to take on greater responsibilities, to accept greater rewards and to meet greater challenges, you need a Greater Reality, which is connected to Knowledge within you. People try to take on big things with a small mind, and as a result they lose sense of what their endeavor might offer them, and everything becomes small.

To go from a little life that is bound by fear and desire to a greater life that is included in the workings of the world requires a Greater Power within you. You are reading these words because you are seeking a Greater Power. You know you need this Greater Power to escape self-doubt and to escape ambivalence, which is indecision. You need this Greater Power to find your foundation, to find the strength you will need to build upon that foundation, and to find the relationships you will need in your life to carry on a greater purpose and to establish a greater meaning. This need is natural.

The blessing of this approach is that your personal mind is not maligned or discredited. It is not repudiated. It is not demeaned. It is not rejected. It is not denied. It is recognized for what it is — an aspect of your mind that is born in the world and conditioned by the world. It is an aspect of your mind that you need to have to be here and to be able to negotiate the particulars of your life. You need the personal mind to govern the body. It is like the switchboard, the control panel for the body. It can become very competent in practical, detailed affairs, but it needs a greater foundation. It needs a

Greater Power. It needs a greater certainty in order to feel certain so that its real capabilities can be realized and applied. It finds its value in this larger context.

This ends the constant struggle with yourself, the constant courtroom battle over what you want and what you don't want, whether you are good or not good, whether you can be trusted or not be trusted, whether you have value or do not have value. These debates can rage continuously within the mind. But when a Greater Reality begins to emerge within you and is recognized not as some distant deity but as a living Spiritual Presence within you, then you can begin to have a real foundation. Your ability to trust this foundation will grow over time. This trust has to be earned. It has to be realized. It has to be exercised until it can become a reliable resource for you.

When people begin *Steps to Knowledge*, they often have great expectations that their lives are going to be transformed in a matter of days or weeks, or maybe months if it takes a long time! But if they stay with their preparation, they realize that this is a process with many stages, and there must be many demonstrations of the power and presence of Knowledge. And their ideas about Knowledge change. And their expectations change. And many of their ideals show themselves to be weak and false. And they realize as they go forward that their personal mind has inflated itself, giving itself divine powers and abilities, giving itself false assurances and grand assumptions about its ability to deal with anything and to handle any challenge.

All these grandiose ideas are a cover for the despair, fear and helplessness which your personal mind feels. It is lost within you and within the world until it finds its foundation in Knowledge. Then it becomes sure and secure, and its little preoccupations and anxieties have less and less of an impact on you.

Perhaps you doubt that this is possible. I understand it if you do. There are very few demonstrations of this in the world. It is understandable to be doubtful. But because something is understandable does not mean that it is correct or meaningful. There is a greater possibility for you because you are reaching out. Perhaps you still have many grand ideas about yourself and what you are going to do in life and lots of plans and goals. Perhaps you have no plans and goals. But you are here reading these words. If you can hear these words and respond to them, beyond the level of your personal mind, then Knowledge within me has reached Knowledge within you, and a real relationship has begun.

You can think of freedom as the escape from ambivalence, which is indecision. You can think of freedom as the escape from self-doubt. You can think of freedom as the escape from the personal mind as the sole authority of your life and the sole determinant of your actions and behavior. All of these definitions are really the same. Perhaps different words strike different responses, but they are all the same.

Your freedom is to find a Greater Power and a greater purpose in life and to join it and bond to it. You will know it is correct because you will know, because it is Knowledge that brings you here. You can doubt, doubt, doubt all along the way, but something deeper in you has brought you here. You can question. You can have fearful anticipations. You can worry that your mind is being taken over, that you are being manipulated—all of these kinds of fears born of the personal mind, fearful because it cannot comprehend the greatness of Knowledge because its own errors are so manifest and because it has no basis for real certainty. It seeks for a Greater Power, but it will not relinquish itself to this Power. And the powers that it will give itself to are no more certain that it is. They are grandiose, but they too are filled with fear and helplessness. The world has many expressions of power and leadership, but without Knowledge they are only pretense—pretense upon pretense. And they must be backed up with force and violence.

How different Knowledge is, which needs neither force nor violence, which needs neither deception nor dominance. Its persuasion is that it is entirely natural to you. It is the absolute essence of everything that is meaningful to you. It comes silently. It lives within you. It awaits the moment when you can begin to accept it. It offers itself at moments of great decision. It comforts you with its silence and reassurance. It abides with you. As you learn to abide with it, come to it, seek it out and learn how to receive it, respond to it and use it, then you become its recipient. Others will shrink away, fearful and doubtful, but you will come forward because Knowledge in you brings you to Knowledge in life. That which is true in you brings you to that which is true in life. The essence of you comes to the essence of life, for there is not only Knowledge within you, there is Knowledge within everything.

Within you there is a seed of Divinity which can grow into a great and bountiful tree of life. That is Knowledge. Trust this. And when you come to a moment of important decision, at a juncture or turning point in your life, you will always see that there are two ways to go: There is the way with Knowledge and there is the other way. The other way may show many possibilities, but there are really only two ways to go.

Sometimes people struggle and fret over meaningless decisions when neither decision is right because they are not patient enough to wait for Knowledge. Indeed, when Knowledge is ready to act, it can move you and everyone around you. It has such great potency. Yet it has such great compassion that it does not exercise its power except to preserve you. But even here its power can be denied and neglected. Recall the time you felt inner restraint when you were about to do something that you would later regret. Recall the time when you felt a nauseousness within you when you were making a decision that would prove itself to be damaging for you. Recall a time when you felt a giddy excitement over something you really wanted, but you later found out that it was empty. If you can learn to face your own experience and to question it objectively, you will begin to see that there is something with you that keeps you on a sure track. There is something living within you that is not frantic, nervous or reactive. Trust this.

Self-doubt will continue, but as Knowledge becomes stronger, your self- doubt will diminish. Then you will see that you have an opportunity to either go with Knowledge or to go without Knowledge when you are required to make important decisions or choices in life. Until you have this foundation in Knowledge, ideas such as peace, equanimity, spirituality and grace are only fleeting experiences, if you experience them at all. They are beyond the realm of possibility as a living reality for you until you build this foundation.

You can receive these things and you can express these things because there is a Greater Power living within you that has now become free to express itself in your life. Your life is no longer governed mindlessly by driving passions, intermittent needs and raging fears. There is more openness in your life, and through this openness comes a Greater Power and grace. You will begin to see its effect on others. And you can begin to see it growing in your life and manifesting itself, in subtle ways at first, until you realize that your life is being moved by something you cannot understand but which you can love and accept because it is natural to do so.

Therefore, doubt what is doubtful. Trust what is certain. Doubt what is temporary. Trust what is permanent. Doubt what is fleeting. Trust that which will last. Then self-doubt will be replaced by wise discrimination. Then fearful perception will be replaced by true discernment. Then doubt will serve you rather than condemn you. This is possible. This is real. This is for you who are reading these words.

You are
right in the middle
of the
Greater Community.
It is here.
Your isolation is over.

Twenty-eight

GREATER COMMUNITY
REALITIES

W E HAVE MENTIONED in many of our presentations the idea that the world is emerging into the Greater Community. What is the Greater Community? What does it really mean? And what are its implications for humanity? We shall speak a little on this now, though we will not give you all the information because there is so much, and so much of it would be meaningless and incomprehensible to you. Instead, we shall focus on the aspects that have bearing on your future and your fate and that have meaning and importance for your education and development now.

The world is emerging into a Greater Community. That does not mean that the world is going anywhere or that you will be penetrating space anytime soon. What it means is that your world is developing into a global community and that you have discovered certain kinds of powers and technology that make you a force to be recognized and reckoned with by other cultures living in your proximity beyond this solar system.

As a primitive race. you offered no threat or competition to your neighbors, and though your world was used as a depository for certain secret devices by various groups and frequently visited in order to gather plant and animal specimens for other worlds, it was not considered a meaningful location until very recently. A turning point came at the beginning of this century with the development of electricity and took another great step forward with the development of atomic power. These represent important milestones in the development of a civilization and, commensurate with this, stimulated greater interest from the Greater Community in the development of your world.

Though the world has been used as a depository and a laboratory for a very long time, there has been no serious intervention here since colonies were established many thousands of years ago. The human race was developed and advanced during this time with the infusion of genetic material from beyond, and this represented a great step forward in humanity's evolution at that time. But since then there has been little or no intervention, with the exception of the introduction of religious symbols and hybrid individuals in order to advance the spiritual understanding of your race. These are not gods or angels but simply individuals who possessed greater understanding and greater intellectual powers. Their infrequent presence in the world is a sign that humanity has a relationship with the Greater Community, a relationship which you must now begin to recognize, accept and cultivate.

Spiritual development has been fostered and furthered here by foreign races so that your race, as it evolves, would have greater promise to be a productive and meaningful part of the Greater Community in the future. This is to counteract the animal nature in human beings so that your higher qualities may be stimulated and developed. Though this shows promise, the acceleration of your technology and its destructive applications, according to your old tribal mentality and your old tribal conflicts and wars, now pose a serious threat to your existence and create an alarm in the Greater

Community. This alarm is not shared by all, and indeed many consider your development something of an opportunity rather than a concern only.

You see, in the Greater Community, particularly in this part of the galaxy, there are many alliances based upon trade and other mutual benefits. There are conflicts as well. It is necessary for you to understand this so that you will not think that everyone and everything revolves around the world you live in. This is an unfortunate remnant of a primitive idea. It is understandable, though, given your isolation in the world and minimal contact with other intelligent life. But it remains a prevailing idea and one that must be seriously challenged and weeded out of your consciousness, or you will have no possibility of understanding the motives or the abilities of those who are visiting the world now and who will visit in the future.

Because you live in a Greater Community reality rather than only in a human reality, the world is influenced by the Greater Community and will be so increasingly as time advances. Greater Community intervention in the world will increase because competing races are here both to safeguard themselves against the destruction of your environment, which they consider to be too valuable to destroy, and to engage in possible resource development and future alliances with humanity should you ever be able to form a world community. Until this community is formed, alliance with the world would not be practical. No foreign power wants to become involved in the intertribal warfare of a domestic race. There is no advantage to this.

There are several different interests which are represented by your visitors. They are not aligned with each other and in some cases are even in competition with each other. Yet, there is a general consensus, given the priorities of advancing races in the Greater Community, that your environment must be preserved even if your race destroys itself. You see, in the Greater Community, environment is considered more important than racial survival. Here you have a natural world with millions of species of plants and animals, a magnificent creation, the result of millions of years of development, all now at risk because of one selfish race that is spoiling the world out of ignorance and greed.

Many people are now becoming concerned for the environment because they are concerned about the future of the race, the future of the availability of resources, the future of the quality of life, and for some even the ability of the race to survive in a declining environment. This, of course, is very important and is born of a greater understanding. It is also important because you live in a Greater Community. Here you must realize that your world is a valuable part of the Greater Community and that it is considered amongst advancing races in the Greater Community that environments such as yours belong to everyone, even though certain races have a stewardship role that is honored.

What this means for you is that should you fail to join as a world community and should your environment be threatened past a point where its reclamation can be assured, then others will intervene, not to conquer you but to preserve the environment. That is why there is a great deal of study by your visitors now on plants and animals, in order to preserve both your race and the environment and to be able to participate in this environment should humanity fail.

Perhaps this seems frightening and too radical for you to consider, but it is the reality in which you live. It gives great impetus and importance to our emphasis on Knowledge and on contribution in the world. People are casual about these things because they do not see their relevance and importance. Many people are casual even about meeting the necessities of their lives because they do not consider the consequences of neglecting them. Many people are casual about their spirituality because they think it is an addendum to their other interests, goals and priorities. Yet, in reality this is not the case.

Your world is an evolving world. It is so considered by your neighbors and by your visitors from afar. Some are here to attempt to rescue things that were buried long ago because they are concerned that the environment of the world may be so compromised that in the future it may not be possible to rescue these things. Others are here to determine ways that they may introduce their genetic materials into the human race in order that the human race may, so to speak, take a quantum leap in its evolutionary development. And other interests are here to discern the possibility of your replacement should you fail. This is a real possibility, and given the events of the last forty years, it has become greater than ever. Because there is not yet a consensus amongst humanity to join together to meet its environmental and social needs, the risks have grown much greater. Therefore, Greater Community intervention in the world has increased dramatically and will continue to do so.

Some people think that these visitors are here to bring enlightenment to humanity. Others think that they are here to take over the world. And of course many people think there is no Greater Community visitation at all! Regardless of what people think and what they like to believe, you live in a Greater Community reality, and you are merging into this reality because you are becoming more involved with it every day. This is a product of your own development and the result of human error. It is also a product of the events and dynamics of Greater Community life.

In the Greater Community, the advancing race of any solar system is considered the master of that solar system and rarely will outside intervention occur. History has proven that the conquest of one race over another is too costly and too destructive. There are more subtle ways to influence nations, and in this, the development of skill in the mental environment has been the great emphasis for those who are interested in conquest and acquisition. Brute force is too destructive, requires too much effort and often produces unwanted results. This is a lesson that most advanced worlds have learned. There are more subtle forms of persuasion in the mental environment, and we have touched upon this in many of our discourses in this book. We have introduced the idea of the mental environment in its relevance to your life. Development in the mental environment and development in Greater Community Knowledge must come about and can only come about through diligent practice and preparation in *Steps to Knowledge*.

What we are introducing here is a larger perspective so that you can understand more completely the predicament of your world and the opportunities that are offered to you now. Understanding should precede action in order for action to be meaningful and wisely employed.

The Greater Community is with you now. You are learning about it. It is influencing your thoughts. It is influencing your images. It is influencing your art and your psychology. It is having an impact on your physical environment. Indeed, around the world individuals are encountering Greater Community intelligences who are either observing them or studying them for various purposes. Yet, because humanity's focus is so diffused and distracted by small and meaningless things and because humanity cannot reach a consensus about even the most obvious things, these Greater Community interventions arouse minimal response, understanding and awareness.

The world here is quite unique in the development of its biology and the temperateness of its climate. This, of course, has been known for some time by races who have visited here. But because of its biological richness, it has been difficult for many races to settle here, because of the world's specific atmospheric conditions and because of the presence of so many biological entities. When you consider that advanced races who are engaged actively in space travel generally live in sterile environments for most of their existence, to enter an environment with such biological diversity poses a tremendous hazard. Even many advanced races live underground where they are able to sterilize their environment and thus protect their populations from disease very effectively. So, as the world is rich and abundant in life, it is also a difficult environment to adapt to for these same reasons.

A great deal of study is being undertaken currently to understand the biological mechanisms here in order to prevent illness so that Greater Community individuals and groups of individuals can temporarily inhabit the world for their own purposes.

Humanity is at a very crucial turning point. It is in an adolescent stage of its development, adolescent in the respect that it is discovering greater technological powers but is lacking maturity, accountability and responsibility, which makes the discovery of these powers very hazardous indeed.

In the world, there is now the capability of not only poisoning the environment but destroying the human race. This is of grave concern to your neighbors, not that they value human existence particularly, but they value this environment. It is in their collective interest to maintain this environment, even if they cannot live within it. The human race, then, poses a threat to Greater Community interests, and given the ethics of Greater Community cooperation and understanding, it is allowable to displace a race that is threatening its own environment. This is admissible within this part of the Greater Community in which you live, which is in no way a remote part of the galaxy.

Another reason there has been limited Greater Community involvement in the world in the past is because other planets in your solar system are inhospitable, and mining and resource development have proven to be more costly than they are worth. Therefore, you have one inhabitable planet alone in a very large solar system. However, even as we speak, there are Greater Community establishments being built on other worlds in this solar system, mostly to observe the earth. Because of this, your visitors do not have to travel very far to reach the surface of your world, and so they can take their data and their specimens to their respective areas of study. Your solar system does afford many opportunities for this. But as a whole your solar system is quite limited in terms of Greater Community interests, with the exception of your planet.

Adaptation to foreign environments is a very serious matter, and many worlds which may be considered rich in resources have proven too difficult to explore and to exploit. Barren worlds are actively exploited if they can be reached and if establishments can be built, either on the surface or underground. They are not considered valuable environments. However, your world is considered valuable, and there is great interest in and emphasis on preserving this environment, whether humanity can evolve successfully or not.

We are not trying to scare you or threaten you by saying these things. We want you to have a greater understanding of the world in which you live and of the Greater Community in which you live. You are not immune from the Greater Community and you are not isolated in the universe. As a matter of fact, human civilization is remarkably accessible, given that you are surface dwellers and do not live underground. Your activities, your communications, your establishments and your conflicts are easily seen by the discreet observer. The fact that human beings are still very superstitious means that your ideas and images can easily be controlled.

One of the important thresholds for people is to learn to distinguish between material reality and spiritual reality. This distinction is clear in the minds of those who have developed this advantage in the Greater Community, and we should mention here that not many races have really been successful in developing this understanding, so it is not universally held. Human beings have difficulty distinguishing between a physical event and a spiritual event. This makes it very easy to fool you. Project an image and people will think that they are having a religious experience! Carry out a physical activity in the world and people may think that it is a projection of their own psychology. These levels of reality, then, have not adequately been distinguished. Therefore, humanity is easily confused by new experiences and strange events.

Those visitors who are investigating the biology of your world are carrying on their work. Their work represents several different motives. These groups are not all in cooperation with each other. They are carrying on their work regardless of whether they are seen or not. There is not that great an emphasis placed on hiding from people because people offer very little challenge, mentally or physically. During the dark nights of the year, visits can be made. Certain people will be aroused, and witnesses will see things, but this in general does not obstruct the activities of your visitors.

In this part of the Greater Community, there is no ruling world or ruling body. There is no center of government. There is only a center of trade between participating nations. This is a great federation, but its primary purpose is to maintain trade. What goes on outside the jurisdiction of this trade is anybody's business. Within the established areas and parameters of trade, there are ruling guidelines for behavior. But this government of commerce, as you could call it, does not interfere in internal affairs. Only if one world is threatening another militarily can there be any possibility of intervention, but this is very rare. Worlds are far too distant from each other to enforce uniformity. Races are far too different from each other to have common values.

There are certain ethical principles that are established for the convenience of interacting with other worlds within a general area. These are more like codes of ethics in order to preserve peace. One of the codes of ethics is the preservation of all biological environ-ments. This holds true in the region in which your world exists. It is enforced for practical and expedient reasons. Terrestrial worlds such as yours are rare and represent valuable biological components that can be duplicated and introduced in other worlds where life is being colonized or is already established.

You see, many races who are now involved in intergalactic travel exhausted their world's resources long ago. In some cases, they have compromised the productivity of other worlds. They are now dependent upon trade for their vital resources. In order to revitalize their own food-processing abilities, they visit worlds such as yours to collect samples. The fact that an indigenous race on earth is threatening such a magnificent storehouse of biological materials is naturally of concern to them. Your conventional warfare in the past, though locally destructive, posed no great threat to the world overall. Therefore, it has not been a cause for intervention. But the development of atomic energy, world pollution and biological war-fare have aroused grave concern for the safety of this world.

Now, this is difficult for people to hear and to understand because they think that they are the most important thing in the universe and that even their natural environment is second to this, as well as everything else that lives in the world. It is generally considered that everything else is expendable as long as humanity is prospering. The environment is being used up and thrown away. Other species are being destroyed at random with very little regard except by a few sensitive individuals amongst you. This recklessness and irresponsibility is generating Greater Community involvement at this time. Ways are being considered as to how to neutralize your destructive behaviors, how to preserve the environment and, by some who have your interests at heart, how to revitalize and intro-duce greater ethical standards and moral strength into your race.

This is very important for you to understand. The great diffi-

culty here, from a human standpoint, is being able to gain a Greater
Community perspective. We are giving you this information so
that you can begin to develop a Greater Community perspective. It
does not matter that you believe what we are saying or not. Much
of what we are saying may challenge many of your ideas and beliefs,
but we are only presenting the facts of the situation. We are not
trying to scare you. You need to gain a Greater Community perspective. Until this happens, you will not understand what you are
doing, what is happening in your world and what its future possibilities are. You will certainly not understand Greater Community
visitations, and you will not understand the emphasis and purpose of
other intelligent life that are interacting with your world.

We are, therefore, very emphatic in encouraging the development of Knowledge, for this is the source of your responsibility
and moral accountability. With Knowledge, you will know what
to do and will be able to do what is right. You will be able to carry
on constructive behavior and activities and divorce yourself from
those things which only hurt you and others. We are emphatic in
encouraging the development of a Greater Community perspective,
for as long as you think within your isolated human perspective, you
will not understand yourself, your capabilities or the events that are
taking place in your world. You must have a greater perspective to
see greater things. You must have a more universal or complete perception and understanding in order to see beyond the limits of your
own thinking. This is possible, and it is most assuredly necessary.

People will always be preoccupied with their own personal
needs and endeavors. Only a few amongst you will look into the
bigger picture to see beyond these preoccupations, to discern the
direction of your world and its possibilities for humanity. This represents a greater perspective. For these individuals, a Greater Community perspective will be particularly helpful because when you
see and accept that you are not the center of the universe and that

not everything that is happening is happening for you, you will be in a position to take greater responsibility for your actions and to see yourself as part of a Greater Community of life.

The Greater Community is not bound by human preoccupations, human ideals, human beliefs or human assumptions. Many of its societies are more advanced than yours — spiritually and technologically. Therefore, developing a Greater Community perspective puts you in a position to learn a great deal, a position that you would not be able to assume otherwise.

Greater Wisdom is possible for humanity, but in order for it to be received rather than denied or resented, a greater reality must be presented — a greater need for humanity, a greater need for your world and a greater possibility given your inherent virtues and abilities. In this, The Greater Community Way of Knowledge is unique. It will take you far beyond what is thought to be humanly possible. It will take you beyond human assumptions, beliefs, ideas, rituals and historical constraints. It is a rare and unique learning opportunity. It begins with what you know and develops your awareness and your perception, your ability to discern, your moral responsibilities, your sense of identity and your concern for your world and your race. It is here for humanity to enable humanity to keep pace with its own development and with the needs of the world. It is spiritual because it recognizes the presence and reality of a Greater Power in your life, not a greater extraterrestrial power but a greater Spiritual Power that is intrinsic to each of you and that you share together. You will need this Greater Power now, for you cannot make this advancement that we have indicated based purely on your human motivation alone. You need greater assistance, for you will need a greater mind, a greater will and a greater responsibility in order to meet the challenges in the future. For this, a Greater Power — the power of the Creator and the presence of Knowledge — is vital for your success.

The emphasis of this spirituality is not to take you away from the world. It is to enable you to be in the world. Its emphasis is not for you to make everything look sweet and lovely. It is to enable you to serve a world in need. Your concern is the world. What goes on in other worlds at this point is not your concern, but the fact that you are part of a Greater Community represents the larger context from which you can see yourself far more clearly and from which you can discern your responsibilities and the needs of the world.

It is easier to see yourself looking from the outside in than from the inside out. For example, people think they are remarkably complex and idiosyncratic, but in reality they are not that complicated, and they are not that different from each other. Your differences are slight and are often environmentally conditioned. This is not to say that you are not wonderful and marvelous, because you are wonderful and marvelous. But do not think that you are inexplicable. To an intelligent observer, human behavior and human thinking are easily discernible. Other races are not dominated by human logic, so they do not depend upon it in order to make their evaluations. You may appear logical to yourself, but that may only mean that you appear foolish to an outside observer. Human beings behave in predictable ways, and this can be easily discerned, especially because you are surface dwellers and all of your activities are out on the surface. In the mental environment, your minds can be read and understood, for you have not yet developed the ability to shield your thoughts, which will be necessary in the future if you are ever to compete successfully with Greater Community forces. Spiritually speaking, you are still very tribal in your outlook. You are very conditioned by the past and by past traditions, many of which are far overshadowed and have no relevance in a Greater Community context.

So, you see, there is a tremendous opportunity and need for advancement. Not everyone has to become engaged in this preparation, but a significant number of people need to. The race is furthered by the actions of a relatively small percentage of the population, but everyone has to be able to go along with it. Do not wait until your environment begins to fail you. Do not wait until your food supply becomes threatened and begins to diminish. Do not wait until your nations are bankrupt from warfare and exploitation. Then the road to recovery will be very difficult and possibly too difficult to achieve.

We have emphasized that you were sent to the world to serve the world. Though people generally believe they are in the world to satisfy themselves, you were sent to the world to serve the world, the whole world. Even if you only work in one little place, you are here to serve the whole world. From a Greater Community perspective, you are all one people. From a Greater Community perspective, you are not seen as being American or Chinese or Brazilian or African. You are all seen as one people, you will all be treated as one people, and you are all accountable as one people. So, the more you can begin to behave as if you were part of one people, which you will naturally do as you grow strong with Knowledge, then things can get done here. Then greater responsibilities can be assumed and shared.

Greater Community reality is not a foreign reality. It is not something that is going on way over there, far beyond your interests and concerns. You are right in the middle of it! You are right in the middle of the Greater Community. It is here. Your isolation is over. No longer will you be left alone to do as you please. No longer will you have a safe autonomy. It is like a little village in the jungle that is being discovered by the outside world. It is forever changed and in some cases may not survive the experience. The world is like a little village that has been left all to itself for these many millennia and now it has been discovered, not for the first time of course, but the intervention here is permanent. It will not go away.

You are involved now. This is your life now. Its problems

are great, but what it offers you is freedom from personal isolation. Your life offers you a chance to become a citizen of the world to serve the world. It offers you an escape from your own little preoccupations. In this, it offers you greatness because it is great. If problems are great, the solutions will be great, the actions will be great, and the individuals who undertake them will be great. Your race needs greatness now because of what it faces. It faces the need to repair its world and to unite its people. It faces competition from the Greater Community. And it faces a requirement to evolve spiritually and psychologically in order to become citizens of the world and to become one race, in order to participate in the Greater Community.

You are now part of the Greater Community. Congratulations! It has arrived. You have arrived. Though many, many people — even some experts amongst you — still think that the nearest life is billions and billions of miles away, it is right in your own back yard. You will see the effect and evidence of this old anthropocentric thinking all around you. People's ideas of themselves and the world offer no place for other intelligent life to exist.

Human beings have never had to compete with other intelligent life. Human beings compete with each other, often destructively, but not with a totally different form of intelligent life. To learn to do this will make you strong and discerning and will expand greatly the boundaries of your awareness and your capability. If your motives are honest, pure and wholesome, then there is the possibility of achieving Wisdom for this race, or at least for many in this race. Yet, if your motive is conquest and domination, then you will fail in the Greater Community because those whom you choose to be your adversaries are far more advanced than you in both their awareness and their capabilities. Their mental and physical abilities will exceed yours.

Your possibility for success rests in Knowledge, for another race can be technologically advanced and even have gained some skill in the mental environment, but that does not mean that they are strong with Knowledge. That is why we emphasize Knowledge, not only for your fulfillment and well-being in the world but also because it gives you a great foundation and the only real advantage you have in terms of competition in the mental environment.

In the Greater Community, warfare as you know it—which is one side destroying another—does occur but is rare because there are other more subtle and less destructive ways of accomplishing the same task. Make others think the way you want them to think. You can do this without firing a shot. Make others respond the way you want them to respond and you can control the outcome. Make others believe what you want them to believe and they are completely pliable. All of these are possible when there is no Knowledge. Without Knowledge, you are easily manipulated. Your behavior can be predicted, and you can be persuaded. Your beliefs, your ideals, your religions and your political conditions can all be used against you. Only when Knowledge is strong within you can you become immune from even Greater Community influences, for Knowledge is the only thing within you that cannot be manipulated or dominated. It is completely free in the physical universe, and that is why the more you are aligned with Knowledge and are in relationship with Knowledge, the more free and free from intervention you become.

Some people think that The Greater Community Way of Knowledge is a way to change human thinking, when in reality it is a way to liberate human thinking, for it emphasizes the only thing in you that is truly free, the only thing in you which has power and real self-determination.

You live in a Greater Community reality. Embrace this reality. Learn of this reality. Become strong in Knowledge. Become a student of Knowledge. Move beyond tribal mentality. Become a citizen of the world. This is the promise, and this is the need for you now. In this, you have great support and true companions.

True inspiration
arises when you are
engaged in the world
in a purposeful way.

Twenty-nine

INSPIRATION

SURELY INSPIRATION is something that must abide with you in meeting great challenges, in exerting yourself, in concentrating your mind and in resolving conflicts in your life. But inspiration will only occur momentarily here and there as a reminder, as something that reconnects you to something greater that represents a larger purpose in life beyond your personal concerns and interests. Inspiration can come from Knowledge. It can come from your Teachers. It can come from your companions. And it can come from very unexpected places. It is a spark that can affect you if your mind is open and receptive to it.

The most important thing, however, is that you are able to inspire yourself. Though you will need inspiration from others, it is your ability to renew your purpose and determination and to remind yourself of your greater responsibilities that will make all the difference. To be self-directed, or inner-directed, requires that your motivation can be renewed and rededicated from within you. Without this, you will not get beyond the first barrier or obstacle that stands in your way. And, indeed, many people do not proceed beyond these first obstacles.

Inspiration is something that you must generate within yourself. You must also seek it in your environment and in your relationships. To seek it in the environment, you must direct yourself to those individuals, to those events, even to those historical accounts, that reinforce your conviction and commitment and remind you that greater things are possible given true determination, true companionship and a worthy goal. Indeed, the lives of inspiring people can serve to help you here tremendously, for they have risen above their own circumstances. They have risen above their own concerns. They have risen above their own priorities to respond to a greater need in the world. They were not that different from you. The thing that distinguishes them from others is an abiding need within them and their ability to respond to the world.

This inner need and outer initiatory stimulation are very essential. You may feel the need, but something in the world has to call it out of you. You cannot call it out of yourself. True inspiration arises when you are engaged in the world in a purposeful way. True inspiration arises in the context of purposeful relationship—with a person, with a place, or with an endeavor. It is not something that is within you alone. It must be sparked by the presence of others and in the context of a greater involvement.

At the outset you will need the accounts of others' lives. You will need encouragement from your companions. You will need to seek out those things that remind you of your purpose and reinforce your conviction that you can carry it out. You will need these external supports and indeed they are there to serve you. If you seek for them, you will find them. Though they might not seem abundant, the truth is that millions of people throughout the ages have done noble and worthy things with their lives, and their examples have been recorded in many cases, certainly enough to provide ample encouragement for you.

At the outset, you will also need real companionship. Here you must distance yourself from people who discourage you and who add to your confusion or self-doubt. You must even distance yourself from people who are going in a different direction, even if their pursuits are worthy. Indeed, you must distance yourself from anyone who cannot support a greater purpose in you. You do not cast them out of your heart or deny your love and appreciation for them, but you must have distance from them in order to proceed. Do not underestimate the importance of this. It is absolutely vital. Without the right companions, you cannot undertake a journey. Without true assistance, you cannot even begin.

Often at the outset, one of the most difficult challenges is to disengage from relationships which cannot accompany you on an important discovery in life. This is often the first great challenge, and many people will not be able to meet it. But you can. And you must. Doing this restores to you the confidence that there is a Greater Power living within you. You side with it. You choose with it. You follow it. Here you may have to give up money, pleasure and even love at the outset, but this strengthens Knowledge within you. Here you realize that you have two choices. It always comes down to two choices: to follow Knowledge or not to follow Knowledge. Now, of course, if you are not aware of Knowledge or don't know what Knowledge is, this may seem incomprehensible to you. But as Knowledge becomes revealed, you will see in every case that you have two choices. To make the right choice, you must find inspiration in your companions and in your life, and you must inspire yourself.

You will always have great support for making the wrong choice. You can always find much companionship in going the wrong way. And you can always receive much consolation for not going anywhere at all. But what value is there in this? Does this inspire you? Does this encourage you to live a greater life and to exercise a greater authority that the Creator has given to you? Is there anything inspiring about being safe and comfortable? Is there anything here that points to a greater life and a greater fulfillment?

We are not suggesting that you throw away all of your se-
curities, but we are saying that at the important junctures in your
life where you have to make an important decision, you must risk
your security to undertake something of a greater magnitude, the
outcome of which you will not be able to see at the outset. Perhaps
you can take many treasured things with you. Perhaps you can take
nothing with you. It depends on the situation and what is required
in your own learning and preparation.

There is something else in your life beyond comfort, pleasure
and security, something of far greater importance and magnitude.
Perhaps you alone amongst all of your acquaintances are feeling
this and can sense this. Here you will need to align yourself with
others who have the same inner need and the same inner conviction, however ill defined it might be. They too are responding to
something. They too are being called in life to follow something,
to find something and to do something beyond the normal range
of human interests and activities. You need these people. You need
their demonstration. You need their reinforcement. You need
their experiences as a confirmation of your own. They can provide
inspiration, for they are doing something that is beyond their personal interests, as you yourself will provide inspiration when you do
something beyond your personal interests.

Inspiration is a natural by-product of selfless activity. It affects
other minds. It leaves its impressions and has its impact. You need
to receive this inspiration at the outset, and later you will need to
give it to reinforce its reality. Inspiration is a reminder that you are
a part of a greater life and a greater purpose, that you are not simply
a human being whose only concern is for survival and self-gratification. This reminder is important, for humanity is preoccupied with
survival and gratification, and you may have to look far and wide
indeed to find those who feel a greater calling and a greater impetus
in life. Those who do not feel this, who do not have this experience

and who are not moved by it cannot go with you on your journey no matter how much you care for them personally. No matter what their wonderful attributes may be, they cannot journey with you, and you must realize this and accept it, or they will either intentionally or inadvertently spoil your inspiration. They will become part of what holds you back rather than part of what inspires you.

To choose that which is inexplicable but necessary is an act of courage and personal integrity. This is inspiring. You can find examples of this if you look for them. You will find what you look for in the world. If you want security and self-gratification only, you will find these up to a point, though there is no real security without Knowledge, and self-gratification is not very gratifying no matter how much you give it to yourself.

It is correct to say that all inspiration comes from Knowledge, but since people do not know what Knowledge is, this is a difficult definition to accept and even more difficult to apply. Let us say for now that inspiration is a reminder. It is a reinforcement. It is a re-membrance. It represents that greater truth of your life that is calling you to recognize it, to accept it and to embrace it. If you feel this, then you must go forward. Do not hold back. If this is moving your life, then move within it, not blindly but wisely, with your eyes open because you are a beginner in The Way of Knowledge.

No matter how advanced you think you might be in spiritual things or in the ways of the world, you are still a beginner in The Greater Community Way of Knowledge. Accept this. It will give you a great advantage in life. Yes, it will humble you, and it will temper your ideas concerning yourself. But it will give you a great advantage because it enables you to become wise and observant. Being a beginner teaches you to use restraint and forbearance in your participation with others. It teaches you to generate inner power and strength rather than throw it away on emotional outbursts or meaningless involvements. It teaches you when to speak and when not to speak, when to act and when not to act, who to be with and who not to be with, which way to go and which way not to go. This is the evidence that Knowledge is becoming active in your life and that you are following it and learning The Way of Knowledge and The Way of Wisdom. This is inspiring.

Inspiration refers to the spirit. It represents a Greater Reality and a greater purpose in life, and it will be manifest if you look for it and if you need it. If you preoccupy yourself with petty interests and little concerns and fearful fantasies, you will not find the inspiration that you need. If you spend all of your time with people who are not responding to this, then you will lose your ability to respond as well. You are not strong enough with Knowledge to initiate these people into Knowledge. No matter how advanced you may think you are, you are not this strong. Accept this. This is Wisdom.

Only a very advanced practitioner in The Way of Knowledge can inspire those who do not feel the call of Knowledge. Only the very advanced can be initiators in this regard, and even here there can be no personal ambition on their part. You must let the Greater Power work through you rather than attempting to use it for your own personal gain or self-validation. By being a beginner you can become a recipient. If you think you are more advanced than a beginner, you will not be in a position to learn or to receive, and then your advancement will only occur at the cost of great disappointments.

As we have said, you will need tremendous reinforcement because you are choosing something that the world does not choose or value. You are choosing something that perhaps many of your companions do not choose or value. You are choosing a direction away from most people's preoccupation with survival and self-gratification. You will not have many models, but you can seek them out. You need others to say to you, "Yes, you are doing something important. Stay with it! It is valuable. Do not rush it. Do not hold it back. Be patient with it. Be observant. Stay with it!"

You who are reading these words have an advantage here, for you have come upon a mysterious and wonderful preparation, something that has recently been introduced into the world to assist humanity, to enable it to advance to meet its own needs and to meet the challenge of living in the Greater Community. You are very fortunate in this regard. These words, then, will serve to reinforce a greater understanding that is seeking to emerge within you. These words will confirm things known in the past that have led you into a greater pursuit in life, a pursuit that has often been compromised and obstructed by personal needs, fears and ambitions.

Therefore, we offer inspiration, not only in the form of encouragement but in the expression of truth. Whenever you speak the truth that is the truth, you provide inspiration. Whether others can accept this inspiration or not is up to them. The important thing is that it has come from you. Often you will say or do inspiring things without even thinking about it. It will happen naturally. For that moment, you are not dominating your own mind and behavior. Something greater is allowed to speak and act through you, something that we call Knowledge, the greater part of you that joins you with all life.

When you speak the truth and do what is correct and real, you provide inspiration. When you deny this or refute it or when you try to mix it with your own personal needs, you deny inspiration. If your life is not inspiring, then it is detracting from inspiration in the world. This is true because inspiration can be equated with value, meaning, purpose and truth. No one is neutral in this regard. You are either adding inspiration or taking it away through the expression of your life. No one is sitting on the sidelines. Everyone is involved. Everyone is making contributions to life, whether it enhances life or detracts from it. This is going on all the time, and everyone is involved.

Do not fall prey to the temptation to judge or discredit people for the lack of inspiration in their lives. This is unnecessary. You have to stay focused on what you have to do and on those few relationships that are capable of supporting you. When you become a critic of humanity, you lose your own meaning and worth. Humanity is what it is. To call it good or bad is meaningless. It is where it is. We do not lie to you and say everything is wonderful and everyone is doing great. Likewise, we do not lie to you and say everyone is stupid and idiotic. People are where they are. Many have not reached the threshold of Knowledge. Many have not responded to a greater need and a greater calling in their lives. Why blame them for this? Accept it. If inspiration were abundant in human life, then the world would look very different than it does today. If Knowledge were being expressed through the lives of many people in a consistent way, the world would look very different than it does today. Accept where people are and concentrate on what you must do. Do not waste your self-worth and your vitality in criticizing others. This takes away from inspiration and makes inspiration more difficult for you to attain or to receive.

Criticism must be replaced with compassion, for compassion is based on understanding. It is understanding where people are in the stages of life. It does not make them right. It does not make them wrong. It does not release them from their responsibilities, but it does not condemn them for their failures. Go back to inspiration. Concentrate on something that is greater, more important, more genuine and more real. It is within you, and you can find it in the world if you look for it, but it will not be obvious. Here you must take responsibility for seeking out people, situations, examples and demonstrations that reinforce a Greater Reality within you, that support you in proceeding forward and that encourage you to do so. You must look for this goodness because you need it. Alone you cannot overcome the world or the world's preoccupations. You need great assistance to do this. You need assistance from beyond the world through your Spiritual Family, and you need assistance within the world through meaningful relationships. And you need to be able to generate it within yourself.

To generate inspiration within yourself, it is necessary to identify those experiences and accomplishments in your life that had a tremendous and positive impact on your development and future possibilities. Perhaps these are only moments in the span of your years, but they stand out in great contrast to your normal range of experience. These are essential for you to remember and to recall. This will give you the strength and encouragement that you need should you be facing an important decision in your life. Then you can choose that which is correct over that which is merely expedient or personally rewarding. You can do something that you feel and know is right over something that merely looks good. Here you go beyond appearances to penetrate the real value of things. You can have this encouragement because you have experienced it before, and you have seen this demonstration in others.

Remember these experiences and do not forget them. Do not deny or discredit them. Sometimes people deny or discredit their inspiring experiences because they did not yield a personal reward that was expected. They say, "Well, I did not make money out of this situation!" or "Gee, I really lost a lot in this situation!" Of course. Doing what is real, what is needed and what is correct does not fill your pockets with money, and it does not enhance your resume in life. Yet, it gives you something greater, so much greater. It gives you reality; it gives you truth and purpose, things which those who are clamoring for wealth — the wealth of money and the wealth of love — cannot find. For this you must have faith. Call upon your earlier experiences to remind yourself. Call upon your relationships to remind you, and seek out the companionship that is worthy of your journey in life.

One wrong companion can spoil the whole endeavor. Think of it like this. You are going to climb a great mountain. This requires equipment and preparation. This requires planning and determination. It requires that you resolve certain conflicts at the outset in order to proceed. The journey is going to require tremendous strength and dedication. It is going to require some very wise planning, and it is going to require worthy and capable companionship. If one companion does not share this, he or she can undermine the whole expedition. One person whose commitment is not genuine can cast doubt upon everyone's focus and purpose.

You *are* on a mission in life, no less great than climbing a great mountain. You have come here on a mission. You do not just simply wash up on the shore of life to live a few years and then pass away. You came here on a mission. Your mission will not garner you wealth, fame or universal appreciation. Instead, your mission will give something back to you that the world cannot provide, something of far greater value that only you will be able to give to the world. This is inspiration, born of Knowledge, realized through genuine decision making and real living, shared through meaningful relationships and passed on through contribution to those who need it everywhere.

This is inspiration, the presence of Spirit in life. Have this Spiritual Presence be with you and have this Presence prepare you. Have this Presence lead you forward. Have it abide with you in your times of doubt, fear and confusion. Have it be evident in your primary relationships. Have this Presence help you determine your priorities and even your practical needs, for this is the Presence of Knowledge living within you and expressing itself through your relationships with others and with the world.

You have the possibility of becoming a messenger of inspiration. This does not mean that you simply say positive things, share exciting or uplifting ideas or promote great ideals for humanity.

No, it is not this. It is that the presence of Spirit is with you, and it is regenerated through your wise decision making and through your selfless activity. Here Knowledge can speak through you, act through you and make a demonstration in the world through you. This is inspiration, yours to receive and yours to transmit into the world. This is possible in The Way of Knowledge, and in The Way of Knowledge this will be your destiny.

*How we
regard you
is a model
for how you
can regard others.*

Thirty

KINDNESS

WHEN YOU ARE WITH KNOWLEDGE, you can afford to be kind because you are not rushing about the world trying to fulfill your goals and assure your security. You are able to be in present time with far greater effectiveness and far greater presence of mind. If you are not rushing about, you become aware of what is here now, and you become responsive to the genuine needs of those whom you are meant to serve.

You can afford to be compassionate when you are with Knowledge because Knowledge recognizes where people are without demanding that they be different. Knowledge fosters understanding based upon acceptance. It does not project hopeful ideas, yet it does not deny the needs of anyone. It moves you towards certain people and away from others without condemnation. It teaches you over time to recognize that there are stages in life, and each stage has its advantages and liabilities.

With Knowledge, you can afford kindness because you want to nurture things, and you want yourself and the people around you to be grounded in what is real and genuine. Here your kindness is not always sweet. Sometimes it is demanding. Sometimes it produces a confrontation, but it is kind because it asks others to honor themselves enough to be real with you and with themselves. It asks this through the way you live, the way you think and the way you interact with others.

You can afford to be kind when you are with Knowledge because you are not trying to change anyone. You are only stimulating their inherent abilities. You are not trying to seduce anyone in order to get things from them, to win their love or to gain their financial assistance. With Knowledge you are not condemning them, and this allows kindness to naturally emerge in all of its vast array of expressions.

To be genuinely kind is to recognize a Greater Reality in another and to nurture and support that without denying that person's present state. To be compassionate is to understand conflict and failure and to realize that until people have gained a foundation in Knowledge, they are prone to self-deception. They will be captured by the fascinations of the world, and they will be prone to all the miseries that attend such fascinations. And they will be fretful, fearful and defensive. You will understand this because you will have experienced it yourself, and having found the way out of this state, you will be able to provide a way for others so that they too may find their way.

Within the greatness of the Greater Community and in the smallness of your individual sphere of life, kindness creates inspiration. It incites in those who are prepared a greater yearning and a greater ability. True kindness is not condescending. It does not patronize people. It does not use affected behavior to win friends or to gain advantages. It is kind because it is understanding. It is compassionate because it is understanding.

In our presentations to you, we challenge you and we nurture you. We acknowledge you and we prompt you forward. We present great challenges and we validate great abilities. We do not value falseness, but we do value sincerity. This is kindness. How we regard you is a model for how you can regard others. We understand the world's tribulations and its little joys. Having found Knowledge and having joined together in true relationship, we can look upon you with great understanding and offer a greater promise. This is kindness.

Do not confuse kindness with being nice to everyone. Do not confuse kindness with acting sweetly or with stimulating people's vanity by complimenting them when compliments have not been earned. Kindness is not about doing good things to feel good. Kindness really comes from having a greater regard for people. This greater regard must contain an understanding of their condition — their weaknesses, those things that threaten them or undermine them and their true abilities and greater possibilities. With this greater regard there can be true value — without deception, without hiding one thing to emphasize another, without concealment at all.

In our presentations to you, we present greater responsibilities and demands in life that require greater aptitude in you, greater sobriety about your life and its value, and a more objective view of the world — its problems and its benefits. This is kindness. If we kept you from your greater duty in life, we would be contributing to your unhappiness and dissatisfaction. But we do not do this. We challenge you. We call you forward. We call upon you, not someone else. Our presentation didn't come to you by accident. It came to you for a purpose. This is kindness. We require more of you than perhaps you think you can give. We require that because we know you can give it, and you need to give it, and you want to give it.

We present greater problems to you because these motivate you to do great things in life. This is kindness. We accept your liabilities without valuing them. We accept your limits without valuing them. This is kindness. We are compassionate because we know what it means to pass through the great threshold from being an isolated and separate individual to becoming a greater participant in the evolution and the expression of life. We know what it means and what it requires to regain full relationship with life and full partnership with others. We can afford to be kind because we have no other intention. If kindness is merely a behavior or an affectation, it is but another ploy to use people for your own personal interests. But kindness arises naturally and is inspired when you are naturally engaged with your life and inspired by your life.

Kindness and compassion are also cultivated because with a greater understanding, you realize how difficult the challenges of life are. You do not underestimate them. You do not hide them. You do not cover them up with a prettier picture. You face them. You do not make them bigger than they are or less than they are. You take your life seriously, and you take your enjoyments happily. When you are not attempting to use your life and other people's lives to fulfill ambitions or to build defenses, then kindness emerges from you. Then you are moved by people. Their needs and their value inspire you, motivate you and encourage you to give something of yourself.

When you are not trying to prove yourself, then your basis of judgment and condemnation of others begins to fall away. If you are not struggling to get somewhere in your life, then you can slow down to understand where people are and how things are at this moment. To be compassionate does not mean that you excuse or justify error. It does not mean that you cover anything up. It means that you understand the nature of another's predicament without justifying it.

To become compassionate with yourself, you must be able to step away from your own suffering and have a greater viewpoint of your life. Then you can say to yourself, "What I am doing here is not right, and I must change it," or "What I am doing here is fine, and I will support it." Here there is no cruelty. There is no punishment. There is only the recognition that when you do what is real and good, you feel real and good, and when you do something that is not real and good, you do not feel real and you do not feel good. How simple this is, and yet how easily it escapes people's understanding and recognition.

Kindness is built on acceptance. Acceptance is built on understanding. And understanding is built on experience. To have this experience, you must be patient and observant. As your own ambitions die and pass from your life, you become present to others. From this, kindness grows and with this compassion grows as well.

You can demand great things from yourself, but you must accept that a certain amount of failure is not only inevitable but necessary. To gauge how much compassion and kindness you have towards yourself, consider how you treat yourself when you make mistakes. Consider what your response to error is within yourself. Can you tolerate making mistakes, even very foolish ones? Can you stand it when you have done something very dumb? How do you face failure in your life when you have attempted something and it did not work, and you tried again and it still did not work, and you couldn't make it work, and you couldn't figure out how to make it work? How do you respond to this? Judgment and condemnation are easy here. Understanding, compassion and kindness are not so easy.

If you become a student of *Steps to Knowledge*, you will learn to become patient because you will see that your life has its own progression, that you learn at a certain pace, and that learning requires periods of re-evaluation and accountability. Learning is not simply collecting ideas or insights or happy experiences. Understanding is the result of coming to terms with things as they really are. It is the result of dealing with reality, and so it has a soundness to it that cannot be dismissed.

Patience, perseverance, stillness, objectivity, observation — these are all very important qualities of a mind that is becoming still. It is not going to sleep. It is becoming awake, present and observant. It is becoming a witness to life rather than attempting to be its master.

Many people are afraid of The Way of Knowledge because they think that it will take away from them things that they want, challenge their goals, threaten their cherished possessions, or disappoint their hopes. This is all foolishness. There is nothing at risk here except the things that you do not really want, the things that you want that you cannot really have and the things that you try to be that are not meant for you. Those are at risk, but it is better that they fail you now rather than later lest you invest more of your life and yourself in them. These are things that cannot yield any real value for you. Coming to terms with this will give you an understanding of yourself that will be profound, and from this you will be able to become compassionate with others because you will understand their predicament, and you will recognize how difficult and magnificent it is to find an escape. Here you not only find an escape for yourself, you forge an escape for others. Here you build a new life. It is not simply given to you. You build it.

With compassion, you will understand your predicament and the tremendous process involved in finding a way out of that predicament. You will understand the challenges because you are experiencing them. You will understand the obstacles because you are facing them yourself. Then you will see why people are not quite ready. You will see why they decline the challenge. You will see why they go back into old patterns of thinking and behavior in order to feel assured and to feel some consistency in their life. You will understand why people cannot face the uncertainty of change and why they cling to old things that remind them of who they thought they were. You will understand all of this. You will understand these tendencies within yourself and within others. And if someone cannot go where you are going, if someone cannot share what you are sharing, you will say, "Oh, well," and you will go on.

You are looking ahead and not backward now. You are not trying to take everything with you. You are not trying to keep all of your loved ones with you. You are not trying to have all the things you want to have. You are going forward with a different emphasis. This is an expression of kindness because you are doing something wonderful for yourself, and this naturally translates to how you relate to other people.

In our presentation to you, we demonstrate kindness and compassion. We challenge you. We call upon you. We do not validate those things that have no meaning. We only validate those things that are intrinsic to your nature. We are not always gentle, but we are never harsh. We are not always sweet, but we are always nourishing. We provide substance not sweets. We give what is life giving, not what is sensational. We give what is constant and real, not what is intriguing and fascinating. This is kindness. This is kindness at work because of the purpose that it acknowledges and supports.

Kindness is demonstrated throughout the Greater Community. It is universal. It represents a universal understanding and a universal language. It represents a universal Knowledge and a universal Wisdom. Though cultures and races in the Greater Community vary significantly, they do have Knowledge and Wisdom in common, and that is why Knowledge and Wisdom are the foundation for real relationship beyond the boundaries of race and place of origin. This is what kindness means in the Greater Community. This is what kindness means right here on earth, right here, right now.

Advance up the mountain of life, and you will understand what is below. You can look and see the difficulty people are having at certain junctures along the way, and you will not condemn them for not being with you or for not being further along because you will understand the reality of advancement in life — not just the concept of it or the ideal of it, but the reality. You will understand what real self-application means, what work means and what contribution means. And though you may encourage these in all people and even demand it of those whom you know are capable of giving it at this moment, you will be compassionate to those who cannot. They call for your understanding not your condemnation. They need encouragement, not rejection. Encourage them by your example. You cannot go down the mountain to help them up. You cannot drop everything you are doing to go back where you used to be in order to help people through that stage of life. You have to keep on going. Signal to them that they can make it, but keep going. Do not stand by the side of the road to help others along. You must make the journey yourself. If you stop by the side of the road to help them along, they will advance and you will not. You must journey on. They will follow, for they will have someone to follow. This is kindness. Do not abdicate your own responsibilities even to help others. Fortify your responsibilities to become a man or a woman of Knowledge, and you will help everyone. Set the pace. Make the demonstration. Let your life be a vehicle for a Greater Reality to express itself through you, and your value to others will have no limit and will be incomparable.

When you are trekking up the great mountain of life, you do need help along the way, but most importantly you need to see that there are those ahead of you and that they are keeping on. Seeing this, you will either choose to go on or you will choose not to, but you will know that it is possible to proceed. If there is no one leading you, how can you know what is up ahead? What greater encouragement is there than to have others walking the path of life ahead of you and motivating you to keep going because they keep going?

Those who are ahead point the way and renew your spirit to proceed. This is kindness. They know that the only rescue is an escape. To find greatness and meaning in your life, you must move into a greater life. You cannot stay where you are and have the greatness, the meaning, the value, and the relationships that you know you need. You must move into a different life. You need to renew yourself and your mind. This is kindness.

God is not coming down the mountain helping everyone up. God is at the top calling you forth. If you can respond to this calling, you can keep going even when it gets difficult, even when you are not sure that you want to make the journey.

How do you become kind and compassionate? You learn The Way of Knowledge. Then kindness and compassion will become natural rather than fabricated. Who takes the journey? Who makes the decisions? You do. You apply yourself. You share your journey with others who can keep pace with you. You give encouragement to those who are just behind you. And you keep your eyes on those who are just ahead. In this way everyone follows and everyone leads. Everyone receives inspiration and everyone gives inspiration at the level of life at which they live. With this, humanity moves forward as a whole. Rather than a few individuals escaping the well of ignorance, everyone takes a step away from it.

Trusting in Knowledge to guide you and to inspire you is important, but you yourself must rise to the occasion by becoming honest and simple in your endeavors. You create the environment in which kindness will emerge, and you develop the compassion that you need. Just progressing in The Way of Knowledge will give you this, for you will have to learn to become kind and patient with yourself.

If you learn to become truly observant, you cannot engage in condemnation. Here you become more concerned with whether something is correct or not, rather than whether it is good or bad. Things are yes or no, not good or bad. Here there is kindness because there is no condemnation. Here there is compassion because there is an understanding about the progress of life.

Your kindness and understanding, your compassion and experience must transcend the conventions that surround and hinder you. They must be great enough and universal enough to apply even in the Greater Community, where the expression of kindness and the demonstration of compassion can be quite different from what they are assumed to be in the human community. You must experience the essence of things here. With Knowledge, this is possible. Without Knowledge, there is only ritual and conventions. With Knowledge, there is penetrating understanding. From this, a greater kindness will emerge.

Concentration
is an act of giving
yourself to something.

Thirty-one

CONCENTRATION

W E HAVE SAID IN MANY DIFFERENT WAYS at many times that concentration is power and that it is a necessary skill to develop over time to achieve a goal of any significance. Concentration is something that everyone who approaches Knowledge must develop because it takes strength of mind and conviction, focus and determination to pass through the thresholds on the way to Knowledge.

But what is concentration? What does it feel like? How is it practiced and applied? Let us address these questions because they are important for you who are considering taking the path to Knowledge. Concentration is focusing the mind on one thing, one goal or one activity to the exclusion of everything else. It is a special activity of the mind and not something that you do at every moment. But it is necessary in order to penetrate both the mysteries and the lies that surround all the great truths of life.

Thinking about one thing, observing one thing or working on one thing for any prolonged period of time produces a result that could not be achieved otherwise. Any craftsperson knows this. Any artisan knows this. Any composer of music knows this. Any builder knows this. You must concentrate on what you are doing. Work demands this concentration. That is why work is redeeming to people. Real concentration is consciously directed. The world can demand your attention for great periods of time, but that does not necessarily cultivate the kind of skills that we are referring to. To develop these skills, the motivation must come from within you, and you must have adequate support on the outside to assist you.

The *Steps to Knowledge* Program provides the structure and the focus for reclaiming and regaining your relationship with Knowledge. In order to follow these steps and to apply the practices adequately, you must develop your concentration. The motivation for this must come from within you. No one is standing over you telling you to do it. No one is demanding it of you and threatening you with the loss of your job or security if your fail. The motivation must come from within you.

Concentration is an experience of single-mindedness in present time. You can contemplate something in the future, but it must have to do with something that relates to a present need. You can concentrate upon something of a practical and material nature, or you may concentrate on an idea, a possibility, an event or a decision you are about to make and its possible outcomes.

Concentration is work. In fact, it is the very essence of work. Concentration, matched with skill and appropriate planning, produces results. It produces the results of work. When we speak of concentration, we are speaking of work for the mind. When the mind is worked and is internally motivated, then great inner strength can be developed. The mind then becomes more powerful, more focused, more dedicated and more determined. This determination and this dedication can be focused in many different directions. If they are focused upon good—upon producing meaning and value for people and upon solving problems in the world in service to humanity—their benefit can have no boundaries.

The concentration of one mind affects other minds and stimulates concentration within these minds. It activates the deeper instincts in others — the desire for contribution, accomplishment, value and meaning. These can all be stimulated by the concentration of one mind. In fact, all great people are always surrounded by people of lesser concentration seeking to benefit from the presence and the productivity of that one concentrated mind. It is natural for people to gravitate towards individuals who are concentrated, for these individuals generate power, meaning and productivity.

Developing concentration requires the ability to release your thoughts and to control your thinking. Because life is filled with so many different kinds of stimulation and presents so many different kinds of problems to consider, it is increasingly difficult to become focused on one thing. Your attention is always being pulled away by many different elements and forces. It is so easily captured by stimulating presentations in the media and events in your immediate environment. Greater and greater problems are presented for you to consider — global problems, community problems, problems in relationships and problems that are psychological in nature. With so much to consider and to think about and with so many stimulations and concerns, how can the mind be focused on one thing?

Instinctively, people know that concentration is valuable. People climb mountains in order to experience concentration. They dedicate themselves to the arts, music or dance, they build things, they invent things — all to have this experience of concentration, this experience of being completely present with no past and no future for those moments in which their mind is fully engaged. This produces relief from the constant vexations of the mind, and it produces inspiration.

Give the mind one thing to dedicate itself to. This produces equanimity because when the mind is focused, it becomes still — even when it is working very hard. This gives you freedom from past regrets and from future anxieties. It takes you away from fear and into a concentrated state of mind. It generates activity, observation and many other specific tasks.

When the mind is focused, it gains greater strength. It is more penetrating. It is more creative. And it is more effective. The importance of concentration can be immediately seen when you realize how much you must apply yourself in life, how much time and energy will be required of you and how focused and determined you must be to resolve the many problems that are genuine in nature and that require your attention.

Consider this, because we are preparing you for the Greater Community. Consider the concentration of those who are joined together in singular purpose and are visiting the world at this time. You cannot yet match their concentration. You are much too distracted. Yet, your visitors can provide motivation for you in this regard: They have achieved concentration. Even if their motives are not pure or beneficial, they have achieved concentration. Only very few people here have achieved this level of concentration. Some of these have been concentrated on good, and some have been concentrated on destruction. Yet, in all cases, they are more powerful and more effective than those around them. They have had an impact on the world. Great conflicts in the world—wars, cultural conflicts and competition for land and resources have all been waged by powerful individuals. Everyone else just goes along or tries to hide and escape.

The world that you live in is governed by individuals. A very small percentage of the population impacts humanity and determines its activities. If you think about this, you will realize that it is true. How important it is, therefore, for you to become a concentrated person—not only for the personal, spiritual and psychological benefits but also to make a difference in the world, to be a force for good and to be a vehicle for Knowledge. You must be concentrated in order for Knowledge to emerge within you. Otherwise, Knowledge will seem too powerful, too threatening or too overwhelming for you to experience.

Those who will visit your world from the Greater Community and those who have visited your world already represent a level of concentration that should incite within you a commitment to develop your mind. Knowledge will direct your mind towards what is good and will purify your motives, clarify your vision and give you direction. But you must desire Knowledge in order to apply yourself. This is not a casual pursuit. This is not being in the receiving line. This is not spiritual welfare. This is the real preparation and accomplishment.

You would not be able to think clearly around a Greater Community presence. You would not be able to make your own decisions. You would not be able to discern the actions and motives of others. You would lose both your concentration and your composure in the presence of a more powerful and focused mind. This is not to say that you are deficient or stupid; it is simply to clarify an important law in life — stronger minds influence and dominate weaker minds, and their strength is a function of concentration and motivation.

If you are to make a difference within the human community, and if you are to succeed and be self-determined in the Greater Community, you must develop this concentration. Perhaps the Greater Community aspect of this Teaching seems beyond your experience or concern. Yet, given even your individual and personal needs, concentration is a necessary requirement. But you must see that there are greater problems and greater opportunities that call upon you. These give you the adequate motivation to develop yourself and to receive the preparation that has been given to you to develop Greater Community Knowledge and Wisdom.

You were not trained to concentrate in your education in the world. You were trained to memorize information for brief periods of time in order to meet certain educational requirements, and then most of these things were forgotten. You were taught to pass tests to meet temporary or expedient needs. You were not taught patience or concentration. You were not taught contemplation or how to abide with greater problems for longer periods of time. You were not taught how to be single minded. Indeed, you were prepared to deal with complexities, but in a very superficial way. Developing the greater powers of mind is not encouraged in your culture. Indeed, the sheer weight of sensory stimulation that you experience every day — being bombarded with images, suggestions and ideas from everywhere — denies you from having access to the greater capabilities that you possess and that you need at this time.

To progress, you must work hard and concentrate. You must stay focused on things. Too much pleasure, too much indulgence or too much stimulation dulls the mind, weakens your perceptual abilities and your discernment and renders you weak and impotent in the face of the events that mark the great turning points and great opportunities in your life. Life gives you this challenge — the challenge to live in the world and the challenge to live in the Greater Community.

How will you understand a Greater Community intelligence? How will you understand what each Greater Community group is doing here and what their purpose is? You will have no possibility of success in finding an answer here if you approach these questions in a casual manner or if you merely attach yourself to pleasing or comforting ideas. You will have to concentrate on, contemplate and live with these questions without an immediate answer. This is how greater truths are revealed and greater discoveries are made. It is possible to know these things, but only with adequate preparation and self-application.

In the Greater Community, the power of concentration is well recognized amongst societies that travel and trade because they have to interact and compete with each other. Here telepathic abilities become important; strength of conviction becomes important; powers of discernment become important and the ability to communicate effectively becomes important. These are all valuable skills, though they are not always used for good purposes. Developing these skills is part of the challenge facing humanity at this time. The challenge is not about personal enhancement. It is not about finding greater satisfaction in life. It is about adapting and surviving. It is a fundamental need. The problems within your world are now too great to solve in easy or convenient ways. They require greater concentration, greater activity and more determination than most people are capable of giving or willing to give at this time.

Concentration is an act of giving yourself to something. If you are holding yourself back in life, afraid to make a commitment to anyone or anything, how can you develop concentration or mental power? You will not be able to mount a sufficient effort mentally or physically to get anything done or to comprehend anything of great importance. Because you were not taught concentration in school, it is important that you learn it now. It is necessary for your spiritual development, and it is necessary to get anything done in your life. This is not an easy task because your world is so distracting.

How do you develop concentration? You must have the right preparation, the right instruction and the right relationships. Let us discuss these now. First, the right preparation is vital. Not only must it teach you concentration, it must aim you towards the source of Wisdom within you and within others. Seeking power alone is not good. Power needs restraint, discernment and wise application. The Greater Community Way of Knowledge is not a path of power. It is a path of Wisdom. Wisdom requires power, but power must be dedicated to the right cause. It must be guided by a greater intelligence within you, which we call Knowledge. It must be inclusive in life rather than exclusive. And it must bring you into life rather than cast you further away.

There are many genuine preparations, and they all have certain things in common. What they have in common is teaching you to concentrate your mind on something beyond your personal sphere—on something bigger than you. They all teach you to quiet your mind and to become more receptive and more discerning. They all advocate that you value your deeper experiences and learn over time how to interpret them and apply their meaning.

The Greater Community Way of Knowledge focuses upon a larger context of life where concentration has increasing value and merit. It is a unique preparation. It teaches concentration because it teaches you how to focus your mind. It teaches concentration because it teaches you to still your mind, which takes great concentration. It teaches you to think constructively, and it teaches you the art of contemplation, where you learn how to think about something in a gradual and penetrating way. These are all part of learning concentration.

To follow a preparation that you did not invent for yourself, you must follow it explicitly and not alter its methods or its prescriptions to meet or satisfy old habits or beliefs. It is not something that you pick apart, keeping the parts that you like and discarding the rest. This never leads to success. This will keep you where you are and disable you from going anywhere else.

To successfully follow *Steps to Knowledge,* follow it as it is given and learn how to work with it as you go along. The preparation does not demand perfection or absolute success. It requires perseverance and determination. You learn to develop these as you learn to concentrate. When you concentrate your mind, you become free of the many little preoccupations that require great amounts of energy but provide little value. You become free of the distractions of the world because you do not have time for them, and you do not choose to devote your energy to them. You become free of your own confusion and ambivalence because you don't have time for these either. You become free of disabling relationships because you recognize they will take you nowhere and will rob you of your vitality and direction.

A mind that is concentrated is free of many of the tribulations and distractions of the world because it is concentrated on something. But a mind that is not concentrated can be captured by anything and held in bondage by random impulses and great anxieties.

Making the mind whole requires concentration in order to bring all of its resources to bear, to develop these resources and to keep them focused on a greater goal. This translates immediately into developing greater abilities in the mundane activities of life. Many things that were difficult before become easier now. Many things that were problems before are not even thought of now. Many things that distracted you before go unnoticed now.

You can experience this for yourself if you associate with those who are concentrated on a task that you admire. Notice the difference between their activity, their concerns, their experience and yours. They do not have time for the things that plague you. They have other problems to solve. Those who are dedicated to serving the world do not have time for the debilitating ideas and preoccupations that keep others in a diffracted and confused state. They are going somewhere while others are standing still. They are concentrated on their goals while others are lost in past recollections or in musings about the future.

As you think about these things, you will begin to see that there is a greater possibility for you. For this possibility to be realized, you will need to receive a preparation and you will need to stay with it. You will need to go past all the thresholds where you quit or gave up on yourself before — past the thresholds where you judged and separated yourself from something that was valuable. The preparation gives you the structure and the focus to do this, but you must generate the effort to proceed.

Development in The Way of Knowledge and in concentration requires instruction. Here it is important to be around individuals who are more concentrated than you are. And they must be significantly more concentrated than you are in order to lift you upwards and to have an effect upon you. Because your lack of concentration will affect them, their impact on you must be greater than your impact on them. They must show you through demonstration what is possible, and if they are true teachers, they will be able to treat you as a unique individual and not as a projection of themselves. They will be able to recognize your path and course of development as unique. You will need individuals such as these as mentors and as companions. Without them, you will try to teach yourself, and that will have only very limited results. True development requires someone else to demand things of you, to demonstrate the path for you and to set the pace at which you must learn to travel. If you select your own path and set your own pace, you will not advance. Someone else must demand things of you and discern the greatness that is within you — things which you cannot do adequately for yourself. Accept this limitation, for it exists. You will need to be around people who are more advanced than you are, not to rob them of their energy or to take advantage of their skill, but to learn from their example.

Next, you will need true companionship. Here you will need people of equal or greater concentration than yourself to be your companions. They will demand things of you, demonstrate things for you and keep you moving forward. Do not choose companions who are less concentrated than you are, for they will take things away from you. They will dilute your focus. They will confuse you. They will generate uncertainty within you, cloud your vision and erode your ability to stay concentrated on your path in life. There are many of these people, and many of them are very charming and lovable, but you must choose your companions wisely. You will not go any further than the weakest relationship that you cherish.

Therefore, all of your close relationships need to be strong and dedicated. Here is where most people falter. Here is where they make their compromises. It is easier and more self-assuring to be around someone who has less strength and concentration than your- self. That may make you look good in comparison, but what value does it give you? If you choose to have weaker companions, make sure that they are committed to the truth so that they may benefit from your presence. Then, whatever you give to them will bear fruit and will be carried on.

You will need very strong companions. You will need people who are dedicated to the truth, to Knowledge and to a greater purpose in life. If this is not the case, you will be fighting a losing battle. For this, you must exercise your inner author- ity. For this, you must discern that which is valuable in others from that which is not and call upon Knowledge to guide you. Here you will need to exercise concentration and determination. Stronger companions will make you stronger. Weaker compan- ions will make you weaker. The choice is yours. Choose well. There is no exception to this rule. Companions of equal strength and ability will be worthy, but you will still need stronger indi- viduals to instruct and motivate you.

It is an unfortunate tendency in your world that people tend to do things for themselves, on their own, at their own pace and in their own way. This is called "personal freedom," but it is really an exercise in futility because you cannot lead yourself into new terri- tory. You cannot educate yourself. You cannot uplift yourself. You cannot prepare yourself. You cannot initiate yourself in anything beyond your past experience. To accomplish these, you will need Knowledge, which represents the Greater Power that lives within you and which represents your promise for redemption. You will also need strong individuals who can challenge you and require you to step beyond your former boundaries and assumptions. And lastly, you will need a preparation that you did not invent for yourself to prepare you for a future life of greater magnitude and dimensions beyond what you have known before.

The Greater Community Way of Knowledge provides the preparation and the foundation for genuine relationships. It produces a learning environment where you can grow and develop if you share it with others and if you apply its principles and its practices adequately and wisely. It will enable you to become a person with greater concentration. If your purpose is genuine and your motivations are born of Knowledge, then your concentration will be a great benefit for the world. During this preparation, you will have times when you will feel very alone, either because others are not with you or because others do not share your growing perception and understanding. But true companions will find you, will be with you and will strengthen you along the way.

To become a man or a woman of Knowledge requires this greater preparation, this greater concentration and this greater dedication. These requirements cannot be escaped. There are no shortcuts. There is no way around them. There are no deals that you can make with the Creator in order to get ahead of everyone else without having to take the journey yourself.

We emphasize concentration here because it makes peace, true strength and greater self-application possible. It is one of the necessary ingredients, one of the fundamental and underlying abilities that has to be present in order for greatness to work through you and for you to find greatness for yourself.

We are concentrated on your well-being and advancement and encourage you to share our concentration. Our concentration is genuine. It is nurturing and empowering for you. As you receive this, you will be able to give it because whatever you receive, you can give. This represents your promise for the world, for you have come from a place from beyond the world where concentration is natural to a place where concentration is lacking. You have come from a place where relationship is natural to a place where relationship is lacking. You have come from a place where natural affinity is ever present to a place where it is lacking. You have come to give something here. What you have to give is with you now. It is your task to find it. To find it, you will need the preparation, instruction and companionship that are necessary. Even with these, you will need to dedicate yourself, which represents an act of concentration.

Pride
is a compensation.
It is something
you give yourself
to make up
for something
that is lost.

Thirty-two

PRIDE

*P*EOPLE HAVE VERY MIXED FEELINGS ABOUT PRIDE. On the one hand, they do not like the appearance of pride because it is arrogant and condescending. It makes others feel smaller or weaker or less capable. It has an insulting quality to it that you can immediately feel in others if they are exhibiting this characteristic. Yet, everyone likes to feel pride because it gives one a temporary sense of power, purpose and meaning. So, while it is unattractive in others, it has its own appeal for each person. But what is pride, what does it mean and how should it be viewed in order to gain a greater perspective in life?

Simply said, pride is a compensation. It is something you seek to offset the pain of your own separation and uncertainty. It is a compensation to offset the grave discomfort that accompanies a feeling of inability, a lack of capacity, and so forth. It is something to offset a weakness and to cover it up. Pride cannot replace the weakness, but it provides an escape. If pride is a compensation, then it makes up for something that is lost.

To be proud of yourself and what you do seems absolutely normal. It even seems to be valuable, for it is thought that when people have pride in what they do, they tend to function more adequately, with greater conscientiousness and greater ability. But being aware of your attributes and feeling confident or satisfied with your creations is not the same as pride itself. You can have the experience of satisfaction in your own accomplishments and the value and excellence of your work, whatever it may be, without demonstrating arrogance, without being condescending to others and without the other forms of conceit that inevitably will turn against you.

Pride is a compensation. It is something you give yourself to make up for something that is lost. For practical purposes, let us say that pride is equivalent to self-importance. The idea of self-importance seems absolutely normal and justifiable as long as it does not become irritating to other people or extreme in its expression. But there is an inherent flaw with self-importance, a flaw which cannot be escaped and which will cast its destructive influence and impact upon everything you do and everything you conceive because self-importance is a compensation making up for something that is lost. It is a weak replacement, for what it replaces is the strength of Knowledge within you which has been lost.

So, we can replace the word "pride" with the word "self-importance." They are really the same. Self-importance works against the reclamation of Knowledge because it continues to assert an idea about yourself that is not consistent or compatible with life. It continues to separate you from life and to make you the central focus. It binds you to your own dilemmas and prevents your escape from them because it leads you to become self-absorbed. It is concentration on the personal mind to the exclusion of life itself, and because the personal mind is inherently flawed and incomplete, its flaws and incompletions will haunt you and dominate your attention. In order to offset this, there are all kinds of demonstrations and expressions of self-importance. This is manifest in every aspect of people's behavior, in their concepts, in their beliefs, in their philosophies, and in their strong adherence to their own ideas and ideals. But underneath this myriad of expressions, there is self-importance. And the importance that is emphasized in this attitude is weak and inconsistent with life.

You are a part of life. You are an expression of life. To a certain degree, you are a unique expression, though do not take the idea of uniqueness too far. You are not the center of life. You are not the center of the universe. You do not have your own universe. You do not create your own universe. You merely interpret the universe that you share with all life. If you interpret life wisely, then you will be able to participate in it and join with it meaningfully. But if you interpret life according to a belief in self-importance, according to the need to assert yourself and to offset your own discomforts, then you will misinterpret life and you will attempt to use it to fortify your self-importance, which denies your access to life and makes your participation within it disassociating and destructive.

Underneath pride is a sense of despair, a sense of despair that cannot yet be faced, and so there is an attempt to run from it, to build something over it, to build a wonderful and beautiful expressive life over an inner reality that is in disrepair and is inherently alone and sad. Observe the desire for pride in yourself. See how it feels to take great pride in yourself or in your accomplishments. See how long this lasts and what it really feels like. Does it give you a sense of inclusion in the world? Does it give you a sense of peace? Does it give you greater equanimity? Or is it a momentary experience of self-inflation which will soon be replaced by the fervent need to reassert yourself in a different set of circumstances? For all that has been devoted to this pursuit and for all that has been invested in it, how much and how great is its reward?

Self-importance is a critical error because it denies the source of your expression. It denies the source of your meaning and purpose in the world. It says that you are the source of your creations. Yet, if the real source of your creations disavowed you or pulled away from you, you would be truly empty and truly impoverished.

What self-importance is there then?

All great contributors in all fields and endeavors must at some point come to terms with the reality and the fact that what they are giving comes from beyond them, that they themselves are a medium, a messenger and a provider for something greater from beyond themselves. This is the reality of their creativity. This is the reality of their desire to give. This is the source and meaning of their contributions, whatever they may be. This is what gives these contributions value and what enables them to be inspiring to others.

But, of course, with pride this is all lost. There is no recognition of the source of your meaning and your value. There is no recognition of the power and the grace that can express itself through you. There are only moments of self-aggrandizement followed by great periods of fearfulness, suspicion, anxiety and conflict.

Yes, you must practice and develop your skills. You must work very hard, and you must rise above the mediocrity that you see around you. But this is only so that you can become a vehicle for a Greater Reality to express itself through you. In this there is real accomplishment. In this there is no pride because when you are in relationship with a Greater Reality, you realize you are but the vehicle for its expression, and you value yourself for this. You do not claim responsibility for its power and its intelligence. You give. You do not claim the glory. What glory is there in giving except the satisfaction of giving itself? If the world honors you and esteems you and even glorifies you, which it does for some people momentarily, what meaning is there in this? A moment of glory for a lifetime of contribution.

There are many creative people in the world who have potential for expressing something of real meaning and value but who suffer greatly because they cannot see that they are but the means for expressing something greater. They believe that they are the source. They feel that they must control their own expression and determine where it is to be given, to whom and for what purpose. They must control the results. They must control the whole process. They must be the authors of their own creations. For this they suffer without seeming limit or end. And their ability and potential are greatly stifled by and wasted upon a self-absorbed approach that can only lead to frustration and disappointment. And so there is this constant attempt to assert oneself, to establish one's value, to declare one's purpose, to gain recognition and even adulation.

This is not the way of Knowledge. It is not the way of happiness, and it is not what the world needs. You do not need recognition from the world. You need to experience the value of your own giving and the meaning of your own work. These can only be recognized when you see that you are the vehicle for something greater, something that loves the world but which is beyond definition, beyond words and even beyond understanding. You do not need to understand the Greater Reality to feel it, to enter into relationship with it, to be part of it and to reclaim the Ancient Heritage which is yours and the power which has been given to you through Knowledge. Let those who cannot be in relationship with life try to understand it. They will not. And their ideas, no matter how seemingly intellectual or perfectly ordered, will not encompass the experience of the Greater Reality of which they themselves are an intrinsic part.

For you who are considering becoming a real student of Knowledge, and for you who have begun the great reclamation of Knowledge according to the preparation that we have provided, you must realize that self-importance is a weakness and a liability. It is not simply the behavior that is associated with it that is the problem. It is the lack of foundation that this behavior expresses.

In becoming a student of Knowledge, you begin to reclaim, slowly and significantly, a real foundation in life. This does not happen all at once. It is not simply an answer or an explanation or something you tell yourself. It does not excuse you from the difficulties of life. It does not raise you above everyone else. It is not about self-importance. Instead, it builds a foundation for certainty — certainty within yourself and certainty within your relationship with life. Over time this certainty begins to permeate all of your thinking and activities, and as it does so, you become stronger and more complete. What need is there then to assert and to prove yourself when this foundation has been established? Indeed, you will see that the pursuit of self-importance takes you away from your foundation, blinds you to your inclusion in life, turns you away from the source of your Wisdom and creativity and places you alone in a seemingly hostile universe, in competition with everyone else who is attempting to assert themselves and to step in line in front of you to compete with you for the world's recognition and rewards.

Turn away from self-importance. Your personal mind will never be significant in the universe. Do not give it this importance. It is not an honor for you or for life. Your personal mind is but a part of the means for expressing a Greater Reality in a temporary reality, for expressing the Knowledge of the universe in the unique opportunity you have to live in the world.

It could be said that there are two things in life that you will see: There is Knowledge and there is self-importance. You will see that without Knowledge people need to be self-important because they feel they are nothing, have nothing and are associated with nothing. And so they associate themselves with their ideas, they develop their relationships in order to support their ideas, and they fortify themselves against loss by desiring money and power, influence and recognition. But no matter how much they acquire or how successful they might be temporarily, underneath all of this is a tremendous sense of emptiness and loss. They are not connected to Knowledge. Yes, they may use intuition here and there, but that does not represent that they have a relationship with Knowledge.

Those individuals who seem more powerful, more grand, more significant, more influential, more beautiful or more handsome than you — consider what you are seeing. Without Knowledge, there are no other advantages in life. Without Knowledge, you will not have a foundation. *Steps to Knowledge* is the means for building a foundation upon which you can live a meaningful life. Without this foundation, you are at sea. Your life is built on quicksand. Anything that you establish can easily be torn down. You are a victim of the world and the forces in the world. You are competing against everyone and everything. You are competing against yourself. Your mind is constantly in conflict. Success and failure are your concern, not contribution.

Into this seemingly hopeless situation come the gift of Knowledge and The Greater Community Way of Knowledge. While people around you are reinforcing their need for self-importance and their investment in their self-importance, you have a greater possibility. You have the gift of freedom to enable you to escape a pursuit that can never be successful. You can never be important enough. You can never be rich enough or famous enough or pretty enough to offset the lack of a foundation within yourself. Without a relationship with the Greater Power that is clearly and properly understood, and without being in a position to give in life, you are at a profound disadvantage, whether you are rich or poor, handsome or not, magnificent or simple. No matter what your station in life, no matter what your appearance to others, without Knowledge you are weak and vulnerable.

But take heart. Knowledge has not left you. It has not gone away. You cannot rid yourself of it, and it will never leave you. It is waiting to be discovered, a living reality within you that confirms your meaning and purpose for coming into the world at this time. It confirms your relationship with your Spiritual Family beyond the world, and it confirms your relationship with the world, for you have come to the world to give. What difference does it make if you are important or not as long as your mission in life can be furthered and accomplished? When you leave this life and return to your Spiritual Family, you will not be interested at all in what you became in the world or what people thought of you there. The *only* thing that will concern you is whether you accomplished your task or not. That is all that matters. And your task will always involve the reclamation of relationships and the expression of Knowledge — no matter what your form of expression or the avenue of life that you participate in.

Find escape from self-importance. Be one of the few who finds an open door away from this hopeless involvement. It is a blessing that your life in the world is temporary. The reason it is temporary is that you have come here to give something, and you do not want to linger too long. It is good that it is temporary because being in physical life is very cumbersome and very complicated. It is diffi-cult. Taking care of a physical body, taking care of all the things you own, taking care of your relationships — all require a great deal of effort.

Therefore, you are given the relief of being able to go back to your Spiritual Family. Your tour of duty here is limited, but you can only appreciate what this means as you come to know and to ex-perience that you have a greater reality beyond the world, a reality that gives meaning and purpose to your being here now. This is not merely a self-comforting idea. This is the fundamental truth of your life.

You see, the world cannot give you meaning, and it cannot give you your purpose. What the world can do is ignite the purpose you have brought with you, that is within you already. The world provides the need, not the answer. You have the answer. The world pulls the answer out of you because of its great needs. That is why coming to the world to do anything but work is absolutely foolish.

What else can the world offer you? Yes, it has beautiful places and it offers some wonderful momentary pleasures, but it is not worth the journey here unless you can get something done. Considering where you have come from and where you will return to, this is most certainly true.

Now, when you ask about finding greater purpose in life and whether you are going to have relationships and how you are going to improve your circumstances, it is very important to consider—since everyone has these questions to one degree or another—why you are asking these questions. What is it you really want? What is the motive behind asking these kinds of questions, which are very fundamental and important questions. What is your motive in asking them?

Knowledge will transform your life. Is this what you want? Or do you simply want to fortify your current position and add to your list of advantages? Do you want to become safer and richer and more imbued with wonderful abilities and more recognized and more valued? What is your motive?

When you ask Knowledge to do something for you, you must realize that Knowledge will give you what it needs for you to have, not what you want from it. Yes, you will want certain things, but understand that Knowledge will transform you. This will not guarantee that you will have any of the specific things that you may want. Yes, you can use your mental power to get things in life. Yes, you can commit yourself to acquisition—the acquisition of objects, the acquisition of people, the acquisition of ideas, the acquisition of truths—it is all acquisition. The acquisition of truths can be as selfish and self-indulgent as acquiring money. If it is for pride and self-importance, it will have the same result and the same disqualifying aspects, preventing you from gaining access to your life and its real meaning and purpose, which is where all the satisfaction in life is. Everything you own, everyone you associate with and everything you do can ultimately only serve the purpose of bringing you this greater understanding and this greater commitment to give to the world. In this, the world serves you by disappointing you, even more than by giving you the things you want. It gives you another chance to see if you want self-importance or if you want to live a life of Knowledge.

Let us give this very great idea from the Greater Community for you to consider. This is a truth that advanced races in the Greater Community have come to realize through life's experience. Because it is a universal truth, it means that it is applicable everywhere. It is a truth that transcends race, culture, temperament and nature. It is true everywhere, whether you are a human being, or whether you are something else. The truth is this: The Wise remain hidden to remain wise. We recommend that you contemplate this idea, but do not be satisfied with your first conclusions. You must go far beyond them to reach the real meaning of this idea. This idea is so important if you can consider it and stay with it long enough because it teaches you about yourself, about the nature of your real ability, about the role of Knowledge and about the reality of the world. Only a person who can penetrate this idea will gain these great results.

Right away you can see that if you are driven by the need to assert yourself and to proclaim and establish yourself, then there is a problem in your approach to Knowledge. With Knowledge, the more powerful you are, the more you conceal your power. With Knowledge, the more influential you are, the more careful you are where this influence is expressed. With Knowledge, you are only given to communicate to certain people for certain purposes. With Knowledge, you are hidden in the world because the world cannot yet accept Knowledge wholeheartedly.

Those who are strong with Knowledge will always guard their gifts and be very discerning where they can be given, how they should be expressed, and so forth. This is Wisdom. This is learning how to get things done in the world, which is what Wisdom is about. Wisdom is also about how to be in the world because being in the world and getting things done are the same.

If you were a man or woman of Knowledge and you did not exercise this Wisdom, the world would attempt to use you for its own purposes. People would use you for this or for that. They would associate with you to try to take from you that which you have. They would try to employ you for their purposes. They would drain you of your ability and your energy. They would rely on you and feed off of you and attempt to manipulate you. And when they realized they could not get any more from you, they would either discard you or attempt to destroy you. This is not because people are evil. It is simply because they do not yet have the ability to receive Knowledge directly. When you cannot receive something directly, it must be given to you indirectly. You yourself cannot yet receive Knowledge directly. You have to receive it incrementally, very slowly. Knowledge has to be applied and demonstrated to you.

The Greater Power in the universe is wise. It does not give things to people beyond their capacity, so the focus is to develop people's capacity, desire and understanding. This is what *Steps to Knowledge* is for. This is what my words are for. They are not to fuel your self-assertion. They are not to make you richer, more grand, more beautiful or more exquisite in life, for these only jeopardize you and make you fall prey to the madness of the world.

The Wise remain hidden to remain wise. What are the prospects for self-importance here? The more powerful you become, the more you have to conceal it. The more complete you become, the greater your influence on others and the more careful you have to be.

With Knowledge and Wisdom, there comes a natural reticence to be part of anyone's need for self-importance. And there is a reticence to give yourself to your own self-importance because you see it as an enemy of your true pursuit. You do not repudiate self-importance. It is not morally unjust. Instead, it is seen as something that works against you, and you do not want to support it either within yourself or with others. Likewise, you do not want others to use you to bolster their self-importance, which is so often the motive in people's personal relationships.

The Wise also remain hidden so they will not abuse or misuse their abilities. It is a safeguard for them and for others. If you seek to become a man or woman of Knowledge in order to become more magnificent, more powerful, more recognized or more beautiful — in other words, if you want to become a man or woman of Knowledge to assert your self-importance — then your learning process will be one of disappointment and disillusionment because you must be freed and separated from your incorrect thinking and your inappropriate motives.

Knowledge will not abide with you unless you are sincere. Knowledge is not simply a power that you can tap into and use, as people so often think. It is an intelligence. You cannot simply get to it and use it as if it were an oil well. It is intelligent. It is smart. It is wise. And it is compassionate. It knows the way to you. Become receptive to it. Let it emerge within you. Take the steps to it, the steps to Knowledge. Do not alter them. Do not try to make your own way. You do not know how to get to Knowledge, but Knowledge can bring you to itself, and that is the way. Relieve yourself of the constant burden of asserting yourself and establishing yourself. Then and only then will you see what real freedom means.

Now let us talk about something else that will perhaps give you a clearer idea of what I am saying. I have said that people try to assert themselves, establish themselves and make themselves more important because they feel a deficiency or a lack within themselves. This is obvious. But what is not obvious is that when you try to compensate for your lack or deficiency, they become stronger. When you try to compensate for your weakness, your weakness is confirmed. As you persist, you will become even more disassociated from yourself. You will start to believe that you are really important. You will start to believe that you are all these things that you are trying to be. But underneath is the reality that you feel weak, deficient and alone. Not only has the error not been corrected, it has been overlaid with a gigantic falsification of your life. Now you are doubly removed from yourself. Now the means for the reclamation of Knowledge within you becomes even more difficult to find and to accept.

Face your emptiness rather than compensate for it. Face your sense of weakness instead of constantly trying to prove it is not true. Face your sense of isolation and loneliness instead of convincing yourself that they do not exist. You face these things in The Way of Knowledge because you must pass through them and go beyond them. They are standing in your way. You must face them. You may say to yourself, "Well, I am really a wonderful person," but this may not be how you really feel inside. Then you will try to use The Way of Knowledge to prove that you are a wonderful person. You may even think that Knowledge is proving that. But there is a fundamental error, and you have to go back to where the error is made. You start from where you are, not from where you want to be.

Becoming honest means that you accept things as they are right now. You accept them not because they are ultimately true but because they represent your starting point. You cannot start the journey from where you want to be. You cannot be at the end of the journey while you are at the beginning. You cannot be at the top of the mountain when you are really at the bottom. When you are at the bottom, be at the bottom! Do not falsify the situation by saying that the mountain isn't important or that it is no problem for you to climb it or that you will climb it some other day because you have more important things to do. Do not falsify the situation. Real effort in life is expended because people recognize a need that *has* to be fulfilled.

The Way of Knowledge fulfills a need. It fulfills an inner need to find purpose, meaning and direction in life. And it fulfills an outer need for your contribution to be given because the world needs it. The world needs it in all walks of life. It needs it in every aspect of its existence.

Those who are meaningfully engaged with the world are freed from the attempt to prove themselves. They are simply doing what they have to do. They can afford to be honest. They can afford to face themselves. They can afford to relax. They can afford to enjoy life. They can afford to dedicate themselves. To them, commitment is not a loss. It is the beginning of reality. To them, commitment is not a relinquishment. It is an opportunity to finally engage with life, not on their own terms but according to Knowledge within them. With Knowledge, they have a firm foundation within themselves and in the world. With a firm foundation, they do not continuously have to prove themselves and to establish their self-importance.

The escape from self-importance is a freedom of unparalleled value. You begin to move towards this freedom in The Way of Knowledge because The Way of Knowledge is not about you. The Way of Knowledge is about life, your place in life and your contribution to life. Your reality is established beyond the world, so you do not need to establish it here. You did not create yourself. You only interpret yourself. But a Greater Power can create through you, and if you are not lost and bound to the need for self-importance, then you can be available and receptive to this Greater Power, which will affirm your true identity and your real meaning in the world at this time. Beyond this, your needs are simple, and you need not suffer over them. Beyond this, you work for accomplishment and for contribution, and this takes all of your energy. You do not have time to suffer over yourself. You do not have time to worry about who you are, for in this situation you are giving yourself appropriately. Learning how to do this is a great enough challenge.

Open yourself to a Greater Reality. Become a vehicle for its expression, even in the most mundane circumstances. Give up the need for recognition. You do not really want it. You only need to be recognized by a few people in life. That is necessary. Beyond that, it is better to be unknown and mysterious. Don't show off! When you do this, it reinforces the idea that your life is meaningless and that you have no intrinsic value. Learn to listen and be observant. Become still, and you will see what I am saying. It is so obvious if you stop and look. If you do not judge or condemn yourself or others, you will begin to see. You will see that people are lost within themselves. You will see that they are bound by motives that are desperate and compensatory. Do not ever condemn someone for this because this is the condition of the world. But be grateful that the possibility of escape has been given to you and that you have an opportunity to share this and its great results and rewards with others.

Your prayers have been answered because The Greater Community Way of Knowledge has been given to you. This is a real answer. The real answer is true assistance and the means of preparation, both within the world and beyond. You are now given a way out of your own self-absorption and a way into the world so that you can accomplish what you came here to accomplish with a minimum of stress and misunderstanding.

Over time, as you become engaged in your true activity in life and become mature enough to engage yourself in it wholeheartedly, you will feel the presence of your Spiritual Family with you. You will feel the abiding presence of Knowledge guiding you. You will feel that you have a destiny and that that destiny is assured. And you will not need to be self-important, for you will not feel weak, vulnerable and worthless. You will have work to reclaim Knowledge, you will have work to rectify the imbalances and the falsities of your own life, and you will have work to assist others. But you can give yourself to this. You cannot hate yourself and undertake the Path of Knowledge because you must love yourself enough to be able to undertake this great journey.

Do not value pride. Uncover it. Let disappointment and even disgrace help you come to terms with your true nature in life. Have no idols. Even the man and woman of Knowledge are not idols. They are people from different walks of life who have made a courageous and vital decision amidst often very difficult circumstances. Value their example and let their rewards be an encouragement for you that there is a greater purpose in life, a greater meaning for being here and a greater opportunity to give that which needs to be given.

*If you
stop climbing,
you don't
get up
the mountain.*

Thirty-three

PERSEVERANCE

PERSEVERANCE IS A VERY IMPORTANT ABILITY, but like all important abilities it must have its right application, and it must be understood within a larger scheme of things—a larger context. Take even the most virtuous ability, set it apart from an important purpose, and it turns into an aberrant form of behavior, a problem to be solved, a liability rather than an asset.

The Greater Community Way of Knowledge takes many years to learn. This requires perseverance. It requires that you stay with it and practice it as it is given. It requires that you continue to move through the stages of development both internally and externally so that a Greater Community perspective may be fostered within you. This represents a greater viewpoint of life and a greater recognition of your abilities and application in the world around you. But if you alter the curriculum, you will not learn. If you do not stay with it, you will not learn.

It is very important in The Way of Knowledge that you carry on and finish what you have started. If you go too far and then quit, it becomes very difficult. It is like following a small footbridge across a great chasm in the earth. If you are going to start, then be determined to reach the other side. Don't go halfway or three-quarters of the way and say, "I think I have had enough!" You must keep going. This requires perseverance.

You will reach several thresholds where you will want to quit. You will have some discouraging moments. You will have some empty moments. You will have moments when you won't know why you are doing this at all. You will have moments when you feel an overwhelmingly personal need to live a normal life, to have simple things and to not take on such difficult and seemingly inexplicable quests. You will have moments when you think that something else looks much more exciting and appealing, and you might think that it will get you to your desired goal much faster. So, you give up being an advancing student here to become a be-ginner somewhere else. You will have times when you think it is not worth it. You will have times when you think you cannot do it. You will have times when you will doubt that it will take you where you really want to go.

All of these experiences can be expected. You are not merely learning new information here. You are not merely adding more ideas and insights to your collection of ideas and insights. You are not merely adding new interesting experiences to your collection of interesting experiences. You are undertaking a great transition — a transition from a limited perspective to a greater perspective, from a life dominated by your personal mind to a life that is fused and joined with Knowledge. You are taking a great journey from being imprisoned in your individuality to using it to express a Greater Reality.

This is the greatest journey. Travel around the world again and again and you will not take such a great journey as this. It is a journey that deepens you and expands your perception. It is a journey that changes your priorities and values simply because it is natural for them to change. It is a journey that takes you beyond who you thought you were and what you thought you were here for. As you pass through the thresholds, you will pass through times of uncertainty and confusion and through times of reorientation and reintegration.

To continue, you must persevere. You persevere when you feel like it and when you don't feel like it, when you are happy and when you are sad, when you are encouraged and when you are discouraged, when you are certain and when you are uncertain. Others will quit along the way because they cannot differentiate themselves from their ideas and their feelings. Yet, you persist because Knowledge keeps you going. Here you are strong with Knowledge and Knowledge is strong in you. Others may fall away because they need to go somewhere else. They are just passing through. But if this is meant for you, you must persevere. How do you know if it is meant for you? Because you *know* to persevere. You give yourself to this. You do not give yourself up to this. You give yourself *to* this. There is a very great difference.

Why is perseverance so difficult? Because human beings have not yet developed enough mental strength. Unless they are confronted by adverse conditions, most people seek what is easy and comfortable by and large. Only certain individuals rise above this and push beyond the boundaries of human behavior.

No one is forcing you to do this preparation and to take this journey. You are not doing it for survival. Something greater is moving you. This is important and you must stay with it.

Perseverance is not trusted because people have given themselves to things of little or no value. They have committed themselves to relationships that could never work—relationships with people, relationships with activities, relationships with places and relationships with causes. And so, to protect themselves from being fooled once again or from making an unwanted declaration, they make their involvement very conditional. They say, "Well, I will stay with this as long as it feels right to me," or "I will stay with this as long as I have the time," or "I will stay with this until I find a relationship." This is not perseverance. You must make the journey.

Do not think that if the journey is meant for you, it will be easy and you will not have times of great conflict. Do not think that if this is meant for you, you will be able to pass through the thresholds without great effort and determination. Do not think that if this is meant for you, you will not have times of great misgiving and doubt. How will you know if this is right for you? Because you will *know*, and as Knowledge becomes stronger in you, you will be able to proceed where others have departed.

There is a popular notion in this day and age that you are always right where you need to be, always doing the thing you need to be doing. This is ridiculous. What an unfortunate thing to think. This robs you of your responsibility and blinds you to the fact that you can make grave and serious errors and miss life-renewing opportunities. People think such things when they do not want to work and apply themselves.

You need to know and to learn the difference between what is right and what is not right. There is a difference. Do not take your life for granted. You are the captain of your ship while you are sailing these waters. You need to take responsibility, become effective and learn to become a leader of your mind and emotions rather than their victim or captive. You cannot tell where you are sailing, and you do not know what is in the cargo of your ship, but you must be the captain on deck, negotiating the changing circumstances of your life and the pleasures and tribulations that present themselves on your voyage.

Do not think that you are always in the right place doing the right thing. If that were the case, your world would be very different from what it is today. You can miss great opportunities. They will not come again. Do not pacify yourself and think, "Well, I didn't get it this time around. I'll get it the next time around."

There may not be another time around. Don't be casual about things that will determine your life. And do not think that Knowledge is guiding you yet. Do not think that Knowledge is determining everything you do, for you are not a master and you are not masterful. Do not take for granted things that require serious decisions and self-determination. Do not give yourself that escape or you will disable yourself from becoming potent and effective in life, and you will not realize your responsibilities.

All around you people are making serious mistakes. Sometimes they have been making the same mistake for a very long time. This is wasteful. Humanity is wasting its great possibilities and its inherent skills. It needs to learn cooperation and to become inner directed and responsible. This opportunity is being wasted. Face this. It is real. Do not make excuses for yourself or for others. Those who make a difference in the world and who find out the important things have exerted themselves, not for pleasure, comfort or self-satisfaction, but for something else. They persevered where others gave up. They stayed with one thing when others went shopping elsewhere. They progressed while others became a beginner at something else. They focused their lives while others became confused.

It is true that you have tried to give yourself to things that were never meant for you. This is necessary to learn. It is true that you have tried to commit yourself to people and to situations that did not work out. This is true. It may happen again, but you must find out.

Do not give yourself the license to think that you do not need others, that you do not need divine assistance and that you do not need education, growth and development. If you become lazy here, life will pass you by, and you will live with a sense of dissatisfaction that nothing will be able to relieve. That is why we are making a very serious statement here. We want you to be serious in hearing it and in responding to it.

Life is not casual. Life has great intention and intensity. Life is vital. It is committed. It is totally involved. It is not holding back and watching from a distance. Look at the plants and the animals in your world. Are they not totally committed to their situation? Are they not vulnerable? Are they not completely involved? Are they spending their lives thinking, "I'm not sure I should be doing this. I'm not sure I want to do this. I don't know what I want. What do I want?" They are not lost in these conversations. They are out in the world living in the process called life.

Life is calling for you to re-establish your relationship with it. Knowledge will take you to life because this is part of the purpose of Knowledge. But Knowledge is not only here to re-engage you with life, it is here to give something to life, something that life cannot give you. You are here to give what you brought from your Ancient Home. It is a set of specific tasks to be carried out with certain people for specific purposes. Do not think you are going to become a spiritual teacher or emancipator or initiator. This is extremely rare. No. True meaning comes from engaging in things that are very specific and often quite mundane. The difference is in the intensity with which you are engaged. That is the difference.

Finding and fulfilling your greater purpose will require perseverance most assuredly. It is easy to quit, and there are always good reasons for quitting. It is always a relief to give up, at least for a short time. Nobody likes to work too hard, but what is too hard? Does it not take more effort and energy to maintain confusion and ambivalence than it does to dedicate yourself to something? The cost of ambivalence is dreadful. It leads to mental and physical illness. It leads to an inability to be in relationship and to communicate effectively. It stifles people's certainty, creativity and ability. And, yet, it is chosen again and again because it seems comfortable and familiar.

If you want to learn The Greater Community Way of Knowledge, you must persevere. Don't just go a little way and say, "Well, this is far enough." Don't just go a little way and say, "Well, I just wanted to try it out." You will not learn The Way of Knowledge if you just try it out. You will not even know what it is. Sometimes people study The Way of Knowledge a little and they think, "Well, this is about intuition. I know all about intuition." This is not about intuition. That is like saying because you can hum a little tune, you are a master musician. That is like saying because you can draw a little face with a pencil, you are a great artist. Experiencing intuition is minute compared to living The Way of Knowledge.

Perseverance requires an open mind and a willingness to live without fixed beliefs because as you go through the thresholds of learning, you will go beyond your former ideas and assumptions. You will pass through periods where you are very confused, where you are not quite sure who you are or what you are doing. You thought you knew, but somehow what you used to think doesn't seem to fit anymore. It all seems too limited and small. Now you are entering into new territory, and you are not sure what it means. You are not even sure if it is all right to do that.

To go from a fixed human viewpoint to a Greater Community perspective represents a tremendous expansion. It requires more effort, more consistency and more determination than meeting even the normal range of challenges. But people want great things. They want magnificent relationships, they want totally satisfying careers, they want Spiritual Wisdom and they want great inner certainty. We say it is very good to want those things, but what are you willing to give for them? You cannot bargain here. You don't get the sale price. You don't get Wisdom at one-half off. You don't buy one and get one free. You have to give what is needed to give, however much that is. Knowledge and Wisdom do not come cheap. Though there is no price tag, they require a great and consistent self-application. You cannot go to a seminar and walk out a man or woman of

Knowledge.

You must give yourself to something. Knowledge will help you choose. Don't give yourself to something to prove anything to yourself. Remember, you are not doing this for self-importance. If there is nothing to give yourself to at this moment, then do not give yourself to anything at this moment. But prepare to give yourself. If you go through life and do not give yourself, you will be like a package unopened. You will be like a plant that never bloomed. You never gave your seed, your gift, your fragrance or your beauty to the world.

You have come to the world to give. But first you must learn about the world, and then you must learn about your gift. You have spent your childhood and your adolescence learning to become a functional human being. Many people do not accomplish this, you know. But if you become a functional human being, then you can begin the next great education in life, which is learning about purpose, meaning and direction. If your purpose, meaning and direction are destined to take you beyond human perspective and human limitations, then you must learn a Greater Community Way of Knowledge.

The Way of Knowledge has been given. *Steps to Knowledge* has been given. You need to follow it, not blindly or foolishly, but wisely with awareness and discernment. If you stop climbing, you don't get up the mountain. There are no elevators or helicopters to take you to the top. Angels do not descend on the mountain to lift you up. You have to make the journey. The journey is everything. The journey is where your gifts are given. The journey is where your gifts are discovered. The journey is where you become stronger and wiser, more forgiving and more compassionate. You came to the world to make this journey. If you do not make it, you have wasted your trip, a fact that you will have to reflect upon when you leave here.

I want you to find a life of fulfillment and satisfaction. I want real happiness to blossom in your life. This is not something that is just given to you. You have to achieve it. You have to make a place for it. You have to build a foundation for it, or it will remain a great ideal, always seemingly beyond your reach.

As you move up the mountain of life, you see more and know more. You begin to understand the lay of the land. You understand the difficulties behind you. You see where they took you, and you understand their value and their relevance to your journey. You do not know what is up ahead, but as you proceed, you learn more about how to climb the mountain of life. If you give up or quit, you stay where you are. Is that okay? Well, you have to answer that question for yourself. I cannot answer it for you.

When you persevere in an endeavor that represents an attempt at establishing your self-importance — an attempt to be, do or have something that is not meant for you — you can become very attached. You can protect and maintain this attachment with great intensity and devotion. But this is not a commitment because when you commit yourself to something that is not destined for success, you are only pretending at commitment. For example, if you commit yourself in relationship to another person, but they are not committed to you, it is an easy commitment to make on your part. You do not have to give anything up. You do not have to burn any bridges in your life. You are giving yourself to something that will not work, so what has been given? This is easy. But to give yourself to something that will flourish and grow, that is important. To give yourself to something that has a real foundation, a real value and a real possibility for success, this will change you. This will take you forward in life. This will show you how to climb the mountain of life. This is not so easy.

There are times when you must give things up, things that

were once meaningful but have exhausted their value. Do not persevere with them any longer. This is not inconsistent with what I have said. Relationships and involvements exist at all stages in learning The Way of Knowledge. Some relationships will stay with you the whole way; most will not. Do not persevere when the direction has changed. In climbing the mountain of life, the trail zigzags, the terrain changes. Some parts are steep, some are not, though they all go up. Do not get stuck in one way of thinking. Do not get stuck with one person and one situation because these will change, and you must learn to change with them.

Along the way, however, you will meet people who are destined to take the great journey with you — all the way. Persevere here. But take caution because they may not be able to proceed. Should this be the case, you will have to go on without them, no matter how difficult or how devastating this may seem.

Some things will require great determination, but only for a short time. Other things will require great determination on an ongoing basis. Knowledge is your guide, but for Knowledge to be your guide, you must become strong with Knowledge. You must become open to Knowledge and able to follow it and to discern its movement and direction. These are not simple things. You cannot simply assume that you have the ability. You must earn the ability. You can imagine that you can do what a great artist or athlete can do, but in reality you haven't developed the skill. It is the same with this. You can imagine you are living a life of Knowledge. You can imagine that you are doing exactly the right thing, but this is imagination.

If your eyes are open, if your mind is open, if your heart is open, then you will find your way. You will make some mistakes. That is guaranteed. But you will not persist in your mistakes, and you will not repeat them endlessly. They will serve to make you stronger, more discerning, more capable and more compassionate towards others. Do not quit if you make mistakes. Making mistakes is part of making the journey. But do not persist in your mistakes or defend your mistakes. Do not say they were perfect for you because in fact you may have suffered greatly for them. Accept them. Benefit from them. But do not glorify them or justify them.

We have created a very great goal for students of Knowledge. We have presented a great preparation and curriculum for learning. We have presented a new tradition of learning and spirituality. We have presented everything you need. Life will give you the relationships and opportunities, but you are the one who must come to work. And your work will not be short lived. It will be ongoing, and it will be good work. It will be the kind of work that brings into being all aspects of you. It is the kind of work that heals the wounds and binds the parts of you that have broken away. It is the kind of work that restores you and renews you and strengthens you. It is the kind of work for which you must persevere.

You show up for Knowledge. You show up for your practice. You give yourself to this—today, tomorrow and the next day. You do not base your participation on whether you are having high experiences. You base your participation on something deeper and more consistent. You move forward and Knowledge grows stronger. If you turn away, you will have to go back to the beginning somewhere else.

If this preparation is right for you, you will know. At first, your sense of it may be very weak and faltering. But as you proceed, it will grow stronger and stronger. And as your sense of commitment and determination is set free from your personal ambitions and need for self-importance, then your commitment and determination will have a strength that will abide with you and that you can rely upon as a foundation for living and progressing in life. All of this is possible for you if you will persevere. You will reach your destination if you keep going. If you allow the journey to be what it is instead of trying to determine what it must be, then you will not lose your way in life. You will not try to take shortcuts which end up wasting your time and energy by leading you nowhere.

You take the path. You follow the path. You persevere on the path. And you learn the path. In this, you are able to help others who lag behind you. Here you are able to encourage and inspire those who have fallen by the side of the road. Here you are able to have compassion for those who have given up and are headed back.

You have come to the world to make a journey. Your journey is your gift, and all along the journey you give those things that are yours to give — things you had never intended to give and things you never knew you had to give. If you persist, others will follow you. They will keep you in their sights, and you will keep them moving forward. There are those who are ahead of you who are persisting, that are keeping you moving forward. When you have relationships like this, then you have a greater accountability in life beyond your own wishes and shifting desires. Here you owe it to others to persevere as much as you owe it to yourself. This is the beginning of real strength and determination. This is the beginning of learning a greater way. It will be your relationships and the needs of the world that will prompt you to undertake a great effort to give yourself more completely than you would ever give yourself for your own purposes alone. We celebrate this great journey because this is a great measure of truth that will measure out happiness and meaning to you.

Think about those things that you stayed with and dedicated yourself to, the places where you did not quit. Think about what you have acquired and developed in terms of your experience and education as a result of this perseverance. A greater education awaits you now. It has been given to you from the Creator. But there is no one forcing you to do it. You are not doing it to get a better job or to make more money. You are doing it for a greater purpose. And as you respond, this greater purpose will become stronger and more evident in you.

You learn The Way of Knowledge because you must, not because it holds some big promise at the end. With a greater motivation that is not contingent upon your ambitions, your feelings, your changing attitudes or the ideas or prevailing beliefs in the world, you will have a strength that the world does not possess. You will have a certainty that the world does not possess. This is evidence of Knowledge. This is the greater seed of truth growing in you now. Its seed has been germinating; it is now spreading forth. If you nurture it, it will grow and become a great tree that provides shade and inspiration for others.

*You must take
the steps to
Knowledge
and learn what they are,
how they work
and where they take you.*

Thirty-four

WALKING THE WAY
OF KNOWLEDGE

WHAT DOES IT MEAN to walk The Way of Knowledge? What is it really like? We shall speak about this to give you a greater idea of what the road ahead looks like and what it means to begin.

Everyone's path is a little different, but be careful here not to make too great a distinction. When you are living in the world and all you see are human beings representing intelligent life — which is not completely accurate because there is other intelligent life in the world — you tend to think the variations between one person and another are quite great. Indeed, within this limited context, the differences between people do seem remarkable. People do seem to be quite distinct from one another. There seems to be great variation in people's nature, temperament, environment, culture, and so forth.

But from a Greater Community perspective, human beings are not seen as really that different. The variations between them are really quite small. In order to have this perception, you will need to stand outside your human context and be able to look at yourself with great objectivity within the context of a Greater Community of life. Indeed, the differences between human beings and even your closest neighbors in the Greater Community would make the distinctions between people individually quite small and insignificant. This is born of a Greater Community perspective, a perspective that you will need to cultivate over time.

So, whereas an individual's preparation can seem somewhat unique, everyone must learn certain basic things. Everyone must develop certain basic skills regardless of his or her nature, temperament, environment, culture, age and generation. These things seem to make a great deal of difference to people, but again we must go back to a Greater Community perspective where the differences between people are not that great. I am making this point at the outset because you must see that though there are slight variations in what people must do for themselves and in what they must emphasize in their learning and preparation, everyone must pass through certain basic thresholds.

For example, everyone must learn to find out what Knowledge is and how Knowledge speaks through them. A great task this is and one with many stages of development. It is something that everyone who begins this great journey must accomplish. And they will experience Knowledge differently, not because Knowledge is different in them, but because their interpretive skills and orientations are different. For example, everyone looks at the same tree but has different experiences. That does not mean there is more than one tree. Everyone looks at the same event and comes to greatly different conclusions, but there is still only one event. People look at one another and have a whole range of responses, but they are all still just people engaged in various activities together.

Within the world, human beings tend to make great distinctions about things that are not of great importance and overlook the things that are of greater significance. The differences between people's mannerisms, behaviors, idiosyncrasies, and conflicts are given great importance here. The greater possibility within each person, which is the presence and emergence of Knowledge, is overlooked. Things that are merely peculiarities in people are elevated to such a point that they seem to define them entirely. For instance, you tend to think of people in terms of their dominant characteristics — their behavior, their mannerisms or even their figures of speech. Is this the truly important part of people? No.

This is a very important point because at the outset in The Way of Knowledge, everyone wants to have his or her individuality accentuated and validated. Everyone wants to be more unique, more important and more special. Of course, while there is a great investment in this, there is also a deeper desire for union, cooperation, community, affinity, shared purpose and shared accomplishment.

So, we have these two purposes. They are in opposition to one another, and this represents the conflict that exists within each individual. People want peace. They want reconciliation. But then they want other things too. This makes peace and reconciliation impossible. This is a fundamental conflict in human beings and, as a matter of fact, in all forms of intelligent life. That is why with the emergence of intelligence there must be the emergence of a greater spiritual understanding; otherwise, your intelligence merely makes you more aware of your pain, your discord, your vulnerability and your mortality. Unless a greater spiritual awareness arises with intelligence, intelligence itself creates a great and oppressive burden upon the individual.

People come to the first gate in The Way of Knowledge wanting more of everything they want. And yet they are moved and feel compelled to seek for something more pervasive, something that is more difficult to define perhaps, something that they yearn for more than they want, something that they need more than they desire. So, at the first gate, you encounter the Teaching and you decide that you are going to try to get something out of it. You want to benefit from it; you want it to do something for you. And of course, you want it to satisfy these two different purposes.

Fundamentally, the difference between these two purposes is that one is the desire for greater separation and the other is the desire for union. Sorting all of this out and making decisions to support one over the other represent a great deal of the work in The Way of Knowledge.

Now, at the outset, many people are very disappointed when they find out that The Greater Community Way of Knowledge is not going to make them richer, or fill their life with love and pleasure, or make them immune to the world, or make them more unique and impressive. Many people fall away when they come to this realization. They turn away to seek other things that seem to promise these rewards. These things are not promised here because they are not genuine. The deeper part of you is looking for a place to give. It is not looking to acquire more of what drives everyone in the world mad.

We present The Greater Community Way of Knowledge — nothing more, nothing less. We do not promise love or money. We do not promise fame. We do not promise immunity from the world. We offer something more enduring, more complete, more genuine and more real. We offer Wisdom, Knowledge, relationship, community, purpose and accomplishment. And commensurate with these we offer courage, consistency, self-trust, inner certainty and, most importantly of all, we offer inclusion in life, which includes all that I have mentioned so far. Now these all may sound fine, but of course there are other desires that seem to prevail. So, let us spare you confusion at the outset to say that The Greater Community Way of Knowledge is not going to add to your self-importance. It is not going to compensate for self-doubt or self-hate. It is not a substitute for an inadequate or incomplete life. It is not a band-aid that you put over the open wound of your own inner conflict.

Even to begin The Way of Knowledge there must be a pure motive. That is not to say there are not other motives. We expect there will be other motives. But it is to say that there is something very genuine calling you here. We do not try to make this a popular movement where we have something for everyone, like a great social event or carnival. We do not promise that we are going to resolve all of your little aches and pains. We only promise what is inevitable if you follow The Way of Knowledge. It is inevitable because of what you will learn to value and because your true motives in life will become stronger and eventually will prevail over all other motives and incentives that you may have created for yourself or that you may have assimilated from the world at large. These rewards are inevitable because you will want them, choose them and walk away from anything that falls short of them or that does not represent them truly.

The Way of Knowledge is the place to learn and to give. And if, in the process of learning and giving, things are lost or given up along the way, then just consider them to be excess baggage because you will want your burden in life to be lightened so that you may have the mental and physical freedom to learn greater things. We do not take anything away. The Way of Knowledge does not despise possessions, it does not encourage you to become ascetic and it does not teach renunciation. What it does emphasize is self-honesty and a practical approach to accomplishing things in life. If these are honored, accepted and followed, then that which you need will become stronger and more amplified, and that which merely burdens you will be discarded along the way. For what creates greater conflict than desiring the meaningless and avoiding the meaningful? This is the source of all confusion. Why would you want the petty trappings of life when the greatness of Knowledge is within you, calling upon you? Of course, you haven't experienced this fully. How could you have experienced it fully? But you have reached a place where you can realize that it is possible and that it is important.

Learning The Greater Community Way of Knowledge means that you are learning to work, focus and be still while you carry on the normal activities of life. It does not mean that you leave aside all the mundane activities that bother you or discourage you. It means that you enter into them with a greater presence of mind. Your life looks the same. There is not a lot of ritual or fanfare. Your behavior doesn't necessarily change. What is changing is something more fundamental and pervasive. It is like growing a great garden. It requires a lot of work, and while you carry on your life, the garden grows. It is the same in The Way of Knowledge. You cultivate a place within yourself for Knowledge, you support this place and you nourish it, and Knowledge grows all by itself.

Important change is gradual. This is change that has had time to integrate itself within you. Change without Wisdom or integration is merely a disassociating force in your life. It does not promise advancement, growth or development. Indeed, you can see that people all around you have undergone tremendous change with very little real effect upon them. Change becomes life giving and life renewing when it is accompanied by a greater purpose and the possibility for Wisdom and meaningful relationships. Then change does something for you. Then it opens new doors and takes you into new areas.

So, living and following The Way of Knowledge does not make things look different. You will still have good days and bad days. You will still have days when you feel certain of what you are doing, and you will have days when you are uncertain. You will still cry and get angry. You will still do silly things. You will still make mistakes. But while all this is going on, something else is growing within you and becoming more powerful, more real and more evident. There is the great garden growing—the garden of Knowledge. There is a fire burning within you — the Fire of Knowledge. It is growing, day by day.

The great change that you will experience will be unlike the big sensations that people usually call self-transformation. The real change happens deep within you. You don't usually see it happening, but you do notice the results. As time passes, you start to feel differently about certain things, not because anyone has told you to do so. It's just something you feel. Time passes, and your values change. You begin to take refuge in the truth rather than attempt to escape from it. You seek quiet more and more as gross stimulation becomes a great aggravation. You look for different things in yourself and in others. You become more aware of the subtle interactions between people. You are more affected by the mental environment and more sensitive to it. You begin to value truth and understanding more than possessions and pleasurable sensations.

This is all natural. Nothing is being imposed upon you here. You are simply coming to terms with a deeper need and a deeper affinity with life. People have great big experiences, and they say to themselves or others, "Oh, my God! This was the biggest experience! I had the biggest experience! It will change my life!" Well, these do not change your life. What they can do, however, is make you aware of a greater change that is occurring within you.

It is true that very intense or demanding experiences do have an impact on people. But real growth and development happen from the inside out. They happen beyond the control of your personal mind, which is why we say that working on yourself should never be your priority because how can you work on yourself? Can you pick yourself up by the scruff of the neck? Can you lift yourself up by the hands? No, of course not. However, many people think that they can. In reality, it takes something else to do this for you.

The real work on yourself involves adjusting your thinking and behavior in relationship to real experiences in life. Going off and trying to change your personality will not be productive. The Way of Knowledge does not ask you to bow out of life and fiddle with yourself. It does not ask you to become more important, more distinct or more unique. It does not ask you to be better than others or worse than others. It does not ask you to be proud and arrogant, and it does not ask you to be weak and self-effacing. These are all attempts to increase your self-importance. They represent attempts to look better to yourself.

The Way of Knowledge does not ask you to look better. It asks you to become open and receptive to Knowledge. The process of doing this will correct the inconsistencies and conflicts within you. It is the process itself that will do this. It is walking up the mountain of life. In doing that, you shed things that are not necessary, and you bond to things that are. You say farewell to certain people, and you join with others. You are not doing this because you are fooling around with your personality. You are doing this because you are going somewhere, and to get where you are going, you have to make certain adjustments. This is the real personal work you do on yourself, and it constitutes a very small amount of your time.

Some people think that they are self-created, so in order to improve, they have to recreate themselves and make a better rendition of themselves, an improved version. Of course, this only darkens their dilemma and makes it more complicated and difficult to escape.

The Way of Knowledge gives you something important to do in life, and as long as you keep doing it and persevere in doing it, things which are unimportant will either be satisfied or forgotten. God does not enter conflict and correct it. God provides purposeful activity to do, and that is what restores self-value and self-awareness to the individual. God does not come into your mind to repair everything and rewire your circuits. God calls you to do something and to respond to something. If you do that, then you will begin a path of resolution.

This is The Way of Knowledge. At the outset, you will not see much change on the surface, unless, of course, you are trying to recreate yourself, restyle yourself or make yourself more attractive to yourself, which is what a great deal of personal growth is really about. It's like a beauty school! How to look better to yourself. What value is there in looking better to yourself? The approval you will get will be temporary, and the problems you encounter will be many. The greater your investment in self-importance, the greater your distance from inclusion in life, and the more remote peace and accomplishment will become for you. The world does not need another tormented life. It needs a life of unity—a unity that has been established through honest endeavor, a unity that has no pretense and is not being used for compensation or justification.

In beginning The Greater Community Way of Knowledge, you begin some new activities. In the *Steps to Knowledge* Program you begin a daily practice. It is not a practice that you govern. It is not a practice that you adapt to yourself. It is a practice that you step up to. It is a practice that you adjust yourself to. You cannot improve it, but you can participate within it. Your practice at the beginning is very small, but it is consistent, and to follow it, you have to persevere and apply yourself. At first, it asks for very little time and attention. But what it does ask for it asks for consistently, not a day here and a day there, whenever you remember or feel like it, but every day. And if you miss a day, you come back and rededicate yourself. Your practice will grow, and as it grows, you will see that it is in keeping with the progress of your life. Yes, you will have days when you do not like it or understand it. You will have days when you feel grave self-doubt or self-deprecation, but as long as you are practicing, you are building a place for Knowledge to emerge within you.

So, you have something new in life. It is called practice. If you stay with it, you will slowly begin to understand it. And if you learn to understand it, you will learn to value it, and your participation will deepen. You will do this without having to believe in any heroes. You will do this without having to have any creation stories. You will do this without having to have any heavens or hells. You will do this because you know you need to develop and you need to gain access to your inner life.

Perhaps you may give a different definition that expresses your motive. But remember that there are only two motives: There is the motive for Knowledge and there is the motive to look good. Look around you. How many people are trying to look good, not only to each other but primarily to themselves? Everyone wants to be liked. Everyone wants to be justified. Everyone wants to be unique. Everyone wants to be validated. This is a desperate and hopeless pursuit, for you will never get enough to satisfy you.

So, while you are going along as a student of Knowledge, not much has changed except that you have this practice. But as you follow this practice, you will begin to experience some very important turning points which we call thresholds. In most cases you will not see the threshold itself, though you may think you have identified it. In most cases, you will experience the result of the threshold, which is a change in your perception and inner orientation. This is the result of a real change. The highs and lows of emotional experience do not constitute thresholds. A threshold happens at a deeper level, beyond awareness. But you will begin to experience its results with a change in your attitudes, your perceptions, your values and your associations. This is gradual. It needs to be gradual in order for you to integrate it and to put it into practice. Sudden change is often more destructive than it is constructive. Gradual change holds the best promise for success and for enduring value.

As you advance, you will begin to have new levels of experience and a greater sensitivity to people and to your own inner state. The development of this sensitivity is natural, but it also requires a certain amount of repositioning yourself in life because human activity is very gross and abrasive, and it will be more difficult in many cases to be around this. This will lead to some new behavior on your part and generally will bring about improvement in the quality of your life. These are all the results of inner development, which is fueled by your practice in The Way of Knowledge.

Thresholds await you down the road. You will pass through them and not know you are passing through them, but their evidence will be unmistakable as you begin to experience their effects and their results. It takes two to three years to assimilate your practice and to experience these kinds of results. Now, of course, most people do not last that long in their attempt to learn The Way of Knowledge. Some stay for a few weeks, some stay for a few months and some stay for only a few days. But they eventually will come back to this or to something else as they experience their inner need and come to realize that they themselves cannot fulfill it.

You are not apart from life, so you cannot fulfill yourself. You are not apart from life, so you cannot complete yourself. You are not apart from life, so you cannot uplift yourself. Life must do these for you — the powerful, important forces in life that represent a Greater Will and a Greater Power. These forces permeate the ignorance, the conflict and the violence of your world and of the Greater Community. They are there for you, you can call to them, and they will abide with you.

After a few months along the road, everything looks kind of the same, but something else is happening. Instead of dressing yourself up on the outside, something is growing and emerging on the inside. Through your practice in *Steps to Knowledge*, you are creating a place for Knowledge to emerge. You are orienting yourself towards Knowledge. You are creating time and space in your mind for Knowledge. You are slowly recognizing your need for Knowledge, and not just a need to have certainty in times of conflict or challenge. The Greater Power offers you more than simply a lifesaver to rescue you from your own catastrophes. Much more is offered.

A few months into your practice, and your friends say, "Well, you look the same to me!" But you begin to say, "Well, yes, but something is happening. I'm starting to feel things. I'm not sure what they are, but I know they are important." It is to allow this emergence of Knowledge that you engage in practice. The practice helps you on many levels. It creates balance and focus for your mind. It creates a meaningful consistency in your daily life. It produces awareness of your inner states and a growing understanding of the distinction between Knowledge and desire. It slowly develops a greater discernment in your relationships and in your perception of the world. It creates a balance where things can be sorted out and order can be established in your own mind and emotions. It does this slowly and gradually. In following *Steps to Knowledge,* you develop a consistency, perseverance and inner determination that are not dominated by your emotional states. You become open to new ideas and experience as you move beyond the boundaries of your former ideas and beliefs. *Steps to Knowledge* will take you beyond them if you follow the steps.

Now, many people are very slow in this respect. They try to use all the steps in order to fortify their fixed beliefs and ideas, especially the beliefs and ideas that they consider to be spiritual and uplifting. They try to fortify what they already know rather than learn something new. Often they can persist in this quite awhile before they come to realize that The Greater Community Way of Knowledge is not here to validate their beliefs. The Way of Knowledge is here to take them on a journey into an entirely different state of awareness where their former beliefs may have little relevance.

The Greater Community Way of Knowledge takes you beyond idealism and speculation into real engagement and greater certainty. You do not need to have a wonderful set of beliefs and ideas about yourself and others in order to advance in The Way of Knowledge. In fact, The Way of Knowledge will free you from the burden of maintaining and believing in these things.

To find the natural goodness that exists within people and within yourself, your mind cannot be encumbered by a great establishment of ideas and beliefs. People usually do not come to The Way of Knowledge in order to become free in this regard. They generally come to build or to rebuild their belief system. The Way of Knowledge provides an escape from this. It enables a more natural belief system based upon real experience and observation to be established rather than something that is simply constructed because it makes you look good to yourself, makes the world look good to you or makes you conform to the expectations and conventions of other people.

Walking The Way of Knowledge can seem very ordinary, particularly at the beginning. There are no great things to be done here. There are no great changes to be made in your life. In fact, you are encouraged not to try to transform yourself. Stop fiddling with yourself and let something real emerge within you. Nurture that. Support that. Like the gardener, you do all the preparation work. You plant the seeds. And then they grow on their own. You just tend to the garden, manage it and maintain it, and wonderful things spring forth. If you do too much, you spoil the garden. If you do too little, you neglect the garden.

Knowledge is like a garden. It will emerge naturally within you as you are capable of receiving it, accepting it and experiencing it. This requires desire and capacity. Progressing in The Way of Knowledge requires desire. This cannot be a casual interest or a fleeting impulse. This must be something that you feel is important.

And then there is the question of capacity. We shall speak a little on this now because this is an important subject. Even given a true desire for truth and purpose in life, one must come to recognize one's current capacity. The only way to recognize your capacity is by taking on more than you have taken on in the past. This shows you your current mental and physical boundaries. Now, many people assume that their capacity is very great when in reality they have no way of determining how great it is. You must be engaged in something of a greater magnitude in order to find out what your capacity is. In the normal range of activities, people never reach their capacity and never have a real basis for understanding what it is. They continue to set arbitrary boundaries for their own experience, believing that they can function within these boundaries, and only through grave disappointment and disillusionment will they find out if they were correct or not.

Developing your capacity is a very slow and gradual process. It happens beneath the level of awareness. It is the result of practice. It is part of the preparation. You were not born with a gigantic capacity. Therefore, you have to cultivate it. Until real cultivation has occurred, people tend to think that either their capacity has no limits or the limits they place upon it are purely emotional in nature. People say, "Well, I can have this, and I can be that, and I can do this," but then they are scared away by something very small. "Oh, I could never do that! I'm no good with this. I can't do that." The truth is, until you are engaged in something that calls upon you and demands things of you, you won't know what you are capable of. You won't know what your capacity is.

This is The Greater Community Way of Knowledge. It requires a far greater capacity than your world's religious teachings do because it accounts for a larger arena of life. It calls for a greater objectivity, a greater tolerance, a greater flexibility, a greater openness, and a greater discernment than any worldly philosophy or religion. The demands upon your capacity here are very great.

So, what is the best way to proceed? The best way to proceed is to start out very small and grow. It is to have a beginner's mind — to be a beginner, to not claim much for yourself, to not give yourself grandiose commendations and to not claim powers, abilities and awareness for yourself. In fact, it is wiser to take the opposite approach — to have a healthy self-doubt, to say to yourself, "I'm not so sure about these things that I believe. I'm not so sure about this. I will have to look more carefully."

Sometimes people go from being self-inflated to being self-denying, missing all that is in between. In this, we take a middle ground. Make few assumptions, keep your eyes open and stay connected to your inner experience. That is not the final answer, but it is a good starting point.

Steps to Knowledge continues for a long time because it is building your capacity while it is nurturing your desire for truth and for reality. Building capacity takes a long time. Do not think that you are going to undo decades of worldly conditioning in a few weeks or months. Do not think that you are going to reverse in a short time all that has built your personal mind since the day you arrived in this world. You can tell yourself anything that you want. You can persuade yourself to believe anything that you want to believe. You can hold any conversation with yourself. Sometimes you can even convince yourself to do or believe things that you know are wrong. But then there is Knowledge, and with Knowledge, there is truth. Accepted or denied, altered or embraced, the truth abides with you.

Developing your capacity to live the truth, to know the truth and to see the truth requires a great deal of time. Consider three years to be a reasonable amount of time to give yourself a good start. Three years of consistent participation and practice. You are building a foundation. Foundations are not built overnight. If you want a quick and easy way, then you will get a result that cannot stand. Do you want to build something solid or something flimsy? Do you want to build something enduring or something that is merely expedient?

So, be patient. Let Knowledge grow on its own. You do your preparation work, which is following *Steps to Knowledge*, considering each step seriously and learning over time how to apply them and how to interpret their application. This takes time, but it develops a real depth and foundation within you. If you must have great results right away, then you will continue to buy books, or take programs or do anything that you think will give you the fast and easy way. And your house will be filled with books, and your mind will be filled with ideas. You will have all kinds of concepts and different points of view, and you will think that you are on a great journey of higher education. But having all of these things does not mean that you have begun the journey.

To begin the journey, you will need to give yourself to something, something you did not invent for yourself. And you will need to stay with it. The things that are valuable in your life have taken time and consistent energy. Your valuable relationships, your children, your careers, your deeper interests are all results of things that have been developed and cultivated over time. Settling down and taking the journey without all kinds of outrageous expectations of yourself and of life is part of the balancing that will enable a real foundation to be established — not something that is fleeting and flimsy and easily altered by circumstances.

Building desire and developing capacity represent the fundamentals of real education. *Steps to Knowledge* gives you more than you are capable of integrating, but it does so in such a way that it expands your capacity. It does this by challenging your beliefs and by nurturing your relationship with Knowledge. Knowledge will change almost everything you think, not because everything you think is wrong, but because much of what you think is unnecessary. This simplifies your mind, and as your mind becomes simplified, it becomes stronger, more focused and more powerful. Now you are not a whole host of sub-personalities anymore, all insanely competing with each other. You are becoming one person, with one point of view, with an openness to learn and a vitality for life. Your point of view is no longer a personal point of view as much as it is an inner orientation. You are able to change your ideas and beliefs as this becomes necessary, and so they are able to serve you as temporary expediencies, which is their highest service to you.

Ideas and beliefs, hunches and associations must be flexible in life because as you develop, you will outgrow the things that you relied upon before. Like a child growing through different sets of clothes, you will outgrow your ideas and beliefs. You are simply too big for them now. They don't fit you anymore. That does not mean they are bad, and it does not mean they are not right for someone else. It means that they have become too tight and too constraining for you.

The Way of Knowledge also requires self-discipline, and self-discipline is something that must be cultivated. Along with self-discipline there is restraint. People have a very odd perspective about restraint. They think it is related to self-denial, but this only represents their point of view. Restraint, in fact, is very important, and if you are to focus your life on anything, then you must curtail your other activities and bring them into your central focus, whatever it may be at that time. You do not have time or energy to waste now because your time and energy are being directed towards something.

The development of self-discipline and the ability to exercise restraint wisely represent growing achievements in The Way of Knowledge. Instead of being driven by passions and desires, compulsions and needs, you begin to function outside of them more and more as you enter into the depth of your own reality. This represents freedom, power and self-determination. Here you can refocus your mind because it is not bound by your former conditioning. So, ideas, beliefs and convictions change in The Way of Knowledge because you are growing.

I said at the beginning that many people come to The Way of Knowledge because they want to fortify what they already believe, and that represents one of their motives, and often their dominant motive. They want to continue to build the point of view that they have been building for so long. But The Way of Knowledge takes them somewhere else. You cannot use Knowledge to build a point of view. You must use a point of view to build access to Knowledge. In this, your point of view must be flexible, changeable and adaptable. This keeps you at the very forefront of learning and develops your ability to interact with life. If everything is used to build a point of view, then you are not involved with life, and your awareness of it will be very selective. You will only want to see the things that represent what you want to see about your life. You will not be able to look at things as they are. You will only look at them as you want them to be or as you demand them to be. How miserable and isolating this is.

The Way of Knowledge leads you in a different direction. It frees you from these encumbrances. As you go through *Steps to Knowledge*, you will see your point of view needing to change here and there, you will see yourself needing to make adjustments in your thinking and behavior and you will see yourself needing to suspend certain ideas that were cherished convictions before. Idealism of any kind stands in the way of the reclamation of Knowledge. It is a choice for belief over experience, for ideas over relationships, for self-importance over truth. Even for those who have very lofty ideas about themselves and the universe, their ideas, which may seem harmless within themselves, become a great restraint in The Way of Knowledge.

To see and to think clearly, one's mind must be unfettered. When the mind is unfettered, it has a greater capacity. It has greater powers of attention, and it is able to exert its will more effectively, which brings about greater self-discipline and the ability to exercise restraint appropriately.

The Way of Knowledge is not about having high spiritual experiences all the time. It is about being real in the moment, being present in the moment, being open in the moment, and being available to learn about the Greater Reality and the Greater Community. It is being open to Mystery and to manifestation without confusing the two. The Way of Knowledge does not mix Spirit and matter together but respects each in its own domain. Thus, the man and woman of Knowledge become more capable in the world and at the same time become more capable at experiencing and penetrating the Mystery and learning beyond current or acceptable boundaries of thought. They become more capable in practical matters and at the same time more pervasive in their perception and discernment.

The Way of Knowledge takes you into the world and prepares you for the world, but it prepares you with a greater state of mind. It is not a form of escape. It does not enable you to escape the mundanities of life. Indeed, it is here to help you contribute to the mundanities of life, for you have come to the world for this purpose.

To experience the things that I have spoken of here and to understand the distinctions that I have made, you yourself must begin and progress in the great journey. You must take the steps to Knowledge and learn what they are, how they work and where they take you. As you climb higher on the mountain of life, you will understand the journey more completely. You will see those far down below who are struggling to progress and to understand,

and you will understand their difficulty. And you will have compassion for them, for you yourself have traveled that way before.

FURTHER STUDY

THERE IS A WAY TO STUDY AND PRACTICE what has been presented in this book. Study of The Greater Community Way of Knowledge is presented in the three texts, *Steps to Knowledge* and *Wisdom from the Greater Community: Volumes I & II*, which comprise the first level of study in the *Steps to Knowledge* Program. Offered in a self-study format, the Program provides the perspective, the insight and the method of preparation necessary to begin learning and applying Greater Community Knowledge and Wisdom.

Steps to Knowledge, the Greater Community Book of Practices, is the map that takes you to the discovery of Knowledge, the Knowing Mind, which is the source of your greater purpose in the world and your true relationships in life. It contains 365 daily "steps," each offering a special teaching and a practice in The Way of Knowledge. By exercising the two natural functions of the mind, stillness and focused inquiry, *Steps to Knowledge* mysteriously opens the mind to revelation, where purpose, meaning and direction become apparent.

The two volumes of *Wisdom from the Greater Community* present the perspective and insight of The Way of Knowledge in its application to the fundamental aspects of daily life. In chapters ranging from "Marriage" and "Freedom" to "Intelligence" and "Greater Community Realities," *Wisdom from the Greater Community: Volumes I & II* create an environment for coming to terms with what you really know about your life and the world around you.

The Sacred Books of the New Knowledge Library are published by The Society for The Greater Community Way of Knowledge. To order copies of *Steps to Knowledge* and *Wisdom from the Greater Community: Volumes I & II* or to learn more about The Society's other publications, educational programs and contemplative services, please contact: The Society for The Greater Community Way of Knowledge, P.O. Box 1724, Boulder, CO 80306-1724, (303) 938-8401.

ABOUT THE AUTHOR

*M*ARSHALL VIAN SUMMERS IS THE FOUNDER
of The Society for The Greater Community
Way of Knowledge and is the primary repre-
sentative of Greater Community Spirituality in the
world today. He is the author of *Steps to Knowledge, Wisdom from
the Greater Community: Volumes I & II* and the other books of the
New Knowledge Library. He lives in seclusion in the Rocky
Mountains where he continues to receive the sacred books of the
Greater Community Way. Several times a year he travels to introduce the Teaching to new audiences and to spread the message
that the world is emerging into the Greater Community and for
this humanity must prepare.

Wisdom from the Greater Community, Volumes I & II, are gifts
from the Creator to prepare humanity for its life in the new mil-
lennium.

ABOUT THE SOCIETY

*T*HE SOCIETY FOR THE GREATER COMMUNITY WAY OF KNOWLEDGE has a great mission in the world. Our world is emerging into the Greater Community of Worlds and humanity must prepare. The Greater Community Way of Knowledge is the preparation. The mission of The Society is to present this message worldwide and to teach The Way of Knowledge through its publications, educational programs and contemplative services. The Society provides the materials, the instruction and the environment necessary for learning and living the greater Knowledge and Wisdom that this teaching and tradition represent.

THE SOCIETY WAS FOUNDED IN 1992 as a religious non-profit organization. It publishes the books of the New Knowledge Library, offers the Greater Community Services and provides special educational programs on Knowledge and Greater Community Spirituality by its founder Marshall Vian Summers. The Society is supported and maintained by people who are committed to learning and living The Way of Knowledge and who recognize that they have a greater purpose in life to fulfill.

AS A RELIGIOUS NON-PROFIT ORGANIZATION, The Society is supported primarily through volunteer activity, tithes and contributions. The Books of Knowledge are finding their way around the world through the power of relationships, where people are sharing the discovery of The Way of Knowledge with others. You can make a difference by reaching those who need

Knowledge and Wisdom now and who feel the need to prepare. Share these books with them.

YOUR FINANCIAL CONTRIBUTIONS will make possible the ongoing publication of all the Sacred Books of Knowledge, many of which are currently awaiting funds for publication. In addition, your support enables The Society to offer the programs and services which make learning and living The Greater Community Way of Knowledge possible.

Announcing
STEPS TO KNOWLEDGE

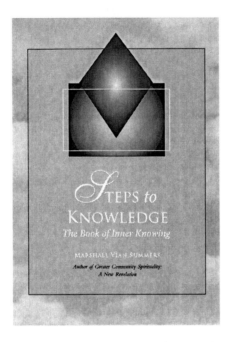

STEPS TO KNOWLEDGE represents the essence of spirituality as it is taught, practiced and shared in the Greater Community of Worlds.

STEPS TO KNOWLEDGE is a gift from the Creator to enable humanity to establish a foundation for peace and cooperation within the human family and to spiritually prepare for its destined encounter with intelligent life from the Greater Community.

STEPS TO KNOWLEDGE provides the lessons and practices that are essential for learning and living The Greater Community Way of Knowledge. In its 365 practices or "steps" it presents the road map to Knowledge, the Knowing Mind, and lays the foundation for learning and applying Greater Community Knowledge and Wisdom.

STEPS TO KNOWLEDGE is for those who have the need to know and who feel the need to prepare.

"These words are a calling. This message is a calling. These ideas are a calling. The world is emerging into the Greater Community. You must prepare. The preparation is here. It is time to begin."

From the Introduction to STEPS TO KNOWLEDGE

Wisdom
from
The Greater Community:
Volume I

ISBN 978-1-884238-28-4

Wisdom
from
The Greater Community:
Volume II

ISBN 978-1-884238-29-1

THE STEPS TO KNOWLEDGE PROGRAM

Steps to Knowledge and *Wisdom from the Greater Community: Volumes I & II* may be ordered individually or as a set:

QTY.   (PLEASE PRINT)

_____ STEPS TO KNOWLEDGE PROGRAM: *Steps to Knowledge* and
          Wisdom from the Greater Community: Volumes I & II @ $70 each   _____

_____ STEPS TO KNOWLEDGE @ $25 each   _____

_____ WISDOM FROM THE GREATER COMMUNITY: VOLUME I @ $25 each   _____

_____ WISDOM FROM THE GREATER COMMUNITY: VOLUME II @ $25 each   _____

          SHIPPING AND HANDLING: $7 for the program; $5 for one book;
          $6 for two books; $7 for three books. Add $1 for each additional book. _____

          Colorado residents please add 4.1% sales tax.   _____

          Boulder residents please add an additional 3.11% sales tax.   _____

          TOTAL: _____

NAME: _____

ADDRESS: _____

CITY/STATE/ZIP: _____

PHONE (optional): _____

Referred by: _____

Please send this order form along with a check or money order payable to:

The Society for The Greater Community Way of Knowledge

P.O. Box 1724, Boulder, Colorado 80306-1724 • (303) 938-8401

THE STEPS TO KNOWLEDGE PROGRAM

Steps to Knowledge and *Wisdom from the Greater Community: Volumes I & II* may be ordered individually or as a set:

QTY.   (PLEASE PRINT)

_____ STEPS TO KNOWLEDGE PROGRAM: *Steps to Knowledge* and
          Wisdom from the Greater Community: Volumes I & II @ $70 each   _____

_____ STEPS TO KNOWLEDGE @ $25 each   _____

_____ WISDOM FROM THE GREATER COMMUNITY: VOLUME I @ $25 each   _____

_____ WISDOM FROM THE GREATER COMMUNITY: VOLUME II @ $25 each   _____

          SHIPPING AND HANDLING: $7 for the program; $5 for one book;
          $6 for two books; $7 for three books. Add $1 for each additional book. _____

          Colorado residents please add 4.1% sales tax.   _____

          Boulder residents please add an additional 3.11% sales tax.   _____

          TOTAL: _____

NAME: _____

ADDRESS: _____

CITY/STATE/ZIP: _____

PHONE (optional): _____

Referred by: _____

Please send this order form along with a check or money order payable to:

The Society for The Greater Community Way of Knowledge

P.O. Box 1724, Boulder, Colorado 80306-1724 • (303) 938-8401